THE ENGINES OF GOD

Jack McDevitt's short stories have appeared in several magazines, notably Asimov's. His first novel, *The Hercules Text*, won the Philip K. Dick Special Award. *A Talent for War*, was a *Locus* bestseller. Recently, McDevitt won the first UPC International Award for his novella *Ships in the Night*.

He lives in the USA with his family.

Voyager

JACK McDEVITT

The Engines of God

HarperCollins*Publishers*

Voyager
An Imprint of HarperCollins*Publishers*
77–85 Fulham Palace Road,
Hammersmith, London W6 8JB

A Paperback Original 1996
3 5 7 9 8 6 4 2

A catalogue record for this book
is available from the British Library

ISBN 0 00 648227 9

Set in Times

Printed and bound in Great Britain by
Caledonian International Book Manufacturing Ltd, Glasgow

For Maureen
with love

I would like to acknowledge the technical assistance of James H. Sharp and Geoff Chester of the Albert Einstein Planetarium at the Smithsonian Institution; David Steitz and Charles Redmond of NASA; and George B. Hynds, Jr., of GBH Fabricating & Packaging, Inc. Dr. Charles Stanmer filled in the gaps in my chemistry, which were considerable. Douglas Myles's excellent *The Great Waves* (McGraw-Hill, 1985) was a valuable source. I hope I got it all straight. And Patrick Delahunt was dead right. Bob Melvin and Brian Cole provided timely help. Mark Van Name was there when I needed him. Thanks also to Ralph Vicinanza, and to Ginjer Buchanan and Carol Lowe at Ace. I am also grateful for the encouragement and understanding of my children, Merry, Scott, and Chris, to whom it must seem as if they were fathered by Lamont Cranston.

Dates are rendered in the standard language of the Christian epoch, out of respect for everyone's sanity.

In the streets of Hau-kai, we wait.
Night comes, winter descends,
The lights of the world grow cold.
And, in this three-hundredth year
From the ascendancy of Bilat,
He will come who treads the dawn,
Tramples the sun beneath his feet,
And judges the souls of men.
He will stride across the rooftops,
And he will fire the engines of God.

—Uranic Book of Prayer (Quraqua)
    (Translated by Margaret Tufu)

To Sagittarius Arm & Galactic Center

VOID

Beta
Pacifica
III

Pinnacle

Quraqua

Nok

Light Years

50

Earth

Archeological Sites, Early 23rd Century

PROLOGUE

Iapetus. Sunday, February 12, 2197; 0845 GMT.

The thing was carved of ice and rock. It stood serenely on that bleak, snow-covered plain, a nightmare figure of gently curving claws, surreal eyes, and lean fluidity. The lips were parted, rounded, almost sexual. Priscilla Hutchins wasn't sure why it was so disquieting. It was more than the carnivorous aspect of the creature, the long slow menace of talons, the moonlight stealth of the lower limbs. It was more even than the vaguely aggressive stance, or the position of the figure in the center of an otherwise lifeless plain beneath the October light of Saturn's rings.

Rather, it seemed to flow from its interest in the ringed world which was forever frozen above a tract of low hills and ridges in the west. Stamped on its icy features was an expression she could only have described as philosophical ferocity.

"I keep coming back." Richard's voice echoed in her earphones. It was filled with emotion. "Of all the Monuments, *this* was the first, and it is the centerpiece."

They stood on a ramp, designed to preserve the tracks of the original expedition. *Here* was where Terri Case had stood; and *there*, Cathie Chung. The heavy bootprints circling the figure, up close, those belonged to Steinitz himself. (She knew because she'd seen the ancient video records countless times, had watched the astronauts clumping about in their awkward pressure suits.)

She smiled at the memory, pushing her hands down into her pockets, watching Richard Wald in his rumpled gray jeans and white sweater, his Irish country hat pressed down on his head. (It didn't quite fit within the bubble of articulated energy that provided breathing space.) He was slightly out of focus, difficult to see, within the Flickinger field. Much as

1

he was in ordinary life. Richard was one of the great names in archeology. He would be remembered as long as people were interested in where they'd come from, as long as they continued to send out explorers. Yet here he stood, as awed as she, momentarily a child, in the presence of this *thing*. Around them, the silence and the desolation crashed down.

Hutchins, on first glance, might have been one of those diminutive women with finely chiseled features and a beguiling smile who seemed more akin to the drawing room than to a bleak moonscape. Her eyes were dark and good-humored, and an initial impression might suggest that they reflected empty conviviality. But they were capable of igniting.

Her black hair was cut short. It peeked out from beneath a broad-brimmed safari hat. Everyone who knew her believed that it was her slight stature that had fueled her various ambitions; that she had chased men, and professional success, and eventually the stars, all out of the same drive to compensate.

She knew it wasn't true, or believed it wasn't. The reality was far simpler, but not the sort of thing she would tell anyone: her father had taken her to Luna when she was eight, and she had felt the full force of the enormous age of the place. It had occupied her dreams and overwhelmed her waking hours. It had driven a sense of her own transience into her soul. *Live while you can, indulge your passions. Make it count.* The ancient storm stirred again while she looked into the frozen emotions of the ice creature. And recognized them.

Richard Wald folded his arms and pressed them against his sweater, as if, inside his energy envelope, he was cold. He was tall, and embodied the kind of self-conscious dignity one finds in those who have achieved a degree of fame and never quite come to terms with it.

Despite his sixty years, Richard was a man of remarkable vitality. And exuberance. He was known to like a good drink, and a good party; and he loved the company of women. He was careful, however, to maintain a purely professional demeanor with Hutchins, his pilot. There was something of the Old Testament prophet in his appearance. He had a thick silver mane and mustache, high cheekbones, and a preemptive blue gaze. But the stern appearance was a façade. He was, in Hutchins' amused view, a pussycat.

He had been here before. This was, in a sense, where he had been born.

This was the First Monument, the unlikely pseudo-contact that had alerted the human race two hundred years ago to the fact they were not alone. Explorers had found thirteen others, of varying design, among the stars. Richard believed there were several thousand more.

The Great Monuments were his overriding passion. Their images decorated the walls of his home in Maine: a cloudy pyramid orbiting a rocky world off blue-white Sirius, a black cluster of crystal spheres and cones mounted in a snowfield near the south pole of lifeless Armis V, a transparent wedge orbiting Arcturus. (Hutchins' throat mike was a cunningly executed reproduction of the Arcturian Wedge.) Most spectacular among the relics was an object that resembled a circular pavilion complete with columns and steps, cut from the side of a mountain on a misshapen asteroid in the Procyon system. ("It looked," Richard had told her, "as if it were awaiting the arrival of the orchestra.") Hutchins had only seen the pictures, had not yet visited these magic places. But she was going. She would stand one day in their presence, and she would feel the hand of their creators as she did here. It would have been difficult to do on her own; there were many pilots and few missions. But Richard had recognized a kindred spirit. He wanted her to see the Monuments, because in her reactions he could relive his own. Besides, she was damned good.

Of all the artifacts, only the Iapetus figure could be interpreted as a self-portrait. The wings were half-folded. The creature's taloned hands, each with six digits, reached toward Saturn. Clearly female, it looked past Richard, arms open, legs braced, weight slightly forward. It was almost erotic.

Its blind eyes stared across the plain. It was set on a block of ice about a third its own height. Three lines of sharp, white symbols were stenciled within the ice. To Hutchins' mind, the script possessed an Arabic delicacy and elegance. It was characterized by loops and crescents and curves. And, as the sun moved across the sky, the symbols embraced the light, and came alive. No one knew what the inscription meant.

The base was half again as wide as Hutchins with arms outspread. The creature itself was three and a half meters high. That it was a self-portrait was known because the Steinitz expedition had found on the plain prints that matched the creature's feet.

The ramp was designed to allow visitors to get close enough to touch the artifact without disturbing anything. Richard stood thoughtfully before it. He pressed his fingertips against the base, nodded, and unhooked a lamp from his belt. He switched it on and played it across the inscription. The symbols brightened, lengthened, shifted.

"Nice effect," Hutchins said.

Each of the Monuments had an inscription. But no two seemed to be derived from the same writing system. Theory held that the objects were indeed monuments, but that they had been constructed during different epochs.

Hutchins stared into its blind eyes. "Kilroy was here," she said.

She knew that all the Monuments were believed to date to a five-thousand-year period ending roughly at 19,000 B.C. This was thought to be one of the earlier figures. "I wonder why they stopped," she said.

Richard looked up at the stars. "Who knows? Five thousand years is a long time. Maybe they got bored." He came over and stood by her. "Cultures change. We can't expect them to do it forever."

The unspoken question: *Did they still exist?*

What a pity we missed them. Everyone who came here shared the same reaction. So close. A few millennia, a bare whisper of cosmic time.

One of the landers from the Steinitz expedition had been left behind. A gray, clumsy vehicle, with an old U.S. flag painted near an open cargo-bay door, it lay two hundred meters away, at the far end of the ramp. Lost piece of a lost world. Lights glowed cheerily in the pilot's cabin, and a sign invited visitors to tour.

Richard had turned back to the inscription.

"What do you think it says?" she asked.

"Name and a date." He stepped back. "You had it right, I think. *Kilroy was here.*"

She glanced away from the figure, out across the plain, sterile and white and scarred with craters. It ascended gradually toward a series of ridges, pale in the ghastly light of the giant planet. (Iapetus was so small that one was acutely conscious of standing on a sphere. The sensation did not bother her, but she knew that when Richard's excitement died away, it would affect him.)

The figure looked directly at Saturn. The planet, low on the horizon, was in its third quarter. It had been in that exact position when *she* was here, and it would be there when another twenty thousand years had passed. It was flattened at the poles, with a somewhat larger aspect than the Moon. The rings were tilted forward, a brilliant panorama of greens and blues, sliced off sharply by the planet's shadow.

Richard disappeared behind the figure. His voice crackled in her earphones: "She's magnificent, Hutch."

When they'd finished their inspection, they retreated inside the Steinitz lander. She was glad to get in off the moonscape, to kill the energy field (which always induced an unpleasant tingling sensation), to dispose of her weights, and to savor the reassurance of walls and interior lighting. The vessel was maintained by the Park Service more or less as it had been two centuries earlier, complete with photos of the members of the Steinitz team.

Richard, buoyed by his excitement, passed before the photos one by one. Hutch filled their cups with coffee, and lifted hers in toast. "To Frank Steinitz," she said.

"And his crew."

Steinitz: there was a name, as they say, to conjure with. His had been the first deep-space mission, five Athenas to Saturn. It was an attempt to capture the public imagination for a dying space program: an investigation of a peculiar object photographed by a Voyager on Iapetus two decades earlier. They'd returned with no answers, and only a carved figure that no one could explain, and film of strange footprints on the frozen surface of the moon. The mission had been inordinately expensive; political cartoonists had loved it, and an American presidency had been destroyed.

The Steinitz group had borne permanent scars from the flight: they had demonstrated beyond all further quibble the devastating effects of prolonged weightlessness. Ligaments and tendons had loosened, and muscles turned to slush. Several of the astronauts had developed heart problems. All had suffered from assorted neuroses. It was the first indication that humans would not adjust easily to living off-Earth.

Steinitz' photo was mounted in the center. The image was familiar; he'd been overweight, aggressive, utterly dedicated, a man who had lied about his age while NASA looked the other way. "The bitch of it," Richard said solemnly, turning toward the windows and gazing out at the ice figure, "is that we'll never meet them."

She understood he was referring to the Monument-Makers.

"It was," he continued, "Steinitz' comment when he first saw her. And he was right."

"Right for his age. Not necessarily for ours." She didn't exactly believe that, since the Monument-Makers seemed to have vanished. Nevertheless it was the right thing to say. She examined her coffee mug. "I'm amazed that they were able to get that kind of articulation and detail into a block of ice."

"What do *you* think of it?" he asked.

"I don't know. It *is* disquieting. Almost oppressive. I don't really know *how* to describe it." She swung the chair around, turning her back to the plain. "Maybe it's the desolation."

"I'll tell you what it is for *me*," he said. "It's her *footprints*. There's only one set."

Hutch didn't quite understand.

"She was *alone*."

The figure was idealized. It watched Saturn with unmistakable interest, and there was nobility and grace in its lines.

Hutch read something else at the juncture of beak and jaw, and in the corners of the eyes: an amalgam of arrogance and distrust laced with stoicism. Tenacity. Perhaps even fear.

"The inscription," she said. "It's probably the thing's name."

"That's the position Muncie takes. If in fact it's a work of art and nothing else, it could be the title of the work. 'The Watcher.' 'Outpost.' Something like that."

"Or," said Hutch, "maybe the name of a goddess."

"Possibly. One of the members of the original mission suggested it might be a claim marker."

"If so," she said, "they're welcome to this rock."

"They were thinking more of the solar system." The plain lay flat and sterile. The rings were knife-edge bright. "Are you ready to take a walk?"

They followed the ramp out onto the plain. Off to one side they could see the booted tracks of the astronauts. Approximately a kilometer and a half west, *her* prints appeared.

There were two sets, going in opposite directions. She wore no shoes, and the length of both the foot and the stride, measured against the anatomy of the ice figure, suggested a creature about three meters tall. They could distinguish six toes on each foot, which was also consistent. "Almost as if," Hutch said, "the thing climbed down and went for a walk."

Chilling thought, that. They both glanced reflexively behind them.

One set of tracks proceeded west into the uplands.

The other wheeled out across the plain, on a course well north of the artifact. Astronaut prints, and ramps, followed in both directions. Richard and Hutch turned north.

"The bare feet shook them up," said Richard. "Now, you and I could match the trick, if we wanted."

After about a quarter-kilometer, the prints stopped dead in the middle of the snow. Both sets, coming and going. "There must have been a ship here," Hutch said.

"Apparently." The snow beyond the prints was untouched.

The ramp circled the area, marking off a space about the size of a baseball diamond. Richard walked completely around the circle, stopping occasionally to examine the surface. "You can see holes," he said, pointing them out. "The ship must have been mounted on stilts. The prints show us where the creature first appeared. It—she—walked off the way we've come, and went up into the hills. She cut a slab of rock and ice out of a wall up there. We'll go take a look at the spot. She fashioned the figure, put it back on board, and flew it to the site." He looked in the direction of the ice figure. "There are holes back there, too."

"Why haul it at all? Why not leave it up in the hills?"

"Who knows? Why put something *here* and not *there*? Maybe it would have been too easy." He tapped the ramp with his toe. "We're in a valley. It's hard to see, because the sides are low, and the curve of the land is so sharp. But it's there. The ice figure is located precisely in the center."

After a while they went back the other way, and followed the tracks into the hills. The walkway plunged through deep snow and soared over ravines. The prints themselves twice went directly up to sheer walls and stopped. "They continue higher up," said Richard.

"Anti-gravity?"

"Not supposed to be possible. But how else would you explain any of this?"

Hutch shrugged.

• • •

They entered the ravine from which the ice and stone for the figure had been taken. A block had been sliced cleanly out of one wall, leaving a cut three times the visitor's height. The prints passed the place, continued upslope, and petered out on thick ice. They reappeared a little farther atop a ridge.

The ground dropped sharply away on both sides. It was a long way down.

Richard strode along the ramp, submerged in his thoughts, not speaking, gazing neither right nor left. Hutch tried to caution him that the energy field provided fair traction at best, that the light gravity was treacherous. "You could sail off without much effort. You'd fall kind of slow, but when you hit bottom, there would be a very big splash." He grunted, and went a little easier, but not enough to satisfy her.

They continued along the crest of the ridge until the tracks stopped. It was a narrow place. But with a rousing view of Saturn, and the breathless falling-off of the worldlet's short horizon.

Judging from the confusion of tracks, the creature might have been there for a time. And then of course she had doubled back.

Richard gazed down at the prints.

The night was full of stars.

"She came up here *before* she cut the ice," said Hutch.

"Very good. But why did she come here at all?"

Hutch looked out across the plain, luminous in Saturn's pale light. It curved away from her, giddily.

The stars were hard and cold, and the spaces between them pressed on her. The planet, locked in place, had not moved since *she* stood here. "The image on the plain," she said, "is terrifying, not because it has wings and claws, but because *it is alone*."

She was beginning to feel the cold, and it was a long way back to the ship. (The Flickinger fields *do* cool off, in time. They're not supposed to, and there are all kinds of tests to demonstrate they don't. But there you are.) Half a dozen moons were in the sky: Titan, with its thin methane atmosphere; Rhea and Hyperion and some of the smaller satellites: frozen, spinning rocks like this one, sterile, immeasurably old, no more capable of supporting a thinking creature than the bloated gasbag they circle.

Richard followed her gaze. "She must have been very much like us." His lined features softened.

Hutch stood unmoving.

The universe is a drafty, precarious haven for anything that thinks. There are damned few of us, and it is a wide world, and long. Hutch wondered about her. What had brought her so far from home? Why had she traveled alone? Long since gone to dust, no doubt. *Nevertheless, I wish you well.*

PART ONE
MOONRISE

1.

Quraqua. 28th Year of Mission, 211th Day. Thursday, April 29, 2202; 0630 hours local time.

Almost overnight, every civilization on this globe had died. It had happened twice: somewhere around 9000 B.C., and again eight thousand years later. On a world filled with curiosities, this fact particularly disturbed Henry's sleep.

He lay awake, thinking how they were running out of time, thinking how the Quraquat had known after all about the anomaly on their moon. They were unaware of the two discontinuities, had lost sight of them toward the end, and remembered them only in myth. But they knew about Oz. Art had found a coin which left no doubt, whose obverse revealed a tiny square on a crescent, at the latitude of the Western Mare. Precisely where Oz was located.

He wondered whether Linda's surmise that the Lower Temple era had possessed optical instruments would prove correct. Or whether the natives had simply had good eyes.

What had *they* made of the thing? Henry buried his head in his pillow. If the Quraquat had looked at their moon through a telescope, they would have seen a city occupying the center of a vast plain. They would have seen long airless avenues and rows of buildings and broad squares. And a massive defensive wall.

He turned over. Eventually Oz would surface in Quraquat mythology and literature. *When we've collected enough of it. And mastered the languages.*

His stomach tightened. There would not be time.

The anomaly was only rock, cunningly hewn to create the illusion of the city. *There* was the real puzzle. And the explanation for Oz lay somehow with the race that had inhabited this world. This was a race that had built complex cultures

13

and developed philosophical systems that had endured for
tens of thousands of years. But its genius did not extend
to technology, which had never risen much beyond a nine-
teenth-century level.

The door chimed. "Henry?" The voice in the speaker was
tense with excitement. "Are you asleep?"

"No." He opened the door. "Did we get in?"

"Yes—"

Henry threw back his sheet. "Give me two minutes. I didn't
think it would be this quick."

Frank Carson stood in the corridor. "You have a good crew
down there." In the half-light, he looked pleased. "We think
it's intact."

"Good. That's goddam good." He turned on his table lamp.
Beyond the window, sunlight filtered down from the surface.
"Did you see it?"

"Just a peek. We're saving it for you."

"Yeah. Thanks." The traditional lie amused Henry. He
knew they had all stuck their heads in. And now they would
pretend that the boss would make the grand entrance.

If there was anyone with the Academy's archeological
teams homelier than Henry Jacobi, he would have been a
sorry sight. In Linda Thomas' memorable phrase, he always
looked as if a load of scrap metal had fallen on him. His face
was rumpled and creased, and his anatomy sagged everywhere. He had slate-colored hair, and a permanent squint
which might have derived from trying to make out too many
ideographs. Nevertheless, he was a master of social graces:
everyone liked him, women married him (he had four ex-
wives), and people who knew him well would have followed
him into combat.

He was a consummate professional. Much like those pale-
ontologists who could assemble a complete brontosaur from
a knee bone, Henry seemed able to construct an entire society
from an urn.

He followed Carson through the empty community room,
and down the stairway into Operations. Janet Allegri, man-
ning the main console, gave them an encouraging thumbs-up.

Creepers and stingfish moved past the wraparound viewpanel. Beyond, the sea bottom was crisscrossed by trailmarker
lamps. The sunlight was fading from the water, and the Temple was lost in the general gloom. They passed into the sea

chamber, and put on Flickinger harnesses and jetpacks. Henry rubbed his hands together in pure pleasure.

Carson straightened his shoulders in his best military bearing. He was a big man with a square jaw and intense eyes that saw the world in sharp colors. That he was a retired colonel in the army of the North American Union would surprise no one. "This is just the beginning, Henry. I still say we should hang on here. What are they going to do if we refuse to leave?"

Henry sighed. Carson didn't understand politics. "They would put a lot of heat on the Academy, Frank. And when you and I went home, we would find ourselves back in classrooms. And possibly defending ourselves in court."

"You have to be willing to take risks for what you believe, Henry."

He had actually considered it. Beyond Earth, they knew of three worlds that had given birth to civilizations. One of the civilizations, the Noks on Inakademeri, still survived. The inhabitants of Pinnacle had been dead three-quarters of a million years.

And Quraqua.

Quraqua, of course, was the gold mine. Pinnacle was too far gone, and since the Noks were still in the neighborhood, the opportunities for investigation were limited. Nonetheless, there was hardly a graduate student who hadn't found a buried city, uncovered the key to a mass migration, tracked down a previously unknown civilization. It was the golden age of archeology. Henry Jacobi understood the importance of saving this world. But he had no inclination to risk anyone's life in the effort. He was too old for that sort of thing.

"Does Maggie know we're in?"

"They're getting her now. The poor woman never gets any rest, Henry."

"She can rest when we're out of here." Maggie was his chief philologist. Code-breaker, really. Reader of Impossible Inscriptions. The lamp on his left wrist flashed green. He activated the energy field.

Carson punched the go pad, and the lock cycled open. Water sloshed in over the deck.

Outside, visibility was poor. They were too close inshore: the marker lights always blurred, the water was always full of sand, and one could seldom see the entire Temple.

The Temple of the Winds.

A bitter joke, that. It had been submerged since an earth-quake somewhere around Thomas Jefferson's time created a new shoreline. The Temple was a one-time military post, home for various deities, place of worship for travelers long before humans had laid bricks at Ur or Nineveh.

Sic transit.

Fish darted before him, accompanied him. Off to his left, something big moved through the water. Carson turned a lamp in its direction, and the light passed through it. It was a jelly. Quite harmless. It rippled, blossomed, and swam lei-surely on its way.

A broad colonnade masked the front of the Temple. They settled onto the stone floor, beside a circular column. It was one of ten still standing. Of an original twelve. Not bad, for a place that had been through an earthquake.

"Frank." Linda's voice broke in on his earphones. She sounded pleased. And with good reason; she had planned this aspect of the excavation. She'd taken a couple of chances, guessed right, and they'd broken in well ahead of schedule. Under the circumstances, the time gained was critical.

"Henry's with me," said Carson. "We're on our way."

"Henry," she said. "We're open as far back as we can see."

"Good show, Linda. Congratulations."

The Temple entrance gaped wide. They swam into the nave. Lines of colored lights trailed off through the dark. It always seemed to Henry that the lamps exaggerated the size of the place.

"Blue," said Carson.

"I know." They followed the blue lamps toward the rear. Only vestiges of the Temple roof remained. The gray light from the surface was oily and thick against the cheerful glow of the markers.

Henry was in poor condition. Swimming tired him, but he had declared jets too dangerous to use inside the excavation. He had to live by his own rules.

The glowing blue track angled abruptly off to the left, and plunged through a hole in the floor.

He could hear Linda and Art Gibbs and some of the others on the common channel. They were laughing and cheering him on and congratulating one another on the find.

He swam down the labyrinthine approach tunnel. Carson stayed to his rear, advising him to take his time, until Henry finally lost patience and asked him to be quiet. He rounded the last bend and saw lights ahead.

They stood aside for him. Trifon Pavlaevich, a husky Russian with a giant white mustache, bowed slightly; Karl Pickens beamed; and Art Gibbs floated proudly beside Linda.

Linda Thomas was a redheaded dynamo who knew what she was doing and didn't mind sharing credit with her colleagues. As a result, they loved her. She stood over a shaft, waving him forward. When he reached her, she shook his hand, and their fields glimmered.

"All right," he said briskly. "Let's see what we've got."

Someone pressed a lamp into his hand.

He lowered it into the darkness, saw engravings and bas-reliefs, and descended into a chamber whose dimensions reached beyond the limits of the light. The walls were busy, filled with shelves and carvings. There were objects on the shelves. Hard to see precisely what. Maybe local sea life, accumulated before the room was sealed. Maybe artifacts.

His team followed. Trifon warned them not to touch anything. "Got to make a chart before anything gets moved."

We know, Tri.

Lights played across the wall-carvings. He could make out animals, but no likenesses of the Quraquat. Sculptures of the intelligent species were rare, except in holy places. In any age. And among most of their cultures. There seemed to be an imperative that prohibited capturing their own image in stone. There would be a reason, of course, but they had not yet found it.

The floor was covered with a half-meter of silt.

Other chambers opened beyond. And voices echoed happily in his phones:

"This used to be a table."

"The symbols are Casumel series. Right?"

"Art, look at this."

"I think there's more in back."

"Here. Over here."

And Linda, in the room on the north side, held a lamp up to a relief which depicted three Quraquat figures. Trifon delicately touched the face of one of the images, trailing his fingers across its jaw, along the thrust of its mouth. The Quraquat had been warm-blooded, bipedal, furred creatures

with a vaguely reptilian cast. Alligators with *faces* rather
than long jaws and mindless grins. These were robed. A
four-legged beast stood with them.

"Henry?" She motioned him over.

The figures were majestic. They radiated power and dignity. "Are they gods?" he asked.

"What else?" said Tri.

"Not strictly," said Linda. "This is Telmon, the Creator."
She indicated the central figure, which was dominant. "She
is the Great Mother. And these are her two aspects: Reason
and Passion."

"The Great Mother?" Henry sounded surprised. The Quraquat at the time of their demise had worshipped a supreme
male deity.

"Matriarchal societies have been common here," she said.
Tri was taking pictures, and Linda posed beside the figure.
For perspective, more or less. "If we ever get a decent analy-
sis on the Lower Temple," she said, "we'll discover *that* was
a matriarchy. I'll bet on it. Moreover, we'll probably find
Telmon in that era as well."

Carson's voice came in on Jacobi's personal channel. "Henry, there's something here you'll want to see."

It was in the largest of the chambers, where Carson waited
before another bas-relief. He waved Henry nearer, and raised
his lamp. More Quraquat figures. These seemed to be set in
individual tableaus. "There are twelve of them," he said in a
significant voice. "Like the Christian stations."

"Mystical number."

Henry moved quietly around the room. The figures were
exquisitely wrought. Pieces had broken away, others were
eroded by time. But they were still there, frame after frame
of the Quraquat in that same godlike dignity. They carried
rakes and spears and scrolls. And, near the end, a fearsome
creature with partially hooded features appeared.

"*Death*," said Linda.

Always the same, thought Henry. Here or Babylon or New
York. Everybody has the same image.

"What *is* this? Do you know?"

Linda was glowing. "It's the story of Tull, the Deliverer.
Here—" She pointed at the first tableau. "Tull accepts the
wine of mortality from Telmon. And here he is behind a
plow."

Quraquat mythology wasn't Henry's specialty. But he knew Tull. "Christ figure," he said. "Osiris. Prometheus."

"*Yes*. Look, here's the visit to the armorer." She drifted along the friezes, pausing before each. "And the battle sequences."

"There's a problem here somewhere," said Carson. "The myth is later than this period, isn't it?"

"We're not sure of very much yet, Frank," said Linda. "And maybe this place isn't as old as we think. But that doesn't matter as much as the fact that we have a complete set of tableaus."

"Marvelous," said Henry. "They'll put these in the West Wing and hang our name on them."

Someone asked what they represented.

"Here," said Linda. "It begins here. Tull is an infant, and he's looking down at the world."

"It's a globe," said Art. "They knew the world was round."

"That knowledge was lost and recovered several times during their history. Anyway, Tull envied the people on the world."

"The Quraquat."

"Yes."

"Why?"

"It's not clear. The Quraquat apparently thought it was obvious why an immortal would behave this way, but they didn't explain it. At least not in any of the records we've been able to find.

"Over here, he's assumed a devotional attitude. He is requesting the gift of mortality from his mother. Look at the universal outstretched hands.

"And here"—she moved past Henry, pointing—"here, he is a teacher."

And here, caught up in war. Arm raised. Expression fierce. His right hand was broken off. "He would have been holding a weapon," she said. "He was at a disadvantage, because when they gave him mortality, they did not deprive him of all his divine attributes. He understood the suffering of his enemies. And he could see the future. He knew that death in battle awaited him. And he knew the manner of its coming."

The crocodilian image of the god-hero was not without its nobility. In one frieze, he contemplates mortality in the presence of dark-robed Death.

"Eventually," said Linda, "he asks that his godhood be restored. Here, look at the supplicating hands."

Henry nodded. "I assume it was restored?"

"Telmon left the decision to him. *I will comply with your wish. But you have chosen by far the better part. Continue in your present course, and you will be loved so long as men walk in the world.* She didn't say 'men,' of course, but used the Quraquat equivalent." Linda illuminated the final tableau. Here, he has made his decision, and puts on his armor for the last time.

"After his death, his mother placed him among the stars." She turned toward Henry. "That's the point of the myth. Death is inevitable. Even the gods are ultimately subject to it. Like the Norse deities. To embrace it voluntarily, for others, is the true measure of divinity."

The dark, robed figure was disturbing. "Something familiar about it," said Henry.

Carson shook his head. "It just looks like your basic Grim Reaper to me."

"No." He had seen the thing before. Somewhere. "It isn't Quraquat, is it?"

Art pointed a lamp at it. "Say again?"

"It isn't Quraquat. Look at it."

"No, it isn't," said Linda. "Does it matter?"

"Maybe not," he said. "But take a close look. What does it remind you of?"

Carson took a deep breath. "The thing on Iapetus," he said. "It's one of the Monuments."

Dear Phil,

We got a complete set of the Seasons of Tull today. I have attached details of the design, and tracings of eight wedges with inscriptions in Casumel Linear C. We are exceedingly fortunate: the place is in excellent condition, considering that it was close to sea water for most of its existence, and in the water for the last few centuries.

Time was, we would have had a major celebration. But we are getting close to the end here. We'll be turning everything over to the terraformers in a few weeks. In fact, we are the last team left on Quraqua. Everybody else has gone home. Henry, bless him, won't leave until they push the button.

*Anyway, your wunderkind has struck gold. Henry
thinks they'll name the new Academy library for me.*

Linda

—Linda Thomas
Letter to her mentor, Dr. Philip Berthold, University of
Antioch. Dated the 211th day of the 28th year of the Quraqua
Mission. Received in Yellow Springs, Ohio, May 28, 2202.

2.

Princeton. Thursday, May 6, 2202; 1730 hours.

Hutch killed the engine and the lights, and watched the first wave of office workers spread out through the storm. Most headed for the train station, an elevated platform lost in the hard rain. Some huddled in the shelter of the Tarpley Building, and a few—the more prosperous—dashed for their cars. The sky sagged into the parking lot, its underside illuminated by streetlights and traffic.

His lights were still on, but the blinds were down. It was a corner office on the top floor of a squat utilitarian building, a block of concrete and glass, housing law firms, insurance agents, and jobbers reps. Not the sort of place one would associate with romance. But for her, just being here again, just *seeing* it, set her internal tides rolling.

People were piling up at the main doors, pulling their collars tight, wrestling with umbrellas. Two or three energy fields blinked on. Cars swung into the approaches, headlamps blurred, wipers moving rhythmically.

Hutch sat unmoving, waiting for the lights to go out, waiting for Cal Hartlett to appear out on the street, wondering what she would do when he did. That she was here at all angered her. It was time to let go, but instead she was hanging around like a lovesick adolescent, hoping something would happen. Hoping he would change his mind when he saw her, as though everything they'd had would come rushing back. But if she didn't try, she would have to live with that knowledge, and she would always wonder.

She shrank down into the front seat, and drew the rain and the night around her.

He had first confessed his love to her in that office. She'd sat in as a systems technician for him one memorable eve-

22

ning, and they'd stayed until dawn.

How long ago all that seemed now. She had been between flights, and when it all ended everything had seemed possible. *We'll find a way.*

The glidetrain appeared in the distance, a string of bright lights against the general gloom. A few people hurrying across the lot broke into a run. It approached on a long slow curve, braked, and whispered into the station.

Cal was a financial analyst with the brokerage firm of Forman & Dyer. He enjoyed his work, loved to play with numbers, had been fascinated by *her* profession. *My star pilot.* He loved to listen to her descriptions of distant worlds, had extracted a promise that one day, somehow, she would take him along. At least, he'd smiled, to the Moon. He had gray eyes and brown hair and good laugh lines. And he loved her.

The lights in his office went out.

He lived eight blocks away. Cal was a fitness nut, and even in weather like this he would walk home.

The glidetrain pulled out, accelerated, and slipped into the storm.

The steady flow of people thinned to a handful. She watched the last of them, several waving down their rides, two breaking into a run toward the station.

And then he came through the door. Even at this distance, and in the blurred light, there could be no mistaking him.

She took a deep breath.

Cal pushed his hands deep into the pockets of his soft brown jacket and strode into the lot, away from her, with a quick step. She watched him cross the plastene, skirting puddles, plowing steadily ahead through the storm.

She hesitated, very deliberately shifted to low feed, and switched on the engine. The car moved silently across the pavement, and drew up beside him. Until the last moment, she was uncertain whether or not she would swerve away.

Then he saw her. Her window was down, rain pouring in. He looked startled, pleased, ecstatic, uncomfortable. The whole range of emotions played across his face. "Hutch." He stared at her. "What are you doing here?"

She smiled, and was glad she'd come. "Want a ride?"

The passenger's door lifted, but he stood watching her. "I didn't know you were home."

"I'm home. Listen, you're getting drenched."

"Yeah. Thanks." He came around the front of the car and got in. The after-shave was the same. "How are you doing?"

"Okay. How about you?"

"Fine." His voice was flat. "You look good."

"Thanks."

"But then you've *always* looked good."

She smiled again, warmer this time, leaned over, and carefully kissed his cheek. Cal had seemed fairly dull when she'd first met him. And his profession had done nothing to enhance that image. But he'd touched her in some primal way so that she knew, whatever happened tonight, she'd never be the same. His appearance, which had been so ordinary in the beginning, was now leading-man, drop-dead caliber. How and when had that happened? She had no idea.

"I wanted to say hello." Swallow. "See you again." Who were the couple who slept with a sword between them to ensure forbearance? She felt the presence of the sword, hard and dead.

He was silent, searching. "Hello."

Rain rattled on the roof. "I missed you."

He frowned. Looked uncomfortable. "Hutch, I have something to tell you."

Up front, she thought. That was his style. "You're getting married."

His eyes widened again. He grinned. It was the sheepish, friendly, disingenuous grin that had first attracted her two years before. Tonight, it reflected relief. The worst of this was already over. "How did you know?"

She shrugged. "People were telling me about it ten minutes after I landed."

"I'm sorry. I would have told you myself, but I didn't know you were back."

"It's not a problem. Who is she?" She negotiated a deep puddle at the exit, and turned onto Harrington Avenue.

"Her name's Teresa Pepperdil. She's like you: uses her last name. Everybody calls her 'Pep.' She's a teacher."

"She's attractive, of course."

"Again, like you. I always restrict myself to beautiful women." He meant it as a compliment, but it was clumsy, and it hurt.

Hutch said nothing.

He looked past her, avoiding eye contact. "What can I tell you? She lives in South Jersey, and, as far as I know, she plans to stay here." He sounded defensive.

"Well, congratulations."

"Thanks."

She turned left onto 11th. Cal's apartment was just ahead, in a condo designed to look like a castle. The pennants hung limply. "Listen," she said, "why don't we stop and have a drink somewhere?" She almost added, *for old time's sake*.

"Can't," he said. "She'll be over in a little while. I need to get cleaned up."

She pulled in at the curb, short of the driveway. Cut the engine. She wanted to back off, let it go, not embarrass herself. "Cal," she said, "there's still time for us." She spoke so softly she wasn't sure he'd heard.

"No." His eyes turned away. She had expected anger, perhaps bitterness, sadness. But there was none of that. His voice sounded hollow. "There never was time for us. Not really."

She said nothing. A man approached with a dog. He glanced at them curiously, recognized Cal, mumbled a greeting, and passed on. "We could still make it work," she said. "If we really wanted to." She held her breath, and realized with numbing suddenness that she was afraid he would say *yes*.

"Hutch." He took her hand. "You're never here. I'm what you do between flights. A port of call."

"That's not what I intended."

"It's what happens. How many times have we had this conversation? I look at the sky at night, and I know you're out there somewhere. How the hell could you ever settle in to hang around Princeton the rest of your life? And rear kids? Go to PTA meetings?"

"I could do it." Another lie? She seemed to be flying on automatic now.

He shook his head. "Even when you're here, you're not here." His eyes met hers, finally. They were hard, holding her out. "When's your next flight?"

She squeezed his hand, got no response, and released it. "Next week. I'm going out to evacuate the Academy team on Quraqua."

"Nothing ever changes, does it?"

"I guess not."

"No—" He shook his head. "I've seen your eyes when you start talking about those places, Hutch. I know what you're like when you're ready to leave. Did you know you usually can't wait to get away? You could never settle for me." His voice trembled. "Hutch, I love you. Always have. Always will, though I won't mention it again. I would have given anything for you. But you're beyond reach. You would come to hate me."

"That would never happen."

"Sure it would. We both know that if I said, fine, let's go back and start again, you call up what's-his-name and tell him you're not going to Quraqua, wherever the hell *that* is, and you'd immediately start having second thoughts. *Immediately*. And I'll tell you something else: when I get out of the car, and you wave goodbye and drive away, you're going to be relieved." He looked at her, and smiled. "Hutch, Pep's a good woman. You'd like her. Be happy for me."

She nodded. Slowly.

"Gotta go. Give me a kiss for the old days."

She managed a smile. Saw its reflection in his face. "Make it count," she said, and drank deep.

Moments later, as she turned onto the Conover Expressway headed north, she decided he was wrong. For the moment, at least, she felt only regret.

Amity Island, Maine. Friday, May 7; 2000 hours.

Hurricanes had been Emily's kind of weather. She'd loved riding them out, sitting in front of the fireplace with a glass of Chianti, listening to the wind howl around the central dome, watching the trees bend. She'd loved them even though they were getting bigger every year, hungrier, wearing down the beach, gradually drowning the island.

Maybe that was *why* she loved them: they were part of the intricate mechanism of steadily rising seas and retreating forests and advancing deserts that had finally forced reluctant politicians, after three centuries of neglect, to act. Probably too late, she had believed. But she heard in the deep-throated roar of the big storms the voice of the planet.

Richard Wald was struck by her in their first encounter. That had come in the days when archeology was still earthbound, and they'd been seated across a table in a Hittite statuary seminar. He'd lost track of the statuary, but pursued Emily across three continents and through some of the dingiest restaurants in the Middle East.

After her death, he had not married again. Not that he'd failed to recover emotionally from his loss, nor that he'd been unable to find anyone else. But the sense of what he'd had with her had never been duplicated, nor even approached. His passion for Emily had dwarfed even his love for ancient knowledge. He did not expect to find such a woman again.

It had been her idea to settle in Maine, well away from D.C. or New York. He'd written *Babylonian Summer* here, the book that made his reputation. They'd been here on Thanksgiving Day, watching a storm like this one, when the announcement came that FTL had been achieved. (At the time neither Richard nor Emily had understood what was so special about FTL, much less how it would change their profession.) That had been just two weeks before she'd died, enroute to visit her family before the holidays.

Rain blew hard against the windows. The big spruce trees in his front yard, and across the street at Jackson's, were heaving. There was no longer a hurricane *season*. They came at all times of the year. Counting from January 1, this was the seventh. They'd named it Gwen.

Richard had been reviewing his notes on the Great Monuments while preparing to write an article for the *Archeological Review*. It was a discussion of the current disappointment that we were no closer to finding the Monument-Makers after twenty years of effort. He argued that there was something to be said for *not* finding them: *Without direct contact, they (the Monument-Makers) have become a considerable mythic force. We know now that it is possible to create an advanced culture, dedicated to those aspects of existence that make life worthwhile, and even noble. How else explain the motivation that erected memorials of such compelling beauty?*

It might be best, he thought, if we never know them, other than through their art. The artist is always inferior to the creation. What after all are Paeonius, Cezanne, and Marimoto when contrasted with the "Nike," "Val d'Arc," and the "Red Moon"? Firsthand knowledge could hardly lead to anything other than disappointment. And yet—And yet, what would he not give to sit here on this night, with the storm hammering at the door, and Beethoven's Fifth in the air, talking with one of those creatures? *What were you thinking atop that ridge? Hutch thinks she understands, but what was really going through your mind? Why did you come here? Did you know about us? Do you simply wander through the galaxy, seeking its wonders?*

Were you alone?

The leading edge of Hurricane Gwen packed two hundred–kilometer winds. Black rain whipped across his lawn and shook the house. Thick gray clouds torn by livid welts fled past the rooftops. The metal sign atop Stafford's Pharmacy flapped and banged with steady rhythm. It would probably come loose again, but it was downwind of the town, and there was nothing the other side of it except sand pits and water.

Richard refilled his glass. He enjoyed sitting with a warm Burgundy near the shuttered bay window, while the wind drove his thoughts. One was more alone in heavy weather than on the surface of Iapetus, and he *loved* isolation. In a way he did not understand, it was connected with the same passions that flowed when he walked the halls of long-dead civilizations. Or listened to the murmur of the ocean on the shores of time. . . .

There was no purification ritual anywhere in the world to match that of a Force 4 hurricane: Penobscot Avenue gleamed, the streetlights glowed mistily in the twilight, dead branches sailed through town with deadly grace.

Keep down.

It was, however, a guilty pleasure. The big storms were gradually washing away Amity Island. Indeed, it was possible, when the ocean was clear, to ride out a quarter mile and look down into the water at old Route One.

He'd been invited to eat at the Plunketts that evening. They'd wanted him to stay over, because of the storm. He'd passed. The Plunketts were interesting people, and they'd have played some bridge (which was another of Richard's passions). But he wanted the storm, wanted to be alone with it. Working on a major project, he told them. Thanks, anyhow.

The major project would consist of curling up for the evening with Dickens. Richard was halfway through *Bleak House*. He loved the warm humanity of Dickens' books, and found in them (to the immense amusement of his colleagues) some parallels to the Monuments. Both espoused, it seemed to him, a sense of compassion and intelligence adrift in a hostile universe. Both were ultimately optimistic. Both were products of a lost world. And both used reflected light to achieve their sharpest effects.

How on earth can you say that, Wald?

Carton in *A Tale of Two Cities*. Sam Weller in *Pickwick*. In Dickens, the point always comes from an unexpected angle.

Richard Wald was somewhat thinner than he had been when he'd walked the ridge with Hutch five years before. He watched his weight more carefully now, jogged occasionally, and drank less. The only thing left for him seemed to be womanizing. And the Monuments.

The meaning of the Monuments had been debated endlessly by legions of theorists. Experts tended to complicate matters beyond recall. To Richard it all seemed painfully clear: they were memorials, letters sent across the ages in the only true universal script. *Hail and farewell, fellow Traveler*. In the words of the Arab poet, Menakhat, *The great dark is too great, and the night too deep*. We will never meet, you and I. Let me pause therefore, and raise a glass.

His face was long and thin, his chin square, and his nose tapered in the best aristocratic sense. He resembled the sort of character actor who specializes in playing well-to-do uncles, Presidents, and corporate thieves.

The storm shook the house.

Next door, Wally Jackson stood at his window, framed by his living-room lights. His hands were shoved into his belt, and he looked bored. There was a push on now to shore up the beach. Harry was behind that. They were losing ground because of the frequency of the storms. People were simply giving up. Real estate values on Amity had dropped twenty percent in the last three years. No one had any confidence in the island's future.

Directly across Penobscot, the McCutcheons and the Broadstreets were playing pinochle. The hurricane game had become something of a tradition now. When the big storms came, the McCutcheons and the Broadstreets played cards. When Frances hit the year before, a Force 5, they'd stayed on while everyone else cleared out. Water got a little high, McCutcheon had remarked, not entirely able to disguise his contempt for his fainthearted neighbors. But no real problem. Tradition, you know, and all that.

Eventually, the McCutcheons and the Broadstreets and their

game would get blown into the Atlantic.

Darwin at work.

The commlink chimed.

He strolled across the room in his socks, paused to refill his glass. Something thumped on the roof.

Three-page message waiting in the tray. The cover sheet caught his interest: the transmission had originated on Quraqua.

From Henry.

Odd.

He snapped on a lamp and sat down at his desk.

Richard,

We found the attached in the Temple of the Winds. Est age 11,000 years. This is Plate seven of twelve. The Tull myth. Frank thinks it's connected with Oz. Date is right, but I can't believe it. Any thoughts?

Oz?

The next page contained a graphic from a bas-relief. An idealized Quraquat and a robed figure. Page 3 was a blow-up of the features of the latter.

Richard put down his glass and stared. It was the Ice-Creature!

No. No, it wasn't.

He cleared off his desk and rummaged for a magnifying glass. This was from *where*? Temple of the Winds. On Quraqua. Oz—The structure on Quraqua's moon was an anomaly, had nothing in common with the Great Monuments, other than that there was no explanation for it. Not even a conjecture.

And yet—He found the lens and held it over the image. Too close to be coincidence. This creature was more muscular. It had wider shoulders. Thicker proportions. Masculine, no doubt. Still, there was no mistaking the features within the folds of the hood.

But this thing is a Death-manifestation.

He slipped into an armchair.

Coincidence, first. Somebody had once shown him an image on the outside of an Indian temple that looked quite like the long-departed inhabitants of Pinnacle.

But *something* had visited Quraqua. *We know that because*

Oz exists. And the evidence is that the natives never approached the technology needed to leave their home world.

Why the *Death* personification?

That question chilled him.

He punched up an image of Quraqua's moon. It was barren, airless, half the size of Luna. One hundred sixty-four light-years away. A little less than a month's travel time. It was a nondescript worldlet of craters, plains, and rock dust. Not much to distinguish it from any other lunar surface. Except that there was an artificial structure. He homed in on the northern hemisphere, on the side that permanently faced the planet. And found Oz.

It looked like a vast square city. Heavy and gray and point-less, it was as unlike the works of the Monument-Makers as one could imagine.

Yet many argued no one else could have put it there. Richard had always dismissed the proposition as absurd. No one knew who else might be out there. But the Tull discovery was suggestive.

He called the Academy and got through to the commission-er. Ed Horner was a lifelong friend. He, Richard, and Henry were all that was left of the old guard, who remembered pre-Pinnacle earthbound archeology. They'd gone through the great transition, had been mutually intrigued by million-year-old ruins. Horner and Wald had been among the first to set down on Pinnacle. Today, they still made it a point to get together for an occasional dinner.

"I don't guess you'll be jogging tonight, Richard." That was a reference to the storm. Ed was slightly the younger of the two. He was big, jovial, good-humored. He had thick black hair and brown eyes set too far apart, and heavy brows that bounced and rode when he got excited. Horner looked reticent and inoffensive, someone who could easily be cast aside. But that pleasant smile was the last thing some of his enemies remembered.

"Not tonight," said Richard. "It's brisk out there."

Ed grinned. "When will you be coming to D.C.? Mary would like to see you."

"Thanks. Tell Mary I said hello." Richard raised his glass toward his old friend. "Nowhere I'd rather be. But prob-ably not for a while. Listen, I just got a transmission from Henry."

"He sent it here, too. I haven't seen it. Something about a Grim Reaper?"

"Something about the Monument-Makers," Richard explained. Ed began to look uncomfortable.

"We've got a problem," he said. "You know we're getting ready to pull the plug on Quraqua."

Richard knew. Quraqua was first in line to be terraformed. It was to be the New Earth. (No other world offered hope of supporting a settlement, save Inakademeri. *Nok*. But that garden world was already home to a civilization.) Now, a wide group of powerful interests saw Quraqua as a laboratory, a place to establish a utopia, a place to start over. "When?"

"Six weeks. A little less. Henry was supposed to be out of there by now. But you know how he is. Hell, Richard, once they start, we're finished. Forever."

Well, for a half-century anyhow. Might as well be forever. "You can't let it happen, Ed. The situation's changed."

"I can't see how. Nobody gives a damn about the Monument-Makers. Not really. You and me, maybe. Not the taxpayers. And certainly not the politicians. But a lot of people *are* excited about terraforming. There won't be any more delays."

"Have you spoken to Caseway?"

"No. And I don't intend to. That son of a bitch wouldn't give us the time of day. No." Horner's eyes flashed. Richard read his old friend's frustration. "Look, you know I would if I thought there was a chance. Why don't *you* try talking to him?"

"Me?"

"Yeah. He thinks you're the big hotshot with this outfit. He's read your books. Always speaks highly of you. Asked me why the rest of us couldn't be more like *you*. Wald wouldn't put his own interests first, he says. Thinks *you* have a sense of decency. Unlike me, apparently."

Richard grinned. "Can't argue with him there." The wind howled over the house. "Ed, can you get me transportation to Quraqua?"

"Why?"

"Because we're running out of time. I'd like to see the Temple. And Oz. Can you do it?"

"We have a flight going out to pick up Henry and his people."

"When?"

"When can you be ready?"

"Soon as the storm blows over. Thanks, Ed."

The corners of Horner's mouth rose. "I want you to do something for me."

"Name it."

"Two things, actually. I would like you to consider talking to Caseway. And, when you get to Quraqua, make sure Henry gets off with time to spare. Okay?"

NEWSDESK

NO END IN SIGHT FOR MIDWEST DROUGHT
Small Farm Bankruptcies Up Ninth Straight Year
NAU, Quebec Promise Help

INFLATION SOARS TO 26%
October Figures Fueled by Food, Medical Costs
Housing, Energy Down Slightly

GREENHOUSE GROUP PESSIMISTIC
Natural Processes Have Taken Over, Says Tyler
"We Waited Too Long"
President-Elect Announces Wide-Ranging Agenda

How You Going to Keep Them Off the Farm?
EUROPEAN URBAN POPULATION HITS NEW LOW
71% Now Live in Rural or Suburban Areas
Similar Trend in NAU
(See related story following)

FOXWORTH REASSURES MAYORS
ON FOOD TRANSPORT
Insists Breakdown Cannot Happen Again
Will Implement Ad Campaign To Halt Flight from Cities

BRITAIN, FRANCE REVEAL PLANS FOR NEW INNER
COUNCIL
"We Can Avoid the Old Mistakes," says Kingsley
Cites "Executive Group with Teeth"
Haversham Warns of World Government

572 DIE IN MIDAIR COLLISION OVER MED
Massive Search on for Black Box

HORNCAF ARRESTED WITH PROSTITUTE
Holovangelist Claims Interest Only in Her Soul
Sex Scandal Latest in Series

WET YEAR PREDICTED FOR MEXICO
Rainfall Expected to Double
Summer Planting in Danger

THIRD WORLD GROUP CALLS FOR SHUTDOWN OF MOONBASE
"Insult to World's Starving Populations"
Demonstrations Scheduled in NAU, UK, Russia, Germany, Japan

MARK HATCHER BURIED IN LONDON
Dead With Six-pack, A Poetic Tour Through the Great Famine
Won Pulitzer in 2172
Had Been in Seclusion 30 Years

MILLIONS DEAD IN INDOCHINA
Drought Worsens Throughout Subcontinent
Council to Consider Options

REBELS SEIZE KATMANDU
Hundreds Die in Street-Fighting

NAU POPULATION REACHES 200 MILLION
Foxworth Promises Action
Propose More Benefits for Childless Couples

POPE ON THIRD DAY OF FRENCH TOUR
Says Mass at Notre Dame Nouveau
Exhorts Faithful on Advantages of Celibacy

GROUND WATER DESTROYING EGYPTIAN MONUMENTS
Ancient Heritage at Risk
Restoration Groups Mobilize

GUNMAN KILLS SEVEN IN LIBRARY
Shoots Self as Police Close In
Former Girlfriend Hides in Stacks

POLL REVEALS AMERICANS TURNING OFF POLITICS
Voters Cynical in Wake of Sex, Money Scandals

ISRAELI LEADER DENOUNCES QURAQUA RELOCATION PLAN
"We Will Wait for a World of Our Own"

NAU WILL CUT BACK STAR FLIGHTS
Move Forced by Budgetary Constraints
(See two related stories following)

LIVABLE WORLDS EXTREMELY SCARCE
Odds Astronomical
Commission Recommends Resources Go Elsewhere
Quraqua To Be Ready in Fifty Years
"One New World Is Enough," Says Hofstadtler

PROTEST PLANNED BY NEW-EARTH SOCIETY
"Don't Abandon the Hunt," Warns Narimata

3.

Arlington. Saturday, May 8; 0915 hours.

The chime brought her out of a warm, silky dream. She fumbled at the lamp stand and touched the commlink. "Yes?"

"Hutch?" Richard's voice. "They tell me you're the pilot for the Temple flight."

"Yes," she said sleepily.

"Good. I'll be going with you."

She came awake. *That* was a pleasant surprise. She had not been looking forward to a month alone rattling around in *Wink.* "I'm delighted to hear it," she said. But she wondered why he'd bother. This was strictly an evacuation run.

"I'd have asked for you in any case," he was explaining.

"And I'd have appreciated the business." Hutch was a contractor, not an employee of the Academy. "Why are you going?"

"I want to see Oz," he said.

Richard signed off. Below, a tour boat with a canvas awning circled Republic Island, leaning to port while its passengers crowded the rail. They carried umbrellas against a light rain that had been falling all morning. They munched sandwiches, and dragged windbreakers for which they had no need. A fat man in a misshapen gray sweater sat in back, feeding gulls.

A brisk wind disturbed the surface of the river. Richard watched from his air taxi. Brightly colored pennants fluttered along both beams. A young couple on the starboard side paid far more attention to each other than to the monument. On the island, a group of kids, shepherded by a harried woman with a cane, trailed blue and red balloons. The fleet of sailboats that usually filled the river had not appeared. The fat man

36

crumpled a white bag and opened another. He looked at peace with the world.

Richard envied him. Feed the gulls, and enjoy the monuments.

The taxi banked west. Constitution Island lay to his right, with its cluster of public buildings. The old Capitol had all but vanished into the rising mist. The Lincoln, Jefferson, Roosevelt, and Brockman monuments stood serenely on their embankments. And the White House: nothing in D.C. quite stirred the emotions like the sight of the former executive mansion, defiant behind its dikes. Old Glory still flew, rippling above the green and white banner of the North American Union. This was the only site in the country where the national colors gave precedence to another flag.

Lights burned in the towers along the Arlington shore.

The air taxi swung in a wide arc toward the Virginia side. Richard reluctantly turned his thoughts to the coming ordeal. He disliked confrontations. He was accustomed to deference, to people who listened politely and, if they disagreed, knew how to respond without being disagreeable. Norman Caseway, CEO of Kosmik, Inc., was the prime mover behind the Second Earth initiative. And he could be expected to show no such fastidiousness. Caseway was no respecter of persons. He was an alley fighter, a brawler who enjoyed leaving hoofmarks on opponents. He particularly relished assaulting academic types, as several of Richard's colleagues had discovered to their dismay.

Richard had never met Caseway. He'd seen his antics on NET. A few weeks ago, he'd watched him demolish poor old Kinsey Atworth, an economist whose tongue was not as quick as his brain. Caseway's strategy was to attack the motives of anyone who opposed him, to mock, to sneer, to enrage. And then to back off coolly while his opponent sputtered and self-destructed. The man enjoyed humiliating people.

Always speaks highly of you, Ed had said. *He's read your books.*

He passed over Potomac Island and the Pentagon, and descended toward Goley Inlet. The taxi rolled in a wide, lazy spiral and landed atop the Crystal Twins.

Richard's restraints snapped open, and the hatch slid back. He inserted his card into the reader. The taxi thanked him, wished him good day. He stepped out into warm, sluggish air, and the taxi lurched skyward, far more quickly than it would have with a passenger aboard. It turned south toward Alexandria and soared quickly over the hotels.

Norman Caseway lived with his wife and daughter in what the Towers was pleased to call its Observatory Suite, a lush penthouse that occupied parts of two floors. He was greeted at the door by an attractive middle-aged woman. "Dr. Wald? We're happy you could come." The smile was perfunctory. "I'm Ann Caseway."

"Pleased to meet you." She did not offer her hand, and Richard detected a stiffness which seemed alien to her appearance. Ann Caseway was, he judged, a woman both congenial and casual. Under normal circumstances.

"My husband's waiting for you in his office."

"Thank you." He followed her into a reception room, tastefully decorated with embroidered wall-hangings and Caribbean basket-chairs, and a curved springwood table.

Long windows overlooked the Potomac, and the ceiling was vaulted glass. The overall display of wealth and success was calculated to intimidate visitors. Richard smiled at the transparency of the tactic. Still, reluctantly, he recognized that it *did* affect him.

"This must be difficult for you," she said smoothly. "Norman hoped it might be possible to talk things out with someone at your level." There was the barest hint of regret, not unmixed with satisfaction, in her voice. Regret perhaps that Richard would be an unseemly victim to throw to her husband, satisfaction stemming from the end of the long argument with the Academy over Quraqua, with its threats of court battles and sequestration of funds. Nice to see the enemy at the door, hat in hand.

Damn the woman.

She led him through a conference room filled with Kosmik trophies and memorabilia, photos of Caseway with famous people, Caseway signing documents, Caseway cutting ribbons. Awards, certificates of appreciation from charities and public organizations, plaques from government agencies, were present in such profusion that they overflowed the walls and lay in piles. An antique dark-stained rolltop desk dominated the room. It was shut, but a framed news bulletin, with a photo, stood prominently on its top. The bulletin, dated thirty years before, read: BRAINTREE MAN RESCUES BOY WHO

FELL THROUGH ICE. The hero in the photo was a young Caseway.

"This way, please." She opened an inner door and sunlight blinded him. This wasn't the feeble mid-May sunlight of Virginia. Nor even of a summer day in New Mexico. This was off-Earth sunlight. Naked white sunlight. She handed him a pair of dark glasses.

"Welcome, Dr. Wald." The voice, rich, precise, confident, came from within the glare.

A sand dune half-blocked the doorway. A hologram, of course. Richard strolled directly through the dune (which was not playing the game), and stepped into a desert. The room was air-conditioned. Flat sand stretched to the horizon.

A few feet away, Norman Caseway sat in one of two wing chairs behind a coffee table. A bottle of Burgundy and two goblets were on the table. One was half-full.

He was well turned-out—red jacket, tie, neatly pressed dark blue trousers. Dark lenses hid his eyes. Behind him, rising out of the desert, was Holtzmyer's Rock.

Caseway filled Richard's glass. "I hope you don't mind that I started without you."

They were on Pinnacle. Holtzmyer's Rock looked like a gigantic washed-out red onion rooted in the sand. It stood more than thirty meters high, eight stories. The original was composed of individual pieces of stone, so cunningly fitted that the seams were not visible without close inspection. The object had been dated at almost a million years. Arnie Holtzmyer, who'd stumbled on it almost twenty-two years ago, had been the least competent professional Richard had known. Had the sand been a little higher, Arnie would never have seen it.

The intent of its builders was unknown. It was solid rock, with four inner chambers but no means of reaching them. The chambers were empty, and did not seem to have any geometric order.

"What did you feel when you came to this place?" Caseway's voice, breaking into his reverie, startled him.

"Its age," Richard said, after a moment's reflection. "It felt *old*."

"You didn't mention that. In your book."

"I didn't think it was important."

"You were writing for the general public. About a structure

that seems to be unique on Pinnacle. Nobody knows what its purpose was. Or anything about it. What else was there to talk about except your feelings?"

The book was *Midnight on Pinnacle*. Richard had dwelt on brick texture, on the discoloration near the top that suggested a long delay during construction. He had made observations relating to the geometry of the object, and drew inferences from the fact that it stood alone. He had traced the geological history of the land on which it rested, pointing out that it had probably been a prairie at the time of construction. He had provided graphs showing how long it had been buried. And described recent wind action which had uncovered the object for Arnie.

"I'd like to go out there myself some day." Caseway rose and offered a hand. "I'm pleased to meet you, Dr. Wald. Glad you could find time to come by."

Richard was thinking of the inadequacies of holograms. You can't sip wine out near Holtzmyer's Rock. On the other hand, when he had stood in a high wind years ago and pressed his fingertips against the blistered stone, he had been shielded from the heat by his Flickinger field. The sand had rattled against the energy envelope, and the wind had tried to blow him over. Like Caseway, he had never *really* been there.

"Yes. Well, I needed to talk to you." Richard was naturally gregarious. Despite the years that make cynics of most people, he believed everyone could be reasoned with. He took the proffered hand and squeezed it warmly.

Caseway was a small, heavy man in late middle age. He reminded Richard of a master chess player he had once known, a man of infinite deliberation. He observed all the courtesies, and his manner suggested that he had taken the moral high ground, and that they both knew it. His voice filled with passion, and Richard understood that he was dealing with no empty opportunist. Norman Caseway perceived himself as a benefactor of the species.

"Please, sit down." His host turned his chair to face him. "I assume you'd like to talk about Project Hope."

Right to the point. Richard tasted his Burgundy. "Apparently, Mr. Caseway, there's been some bitterness."

"My friends call me Norman. And that's something of an understatement, Richard."

Richard folded his hands across his waist. "I would have preferred it otherwise."

"Doubtless. So would I. You should know Horner went behind my back. Tried to pull political strings."

"Ed means well. Maybe it didn't occur to him to just ask."

"I think he needs new advisors." Caseway looked out across the desert. "Does he listen to *you*?"

"Sometimes."

"Tell him that if it had been possible to oblige him, I would have done so. *If he had been willing to approach me directly. And talk to me.*"

"What you're saying is that it would have made no difference."

Caseway's lips tightened. "None," he said. "Under the circumstances, I really have no choice but to proceed."

"I see."

"If it's any consolation, I take no pleasure in this. I understand the archeological value of Quraqua. And I have a reasonable idea what we stand to lose. But you have had *twenty-eight* years on that world—"

"That's a long time in a man's life, Mr. Caseway. But it is very short when we are trying to reconstruct the history of an entire world."

"Of course." He smiled at Richard's persistence in using the formal address. But he refused to take offense. "Nevertheless, there are pressing considerations. We are not entirely free to choose our time frames." He sipped his drink. "What a marvelous place Pinnacle must be. I wonder what they were like."

"We'll know eventually. We are already able to make reasonable assumptions. We know they believed in survival beyond the grave. We know they valued mountaintops and seacoasts. We know they succeeded in eliminating war. We even know something about their music. Fortunately, we don't have to worry about a private corporation seizing the world."

"I understand." Caseway looked genuinely regretful. "I envy you. I don't know anyone who has a more interesting line of work. And I would oblige you in a moment, if I could."

"It would be to everyone's benefit." He wished they were somewhere else, away from the glare. He would have preferred being able to see Caseway's eyes. He took his own glasses off to emphasize the gravity of the moment. "The last of the natives on Quraqua died off probably about the middle of the seventeenth century. They were all that was left, scattered in dying cities around their world, of a prosperous and vital web of civilizations that spanned their globe only three thousand years ago. We don't know what happened to them. They collapsed, over a short period of time. Nobody knows why. They were technologically backward, by our standards. Which should have helped them survive, because they were still close to their roots, and not vulnerable to the kinds of problems we've experienced."

"It wasn't all that sudden," Caseway said. "It happened over centuries."

"No." Richard took the initiative. "Those are assumptions, put out by people who think it *had* to happen that way, because some of these civilizations were not connected, and should not all have gone down at the same time. But it's as if someone turned off a light."

Caseway thought it over. "Epidemic."

"Maybe. Whatever it was, the old order went to its knees, and never recovered. Twenty-five hundred years later, the species became extinct."

"Well." Caseway crossed one knee over the other, and scratched an ankle. "Maybe it's the Toynbee factor. Their species exhausted itself."

"That's a non-explanation."

"Richard—" Caseway paused. "I would like to know what happened on Quraqua as much as anyone. But the deluge is upon us. We have no time left for academic niceties."

"*What* deluge?"

Caseway looked momentarily startled. "Tell me," he said, "what you see in the future for us? For mankind?"

"We've always blundered through. I'm optimistic."

"I fear I have the advantage of you: I've read your books, and you speak often of the future. Unusual in an archaeologist, I would think. No, no; no protest please. I'm less sanguine than you are. And perhaps more of a realist. We have virtually unlimited power now. And we have the experience of the convulsions of the last two centuries. What good has it done us? You and I live well. But people continue to starve in frightful numbers; much of the damage to the environment has proved remarkably intractable; population is approaching the levels that preceded the Collapse." He stared pensively into his wine. "We *have* eliminated active warfare, but only because the League has the weapons. The Poles still hate the Russians, the Arabs hate the Jews, the People of Christ hate everybody. It's as if we've learned *nothing*."

"And the only solution is your utopia on Quraqua."

"Yes. We select a small group. Leave the old animosities behind. Start over. But start over, knowing what we know now. *That* way, we may have a future. Earth surely does not."

Richard shrugged. "It's an old idea, Norman. But even if I grant you the premise, why the big hurry? Why not take the time to see what we can learn from Quraqua? *Then* terraform away."

"Because it may already be too late."

"Nonsense."

"Not at all. Listen: the first step, which will happen in a few weeks, is to melt the icecaps. From that moment, it will be a half-century, at best, before the first member of the pilot colony sets foot on Quraqua. *Fifty years, Richard.* Middle of the century. What do you suppose will be going on by then?"

"Who knows?"

"Who indeed? Will political conditions be stable? Will there be money? Will the technology still exist?" Caseway shook his head. "Our experts predict a second Collapse within thirty years. Time is very much against us. Even today, we will be fortunate to bring this off. To create and populate a new world. But if we don't, I suspect we'll end very much like your Quraquat."

"It's a *scheme. Leave the old animosities behind.* You can't do that unless you find a way to leave their human nature behind. And you're prepared to sacrifice a major source of knowledge to this aberration." Damn the man and his arrogant smile. "Granting your premise, there *will be* other worlds. Why not be patient? Why not wait for a world you won't have to terraform?"

"Can you guarantee the discovery of a reasonable habitat within the next half-century?"

"Guarantee? Of course not. But there's a good chance."

"Perhaps you wouldn't object if we settled on Inakademeri? And kicked the Noks off?"

Richard stood. "I'm sorry to find you so determined."

"And *I* to find you so obtuse. But you're right: I am determined. Determined to see that we get another chance. And you must understand, this may be the only window. Delay, back off to save your pots on Quraqua, and someone may find a better way to spend the money. Once that happens, the game is over."

"It is *not* a game." He banged the glass down, shattering it. Gingerly he released the broken stem and mumbled an apology.

Caseway laid his handkerchief on the spilled wine. "It's quite all right," he said. "You were saying—?"

Richard plunged ahead: "*Norman, there is potentially explosive information at the Temple of the Winds.*"

Caseway nodded. "And what is the nature of this information?"

"We have evidence there was a contact between the Quraquat and the Monument-Makers."

His eyebrows rose. That had hit home. "What sort of evidence?"

Richard showed him a copy of the Tull bas-relief.

"It's hard to be sure," Caseway said. He pointed over Richard's shoulder and the desert vanished. They were seated in a modest wood-paneled room, bare save for the two chairs and the coffee table. "Not that it matters. There are *always* good reasons to delay." His eyes narrowed. "Money. Political considerations. The promise of better technology *next* year. Did you follow the debates over whether we have the moral right to destroy an extraterrestrial ecology? The Committee for Common Decency almost got us canceled because we are subverting God's plan for Quraqua. Whatever that might be." His brow creased. "I know what you're saying. I even agree with you, up to a point. I should tell you that if I had my choice, I would go to Nok, take it over, and leave the Temple to you."

Later, when Richard replayed the conversation, the final remark chilled him, because it came from a man he had begun to like.

NEWSDESK

17 DEAD IN TEXAS TORNADO
Second Twister in Eight Days Levels Austin Modpark

HANNIMAN EXECUTED IN TENNESSEE
Accused Killer of 38 Defiant to the End
Small Group Protests Outside Prison

ITALY INDICTS SIX IN PAN-ARAB CASE
Chairman of Courleone Chemical Faces Twenty Years
(Related Story Follows)

BEN-HASSAN DENIES BIO-WARFARE CHARGES
Says Pan-Arab Union Wants Chemical Plant for Peace-
ful Purposes
Charges Mossad Plot

"SISTER SANDWICH" RECEIVES LEGION OF MERIT
French Recognize American Nun Who Brought
Food to Paris During Famine
Sister Mary of the Cross Led Thousands of Volunteers

ANTI-GRAVITY SAID TO BE POSSIBLE
Research Team at Berlin May Be Closing In

Agriculture Moves North
RUSSIANS, CANADIANS DISCOVER CLIMATE SHIFT
PROVIDES NEW FARMLANDS
Farmers in Both Areas Are Staking Claims
(Related story follows)

MIDWEST WHEAT BELT MAY BE GONE FOREVER
Most Experts Say Changes Are Permanent
NAU Now a Major Food Importer

WEINBERG METEOR LANDS ON MOON
Observers On Hand To Watch It Come In
First Time Ever That We Had Advance Information
(Related story follows.)

MOONBASE DEFENDERS WARN OF DANGER FROM ASTEROIDS
Lunar Teams Provide Safety from Falling Rocks, Says Vice-President

20 MORE SPECIES DECLARED EXTINCT IN OCTOBER
BOLLIER QUITS AMID TEMPEST
Says Forests Beyond Recovery, Attacks Sanchez
Brazilians Charge Theft of Foundation Funds

4.

NCA Winckelmann. *Wednesday, May 12; 1410 GMT.*
Earth and moon fell behind.

Hutch sat on the bridge of the *Johann Winckelmann*, watching the familiar globes fade to bright stars. *Once more into the breach, dear friends.* Already Cal was receding, growing hazy, as if his existence were a Schrödinger effect, dependent on her presence. Maybe he was right about her.

Richard was moving around in back, unpacking, getting settled. She was grateful for the last-minute change in plans, which had saved her from a solitary ride out to Quraqua. In her present mood she needed a diversion. And her passenger was the perfect prescription: she knew him well enough to tell him everything, and he would tolerate no self-pity.

They'd had breakfast before departure, and then he'd disappeared into his notebooks. He was excited about something, which was another reason she was delighted to have him aboard. Richard was always on a crusade. He did not come forward after launch, but that was not unusual behavior either. At some point he'd wander up, probably when he got hungry, because he didn't like to eat alone. And he'd explain everything.

She knew about the enigma on Oz, of course. She was pleased that Richard was going to take a look at it, and she looked forward to hearing his ideas on the subject.

But seven hours out he still hadn't appeared, and she informed him they were about to make the jump. "Ten minutes," she said, over the ship's comm. And added: "Estimate twenty-five days to Quraqua."

"Thanks, Hutch." He sounded disgusted. That would be because he was anxious to get started. By the second day he would begin to prowl the ship and challenge her to chess matches and bemoan his inability to get around more quickly. He'd stand on the bridge and watch the transdimensional mists drift past while *Wink* proceeded with the apparent velocity of a flatboat.

He came forward carrying a package of cinnamon buns. "How we doing?" he asked.

"Fine. Buckle in."

He sat down, secured the web, and offered her one of the pastries. "Good to see you again."

The wraparound viewpanel was open. The stars were bright and lovely. Their soft glow suffused the bridge. The interior lights were off, save for a few of the status lamps. They might easily have been outdoors on a terrace.

Richard made small talk for a few minutes. And then, when she saw an opportunity, Hutch wondered aloud about Oz. "It's not really a product of the Monument-Makers, is it? I mean, it's not at all like the other stuff."

His expression clouded. "Until a few days ago, I wouldn't have thought so. Now I'm not so sure." He passed her Henry's transmission.

The similarity was quite clear. "They found this in an eleven-thousand-year-old excavation?"

"Yes. What do you think?"

"It's one of them." She chuckled. "They went down and got their picture taken. I'll be damned."

Hutch went through her checklist prior to insertion. "I always thought it had to be them," she said. "That built Oz, I mean. Who else is there?"

Richard looked disappointed. "We don't really know, do we, Hutch? Anyway, to be honest with you, Oz is a place that I've preferred to ignore. It doesn't fit any kind of rational scenario I can think of."

Hutch looked back at the Death-image. It touched something deep in her soul.

"Well," said Richard, "I'm sure Henry's people will have some ideas."

An amber lamp began to glow. "Insertion coming up," she said quietly. Power couplings activated. "Ten seconds."

Richard settled back into his web. "If it's really them, it might mean they suffered some sort of precipitous decline." His eyes drifted shut. "I hope not."

The engines fired, and the stars went out. That was the only

physical effect of the leap into transdimensional space. There
was not even a sense of motion. Some claimed to feel a slight
vertigo, but Hutch thought they were generally overwrought
types anyway.

It was a little like passing through a tunnel. When the
tunnel faded, a process that might require anywhere from
half a minute to almost an hour, it had given way to the
gray mist.

Systems went green, and she closed off the forward view.

"—I'd hate to think that, in the end, they went mad."

"Isn't that a little strong?" She had waited on the pastry.
Now she poured fresh coffee and helped herself.

"*Mad*? You won't think so when you've seen Oz."

LIBRARY ENTRY

WHERE IS THE PAYOFF?

*... The wealth that was to accrue from interstellar
flight has never materialized. We have had minor technological advances that might have been achieved anyway, at a fraction of the cost. We have learned that
intelligent species existed on two remote worlds, and
that they exist no longer; and that, on a third world,
another species is currently waging a global war. One
might argue that these results (combined with our own
failure to respond to deteriorating conditions on Earth)
suggest that what we have really learned is that intelligence is rarer than we thought. There is some reason to
suppose it has yet to evolve. Anywhere.*

*The annual cost of maintaining the interstellar pro-
gram at its current level would feed every man, woman, and child in India and Pakistan. Currently, there
are eighteen thousand researchers in extrasolar stations.
Many of these stations have been in place for thirty
years, since the dawn of the Interstellar Age. And we
have reams of esoteric material describing climatic conditions and tectonics on other worlds. The Globe has no
quarrel with this acquisition of scientific knowledge. But
it is time, and more than time, to strike a balance.*

*We are in deep trouble. We cannot feed, or house, or
care for, a substantial portion of the global population.
Those who smirk at the Noks and their World War I-style*

conflict might note that the daily toll from famine and malnutrition in China is higher than the total dead in the Nok War last year.

Meantime, PSA lobbies for more funds to build more ships. It is time to call a halt.

—Editorial, *The Boston Globe*
May 22, 2202

5.

Quraqua's Moon. Sunday, June 6; 0734 hours.

Quraqua had a single satellite, roughly half the size of the Moon, ash-gray, scarred, airless. Tonight it was a bright yellow crescent, friendly, luminous. Inviting. But it was a moon with a difference. Six years ago, the pilot of an incoming packet had noticed what he thought was a city high in its northern quarter.

"Richard?"

He was absorbed in a hand-drawn chart spread out on his knees and across a sizable portion of the instrument panel. He waggled his hand to indicate he'd heard. "Let Henry know we're here," he said. "And make for Oz."

Beneath the red sun Bellatrix, and cloud-shrouded Quraqua, *Winckelmann's* shuttle *Alpha* (there was no *Beta*) glided over the moonscape. Peaks and gorges and craters merged with glare and shadow. The shuttle crossed a low mountain range and hurtled out over a sea of flat polished rock. Richard sat quietly, as he always did at such times, leaning forward against his restraints, gazing placidly out the window. Hutch was uncomfortable with his insistence on coming *here* first. She would have preferred to complete preparations for the evacuation before they undertook any side adventures. There would be cargo to load, and last-minute problems, and she wanted all that worked out well in advance. Instead, she could imagine Richard getting caught up in the anomaly, and adding complications.

His attitude did nothing to dispel those fears. "Plenty of time," he said. "We have until the eleventh." Five days.

A ridge appeared, swept toward them, and vanished. The mare was heavily pocked. The *Guide Book*, which she had posted on her overhead display, indicated it was the oldest surface area on the moon. "Some of these craters," she said, "are two billion years old."

Richard nodded, not listening. He wasn't interested in geology.

A sensor lamp blinked on.

"Ship on the scope. Henry's shuttle."

"Good." His expression warmed.

"It's about twenty minutes behind us." Hutch switched to manual, noted her position on the navigational displays, and throttled back.

"Be good to see him again." His eyes brightened. "This has to be a hard time for him. We thought we had forever to excavate Quraqua. Nobody believed we'd be ordered off. It turns out we were too cautious. Should have plowed right in. Like Schliemann."

Hutch had met Henry twice. He was an odd, rumpled little man who had given a lecture she'd attended when she was trying to learn enough archeology to persuade the Academy that she could be an asset. Two years later, when they'd shared passage on the Moon relay, he'd surprised her by remembering who she was. He even knew her name. Priscilla.

The ground began to break up into canyons. A range of needle peaks swept past.

"What were they like?" she asked. "The Quraquat?"

"They lived a long time. Individually, I mean." He fumbled in his jacket. "I should have a sketch here somewhere—must have left it in my room. Or"—sheepishly—"at home." He kept searching pockets. "They looked like furry gators. But they were warm-blooded—"

"No: I mean what were they *like*? What did they *do*? I know they had two sexes, and they had long life spans. What else?"

"They had a lot of dark ages. Not as barbarous as Earth's, not as military. But stagnant. Sometimes nothing would happen for a thousand years. No political development. No science. Nothing. They also had a talent for losing things. For example, we know of three different occasions on which they discovered Quraqua was *not* the center of the universe."

"Why? Why all the dark ages?"

"Who knows? Maybe we'll go through them too. We just haven't been around very long. In the case of the Quraquat, they might have been victims of their life spans. The wrong people succeed to power and don't die. Not for a *long* time." He tried unsuccessfully to brush his hair out of his eyes. "Think about *that*. Imagine having to deal with Hart for the next sixty years." (Adrian Hart was the current chairman of the Academy Board of Trustees. He was fussy and vindictive, a micro manager with no ideas.)

An amber lamp started to blink. "Coming up," she said.

Sunlight danced off the rocks ahead. The reflection splintered, and raced in both directions across the plain. They might have been looking at an illuminated highway, bright, incandescent.

Richard leaned forward expectantly.

The light grew solid. It became a *wall*. Bone-white against the gray moonscape, it extended from a low range of hills on the south to the horizon on the north. Hutch throttled back, fired a series of quick bursts from the maneuvering rockets. She took them down near the surface.

The wall grew, and began to crowd the sky. It was *enormous*. The scale of the thing, as they drew closer, reminded her of the old textbook representations of Troy. She powered up the scopes, put the picture on the monitors: the thing appeared to be seamless.

Except that there were holes punched in it. Long sections had fallen away, and there were places where the wall appeared to have been hammered into the ground. Rubble lay along its base.

"Look," Richard said. The structure was seared, scorched.

"It *does* look as if somebody tried to knock the thing down."

"One would almost think so."

"What kind of fire would burn out here?"

"Don't know." He folded his arms and canted his head. "I was wrong to neglect this place all these years. This is a *fascinating* site."

"So what happened here?"

"I have no idea." He sat looking for several minutes. "Frost," he said.

"Say again?"

"I keep thinking of Robert Frost. 'Something there is that doesn't love a wall—' " He sank back, placed his fingertips together, and let the moment wash over him. "Magnificent," he breathed. "An utterly sublime mystery. It is really no more than a rock sculpture in an airless place. Why was it built? And who would assault it?"

It towered over them.

The only reasonable explanation was that it had been hit by a swarm of meteors. There was indeed meteoric rock in the area. And a lot of craters. But there seemed something *purposive* in the assault.

"It's probably an illusion," said Richard, who seemed always able to read her thoughts. "It's the only artificial structure out here, so there's nothing to contrast it with except the random chaos of the moonscape. Still—" He shook his head. "It's hard to know how to read this."

It had been built, Hutch knew, between eleven and twelve thousand years ago. "Its age matches the Tull set."

"Yes," he said. "There may be a connection."

It was eerie, and she found herself scouring the plain for oversized footprints.

The wall was 41.63 meters high, and 8.32 kilometers on a side. It enclosed a perfect square. "The length of a side," she read off the display on the monitor, "is precisely two thousand times the height."

"Base ten," said Richard.

"How many fingers did the Quraquat have?"

"They weren't exactly fingers. But four."

"The Monument-Makers had *five*."

The shuttle nosed up to the wall. It hovered a few meters away. "Do we want to land?"

"No. Not out here."

The wall had been old before there were pyramids in Egypt. Hutch floated before it, and felt the transience of her own mayfly existence as she never had on Iapetus, or at the other ancient sites. She wondered what the difference was. *Maybe it is bracing, encouraging to know that beauty somehow survives. But to be outlived by such primal madness—*

"This thing," said Richard, "is so different from everything else they left. If it is indeed theirs. The Monuments are light, exquisite, elegant. The race that created them enjoyed being alive. *This thing*: it's grim. Irrational. *Ugly*. A fearful creation." He pushed back in his chair the way people do during a simmy when the werewolf is approaching. "Take us up," he said.

She complied, moving at a leisurely pace.

Richard unrolled his chart again. "What've we got on the building materials? Where did the stone come from?"

She dug out the engineers' report. "All local. Quarries were found in several places, but nowhere closer than six kilometers."

"They didn't want to spoil the appearance by chewing up the landscape. That's consistent, at least, with what we've seen elsewhere."

"I guess. Anyway, they must have modified the rock. One theory is that they reworked it using nanotech. There's a lot of feldspar and quartz lying around. Apparently waste material. The wall itself is a kind of enhanced calcite."

"Marble."

"Yes. But better. More durable. More reflective."

"They wanted it to be seen from Quraqua."

"Apparently." They were near the top now.

They closed in on a section that had been burned. "Henry thinks," Richard said, "that the damage dates to around 9000 B.C."

"That's when it was built," she said.

"Somebody got right after it, didn't they?"

"Maybe the builders had a falling out. Quarreled over their little amusement park."

Richard held out his hands in supplication. "As good a guess as any."

She went back to her screen. "There's a fair amount of trioxymethylene in the soil. Formaldehyde. But only around here. Near Oz."

"That doesn't mean a damned thing to me. My chemistry's godawful. What are the implications?"

"This thing"—she jabbed a finger at the screen—"offers no theories."

The pseudo-city appeared beyond the wall: a dark cross-hatch of wide boulevards and blunt, broad buildings and long malls. A city of the void, a specter, a thing of rock and shadow. Hutch's instincts demanded lights and movement.

"Incredible." Richard barely breathed the word.

It was immense. She took them higher, and simultaneously switched the cabin heater to manual, moving the setting up a notch. The city, like the wall, lay in ruins.

"Look at the streets," he whispered.

They were designed in exact squares. Kilometer after kilometer. All the way out and around the curve of the horizon. Oz was a place of numbing mathematical exactitude, overwhelming even in its state of general destruction. Avenues and cross streets intersected at precise 90-degree angles. She saw no forks, no gently curving roads, no merge lanes. City blocks had been laid out to the same rigorous geometry.

"Not much imagination here," she said.

Richard's breathing was audible. "If there is anything more at war with the spirit of the Great Monuments than this place, I can't imagine what it would be." No burst of inventiveness appeared anywhere. No hint of spontaneity. They called it Oz. But that was a misnomer. If Oz, the original Oz, was a land of wonder and magic, this place was pure stone. Right to the soul.

Hutch disconnected from the vision, and withdrew into the cockpit. The gauges and keyboards and status lamps were all familiar and warm. The aroma of coffee floated in the still air.

Oz had never been intended to shelter anyone. The structures that from a distance resembled houses and public buildings and towers, were solid rock, without even the suggestion of door or window. No bubble, of either plastene or energy, had ever protected the artifact. Henry's teams had found no machinery, no devices or equipment of any kind.

They drifted down the long avenues. Across the tops of marble block-buildings. Many of the blocks were perfect cubes. Others were oblongs. All were cut from flat polished rock, unmarked by any ripple or projection. They came in a multiplicity of sizes.

Hutch looked out over the network of streets. In its original form, before whatever destruction had come on it, the stones had stood straight. No arc curved through the parallels and perpendiculars. No avenue sliced abruptly right or left. No rooftop sloped. No decorative molding or door knob existed anywhere.

They floated down the streets at ground level. The blocks rose above them, ominous and brooding. They passed through an intersection. For the first time, Hutch understood the meaning of the term *alien*.

"The dimensions of the blocks are multiples of each other,"

she said. She brought up the numbers. Every block in the construct was divisible into cubes that measured 4.34 meters on a side. Thus, the various calcite forms that lined the squares and avenues could be perceived as so many units high by so many wide. Streets and open areas were divisible in the same way and by the same dimensions.

The commlink chimed. "Dr. Wald, are you there?"

"I'm here, Frank. Hello, Henry."

Hutch activated the video. Only one man appeared, and it was not Henry Jacobi. Frank Carson was about fifty, a trifle beefy, with an open, congenial countenance. He leveled a steady blue gaze at them, appraised Hutch without reaction, and spoke to Richard. "Henry's not here, sir. Things have got a little hectic, and we couldn't spare him."

Richard nodded. "Anything new on the Monument-Makers? New images?"

"Negative."

Richard seemed almost entranced. "Anybody have any ideas what all this means?"

"No, sir. We were hoping *you* could tell *us*."

Richard brought up the scheduling for Project Hope on his monitor. They were to blow the icecaps sometime Friday. "I don't suppose Kosmik has changed anything."

"The deadline? No." Carson's expression showed disgust. "They're on the circuit every day with a fresh warning and countdown status."

Hutch glanced reflexively at the ship's clocks. Not a lot of time.

"Henry asked me to express his regrets. He would have liked to meet you here, but we just have too much happening." He spoke with military crispness. "What would you like to see?"

"How about the center of this place, for a start? And I'm open to suggestion."

"Okay. I assume your pilot has me on her scope?"

Hutch nodded.

"Why don't you follow me?"

She acknowledged, signed off, and fell in behind. "Tell me about Carson," she said.

"You'll like him. He's retired army. One of those gifted amateurs who are a tradition in archaeology. Like yourself." His tone was light, but she understood he was quite

serious. "He's Henry's administrator and executive officer."
He looked squarely at her. "And his pilot. If Frank weren't
around, Henry would have to behave like a manager. As it
is, Frank does all the routine stuff, and Henry gets to be an
archeologist."

"Carson doesn't object to that?"

"Frank likes the arrangement. He's a little rough around the
edges, and he has a tendency to overreact. But he's easygoing,
and he can get things done without ruffling egos. He enjoys
the work. The organization could do a lot worse."

Carson's vehicle was starting to descend. "Downtown Oz,"
said Hutch. The blocks were a little higher here than they
were out near the wall. Other than that, the sameness was
deadening.

There was a central square, anchored on each corner by a
squat tower, or by the ruins of one. The square was about a
half-kilometer on a side. A fifth tower, a unit shorter than
the others, had been raised in the exact center. Each was as
quadrilateral as everything else in Oz.

Richard was half out of his seat, trying to get a better look.
"Tilt this thing a little, will you? My way—"

Hutch complied.

Two towers were piles of rubble. A third, on the southwest,
was scorched. Burned black from the base up. The fourth
was almost untouched. "There," Richard said, pointing to the
black one. "Tell him to land *there*."

She relayed the message, and Carson acknowledged. "What
are we looking for?" she asked.

He looked pleased. "How much do you know about the
symmetry of this place, Hutch?"

"Not much. Just that it's there. What's to know?"

"Put a few square kilometers on the screen."

"Sure." She brought up a view centered on the middle
tower.

"Now. Pick a target. Anywhere."

"Okay." She zeroed in on a cluster of oblongs forming a
letter H. They were approximately two kilometers north.

"Draw a line from the group directly through the central
tower. And keep going."

On the opposite side of the screen, the line touched another
H. At the same range. "It's a reverse image," she said.

"Surprised?" Richard couldn't suppress a smirk.

Yes. The records she'd examined hadn't mentioned it. "Maybe it all has religious significance. Some high-tech species doing penance. That make sense?"

"Not to me."

Carson's shuttle was almost down.

Hutch turned the short-range scanners on the complex. "The central tower is nine units high, defining a unit as our basic block, four point three four meters on a side. The outer towers are ten. Like everything else here, they're solid. There's no evidence of any interior space." Carson landed, and she started her own descent. "Funny: you'd expect the central tower to be the tallest of the group. Not the shortest. They just don't think the way we do."

Carson had parked close to the edge. Hutch's lights touched the Temple shuttle. It was streamlined, intended for heavy atmospheric use. That meant a sacrifice in payload capacity. It was flashier than *Alpha* in another way too: the Academy had begun painting its spacecraft and CATs in an effort to shore up morale at remote field sites. The vehicle on the rooftop was a bright blue and gold. The Academy's colors. Probably another one of Adrian Hart's decisions.

She rotated the shuttle to bring the passenger's hatch inboard, toward the center of the roof. Give her preoccupied boss as little opportunity as possible to fall over the side. Carson climbed out and waved. She blinked her lights, and sliced down with easy skill, tread to tread.

Richard released his restraints, and reached back for his Flickinger harness. Hutch struggled into her own, pulled it over her flight jacket. Air tanks were okay. She activated the energy field, and helped Richard with his. When they were ready, she decompressed the cockpit.

Carson's military background showed. He wore crisply pressed khakis and a baseball cap, stenciled *Cobra II*, with a coiled serpent and lightning-bolt logo. His name was prominently displayed over the left breast of his jacket. He was a big man, broad in the shoulder, waist beginning to thicken. In the style of the time, he was clean-shaven, with black hair cut short and just beginning to gray. He stood waiting, legs spread, hands clasped behind his back.

Pressure went to zero, and both hatches swung open. Richard was not precisely clumsy, but *Alpha* seemed to have been designed with athletes in mind. To debark, it was necessary to climb out onto a stubby wing, and descend via handholds in the fuselage. Variations in gravity tend to confuse *any* passenger, but particularly someone like Richard, who was well along in years, and had never been light on his feet to begin with.

Carson appeared below the wing, and stood by, but made no actual move to help the older man. That was prudent: Richard did not like being helped. But he was there if needed. Hutch approved.

When her passenger was safely down, Hutch dropped lightly beside him. She clipped a tether around her left wrist and attached it to the shuttle. Take no chances on a rooftop in this gravity.

Richard was already on one knee, examining the charred stone. "What *happened* to this place?" he asked Carson. "Does anybody have any idea?"

"None. Nobody has been able to put together even a reasonable hypothesis."

"Maybe the construction ship blew up," Hutch suggested.

Carson frowned. "Doesn't seem like the kind of damage that would come from a single blast."

Richard got up and walked solemnly toward the edge of the roof. Carson moved as quickly to his side as the low gravity would permit. Hutch stayed a step behind.

"Spooky place," she said.

Carson smiled. His expression suggested he could see that someone might think so.

Richard did what people always do in high places. He leaned out and looked down. A plunge into the street, even from this height, wouldn't be fatal, unless you landed on your head. But you would sure as hell develop a limp. "Careful," said Carson, staying close.

"Is there a team currently working here?" Richard asked.

"No. There hasn't been any kind of presence in Oz for months. We pulled everybody out after we got the Temple deadline."

"There's not much traction up here," cautioned Hutch.

Richard stared out over the city. "Did you ever find any wreckage? Any trace of whatever was here?"

Carson shook his head. No.

"Anything at all left behind? Footprints? Marks in the ground—?"

The two spacecraft stood against the endless cubes and oblongs. Their fuselages and wings and pods were all rounded. A red guide lamp mounted between *Alpha*'s treads blinked softly. Cabin lights in both vehicles spilled out onto the seared rock.

"There's nothing. Wish there was, Doctor." Carson glanced at Hutch, and returned his attention to Richard. "Did you want to see the quarries? Where the rock came from?"

"No. Thank you. What else here is worth seeing?"

"There's an inscription."

"Inscription?" Richard's interest soared. "Why didn't you say something before? The *Abstracts* don't mention it."

"The *Abstracts* are a year old. We've been a little too busy to monkey with updates."

Richard rubbed his hands together. An expression of beatific pleasure lit his features, and he waved an arm, a gesture which was too sudden and sent him reeling sideways and over the edge. Hutch and Carson both grabbed for him. They weighed so little in the low gravity, which was about one-tenth standard, that they'd all have gone down had Hutch's tether not taken hold. Richard let out a whoop, and they scrambled for balance, but he never missed a beat. "Thanks, Frank," he said. And, after righting himself: "What does it say? Have you been able to read it?"

"Not a word," said Carson, looking apologetic. "But you'll find it worth your time."

Hutch decided Richard was right. She did like Carson. He had not hesitated to risk his neck. That impressed her.

They flew west, using both shuttles.

The height of individual blocks gradually decreased as they proceeded away from the center, although there was no regularity in the process. Near the wall, at the limits of the city (Hutch could not help thinking of it in those terms), single-unit pieces had come to dominate so thoroughly that anything higher stood out.

They passed a section in which a chasm had opened. The land had dropped several meters. Avenues were broken off, blocks tossed about. "There are several craters within the walls," said Carson, speaking over the link. "Most of them came *after* the construction. In this case, the crater was already here, and they built over it. They filled it in, but the land eventually gave way. There are a few other places where the crust has simply collapsed under the weight of the blocks."

"The meteors that struck the city: have you been able to determine when they hit?"

"No. We can't date them with any degree of accuracy. We know that the craters in and around the anomaly are considerably younger, though, than they are anywhere else."

"How much younger?"

"Most of the cratering took place between one and two billion years ago. But the local holes are, at most, fifty thousand years old. Of course, the ones *in* the city must have fallen *after* 9000 B.C. Incidentally, we don't understand where the burn marks came from, but we do know that whatever the nature of the fire, it came *twice*."

"Twice?"

"In 9000 B.C., and again around 1000 B.C."

Richard's brow crinkled. "This is certainly," he said with relish, "very puzzling."

"There's more," said Carson, "although it would have to be coincidence."

"What's that?"

"The dates coincide with widespread disruptions on Quraqua. Peoples vanishing from history, states collapsing, that sort of thing."

"That's right," said Richard, remembering the discontinuities. He lapsed into silence.

The somber gray cityscape moved beneath them. Ahead, Carson's navigation lights blinked red and white. Cheerful and brave against the eeriness. Hutch brought Carson up again on the display. "How long have you been out here, Frank?"

"Six years," he said.

"Long time."

"I guess." His features betrayed no emotion. They were shadowed and highlighted by the illumination from his control panel.

"Where's home?"

"Toronto. I was born in Edinburgh, but I don't remember any of it."

"Have you been back at all? For a vacation?"

"No. I've been busy."

Hutch knew that was unusual. Academy personnel were

granted six weeks annual leave plus travel time. Carson was a workaholic.

Richard had been watching the patterns of blocks. "I wonder," he said, "why they're all cut to the same dimensions? Might they have had some sort of inflexible rock scoop? Only cuts one size? Then welds them together?"

Hutch put one of the blocks on the display.

"No," said Carson. "That's not it. The larger blocks aren't made of smaller pieces. They're just cut to be three, or eight, times as big. Whatever. Anyway, we're here. Look over to your left."

A tower rose from the general pattern of low-level obloids. But it was a tower with a difference: the thing was *round*. It was short, squat, about four stories high. It stood alone in a square.

Its roundness was remarkable. In that numbing display of parallel lines and right angles and precise intersections, its simple circularity was a marvel, a masterpiece of invention.

They landed. Richard could barely contain himself during the cycling process, waiting for pressure to drop and hatches to open. Hutch, secure within her energy field, placed a restraining hand on his shoulder to remind him of the need for caution.

The tower was charred on the north side.

Carson opened his cargo door, and emerged with a small stepladder. Richard reassured his pilot, climbed out, and descended the handholds. A layer of dust covered the square.

At ground level, and out of the shuttle, Hutch felt the weight of the ages, empty streets and mock houses, mad geometry and long shadows that had waited through the whole of human history.

Carson knew precisely what he was looking for. He walked to the tower, placed the ladder against it, adjusted it, tried it himself, and then stood aside and invited Richard to mount. "Careful," he said.

About five meters up, four lines of symbols protruded from the marble. Richard climbed until he was at eye level with them, and used his lamp.

They possessed no resemblance to the exquisite symbols on Iapetus. These were heavy, solid, blunt. Direct, rather than suggestive. Masculine. While he appraised them, Carson dropped a bombshell: "It's a Quraquat language."

Richard swayed on the ladder. "Say again? My understanding was that no one on Quraqua ever developed space travel."

"That's correct, Dr. Wald. We don't know much about these people, but we're sure they never had *that* kind of technology."

Hutch stood back to get a better look. "Maybe another kind of technology, then. Something we're not familiar with."

"Like what?"

"I don't know. If I could tell you, I'd be familiar with it."

"Well, it doesn't matter." Carson cut her off impatiently. "We know they had a horse-drawn civilization when people were speaking *this* language."

Richard was inspecting the symbols through a magnifier. "When would that have been?"

"Ninth millenium, B.C."

Same era. Hutch looked around at the blind oblongs and the long quiet streets. A chill worked its way up her spine.

"Would the speakers of this language," Richard asked, "be the same people who engraved the image of the Monument-Maker in the Temple?"

"Yes," said Carson. "The language is Casumel Linear C. It was spoken only over a range of about four hundred years."

Richard, still perched on the ladder, leaned back and peered up at the top of the tower. "Is *this* why Henry has pushed so hard at the Temple?"

Carson nodded. "Can you imagine what it will be like having an inscription from this place, and not be able to read it?" He shook his head in disgust. "The people who spoke the language inhabited the country around the Temple of the Winds. And they controlled the Temple itself at one point. We've been hoping to find a Rosetta stone. Or, failing that, to get enough samples of the writing to allow us to decipher it."

Hutch broke in. "I don't understand this at all. If the Quraquat never came here, how could they possibly have left a sample of their writing? Are you *sure* this is what you think it is?"

"No question," said Carson. "It's a perfect match."

"Then what are we saying—?"

"I would think," Richard said, "that the builders of this—

monstrosity—left a message for the inhabitants of Quraqua. To be read when they got here."

"About *what*?" Hutch could scarcely contain her impatience.

"An invitation to join the galactic club," suggested Carson.

"Or an explanation for Oz." Richard started down. "Who knows?"

Hutch looked at Carson. "Frank, how many of these ancient languages can we read?"

"A few. Not many. Almost none, actually."

"None." She tried to shake the fog from her brain. "What don't I understand? If we can't read *any* of these languages, what difference does it make whether we find a Rosetta stone? I mean, we're not going to be able to read the Rosetta, either. Right?"

"It won't matter. If we get the same text in three or more languages, we can decipher all the languages involved. Provided we get a sample of reasonable size." Richard was back on the ground now. "If you've seen enough," Carson said, "there's something else you'll want to look at."

"Okay."

"We need to go to the top of the tower." They walked back toward the shuttles. "We can use mine."

They climbed in. Carson left the hatch open. He adjusted his cap, and activated the magnets. The vehicle floated up the face of the tower.

"Is there," asked Richard, "another of these things on the other side of Oz?"

"Another round tower? Yes, there is."

"Another inscription?"

"No. Not another inscription."

"Interesting." Richard looked down. "Hey," he said, "the roof isn't level." He leaned out to get a better view. "It's the first slope of any kind we've seen here."

"There's another," said Carson.

"The other tower."

"Yes." They hovered just over the roof.

"Frank." Richard Wald's silver eyebrows drew together. "Is the location of the other tower a reverse image of this one?"

"No."

Richard looked delighted.

Hutch saw the point. "It breaks the pattern," she said. "A straight line drawn between the round towers does not pass through the central tower."

"A unique condition in Oz. Frank, does it happen anywhere else?"

"Nowhere that I know of."

"Good. Then we have only these towers to concentrate on." He swung around, trying to get his bearings. "The center of the city is where?"

Carson showed him.

"And the other tower?"

"Toward the north." He pointed. "Why?"

"Don't know yet. Frank, have you measured the angle of the roof?"

"No. I don't think anyone measured it. Why would we?"

"I don't really know. But look at it. The lowest part of it lies on the side closest to the center of the city. As you look out toward the wall, the slope rises."

"I don't follow."

"All guesswork so far. Is the same thing true of the other round tower?"

"I'm not sure I understand the question."

"You said the roof there is also angled. Is the roof on the other tower lowest where it's closest to the middle of Oz?"

"I don't remember." *Why would anyone*, his tone suggested, *bother with such a thing?* "Do you want to set down and look around on the roof a bit?"

"No, I've seen quite enough, thanks. We have one more job to do, and then I'd like to go with you back to the Temple."

"Richard." Hutch, who had guessed this was coming, tried to use her most serious, don't-screw-around-with-me voice. "Don't forget we're supposed to be here to take these people off. Not augment them."

"I know, Hutch. And I won't forget." He took her hand, squeezed it. Their Flickinger fields flashed.

"Be careful," she said.

"What's the other job?" asked Carson.

"We need as precise a measurement of the inclination as we can get. On both round towers. And we need to ensure that the lowest point on each roof really does match up

with the central square." He winked at Hutch. "Maybe"—
he beamed—"we have something."

June 6, 2202

Dear Dick,

*   . . . Thank God for the round towers and the slanted
roofs. It is all that adds any touch of reason to the entire
business.*

*   You would have been amused at how we behaved.
Very quiet. We kept our voices down, as if we were all
afraid someone might be listening. Even Frank Carson.
You haven't met him. He's not the sort of man to give
way to anyone. But even he kept looking over his shoulder.*

*   Truth is, there is a presence in those streets. You can't
help but feel it.*

*   Poor Hutch. She sees no rationale whatever, and consequently she was damned near unhinged at the end
of our tour. Even with the small insight I have (and
I know you have guessed what it is), I too feel unsettled.
Oz is not a place for anyone with a halfway active
imagination. . . .*

Richard

—Richard Wald to his cousin Dick
Received in Portland, Oregon, June 24

PART TWO

TEMPLE OF THE WINDS

6.

Hutch was glad to get back to the *Winckelmann*. It was an ungainly, modular vehicle, little more than a set of rings (three on this voyage) connected to a central spine. She activated its lights as she approached. They illuminated the shuttle bay and silhouetted arrays of sensors and maintenance pods and antennas. The ship was warm and familiar, a utilitarian and undeniably human design floating against a starry backdrop rendered suddenly unsettling.

The moods of deep space didn't usually affect her as they did many others who traveled between the worlds. But tonight, ah tonight: the ship looked *good*. She'd have liked company, somebody to talk to, someone to fill up the spaces in the vessel. But she was nevertheless relieved to be home, where she could lock doors and do a simmy.

The Academy seal, a scroll and lamp framing the blue earth of the United World, was emblazoned prominently on the A ring, near the bridge.

The moon and the planet floated in a black, starless sky. Quraqua lay on the edge of the Void, the great rift that yawned between the Orion and Sagittarius Arms. The opposite shore was six thousand light-years away, visible only as a dim glow. Hutch wondered about the effect on a developing species of a sky half-crowded with stars and half-empty.

Alpha entered B ring, and settled into its cradle. The big doors swung satisfactorily shut on the night. She pulled off her Flickinger harness and stowed it in the compartment behind her seat. Five minutes later, she was on the bridge.

The message board blinked. There was a transmission in the holding tray from the Temple site, routine precedence. Too soon for Richard to have arrived. Time enough to look

71

at it later. She went to her quarters, removed her work clothes, and stepped into the shower. The spray felt good.

Afterward, still dripping, she ordered steak. Her cabin was decorated with pictures of old friends, of herself and Richard on Pinnacle, of *Alpha* floating nose to nose with the Great Hexagon Monument near Arcturus, of a group of planetologists whom she'd joined for a beach party at Bethesda (and who had hoisted her on their shoulders for the photo). The air was sweet with the breath of green plants, lemon thyme and bayberry and honeysuckle.

The demon moon rolled across her view. Oz, on the far side, was not visible. Annoyed at her own disquiet, she closed the panel.

Richard had given her a medallion years earlier, a lovely piece of platinum, a copy of a talisman he'd brought back from Quraqua. This was in the days before Oz had been found. A winged beast and a six-pointed star were engraved on one side, and a gracefully curved arch on the other. Arcane symbols lined the rim. The beast and the star designate love, Richard had told her, and the arch is prosperity. *Both will be yours as long as you wear the medallion.*

Tonight, it was soothing. She looped it over her shoulders. Local magic.

She dressed and, when the dinner bell rang, strolled by the galley to pick up her steak. She added a bottle of wine, and took everything to the bridge.

The message board was still blinking.

She sliced off a piece of meat, tasted it, and opened the bottle. It was a Chablis. Then she keyed the message, and got a trim, blond female with spectacular good looks. "*Winckelmann*," she said, "my name is Allegri. I'll be coordinating the evacuation. We have fourteen people to take off. Plus Dr. Wald, who is enroute here now. We want to begin departures in forty-eight hours.

"I know that's later than the original plan, but we've still got work to do. For your information, Kosmik will begin operations at ten A.M. *our* time Friday. Temple time. This transmission contains time equivalents. We want to be out with twenty-four hours to spare. We also have artifacts to move, and we should start with those as soon as possible. Please contact me when you can."

The screen blanked.

Hutch pushed back in her chair. People in these remote places usually took the time to say hello. She wondered whether Allegri had been underwater too long.

She put Quraqua on the main display, went to mag 32.

Sunlight flooded the cloud cover, illuminating a world of mud-colored prairies, vast green forests, sprawling deserts, and winding mountain chains. Neither of its oceans was visible. There were two, both shallow, and not connected. It was generally a parched world, a condition that Kosmik hoped to cure during the first phase of its terraforming operation, which it had dubbed Project Hope.

The southern ocean surrounded the icecap, creating a circular body of water averaging about five hundred kilometers in width. Beyond, several finger-shaped seas pushed north. The longest of these was Yakata, a local term meaning Recreational Center for the Gods. It penetrated about three thousand kilometers into the land mass. At its northernmost extremity, just offshore, lay the Temple of the Winds.

She'd read somewhere that Quraqua was thought to be entering an ice age. Whether true or not, both caps were quite healthy. When they went, they would make a substantial splash. And, if the experts were right, Quraqua would get instant oceans.

Ten o'clock Friday morning, Temple time. When was that? She called up the data Allegri had sent.

Quraqua's day was twenty hours, thirty-two minutes and eighteen seconds long. Everyone understood the psychological importance of using the familiar twenty-four hour clock, but adjustments were necessary whenever humans set down for an extended stay on a new world. On Quraqua, timepieces were set to run until 10:16:09, A.M. and P.M. Then they leaped forward to noon and midnight. This method eliminated time from both sleeping and waking cycles.

Coincidentally, it was now Sunday at the Temple of the Winds, just as it was on *Wink*. Terraforming would begin in something over ninety hours. Henry Jacobi wanted to complete the evacuation with a one-day safety margin. And they had two shuttles to work with. It would be easy.

But she was uncomfortable. It did not look as though getting clear was at the top of Jacobi's agenda. She directed the navigational computer to lift *Wink* out of lunar orbit and make for Quraqua. She entered both deadlines into her personal chronometer, and set the ship's clocks to correspond to Temple time.

The navigation display warned her that the ship would leave orbit in thirty-six minutes.

Hutch finished her dinner, and swept the leavings into the vacuum tube. Then she switched on a comedy and pushed back to watch. But by the time the boosters fired, and the ship began to move, she was asleep.

She woke to a chime. Incoming transmission.

The lights were dim. She'd slept seven hours.

Richard appeared on the monitor. "Hello," he said. "How are we doing?"

"Okay."

He looked troubled, in the way that he did when he was about to tell her something he knew she wouldn't like. "Listen, Hutch, they're in a bad way here. There are several sites beneath the Temple. The one we're all interested in is down deep, and they're just now getting into it. We need to use all the time we have available. The shuttle that they've got here will accommodate three people plus the pilot. Figure out a schedule to get everyone out. But leave us the maximum working time."

Hutch let her exasperation show. "Richard, that's crazy."

"Probably. But they could be very close. They're almost into the Lower Temple. Hutch, it dates from 9000 B.C., the same era as the construction on the moon. We need to get a look at it. We can't just leave it here to be destroyed."

Hutch disagreed. "I think our first priority is to get out before the water rises."

"We *will*, Hutch. But meantime we have to make every day count."

"God damn it."

Richard smiled patiently. "Hutch, we won't take any chances. You have my word. But I need you to help me. Okay?"

And she thought: *I should be grateful he's not refusing to leave the surface, and daring Kosmik to drown him.* His inherent belief in the decency of other people had led him astray before. "I'll see what I can do," she said. "Richard, who's running the Kosmik operation here? Do you know?"

"The director's name is Melanie Truscott. I don't know anything about her. She's not very popular with Henry."

"I don't suppose she would be. Where's her headquarters?"

"Just a minute." He turned aside, spoke to someone. "They've got an orbiter. It answers to Kosmik Station." Suspicion filled his eyes. "Why do you ask?"

"Curiosity. I'll be down in a few hours."

"Hutch," he said, "don't get involved in this. Okay?"

"I *am* involved, Richard."

A wispy ring circled Quraqua. It was visible only when sunlight struck it at a given angle. Then it glowed with the transient beauty of a rainbow. The ring was in fact composed primarily of ice, and it was not a natural feature. Its components had been brought in—were still gliding in—from the rings of the gas giant Bellatrix V. Several Kosmik tugs had gone out there, extracted chunks of ice, and launched them toward Quraqua. These were "snowballs." They were intercepted, herded by other tugs, and placed in orbit, where they would be used to provide additional water for the planet. At zero hour, Kosmik would melt the caps, and slice the snowballs into confetti, and start them down. Estimates indicated it would rain on Quraqua for six years. Terrestrial forms would be seeded, and if all went well, a new ecology would take hold. Within five decades the first human settlers could claim a world that would be, if not a garden, at least manageable. *Wink's* sensors counted more than a thousand of the icy bodies already in orbit, and two more approaching.

Hutch had been around bureaucracies enough to know that the fifty-year figure was optimistic. She suspected there'd be no one here for a century. And she thought of a remark attributed to Caseway: "It is now a race between our greenhouse on Earth and the greenhouse on Quraqua."

Wink had entered orbit.

The world looked gray and unpromising.

Who would have believed that the second Earth would be so hard to find? That in all those light-years there would be so little? Pinnacle's gravity was too extreme, Nok was already home to an intelligent race from whom humans kept their existence a closely guarded secret. And one other habitable world she'd heard about circled an unstable star. Other than those, there had been nothing.

The search would go on. Meanwhile, this cold, bitter place was all they had.

Kosmik Station was a bright star in the southern skies. It was a scaled-down version of IMAC, the terrestrial space station, twin wheels rotating in opposite directions, joined by a network of struts, the whole connected to a thick hub.

Its lights were pale in the planetary glow. A utility vehicle drifted toward it.

She ran Melanie Truscott's name through the computer.

b. Dayton, Ohio. December 11, 2161

Married Hart Brinker, then account executive with banking firm Caswell & Simms, 2183. Marriage not renewed, 2188. No issue.

B.S., Astronomy, Wesleyan, 2182; M.S. and Ph.D., Planetary Engineering, University of Virginia, 2184 and 2186 respectively.

Instructor, UV, 2185–88

Lobbyist for various environmental causes, 2188–92

Northwestern Regional Commissioner, Dept. of the Interior, North American Union, 2192–93

Nuclear Power Liaison to UW, 2193–95

2195–97: Gained reputation as chief planner for the (partially) successful North African and Amazon basin reclamation projects.

Consultant to numerous environmental causes, and to Kosmik, 2197–99.

Has written extensively on greenhouse, and changing climatic conditions in the oceans. Longtime advocate of population reduction by government decree.

Arrested on four occasions for protesting wetland and endangered species policies.

The remarks section revealed that Truscott was a member of numerous professional organizations. Still active with the International Forest Reclamation Project, the Earth Foundation, and Interworld.

Once intervened in an attack by a gang of toughs on an elderly man in Newark. Was knifed in the process. Took a gun from one gang member and shot him dead.

During the Denver earthquake of '88, she'd directed traffic out of a collapsing theater.

No shy flower here.

Hutch brought up Truscott's image: she was tall, with a high forehead, and laser eyes. Dark brown hair and lush complexion. She might still be described as attractive, but she had somewhere acquired a hard edge. Accustomed to command. Nevertheless she looked like a woman who knew how to have a good time. More significant, Hutch could see no give in her.

She sighed and opened a channel to the orbiter. The screen cleared to the Kosmik emblem, the torch of knowledge within a planetary ring. Then a beefy, bearded man gazed at her. "Kosmik Station," he said. "What do you want, *Winckelmann*?"

He was big-bellied, gruff. The sleeves of a loud green shirt were rolled to his forearms. His eyes were small and hard, and they locked on her. He radiated boredom.

"I thought you might like to know I'm in the area." She kept her voice level. "If you have ships operating nearby, I'd appreciate a schedule."

He appraised her with cool disdain. "I'll see to it."

"I have commencement of blasting Friday, ten hundred hours Temple time." She used the word "blasting" sweetly, suspecting it would irritate the beefy man, for whom the correct terminology was *surgery*. "Confirm, please."

"That is correct, *Winckelmann*. There has been no change." He glanced aside, and nodded. "The director wants to speak with you. I'm going to patch you through."

Hutch mustered her most amicable smile. "Nice talking to you."

His expression hardened. The man lived very close to the surface. No deep contemplative waters.

His image gave way to a Melanie Truscott who looked somewhat older than the pictures Hutchins had seen. This Truscott was not so well-pressed, not quite so imperial. "Glad you're here, *Winckelmann*." She smiled pleasantly, but it was a smile that came down from a considerable height. "You're—?"

"—Priscilla Hutchins. Ship's captain."

"Good to meet you, Priscilla." The older woman's tone was casual. "Do you have any objection if I record the conversation?"

That meant this was going to be CYA. Get on the record in case there are court proceedings later. "No," she said. "That's fine."

"Thank you. We've been expecting you. Do you need assistance getting your people off?"

"Thanks. There are only a handful, and we have two shuttles."

"Very good. You should be aware that the initial phase of Project Hope involves nuking the icecaps." She looked pointedly at Hutch. "The Academy team still seems to have most of their equipment at the site."

"That could be. I haven't been down there yet."

"Yes." Her voice took on a confidential tone. As if there were foolishness abroad that required immediate attention by the two of them. "I've spoken with Dr. Jacobi. He is aware that destruction at the Temple site will be total." She paused. "The Yakata is open water all the way to the cap. That entire coastline will be rearranged. You understand what I'm saying?"

"I understand." Hutch did not need to inject concern into her voice. But she let the woman see she was doubtful. "What *you* need to be aware of is that they are close to a major discovery down there. There's a possibility I may not be able to get them all off in time."

Truscott's eyes momentarily lost their focus. "Priscilla, they are always close to a major discovery. *Always.* You know how long they've been there?"

"Almost thirty years," said Hutch.

"They've had plenty of time."

"Not really." Hutch tried to keep it light. Avoid being confrontational. "Not when you're trying to excavate an entire world. The Quraquat have three hundred centuries of history behind them. That's a lot of digging."

"Whatever." Truscott dismissed the discussion with a wave. "It doesn't matter. What *is* important is that I have no authority to postpone the start of the project. The Academy has agreed to evacuate; we've given them appropriate advance notification of operations. I am offering assistance, if you wish. And I will expect you to have your people safely away."

"Dr. Truscott, they may have a key to the Monument-Makers."

The director looked annoyed now. "Please understand," she said. "I have no discretion here." She found Hutch's eyes and held them. "Do what you have to. But get them off."

Ship's Log

Johann Winckelmann

Monday, June 7

Melanie Truscott is overbearing, and takes herself quite seriously. She shows no flexibility about the timing of the evacuation. Nevertheless, I am hopeful that she will build an emergency delay into the operation—if she has not already done so. I have described our conversation to Dr. Wald, warning him that it is my opinion that the Friday deadline should be treated with the utmost respect.

PH

Kosmik Station. Monday, June 7; 1050 hours.

Melanie Truscott would have liked to walk on real ground under a real sky. Leave the cramped spaces and gleaming walls and synth meals behind and stride off the station into the night. For God's sake, she was sympathetic, but where did the Academy get these people who thought the entire world should stand aside while they dug up pots and idols?

She stared at the blank screen. When Harvey broke in to inform her that he was talking to the pilot of the Academy ship, she had been paging through the most recent queries and demands for access to the New Earth: Islamic militants, white supremacists, Chinese nationalists, black separatists, One-Worlders, New Hellenes, a vast assortment of ethnic groups, tribes, oppressed peoples. Corporate interests. People with ideas for social experiments. Norman Caseway, who had forwarded the material, had his own plans. She was less optimistic than he. Actual settlement was far in the future. She would be long gone before it happened, as would Norman, and most of the others who had crusaded for the Project. Who knew how it would turn out?

She wondered whether the world's problems might be solved by access to the stars. Or simply exported.

"What do you think, Melanie?"

Harvey Sill stood in the doorway. He was the station chief, the beefy man with whom Hutch had spoken. Truscott had worked with Harvey on and off for years. She liked him; he was an able administrator, and he was a good judge of people. And he was that most valuable of all subordinates: a competent man who was not afraid to express his opinion.

Melanie rocked back in her chair. "I'm not comfortable."

Harvey sat on the table. "They're going to be a problem right to the end."

"There's something you should see, Harv." She called up a two-week-old transmission.

Norman Caseway's congenial features appeared. He was seated at his desk in front of the organizational banner. "Melanie," he said, "I had a visit from Richard Wald recently. He tried hard to get a delay on Hope. Yesterday, I heard he had left for Quraqua. I don't know what he has in mind, but he may defy the deadline. He seems capable of doing it." Caseway looked unhappy. "I hope I'm wrong. But there *is* a possibility he will announce to us, and to the world, that he's going to stay at the Temple. And challenge us to proceed."

"He can't do that," said Harvey.

"If so," continued the recording, "we'll have to be prepared to respond.

"This is not an easy call. If such an announcement is made, we'll handle the public relations end of it here. You will not commence operations until you are certain everyone is off Quraqua. I know that creates coordination problems for you, but I do not want anybody killed. If it happens, if Wald states his intention to stay beyond the deadline, you will inform him you have no authority to act at discretion, which is true; and tell him further that Project Hope will proceed on schedule, and that you expect him to leave in accordance with the court order and the terms negotiated with the Academy. Then you will notify me. Please acknowledge receipt of these instructions. And by the way, Melanie, I'm glad it's *you* who's out there."

"Could be worse," said Harvey, sliding into a chair. "He might have told you to pull the switch no matter what."

"I'm not sure I wouldn't have preferred that." *She had been here three years, and the archeologists had used one delaying tactic after another*. "It's the right decision," she admitted. "But the sons of bitches are going to put it to us again." She got up, walked toward the viewport. "I just can't believe this keeps happening to us."

Melanie Truscott, Diary

The whole history of "negotiations" between the Academy and Kosmik has been a chain of demands, lies, threats, and finally the lawsuit that forced the Academy off Quraqua before they were ready to go.

Nevertheless, if I could, I would grant their request and give them another month or two—it really wouldn't create insurmountable problems for us—but the legal decisions have come in, and I would be, in effect, setting the court's decision aside and opening the door for more litigation.

So I will follow my orders to the letter.

How does it happen that the most intractable types always rise to the top? No give at all.

The young woman I spoke with today, on the Academy evacuation vessel, seemed reasonable enough. She and I could easily have worked out an agreement—I believe—avoided a lot of rancor, and saved a lot of money. And maybe even found the way to the Monument-Makers. But it won't happen.

June 7, 2202

7.

On board Alpha. *Monday; 2205 hours, Temple time. (Eleven minutes to midnight.)*

The shuttle fell away from *Winckelmann*, dropping into a leisurely pursuit of the setting sun. The cloud cover was streaked with pink and purple; storms troubled a narrow belt just north of the equator. Hutch turned control over to Navigation, and tried keying into Kosmik communications. They were scrambled, another measure of the depth to which relations had deteriorated.

From the Temple site, she could pick up the common channel, listen to them calling one another, directing work, asking for assistance. Occasionally, they vented their frustration. *I say we stay put and finish the job.* A female voice. Hutch wondered whether remarks like that were being deliberately broadcast for the benefit of Truscott's people, who would also be listening in. No wonder the woman was getting nervous.

Atmosphere began to grab at the shuttle. Wisps of cloud streaked past. Navigation cut forward speed. She glided into twilight, passing high above blue mountains, descending into fading light. A wide river wandered into the gloom. The Oz moon, a witch's crescent, rode behind her.

She saw occasional reflections, water perhaps, or snow, sparkling in the starlight. Her scanners revealed an uneven sterile landscape, broken by occasional lakes and lava-beds.

A major ruin lay at Kabal, by a river junction. She went to manual, and took the shuttle to ground level. Her navigation lights flashed across half-buried stone walls. There was nothing else—no wharf, no boats lying inshore, no buildings. No hint of a track through the wilderness to mark the inhabitants' route to the next town. Kabal was celebrated because it was among the most recently abandoned of Quraquat cities.

They had been here when Columbus sailed, the remnants of a once-glittering, if loosely connected, global culture. She wondered what their last moments had been like, clinging to their town against the encroaching wilderness. Did they know they were on the edge of extinction?

She looked for a clear space, found it in the middle of the ruin, and landed. The treads pressed down on tall grass. She started the recycle process, intending to get out and look around. But something whipped through the stalks. It was out near the limit of her lights, and too quick to follow. She turned on the spots: nothing but tall dry grass gradually straightening.

Hell with that.

She aborted, and moments later was back in the air, heading southwest.

Snow fell on the plain. Woody plants began to appear. Their branches were thick and short, covered with green spines and long needles. The flat country gave way to a confusion of rolling hills, populated by grotesque growths connected by ropy, purple webs. The local variant of trees, she thought, until one of them moved.

Further south, she flew over thick-bolled gnarled hardwoods. They were enormous, bigger even than California's redwoods, and they stood well apart from each other.

The air temperature began to drop, and she cruised above a snowstorm. Mountains rose through the clouds, broad rocky summits wrapped in white. Hutch had known a few climbing enthusiasts. *These* would be an interesting challenge.

She went higher, across the top of the world, through yet another storm. There was open water beyond, a sea, dark and reflective, veiled in light mist, glass-smooth. The peaks curved along the coastline. She had arrived at the northern end of the Yakata. Where the gods play.

She opened a channel to the Temple. "This is Hutchins on *Alpha*. Anybody there?"

"Hello, *Alpha*." She recognized Allegri's voice. "Good to see you. You are sixty kilometers east of the Temple. Just follow the coast." Pause. "Switching to video." Hutch activated the screen, and looked at Allegri. It was hard not to be envious of those blue eyes and perfect features. But she appeared a little too socially oriented for this line of work.

This was not the sort of person who would stand up gladly to the rigors of modern archeology.

"You're about fifteen minutes out. You want me to bring you in?"

"Negative. Do you have a first name?"

"Janet."

"Glad to meet you, Janet. My friends call me 'Hutch.'"

Allegri nodded. "Okay, Hutch."

"What's the drill? Do you use an on-shore hangar? What am I looking for?"

"We have a floatpier. Watch for three stone towers in the water, about a hundred meters offshore. The floatpier's just west of them. Our shuttle will be there. Put down beside it, and we'll do the rest. It's the middle of the night here. You want breakfast ready?"

"No, thanks."

"Suit yourself. See you when you get in." She reached up, above the screen, and the monitor blanked.

Hutch glided over snow-covered boulder-strewn beaches, over long uncurling breakers and rocky barrier islands. She flew past Mt. Tenebro, at whose base lay a six-thousand-year-old city, most of it now under the sand or in the sea. Its minarets and crystal towers and floating gardens had been recreated in a series of paintings by Vertilian, one of which now hung prominently in the main lobby at the Academy's Visitor Center. She trained the scopes on it, but could see nothing except lines of excavation ditches.

She promised herself that when time permitted, she'd come back for a closer look.

Minutes later, the three towers came into view. They were massive, not mere pillars (as she had expected), but black stone fortresses rising about twenty meters above the waves. The tide rolled over the remnants of a fourth. They were circular, somewhat tapered, wide enough that twenty people could have sat comfortably atop each. A stiff wind blew snow off their crests.

Hutch unmasked the external mikes, and listened to the rhythmic boom of the surf and the desolate moan of the wind off the sea. She eased close to one of the structures. Something screeched, leaped clear, and fluttered away. Lines of symbols and pictographs and geometric designs circled the towers. Most appeared to be abstractions, but she could see representations of birds and squidlike creatures and other beasts. In a niche just above the water, a pair of reptile legs were broken off at the knees. There must have been a shaft or stairway within. Her lights penetrated two embrasures and she caught a glimpse of stone walls. A Quraquat female with wings and a weapon, a sword probably, stood atop one crest. An arm was missing. The remaining hand shielded its eyes. She knew the Quraquat had not been winged creatures, smiled at the concept of a flying gator, and wondered whether all intelligences dreamt of angels.

At the water line, the towers were worn smooth by the sea. Wide wakes trailed toward shore, as if the hoary sentinels were on the move.

The floatpier lay a short distance beyond. It was U-shaped, and big enough to accommodate several vehicles. The Temple shuttle lay on the shoreward side. *Alpha's* lights skimmed across its blue-gold lines.

She drifted in, and slipped into the water. Moonlight fell on the coastal peaks. She opened a channel to the Temple. "I'm down," she said.

The shuttle rocked. "Welcome to the Temple of the Winds, Hutch. Frank's on his way."

The outside temperature was 30° below, Celsius. She activated her Flickinger field, opened up, climbed out. The floatpier rolled with the tide, but it had good footing. It was wide, maybe three meters, equipped with thermal lines to keep ice from forming. And it had a handrail. The sea was choppy, and spray flew, but the field kept her dry.

Alpha's lights cast a misty glow across the two shuttles and the pier. Beyond, the towers were murky shadows. Lines of waves broke against the shoreline.

"Look out you don't fall in." Carson's voice came out of her earphones. But she didn't see him.

"Where are you?"

"Look to your left."

Lights were rising out of the water. Carson sat inside a bubble housing. It surfaced near *Alpha's* prow, followed by a long gray hull. Steam drifted off the deck, and the sea washed over it. The submersible rolled, righted itself, and drew alongside the pier. The bubble opened. Carson paused, timed his move, and strode onto the planks with a grace born of long experience. "Temple Limo Service," he said lightly. "Stops at 8000 B.C., Henry's Hotel, the Knothic Towers, the Yakatan Empire, and points south. What's your pleasure?" The engines gurgled, and the boat rocked.

"The hotel sounds good." The vessel was low in the water.

Its cargo hatch, located on the afterdeck, swung open. Barrel-shaped containers lined the interior. Carson removed one of the containers, lifting it with surprising ease, and muscled it onto the pier. "I've got six of these," he said. "Can we put them in *Alpha*? Thought I'd save a trip."

"Sure." She watched him go back for a second barrel. Each of the containers was almost as big as he was. "Don't break anything," she said. They were big and awkward, but light. She starting moving them off the dock and into the shuttle's storage bay.

"Most of it's foam," said Carson. "And artifacts."

She felt cozy and safe, wrapped in the warm, dry cocoon of the energy field. The wind sucked at her, and mournful cries floated over the water. "Chipwillows," said Carson. "Oversized, ungainly carrion-eaters. They raid the beach every morning."

"Birds?"

"Not exactly. More like bats. They like to sing."

"Sounds like something lost."

"They make the sound by rubbing their wings together."

She drank in the night. It was good, after all these weeks, to be out in the open.

"What's it been like, Frank? Closing down, I mean?"

He moved next to her and leaned on the handrail. "We do what we have to. It would have helped if we'd known six months ago we were going to get thrown out. We could have done things differently. But the word we kept getting was that the Academy was going to win. 'Don't worry,' they said."

"It's a pity."

"Yeah. It is that." The pier rode over a wave. The comber broke, rolled toward the beach, and lost its energy against the outgoing tide. "I'm ready to go home. But not like this." He looked discouraged. "We've put a lot of work in here. A fair amount of it will go for nothing."

Something luminous swam past, approached the sub, and sank.

"What will you do next? Where will you go now?"

"They've offered me a division director's job at the Academy. In Personnel."

"Congratulations," she said softly.

He looked embarrassed. "Most of the people here are disappointed in me."

"Why?"

"They think it's a sell-out."

Hutch understood. Only the people who couldn't make it in the field, or who were less than serious professionals, went into administration. "How do *you* feel?"

"I think you should do what you want. I'd like regular hours for a change. A clean, air-conditioned office. A chance to meet new people. Maybe watch the Sentinels on Sunday." He laughed. "That shouldn't be asking too much. After all these years."

She wondered whether he had a family to go home to. "I wouldn't think so," she said.

The western sky was starless. The Void. She looked into it for a few moments.

He followed her gaze. "Spooky, isn't it?"

Yes. Somehow, it looked more *arresting* from a planetary surface than it did from space. She had noticed the same phenomenon from Nok and Pinnacle, which also floated on the edge of the galactic arm. She could just pick out the dim smear of light from stars on the other side. "According to the Quraquat," Carson said, "that's Kwonda, the home of the blessed, the haven for all who have fought the good fight. On nights when the wind is still, you can hear them singing. Kwonda, by the way, means 'Distant Laughter.' "

The pier rose and dipped. "That was a big one," said Hutch. "How old is the Temple of the Winds?"

"The main temple, what we call the Upper Temple, was built somewhere around the thirteenth—" He stopped. "Difficult to translate time. Around 250 B.C., our calendar. Those"— he indicated the towers—"are *not* the Temple of the Winds. You know that, right?"

"No, I didn't."

"They're the Knothic Towers. Sacred ground, by the way. Built approximately 8000 B.C. They were used for worship, and were maintained as a historical site, one way and another, for seven thousand years."

"So where's the Temple of the Winds?"

He looked at the water. "Believe it or not," he said, "The Temple of the Winds is in the drink." He tied down the last of the containers. "And we should probably get moving. Where are your bags?"

"Only one." She got it out of the *Alpha*, and allowed him to take it.

"This area used to be a crossroad between empires," he said. "It must always have been of strategic importance. And we know settlements thrived here almost right up until the species died out. At the end," he continued, "the Quraquat had no idea why the Towers had been built, or what they'd meant."

"That's very sad," she said. "To lose your heritage."

"I would think so."

"Are we sure the Quraquat are really extinct?"

"Oh, yes. There was a long-running debate over that for several years. It seemed unlikely that we could have missed them by so short a time. Ergo, they had to be here somewhere. Watch your step." He planted a foot on the deck of the submarine as if that would steady it, and offered his arm. "There was always at least one team looking for survivors. We got so many false alarms it got to be a joke. Quraquat seen here, seen there. Seen everywhere. But never any living natives." He shrugged. "They're gone."

They lowered themselves into the cockpit and drew the bubble down. The interior lights dimmed. The sea rose around them. "The Towers are by no means the oldest structures here. This was a holy place long before they were built. There's a military chapel and outpost in the Lower Temple which predate them by millennia. We're excavating it now. In fact, the artifact that brought Richard Wald out here is from the Lower Temple. And there's a lot more that we haven't got close to yet. We know, for example, that there's an old electric power plant down there."

"You're kidding."

"That's what it looks like. It goes back somewhere in the range of nineteen thousand years. There's not much of it left, of course, and we don't get very good pictures. But I don't think there's any question."

The water was dark. The sub's navigation lamps punched into the general gloom. Lines of yellow light appeared. "They connect the Temple with Seapoint," Carson explained. "The base."

He turned toward the track, and within minutes, they had arrived over a complex of domes and spheres. They were brightly illuminated, but many of the windows were dark. Seapoint looked inactive.

Carson took them beneath a shell-shaped structure, and undersea doors opened. They ascended, and surfaced in a lighted bay.

Janet Allegri was waiting with fresh coffee. Hutch disembarked. Carson handed her overnight down and Hutch slung it over one shoulder. She noticed that the walls were lined with containers similar to the ones they'd unloaded. "Is this the cargo?" she asked.

"This is *some* of it," said Janet, passing them cups. "Now, if you like, I'll show you to your quarters."

"I'd appreciate that." Turning to Carson, she said, "Thanks for the ride, Frank."

Carson nodded. "Anytime." And, with a meaningful glance, he added, "You'll want to get a good night's sleep."

Janet and Hutch exited into a short passageway, mounted a flight of stairs, and emerged in a plant-filled chamber furnished with chairs and tables. The lights were dim. Two large windows looked out into the sea, and there was a glow in an artificial fireplace. A half-finished jigsaw puzzle occupied one of the tables. "The community room," Janet said. "If you come here in the morning, we'll introduce you around, and see that you get breakfast."

"You have people working now, right?"

"Yes," Janet said. "We've been operating round the clock since we were ordered off. We used to run a fairly leisurely show. No more."

"What specifically are you looking for?"

"Casumel Linear C," Janet replied. "We want to read the inscription." Her liquid eyes watched Hutch. "There's a military post buried beneath the Lower Temple. The race that operated the post *spoke* Linear C."

"Frank told us about that. You're hoping to find a Rosetta stone."

Several passageways opened off the community room. They exited through one into a tube. The walls were transparent, and the visual effect, enhanced by strategically placed outside lighting, and luminous fish, was striking. Seapoint was a lovely place, although it had a claustrophobic aspect.

"A Rosetta stone is probably too much to ask for," Janet said. "Some more samples might be enough."

"How much success are you having?"

"Some. We've found a couple of inscriptions. What we really need to do is penetrate the lower sections. But there are engineering problems. We have to cut under the Upper Temple. It's shaky, and it wouldn't take much to bring everything down. So it's slow going. Moreover, the sea bottom is filled with silt. The tides throw it back into the excavations as quickly as we can remove it." She looked tired. "The answers are here, Hutch. But we won't have the time to get at them."

They crossed into a dome. Janet opened a door, turned on the lights, and revealed a pleasant, and reasonably spacious, apartment. "VIP quarters," she said. "Breakfast is at seven. If you want to sleep late, that's fine. The duty officer's available on the link."

"Thank you."

"There's a dispenser in the community room if you get hungry. Is there anything you need?"

"I think I'm fine."

"Okay. My first name activates my private channel. Don't hesitate to call if you need anything." She hesitated in the doorway. "We're glad to have you aboard, Hutch. This place has become something of a strain. I think we need some new people." She smiled. "Good night."

Hutch closed the door behind her, and tossed her bag onto a divan. Curtains covered one wall. She opened them and looked into the living sea. Small fish, startled by the sudden movement, darted away. A pseudo-turtle swam slowly past; and a diaphanous creature with large disc eyes, drawn by the light, poked at the plastene. "Hello," she said, knocking at the barrier. There was a control for outside illumination. She reduced the intensity, but did not turn it off.

She unpacked and showered and took a book to bed, but was too tired to read.

There were a host of sounds at Seapoint. In the dark, the walls creaked and groaned, things bumped against the hull, electrical systems came on and went off throughout the night. It occurred to Hutch, as she drifted off, that this entire complex would shortly become part of the wreckage at the Temple of the Winds.

She woke shortly after six, feeling uneasy. The windows and the sea were illuminated by wide shafts of sunlight.

Time to get to work. She dressed rapidly, as if she were running behind schedule, and went to the community room. Despite Janet's assurances, it was empty. She ate a leisurely breakfast and, when she'd finished, opened a channel to the duty officer. Janet was still on duty. "Don't you ever sleep?" Hutch asked.

"Good morning, Hutch. I get plenty of sleep; I just don't get to my room much. How was your night?"

"Fine. Real good. What do you have for me?"

"Nothing for the moment. You are going to *be* busy, because we have a lot of artifacts to move up, as well as people. Frank will be helping with the Temple shuttle, by the way. But we haven't quite got things organized yet. I'd say your morning's free. We'll call you when we need you."

It would be nice to see the Knothic Towers in the sunlight.

"Okay," she said. She thought about asking whether the sub was available, but decided against any action that would brand her early on as a nuisance. Instead, she retrieved her harness, and found an exit pool. She checked her air supply. It was ample. She looped her commlink around her throat, and activated the field. Then she slipped into the water, opened the outer doors, and swam out of the dome.

Thirty minutes later, she surfaced a half-kilometer from the floatpier. It was a glorious morning. The sun blazed over silver peaks, broad white beaches, and blue sea. Long breakers rumbled against black rocks. Creatures that bore a close resemblance to pelicans patrolled the surface, occasionally dipping into the water for a squirming meal.

And the Towers: they rose out of the boiling sea in magnificent defiance. The last stronghold. They were as black by day as they had been by night.

Hutch was a good swimmer, and she set off toward the floatpier with a steady stroke. The tide was running against her, but not so swiftly that she couldn't make headway. She settled into her rhythm. The pelicans wheeled and flapped. Pity it was so cold; she'd have liked to dispense with the energy field. A swim during which you stayed perfectly dry lacked a little something.

Minutes later, she climbed out onto the planks with a sense of exhilaration, and took a deep breath from her bottled air.

The field clung to her, soft and warm.

The sea was calm. She sat down on the pier.

The lower sections of the Towers were polished by the constant wave action. Like the Temple, they too had been on dry land in the recent past, sacred markers at a crossroads on highways connecting empires. A place for travelers to stop and contemplate the majesty and kindness of the gods. Atop the nearest, she saw movement. Something with white feathers stretched and fluttered.

Hutch had consulted maps before coming out, and knew where to look for the old imperial road, which was now only a steep defile northbound through the mountains that lined the shore.

The strategic value of the intersection had been guarded by a fort, as well as by the gods. By a succession of forts, actually, over the millennia. The forts now lay beneath the Temple. And the Temple lay beneath the sea.

She wondered what might have prompted a meeting between the relatively dormant Quraquat and the star travelers?

On the beach, something caught her eye. Movement. Something like a man.

It walked upright toward the water's edge. Two more followed. They were hard to see clearly against the sand, and only when they passed in front of a cluster of rocks could she make out their white fur and sloped, horned heads. Well down the beach, another of the creatures stooped over a tidal pool.

She couldn't see their eyes, but they had large floppy ears, and the one by the tidal pool carried a stick. Others were descending from the pass which had once been the northern road. Several were half-grown.

They fanned out along the beach, the adults keeping the young firmly in tow. Three or four took up stations well apart, and looked out to sea. Then, as if someone had given a signal, the cubs charged across the sand, whooping and cackling and pursuing each other. Some stopped to poke at objects lying on the beach; others bolted into the waves.

Behind her, *Alpha* rose on the tide, and the Temple shuttle nosed gently into the pier.

The creatures on the beach seemed to be having a pretty good time. Hutch became gradually aware of a thin piping sound, a high-pitched trill almost lost in the brisk wind and the roar of the morning. It was birdlike, and she looked overhead for its source but saw only bright sky and a few snowflakes.

One of the animals stood quietly by the water's edge. It seemed to be looking directly at her. Hutch stared back. When finally she grew uncomfortable under its gaze, she drew her knees up tight. *It raised both forelimbs in what was unmistakably a greeting.*

The warmth of the gesture startled her, as if she'd met an acquaintance in a distant place. She waved back.

It turned away, scooped a wriggling sea creature out of the surf, dunked it in a wave, and dropped it into its wide mouth. It looked again toward Hutch, with evident satisfaction, and threw several handfuls of water into the air.

She splashed a little water on herself. *But I draw the line at the quick lunch.*

A screech shattered the general tranquility. It echoed off the cliffs. The creatures froze. Then a general rush began. Inland, toward the pass. Several herded cubs before them. One adult went down. Hutch couldn't see what was happening to it; but it was struggling in shallow water, yelping pitiably, its limbs jerking and twitching.

Hutch raised a hand to block off the sun's glare. And sensed a presence near her left shoulder.

An eye.

Green and expressionless. It was mounted on a stalk.

Her heart froze. She could not breathe and she could not move. She wanted to throw herself into the sea, hide from this *thing* that had risen beside her.

The eye watched her. It was the color of the sea. A section was missing out of the iris, rather like a piece out of a pie. As Hutch tried to get her emotions under control, the piece widened, and the iris narrowed. Slowly, a nictitating membrane closed over it, then opened again.

A second stalk-mounted eye appeared beside the first, somewhat higher. And another beyond those. The stalks moved like long grass in an uncertain breeze.

During those long, dazed moments, she caught only aspects of the thing that had approached her. Four eyes. A broad flat

insect head, to which the eyes were attached. A hairy thorax.
Segments. The creature was gray-green and chitinous. Hutch
saw mandibles and tentacles and jaws.

The thing *stood* on the water, stood *upright* on a set of
stick legs. The shuttles and the pier rose and fell in the light
chop, but the creature remained motionless. It seemed almost
disconnected from the physical world.

Hutch fought down her panic. And in a voice surprisingly
level, she spoke into her throat mike: "This is Hutchins.
Anybody there?"

"Hutch, what's wrong?" It was Janet.

"Janet," she said, softly, as if the creature might hear through
the Flickinger field, "I'm looking at a big bug."

"How big?"

"*Big.* Three meters." Pause for breath. "Mantis. Squid.
Don't know—"

"Are you *outside*?" Janet's tone turned vaguely accusing.

"Yes." Whispered.

"*Where* outside?" There was a hint of anger in the voice
before it regained its professional calm.

"The floatpier."

"Okay. It's not dangerous. But don't move. Okay? Not a
muscle. I'm on my way."

"*You?*"

"You want to hang on while I look around for help?"

Thick fluid leaked out of the bug's mouth.

"No," she said.

The goddam thing sure *looked* dangerous.

Hutch was acutely aware of the piercing screams from the
beach. She had an iron grip on the guardrail, and could
not have let go under any conceivable circumstance. Limbs
flexed; three of the eyes swiveled away, came back.

The Flickinger field wouldn't be much help here, no more
likely to protect her against the razor thrust of those jaws than
an old pressure suit would. "You may want to hurry," she said
into the mike, detesting the whimper in her voice.

"It's only a strider. I'll be there in a minute. You're doing
fine."

If it wasn't dangerous, why did she have to keep still?

With her eyes, Hutch measured the distance to the *Alpha*
cockpit. About fifteen meters. She could open the hatch from
here by voice control. And she thought she could sprint the

distance and get into the spacecraft before the thing could react. *But* the hatch would need about fifteen seconds to close. Would the beast give her that kind of time?

The thing touched some deep primal nerve. She would have been frightened of it had it been only a few centimeters tall. "*Alpha*, open cockpit."

She heard the pop of the hatch.

Three of the eyes turned toward the sound.

"Hutch." Janet again. Her voice flat. "Don't do anything. Wait for me. Just stay put and don't move. Okay?"

The creature watched the shuttle.

The shrieks from the beach had stopped. She wasn't sure when, but she didn't dare look away to see what was happening. She was breathing again. Barely. She braced one foot so she could get up.

She literally *saw* a quickening of interest in the eyes.

The jaws twitched. A tentacle unrolled.

She wanted to look away. But she could not disengage.

Janet, where are you? In her mind, she traced the steps. The duty officer had probably been at her station, which was less than a minute from the sub bay. Stop to pick up a pulser. Where did they keep the pulsers? The voyage last night from the pier to Seapoint had taken between eight and ten minutes. But Carson had been in no hurry. Surely the sub could make the trip in five or less. Say seven minutes altogether.

The wind blew, and one of the pelicans flew past.

How many pictures do you get with four eyes capable of looking in different directions? What is it *seeing*?

Why had she come away without a weapon? She knew the drill. But she had never been attacked, *anywhere*. Dumb.

One of the eyes rose. Gazed over her shoulder at something behind her.

"Right with you." Janet's voice again. "We're in good shape." She heard the whine of the sub, and the hiss of an air exchanger.

The creature was inside the U, separated from the open sea by the dock. It would be difficult to bring the sub to bear against it directly. But that shouldn't matter. Hutch waited for the crackle of a pulser.

Instead the sub banged into the pier. The stalk-eyes turned away from Hutch. "Okay." Janet's tone changed, acquired the weight of command. "Get away from it. Into the shuttle. *Move.*"

Hutch broke and ran. In the same moment, she saw Janet leap from the cockpit of the sub, swinging a wrench. The creature turned to face her. Tentacles whipped, jaws opened, and the eyes drew back. Janet, lovely, blond, drawing-room Janet, stepped inside the writhing tangle and brought the wrench down squarely on the thing's head. Green syrup exploded from the skull, and it staggered. They went down together and fell into the water. The struggling mass slipped beneath the surface.

Hutch gasped and raced back to help. The water thrashed. They came up. Janet grabbed the pier, and nailed it again across one mandible. The thing collapsed into a pile of broken sticks, and drifted away on the current.

Hutch went down on her knees and held Janet while she caught her breath. When she did, she demanded whether *Hutch* was okay.

Hutch was humiliated. "Why didn't you bring a weapon?" she demanded.

"I did. Brought the first one I could find."

Now it was Hutch's turn to be angry. "Don't you people have any *pulsers?*"

Janet grinned. She was bruised and still breathing hard. Her hair hung down in her face and she was bleeding from a couple of cuts. But to Hutch she looked damned good. "Somewhere. But I thought you'd want me out here quick."

Hutch tried to check her for damage, but Janet insisted she was okay. The cuts looked minor.

"Thanks," said Hutch.

Janet put an arm around her shoulder. Their energy fields flashed. "You get one on the house," she said. "But don't do it again. Okay?"

"Was it really dangerous?" asked Hutch. "I mean, all it did was stand there."

The battle ashore had also ended. Several of the furry creatures watched the sea from a rocky shelf well out of harm's way. "These things snack on the beach monkeys," she said, indicating the creatures. "I guess this one didn't quite know what to make of you."

• • •

Kosmik Ground Control South. Tuesday; 0900 Temple Time.

Living worlds were exceedingly rare. The reason seemed to be that Jovian planets were also quite rare. In the solar system, Jupiter's comet-deflecting capabilities had reduced the number of major terrestrial impacts to a quarter percent of what could otherwise have been expected. And made life possible on Earth.

Quraqua, with its functioning ecosystem, its near-terrestrial gravity, its abundance of water, its lack of an owner, was a godsend to the harried human race. It was inevitable that the first full-scale terraforming effort would take place here. This was the Second Chance, an opportunity to apply lessons learned painfully on Earth. It would be home to a new race of humans.

Idealists had created an abundance of plans to ensure that the children of Quraqua would treat this world, and each other, with respect. There would be no nationalism exported to the stars, no industrial exploitation. Poverty and ignorance would not be permitted to take root. The various races and faiths would live in harmony, and the ideologies that had fostered divisiveness in the bad old days would find rocky soil.

Ian Helm, like a multitude of others, would believe it when he saw it.

Quraqua might work, but it would be on its own terms. It would never be the utopia its proponents promised. He knew that. The fact that so many of the people making the Project's decisions apparently did not led him to question either their competence or their integrity.

Project Hope had not reached the brink of this first phase of its existence easily. Environmentalists had decried the diversion of funds from desperately needed efforts at home; the People of Christ had denounced any notions of moving off-world as not in accord with God's plan and therefore sacrilegious; nationalist and racial activists demanded exclusive rights to the new world. Moralists railed against the annihilation of entire species that would inevitably result from terraforming. There were serious doubts that the political will, or the money, would be available over the long term to ensure even a chance of success.

Still, Helm was prepared to concede that he had no better idea. Deforestation, pollution, urbanization, had all progressed so far now that various points of no return had been passed. There was reason to believe that if every human being disappeared tomorrow, the Earth would still require millennia to return to what it had been.

There was a positive side to all this: Helm had built a lucrative, and satisfying, career out of his specialty. He was a planetary engineer, had got his degree in the late sixties, when only astronomers were thinking seriously about the stars. He had done his graduate work on the Venusian problem, where estimates for creating a habitable world ranged into the centuries. (Mars, of course, was out of the question, since there was no way to overcome its crippling light gravity.)

Nok was a second candidate. But it was inhabited. And while there was a movement that favored settlement and exploitation of that garden planet, nonintervention would continue for the foreseeable future.

One more reason why Project Hope had to be made to succeed.

Almost forty percent of Quraqua's water was frozen at the poles. The initial phase of Project Hope was directed at releasing that water. The oceans would fill, new rivers would spread across the land, and, with proper management, climate modification would begin.

Helm often reflected on the fact that other men had controlled more sheer firepower than he, but none had ever used it. No one had ever made a bigger bang than Ian Helm would deliver when, in three days, he activated his arsenal of nuclear weapons, and on-site and orbiting particle beam projectors. Even Harding, at the other pole, would be outclassed. This was true even though the reconfiguration systems were allocated equally. But the ice sheets in the south were unstable atop their narrow strips of land, and the ocean floor was saturated with volcanoes. Helm believed he could coax some of the volcanoes to contribute their own energy to the effort.

The caps were to be melted simultaneously. No one was sure what might happen to rotation if weight were suddenly removed from one pole and not from the other.

Helm returned to his headquarters from a field survey at about the same time Janet Allegri was taking a wrench to the strider. He was satisfied with his preparations, sanguine that the ice sheets would melt on signal.

He drifted in aboard his CAT, circling the half-dozen red-stained shacks and landing pads that made up Southern Hope. The snowfields rolled out flat in all directions. The sky was hard and clear, the sun beginning to sink toward the end of its months-long day.

He descended onto his pad, climbed out, and cycled through the airlock into the operations hut.

Mark Casey sat alone among the displays and communications equipment, talking to his commlink. He raised a hand in his boss's general direction and kept talking.

Helm sat down at his desk to check his In box. He could overhear enough of Casey's conversation to know that his Ops officer wasn't happy.

Casey was a tall, narrow, spike of a man, hard and sharp, given neither to superfluous gesture or talk. His thin hair was combed over his scalp, and he wore a manicured beard. His eyes found Helm, and signaled that the world was full of incompetents. "Another dead core," he said, after he'd signed off. "How was your trip?"

"Okay. We'll be ready."

"Good. Everybody's checked in." Casey scratched a spot over his right eyebrow with an index finger. "If we keep burning up cores, though, we'll have a problem. We have one spare left."

"Cheap goddam stuff," said Helm. "Somebody in Procurement's making a buck."

Casey shrugged. "It's forty-five below out there. Amazes me anything works."

An electronic chart of the icecap was mounted across the wall opposite the airlock. Colored lamps marked nuke sites, red where weapons had been placed inside volcanoes, white where placed within the ice sheets themselves, and green for those locations where teams were still working. There were five green lights. "Anything else I should know about, Mark?"

"Jensen called in just before you came. They've been having equipment problems too, and she says she's running behind. About eight hours. It's not on your board yet."

Helm didn't like that. His intention was to be set up and ready to go with thirty hours to spare. That would allow time for things to go wrong and still leave a decent safety margin to extract the teams. Jensen directed the 27 group, which was tasked with sinking a nuke into the ice on the far side of the pack. Eight goddam hours. Well, he could live with it. But if it got worse, he would have her head.

He thumbed through his traffic. One message caught his attention:

TO: DIRECTOR, NORTHCOM
             DIRECTOR, SOUTHCOM
             CHIEF PILOT
FROM: DIRECTOR, PROJECT HOPE
SUBJECT: ADMINISTRATIVE PROCEDURES
WE ARE INVOLVED IN AN ENDEAVOR THAT IS BOTH UNPRECEDENTED AND COMPLEX. STATUS REPORTS WILL NOW BE UPGRADED AS PROVIDED IN MANUAL SECTION 447112.3(B). REQUESTS FOR SPECIAL ASSISTANCE WILL BE CHANNELED THROUGH OPCOM AS PROVIDED. WE STAND READY TO HELP WHERE NEEDED. IN ADDITION, ALL DETONATION PROCEDURES ARE TO BE DESIGNED TO PERMIT INTERVENTION UNTIL THE VERY LAST INSTANT. ACK.

                                        TRUSCOTT

Helm read it through several times. "You see this, Mark? 'The very last instant'?"

Casey nodded. "I've already sent the acknowledgment."

"She knows we built that in as a matter of course. What the hell is *this* all about?"

"Got no idea. I just work here. CYA, probably."

"Something's happened." Helm's eyes narrowed. "Get her on the circuit, Mark."

Melanie Truscott's image blinked on. She was in her quarters, seated on a couch, a notepad open on her lap, papers scattered across the cushions. "Ian," she said, "what can I do for you?"

Helm didn't like Truscott's regal manner. The woman loved to flaunt her position. It was in her smile, in her authoritarian tone, in her refusal to consult him before formulating policy or issuing directives. "We're ready to cancel at a moment's notice," he said.

"I know." She closed the notebook.

"What's going on? Is somebody putting pressure on us?"

"Corporate is concerned that one or more of Jacobi's people may refuse to leave by the deadline. They want to make sure nobody gets killed."

Helm's temper flared. "That's a goddam joke, Melanie. They might try to bluff, but you can be damn sure none of them wants to be there when that wall of ice and water rolls over the site."

"That's not all." Truscott looked worried. "I talked to their pilot. She says something big is happening, and it sounds as if they may be cutting it too close. We've picked up some of their traffic which implies the same thing."

"Then send them a warning. Remind them what's at stake. But for God's sake, don't back off now. Do that, and we'll never be rid of them. Listen, Melanie, we can't just go on forever like this. The climate here is hard on equipment, and the goddam stuff isn't much good to start with. We put a hold on this operation, even for a couple of days, and I won't guarantee everything's going to fire in sequence." Casey raised an eye, but Helm ignored him.

"Can't help that." Truscott rearranged herself, signaled that the interview was over. "We'll comply with our instructions."

When she was gone, Casey grinned. "That stuff isn't top of the line, but it's not really coming apart."

"A little exaggeration is good for the soul. You know what's wrong with her, Mark? She doesn't know the difference between what management *tells* her to do, and what they *want* her to do. Caseway's covering his ass, just in case. But he wants the job done. If this thing doesn't go on schedule, Truscott's not going to look so good. And neither am I."

"So what are you going to do?"

Helm stared out the window. The sky and the ice pack were the same color. "I don't know. Maybe I'll make her a good manager in spite of herself."

Truscott knew Helm was right. The son of a bitch wasn't worth the powder to blow him to hell. But he was right. She had known it herself, had always known it. *They won't move voluntarily. They will have to be pushed off.*

Damn.

She punched Harvey's button. "When you have a minute," she said.

ARCHIVE

PROJECT HOPE

Phase One Projections

We estimate that nine hundred million tons of ice will be melted at either end of the globe within the first sixty seconds after initial detonation. Reaction to heat generated by nuclear devices will continue at a high level in the south for an indeterminate period, based on our ability to ignite the subsea volcanoes. Best-guess projections are as follows:

(1) Earthquakes up to 16.3 on the Grovener Scale along all major fault lines within 50 degrees of both poles;

(2) Tsunamis throughout the Southern Sea. These will be giant waves, unlike anything seen on Earth during recorded history. In effect, large areas of the sea will simply leave the basin and inundate the land masses, penetrating thousands of kilometers.

(3) Rainfall, even if not abetted by the insertion of snowballs, will continue for the better part of a year. It will remain at a high level for ten to fifteen years, before stabilizing at a global mean approximately 35% higher than the current standard.

It needs to be noted, however, that the presence of volcanoes in the south polar area, joined with our lack of experience in operations of this scale, and the variables listed in Appendix (1), have created a situation which is extremely unpredictable.

(Ian Helm)

8.

The snowball tumbled slowly through the sunlight, growing in his screens. Lopsided and battered, it dwarfed his tug. One end looked as if a large piece had been knocked off. *Big son of a bitch, this one.* Navigation matched its movement, brought him in over scored white terrain. It stabilized, and the scan program activated. Jake Hoffer slowed his approach, his descent, and chose the contact point. About midway along the axis of rotation. *There.* A sheet of flat, unseamed ice.

He watched the readings on his status board. He was, in effect, landing on a plateau whose sides dropped away forever. Quraqua rolled across the sky. The moon rose while he watched, and the sun dropped swiftly toward the cliff-edge "horizon." The effect inevitably induced a mild vertigo. He buttoned up the cockpit, sealing off the view, and watched on the monitors. The numbers flickered past, and ready lamps went on at a hundred meters. Moments later, the *Jack Kraus* touched down with a mild jar. The spikes bit satisfyingly into the ice.

Lamps switched to amber.

The realignment program took hold. Sensors computed mass distribution and rotational configuration, and evaluated course and velocity. The first round of thrusters fired.

Four hours later, he was riding the snowball into its temporary orbit around Quraqua.

Within a few weeks, he and the other tug pilot, Merry Cooper, would begin the real bear of this operation: starting the two-hundred-plus pieces of orbiting ice down to the planetary surface, *aiming* them just as he was doing now, by digging in and dragging them toward their targets. Once that final descent had begun, they would use particle beams to

103

slice them into rain. It pleased him to know that this massive iceberg would eventually fall as a gentle summer shower on a parched plain.

His commlink beeped. "Jake?"

He recognized Harvey Sill's gravelly voice. "You're five-by, Harvey."

Jake switched to visual. Sill was giving directions to some-one off-camera. Usually, the station chief's post in the com-mand center was quiet. But today there were voices and technicians and activity. Getting close.

Sill scratched his temple. "Jake, are you locked onto two-seventeen?"

"Two-*nineteen*."

"Whatever. You got it?"

"Yes—"

"Okay. I want you to *drop* it."

Hoffer leaned forward, adjusted his gain. "Say again."

"I want you to put it into the Southern Sea. The Yakata."

That couldn't be right. "Harvey, that's where the Academy people are."

"I know. Insert it sixteen hundred kilometers south of the Temple site. Can you do that with reasonable accuracy?"

"I can." Hoffer was horrified. "But I don't want to."

Sill's expression did not change. "Do it anyway."

"Harvey, it'll kill them. What have you guys done over there, lost your minds?"

"For God's sake, Hoffer, it's only one unit. Nobody's going to get hurt. And we'll see that they get plenty of advance warning."

"You want me to cut it up?"

"Negative. Insert it as is."

Jake was breathing hard. "Suppose they don't get every-body out? Or can't? Son of a bitch, this thing's a *mountain*. You can't just drop it into the ocean."

"They're *underwater*, goddammit. They'll be safe enough."

"I doubt it."

"Have you got something smaller, then?"

"Sure. Damned near everything we have is smaller."

"Okay. Find something smaller and do it. Don't forget we'll lose a lot of it on the way down."

"Like hell. Most of this bastard would hit the water. Why are we doing this?"

Sill looked exceptionally irritated. "Look, Jake. Those people are playing mind games with us. Right now, it looks as if they'll stay past the deadline. We're sending them a message. Now please see to it."

Hoffer nodded. "Yeah. I guess so. When?"

"Now. How long will it take?"

"Hard to say. Maybe ten hours."

"All right. Keep me posted. And, Jake—?"

"Yes?"

"Get us a decent splash."

The Temple of the Winds lay half-buried in ocean bottom, a polygon with turrets and porticoes and massive columns. Walls met at odd angles and ran off in a confusion of directions. Staircases mounted to upper rooms that no longer existed. (The stairs were precisely the right size for humans.) Arcane symbols lined every available space. Arches and balustrades were scattered everywhere. A relatively intact hyperbolic roof dipped almost to the sea floor, giving the entire structure the appearance of a turtle shell. "All in all," Richard told Hutch as they approached on jets, "it's an architecture that suggests a groundling religion. It's cautious and practical, a faith that employs gods primarily to see to the rain and bless marriages. Their concerns were domestic and agricultural, probably, in contrast to the cosmology of the Knothic Towers. It would be interesting to have their history during this period, to trace them from the Towers to the Temple, and find out what happened."

They shut down their jets and drifted toward the front entrance. "The architecture looks as if it was designed by committee," said Hutch. "The styles clash."

"It wasn't built in a single effort," he said. "The Temple was originally a single building. A chapel on a military installation." They hovered before the immense colonnade that guarded the front entrance. "They added to it over the years, tore things down, changed their minds. The result was a web of chambers and corridors and balconies and shafts surrounding the central nave. Most of it has collapsed, although the nave itself is still standing. God knows how. It's dangerous, by the way. Roof could come down any time. Carson tells me they were on the verge of calling off work and bringing in some engineers to shore the place up."

Hutch surveyed the rock walls doubtfully. "Maybe it's just as well we're being forced out. Before somebody gets killed."

Richard looked at her with mock dismay. "I know you've been around long enough not to say anything like that to these people."

"It's okay," she said. "I'll try not to upset anybody."

The top was off the colonnade, and sunlight filtered down among the pillars. They stopped to look at the carvings. They were hard to make out through caked silt and general disintegration, but she saw something that resembled a sunrise. And either a tentacled sea-beast or a tree. The Temple of the Winds was, if anything, solid. Massive. Built for the ages. Its saddle-shaped design, had the structure remained on dry land, would have provided an aerodynamic aspect. Hutch wondered whether that accounted for its designation.

"Who named it?" she asked. She understood that native place names got used when they were available (and pronounceable). When they weren't, imagination and a sense of humor were seldom lacking.

"Actually," said Richard, "it's had a lot of names over the centuries. Outlook. The Wayside. The Southern Shield, which derived from a constellation. And probably some we don't know. 'Temple of the Winds' was one of the more recent. Eloise Hapwell discovered it, and she eventually made the choice. It's intended to suggest, by the way, the transience of life. A flickering candle on a windblown night."

"I've heard that before somewhere."

"The image is common to terrestrial cultures. And to some on Nok. It's a universal symbol, Hutch. That's why churches and temples are traditionally built from rock, to establish a counterpoint. To imply that they, at least, are solid and permanent, or that the faith is."

"It's oppressive," she said. "They're all obsessed with death, aren't they?" Mortality motifs were prominent with every culture she knew about, terrestrial or otherwise.

"All of the important things," Richard said, "will turn out to be universally shared. It's why there will be no true aliens."

She was silent for a time. "This is, what, two thousand years old?" She meant the colonnade.

"Somewhere in that time frame."

"Why were there *two* temples?"

"How do you mean?"

"The Knothic Towers. That was a place of worship too, wasn't it? Were they all part of the same complex?"

"We don't think so, Hutch. But we don't really know very much yet." He pointed toward a shadowy entrance. "That way."

She followed him inside. Trail markers glowed in the murky water, red and green, amber and blue. They switched on their wrist-lamps. "Did the Temple and the Towers both represent the same religion?"

"Yes. In the sense that they both recognized a universal deity."

"No pantheons here."

"No. But keep in mind, we don't see these people at their beginnings. The cultures we can look at had already grasped the essential unity of nature. No board of gods can survive that knowledge."

"If I understood Frank, there's an ancient power plant here somewhere."

"*Somewhere* is the word. They don't really know quite where. Henry has found bits and pieces of generators and control panels and conductors throughout the area. You probably know there was an intersection of major roads here for several thousand years. One road came down from the interior, and connected with a coastal highway right about where we are now."

"Yes," she said. "I've seen it."

"Before it was a highway, it was a river. It would have been lower then than it is today. Anyway, the river emptied into the sea, and the power plant must have been built somewhere along its banks. But that's a *long* time ago. Twenty-five thousand years. Maybe more." His voice changed subtly. She knew how Richard's mind worked, knew he was feeling the presence of ghosts, looking back the way they'd come, seeing the ancient watercourse, imagining a seaside city illuminated by electric lights. They had paused by an alcove. "Here," he said, "look at this." He held his lamp against the wall.

A stone face peered at her. It was as tall, from crocodilian crown to the base of its jaws, as Hutch. It stared past her, over her shoulder, as if watching someone leave.

The eyes were set in deep sockets beneath a ridged brow. Snout and mouth were broad; the skull was flat, wide, smooth. Tufts of fur were erect across the jaws. The aspect of the thing suggested sorrow, contemplation, perhaps regret.

"It fits right in," she said. "It's depressing."

"Hutch, that's the response of a tourist."

"Who is it? Do we know?"

He nodded. "God."

"That's not the same as the one in the Lower Temple."

"No. This is a male version. But it comes a thousand years later."

"Universal deities—"

"What?"

"—never seem to smile. Not in any culture. What's the point of having omnipotence if you don't enjoy it?"

He squeezed her shoulder. "You *do* have your own way of looking at things."

They descended to ground level, picking up a track of green lights. "What happened to the industrialized society?" she asked. "The one with the power plant?"

"It ran out of gas. Literally. They exhausted their fossil fuels. And developed no replacements."

"No atom."

"No. They probably never tried. It might be that you only get a narrow window to do it: you can't run your motors anymore, and you need a major, concerted effort. Maybe you need a big war at exactly the right moment." He grew thoughtful. "They never managed it on Nok either."

They were still in the central nave. The roof blocked off the light, and it was dark in spite of the trail markers. Occasionally, sea creatures touched them. "It's a terrible thing," said Richard, "to lose all this."

They paused periodically before engravings. Whole walls were covered with lines of symbols. "We think they're stories," he said. "Anyhow, it's all been holographed. Eventually we'll figure it out. And *here's* what we've been looking for."

A shaft opened at their feet. The green lamps dived in, accompanied by a pair of quivering tubes, each about as wide as a good-sized human thigh. "Extracting sand," said Richard.

He stepped off the edge. His weights carried him down. Hutch waited a few moments, then followed. "We are now entering the Lower Temple," he told her. "Welcome to 9000 B.C."

The shaft was cut through gray rock. "Richard," she asked, "do you think there's really a chance to find a Rosetta stone in here anywhere? It seems like a long shot to me."

"Not really. Remember, this was a crossroad. It's not hard to believe they would have carved a prayer, or epigram, or inspirational story, on a wall, and done it in several languages. In fact, Henry's convinced they *would* have done it. The real questions are whether any of it has survived, and whether we'll have time to recover it if it did."

Hutch could not yet see bottom. "The stone wall behind you," Richard continued, "is part of the outer palisade. We're *outside* the military post." A tunnel opened off the shaft. The green lights and the tubes snaked into it. "This is just above ground level during the military era." He swam toward the passageway. "They're pumping sediment out now. It's a constant struggle. The place fills up as fast as they pump."

She followed him in. Ahead, past his long form, she could see white lights and movement.

"George?" Richard was now speaking on the common channel. "Is that you?"

An enormous figure crouched over a black box. It stirred, and looked up. "Damn," he said. "I thought you were the relief shift. How you doing, Richard?"

She could hear the soft hum of machinery, and the slush of moving water.

"Hutch," Richard said, "this is George Hackett. Project engineer."

Hackett must have been close to seven feet tall. He was preoccupied with a device that was probably a pump, and tried to say hello without looking away from it. It was difficult to see him clearly in the uncertain light, but he sounded friendly.

"Where's your partner?" Richard asked.

Hackett pointed at the tubes, which trailed off into a side corridor. "At the other end," he said.

"We're directly over the military chapel," Richard told Hutch. "They're trying to clear the chambers below."

"What's in them?" she asked.

"We don't know yet," said George. "We don't know anything, except that they're located at the western limit of the palisade. They were probably a barracks. But they could also be part of the original chapel."

"I thought you'd already found that," said Hutch. "That's where the Tull tableau was, right?"

"We've got into part of it," said George. "There's more around here somewhere. There's a fair chance this is it."

The silt in the passageway was ankle-deep. They stood amid the clutter of electric cables, collection pouches, bars, picks, rocks.

"Why is the chapel important? Aside from finding samples of the Casumel series?"

George spoke to someone else on a private channel. The person at the other end of the tubes, Hutch assumed. Then, apparently satisfied, he turned toward her. The pressure in the tubes subsided. "This was an outpost of a major civilization, Hutch. But we don't know anything about these people. We don't know what was important to them, how they thought about themselves, what they would have thought about *us*. But chapels and temples tend to be places which reveal the highest values of the civilizations they represent."

"You can't be serious," said Hutch.

"I don't mean *directly*. But if you want to learn what counts to people, read their mythology. How do they explain the great questions?" He grinned, suddenly aware that he had become pedagogic. She thought his eyes lingered on her, but couldn't be sure.

"Hutch," said Richard, "Henry is up forward, in one of the anterooms. Where they found the Tull series. Would you like to see it?"

"I think I'll pass," she said. "I'm out of time."

"Okay. You know how to get back?"

"Sure." She watched Richard swim past George, and continue down the tunnel. Moments later, he rounded a bend and was gone.

Hutch listened to the faint hiss of her airpack. "How are we doing?" she asked.

George smiled. "Not so good."

"I expected to find most of the team down here. Where is everybody?"

"Frank and Linda are with Henry. The rest are at Seapoint. There's really not much we can do until we get things cleared out below. After that, we'll do a major hunt for more Casumel C samples. When Maggie—You know Maggie?"

"No."

"Maggie Tufu's our exophilologist. We've got several hundred samples of Casumel Linear C from around the area. But most of the samples are short, only a few words. When she tells us she's got enough to start reading it, that will be the signal to pull out." He sounded weary.

"You okay?"

"I'm fine." He glanced down at the tubes, which had collapsed. They were blue-black, flexible, painted with silver strips at intervals of about one meter. The strips were reflective.

He didn't seem to have anything to do except sit by the device. "I'm just collecting data from Tri's monitor," he said. "Tri holds the vacuum, and I sit here in case the Temple falls in on him. That's so we know right away." He turned toward her, and she got her first clear look at him.

George had good eyes, dark and whimsical. She could see that he enjoyed having her there. He was younger than she would have guessed: his brow was unfurrowed, and there was something inescapably innocent in his demeanor. He was handsome, in the way that most young men are handsome. But the smile, and the eyes, added an extra dimension. He would be worth cultivating, she decided.

"How unsafe *is* this place?" she asked.

The passageway was too small for him. He changed his position, trying to get comfortable. "Normally, we'd have taken time to buttress everything, but we're on the run. We're violating all kinds of regulations being in here at all. If something goes, somebody may get killed." He frowned. "And I'll be responsible."

"You?"

"Yes."

"Then close the place down."

"It's not that easy, Hutch. I probably *should* do that. But Henry is desperate."

Eddie Juliana had no time to waste. "Red tags first," he said. Hutch glanced around at stacks of cases, most of them empty; and at rows of artifacts: clay vessels, tools, machines, chunks of engraved stone. Some cases were sealed. These were labeled in red, yellow, and blue.

"Okay," she said, not certain what she was to do with the red tags.

Eddie moved around the storeroom with the energy of a rabbit in heat. He ducked behind crates, gave anxious directions to someone over his commlink, hurried in and out checking items on his inventory.

He stopped and gazed at Hutch. "You *were* planning on helping, right?"

Hutch sighed. "Tell me what you want done."

He was thin and narrow with red hair and a high-pitched voice. More than any of the others, he seemed driven by events. Hutch never saw him smile, never saw him relax. He struck her as one of those unfortunate people who see the downside of everything. He was young, and she could not imagine his taking a moment to enjoy himself. "Sub's waiting," he said. "There's a cart by the door, ready to go. Take it over. Carson'll be there to unload. *You* come back. I need you here."

"Okay."

"You really did come in the *Wink*, right?"

"Yes."

"That's good. I didn't trust them not to change their minds, try to save a buck, and send a packet for the evacuation."

She looked around at the rows of artifacts. "Is this everything?"

"There are three more storerooms. All full."

"Okay," she said. "We've got plenty of space. But I'm not sure there's going to be *time*."

"You think I don't know that?" He stared morosely at a cylindrical lump of corrosion. "You know what that is?"

"No."

"It's a ten-thousand-year-old radio receiver." His fingers hovered over it, but did not touch it. "This is the case. Speaker here. Vacuum tubes back here, we think. It was a console." He swung toward her, and his brown, washed-out eyes grew hard. "It's priceless." His breast heaved, and he sounded very much like a man who was confronting ultimate stupidity. "These cases are filled with artifacts like this. They are carefully packed. Please be gentle with them."

Hutch did not bother to take offense. She drove the cart to the submarine bay, turned it over to Carson and a muscular graduate student whose name was Tommy Loughery, got Carson's opinion that Eddie was a basket case, and came back. "We have room on the sub for two more loads," she said.

"How much can your shuttle carry?"

"About two and a half times the capacity of the sub."

"And ours will carry about half that much." He looked around in dismay. "We're going to have to make a few trips. I'd hoped you'd have more capacity."

"Sorry."

Stacks of tablets piled on a tabletop caught her eye. They were filled with symbols, drawn with an artistic flair. "Can we read them?" she asked.

"No," he said.

"How old are they?"

"Six thousand years. They were good-luck talismans. Made by mixing animal fat with clay, and baking the result. As you can see, they last a long time."

Hutch would have liked to ask for a souvenir. But that was against the rules, and Eddie looked as if he took rules very seriously.

"And this?" She indicated a gray ceramic figurine depicting a two-legged barrel-shaped land animal that resembled a Buddha with fangs. It had large round eyes and flat ears pressed back on its skull like an elephant's. The body was badly chipped.

Eddie glared at her, angered that she could not see the need for haste. But it was also true that he loved to talk about his artifacts. "It's roughly eight hundred years old." The object was intricately executed. He held it out to her. It was heavy. "The owner was probably one of the last priests." A shadow crossed his pinched features. "Think about it: the Temple, or some form of it, had been there since time immemorial. But somewhere toward the end of the fourteenth century, they closed it up. Locked the doors, and turned out the lights. Can you imagine what that must have meant to that last group of priests?" The ventilators hummed in the background. Eddie studied the figurine. "This is not a sacred object. It had some personal significance. We found several of these in one of the apartments. This one was left near the main altar."

"Company for the dying god," suggested Hutch.

He nodded, and she realized at that moment that whatever else he might be, Eddie Juliana was a hopeless romantic.

Two hours later, she was in the air, enroute to *Wink*.

"Janet, are you there? This is Hutch."

"Negative, Hutch. Janet's asleep. This is Art Gibbs."

"Pleased to meet you, Art."

"What can I do for you?"

"Uh, nothing. I was just bored."

"Where are you now?"

"Chasing my ship. But I won't catch her for another few hours." Pause. "What do *you* do with this outfit, Art?"

"Dig, mostly. I'm sorry I missed you today. I hear you're a knockout."

Hutch smiled and switched to video. "Dispel all illusions," she said. "But it's nice to hear."

Art beamed at her. "The rumors are short of the mark," he said gallantly. Art Gibbs was in his fifties, hair gone, a roll of flab around his middle. He asked whether she had been to Quraqua before, what she had done that had so impressed Richard Wald, what her reactions were to the Temple of the Winds. Like the others, he seemed stricken by the impending evacuation.

"Maybe it'll survive," she said. "It's underwater. And the Knothic Towers look pretty solid."

"No chance. A few hours after they knock the icecap into the ocean, we'll get huge tidal waves here—"

She had lost the sun now, was gliding through the dark. Her left-hand window looked out on the Void. She caught a glimpse of the Kosmik space station, a lone brilliant star.

"Somebody else," continued Art, "will be along in a few thousand years to try again. Be an interesting puzzle, I'd think: hi-tech wreckage on a low-tech world."

"Art, have you been to Oz?"

"Yes."

"What did you think of it?"

"I don't think we'll ever know what it's about."

"Doesn't it strike you as odd that it got burned at the same time that the military post was destroyed?"

"It burned during the same *era*," he said gently. "Don't forget that the fort disappeared during an epoch of worldwide destruction."

"That's my point. I think. Doesn't it seem likely there's a connection?"

"I don't see how there could be." He stuck his tongue in the side of his cheek and frowned. "I really don't."

"Frank Carson mentioned the connection between the events at Oz and widespread destruction on Quraqua."

"What could it be? There's only a connection in very general terms, Hutch. The discontinuities occurred over long stretches of time. For all we know, so did the damage inflicted on Oz. But they didn't necessarily happen at the same time. Only during the same era. There's a difference, and I think we fall into a trap when we confuse the two." He paused. "Are you interested in the discontinuities?"

"Yes."

"Then I'll tell you something else. It's coincidence, of course."

"What is?"

"There's a poem that we have in translation. Wait a minute, let me find it."

Art walked off-screen. "Have you ever heard of the Scriveners?"

"No."

"They dominated this area between approximately 1400 B.C., and the collapse of the Eastern Empire, about four hundred years later."

"Scriveners?"

"So named because they kept records of everything. Detailed commercial accounts, inventories, medical records, vital statistics. They were quite advanced." He grinned. "In a bureaucratic way. They were a lot like us. They even seem to have had insurance policies. Now, their demise, the fall of the Eastern Empire, and the Second Discontinuity all seem to have occurred around 1000 B.C."

"Okay." Ten lines of text had appeared on Hutch's monitor.

"Judging from the commercial nature of the writings they left behind, the Scriveners appear to have been neither philosophical nor religious. The Temple was relegated to a historical curiosity during their period of ascendancy. But we *did* find a book of devotions in one of their cities. Valdipaa. Not far from here. Next stop on the trade route west. The verse on your screen is from the book."

> *In the streets of Hau-kai, we wait.*
> *Night comes, winter descends,*
> *The lights of the world grow cold.*
> *And, in this three-hundredth year*
> *From the ascendancy of Bilat,*
> *He will come who treads the dawn,*

Tramples the sun beneath his feet,
And judges the souls of men.
He will stride across the rooftops,
And he will fire the engines of God.

She read through it twice. "What are the engines of God?"
Art shrugged.

"Then what's the point?"

"Bilat. He was a hero. He was used for a time to mark the
beginning of the Scrivener era. He seized power somewhere
around 1350 B.C., our time. Hau-kai, by the way, was a kind
of Jerusalem, a holy city, symbolic of the best that the faithful
could hope for in this world."

Hutch reread the verse. "Three hundred years later would
take them close to the Second Discontinuity." She exited
from the screen, and brought Art back. "You're suggesting
somebody predicted the event?"

"We've dated the book. It's one of the oldest we have.
Can't read much of it. What we *can* read is mostly devotional."

"Who did the translation?"

"Maggie Tufu. Have you met her? Well, anyway, she con-
verted the time references. The term that reads as *men* actually
refers to all the inhabitants of the planet, male and female,
past and present. And the verb that's rendered as *judges*
seems to imply both judge and executioner." Art seemed
simultaneously amused and perplexed. "And, yes—the prediction is right on the money."

"Prophecy's a tricky game," said Hutch. "It's common for
religious groups to predict catastrophic events. Get enough
predictions, and somebody's bound to hit it right."

Art nodded. "That would be my guess. But some people
here have wondered whether the thing on the moon doesn't
in some way mark this world for periodic destruction."

By 1900 hours, the Temple shuttle was loaded and ready
to follow *Alpha*. Carson checked everything to ensure that
the containers wouldn't shift, and watched the sub draw away.
Eddie sat stiffly in its bubble with his arms folded, staring
straight ahead.

Carson powered up, informed the watch officer he was on
his way, and lifted off.

The sun had moved behind the peaks, and a cold wind blew across the gathering darkness. The tide was out, and wide stretches of sand glittered in the failing light. Waves broke around the Towers. Carson would be glad to be away, to get to D.C. and to walk in the sun without needing a Flickinger harness.

Still, he was angry. When he had first come here, six years ago, he had thought of the Temple, with its rock walls, as timeless. Long after he passed to a happier existence, it would be here, as it had been here for millennia. It was a symbol, for all of them, of stability. Of the idea that things that really matter live on.

He drew back the yoke. The shuttle sailed through the clouds.

Below, the Knothic Towers were already lost in twilight.

LIBRARY ENTRY

When, in the spring of 2187, Alexander LaPlante completed the first phase of the excavation of Sodom, he concluded that the city had been burned, a fate not uncommon in Biblical times. But he offered two additional opinions which created a storm of controversy:

(1) that the site was far older than had been expected, dating to approximately 5000 B.C.; and

(2) that a computerized reconstruction of the damage suggested the city had been shattered by something akin to modern weapons.

LaPlante's grant was cut off in 2189. A second expedition, led by Oliver Castle and Arian Adjani, examined both propositions. They confirmed the earlier date, but found no compelling evidence to support what had by then become known as the bomb thesis.

LaPlante lost his tenure at the University of Pennsylvania in 2195, and is now teaching at Radison University in London.

—Marjorie Gold
Dead Sea Excavations
Commonwealth, New York, 2199

9.

Quraqua. Tuesday; 2148 hours. (Twenty-eight minutes before midnight.)

Both shuttles had unloaded their cargo on the *Winckelmann*, and were on their way back to the surface when the eleven-ton block of supercooled ice that was designated #171 in the Kosmik inventory crossed the equator into the southern hemisphere. With a whisper, it passed over moonlit tundra and pulpy forests, something not quite heard. Shining splinters fell away, and the arid landscape momentarily brightened.

Snow blew against *Alpha*'s windscreen. Hutch (who had waited for Carson at *Wink*, and then followed him down) could see the sub and the Temple shuttle, haloed by their lights, docked at the floatpier. The shuttle's cargo door was open; Carson and Loughery were working to move a stack of containers off the pier into the spacecraft.

Janet Allegri blinked onto her overhead display. "Hello, Hutch," she said. Her hair was pressed down by an energy field. She was speaking from the sub. "We seem to have got a little behind with Plan A." They had intended to pile cases on the floatpier, and have two more complete shipments ready to go when the shuttles arrived. But not very much had made it topside.

"Weather been bad?"

"It's been wet. But the problem is *people*. Everybody's hunting artifacts."

Well to the south, lightning struck the ocean.

Hutch understood. Under extreme pressure, Henry was willing to risk the artifacts he already possessed—which were after all duly recorded on hologram—to increase his

118

chances of finding what he was *really* looking for. "Coming down," she said.

She settled smoothly into the sea, and drifted into the magnetic couplers, which locked the shuttle against the pier. Carson was loading the last container, and his hold was still half-empty.

Loughery smiled shyly. He was loading a dolly into the sub. The snow slid down his energy envelope.

"How can I help?" she asked.

Janet came out of the sub. "Just in time," she said lightly. "We were running short of peasants."

The sea was calm, but the peaks along the shore, and the Towers, were lost in murk. Carson, who seemed to wear his feelings close to the surface, looked unhappy. "Good to see you," he said, cheering up. "Roll up your sleeves."

Moments later, they submerged and headed at high speed for Seapoint.

If the skies had been clear, and if they'd been six minutes slower to leave, they would have seen a fireball glide silently out of the northeast. They would have seen it arc out to sea, and pass below the horizon. And anyone standing on the pier, even in the thick gloom, would have noticed a sudden brightening of the southern sky.

She had slept during most of the flight down from *Wink*, so she was ready to work. Since she was too small to be of much assistance lugging containers around, she asked Eddie whether there wasn't something she *could* do. He directed her to a storeroom where she found Tommy Loughery.

"Eddie asked me to get you started," he said. His black hair was in disarray, somewhat in the sloppy style common to graduate students in those times.

"Okay," she said. "What do I do?"

He pointed at a table loaded with artifacts. There were wedges, pieces of masonry, pottery. "Most of this just came down from Maggie's operation. They're all from the Lower Temple. And priceless. They get red-tagged. There'll be more later. All of this is high-priority, and should go up on the next shuttle. We need to pack it."

"Show me how," she said.

He produced a stock of plastic cloth and dragged over two of the barrel-shaped containers, which he loaded onto a motorized cart. He held an artifact up to the light, turned it so she could read the four digits on the red tag. "That's the catalog number," he said. "Record it on the packing list." Then he wrapped the artifact in plastic, taped it, and placed it in the container.

It was simple enough, and she proceeded to clear the table, while Tommy found other things to do. When she'd finished filling both containers, he returned..

"What next?"

"We seal them." He picked up a spray gun. It was fed by a short hose that connected to a pair of drums, labeled "A" and "B." He pulled the cart closer, and pointed the gun into one of the containers. "Stand back," he said. He pulled the trigger. A thick white stream slushed out and rolled over the packages.

"It's poly-6, a low volume, expanding rigid urethane," he explained. "Great packing material. It's biodegradable. And it sets quickly. As you can see." He snapped off the flow.

"You didn't put much in," said Hutch.

"Only needs about five percent of volume." He threw the gun aside, clamped the lid down and locked it.

"The merchandise is fragile. Won't it get crunched?"

"No. The poly-6 doesn't apply pressure. When it meets resistance, it stops." He handed her the gun. "Just leave the containers on the cart. When you're finished, call me and we'll take them over to the sub."

George Hackett removed the last of the petrified timbers, held his breath, and smiled with satisfaction when nothing happened. This was as deep as they'd penetrated into the Lower Temple. Beyond, a hole in the wall opened into a chamber that was three-quarters filled with silt. "We'll need to brace the roof, Tri," he said. "On both sides of the opening."

"Okay. Hang on. Braces coming."

While he waited, George thrust his lamp forward. This could be the inner sanctum of the military chapel, the chamber in which priests prepared to conduct services, where they perhaps stored their homilies and their sacred vessels.

"Can you see anything?" Tri called.

Yes. There was something, a piece of furniture probably, to his right, half-buried, just out of reach. It had been metal once. "Something," George said. "A washstand, maybe. Or a cabinet. Can't tell."

Tri moved forward with a pair of braces. "Let's get these up first," he said.

"Just a second." George inched into the space. He was acutely conscious of the weight of the Temple hanging over him. "I think it's a machine."

"In here? What kind of machine?"

"I don't know. But there *is* a housing. Wait." The hole was too narrow for him. He pulled back, scraped out silt and loose rock, and tried again.

"That's enough, George," said Tri. "Let's do it right."

He got his shoulders through the entrance, and pushed forward. "There's a metal framework here. With, uh—Hell, Tri, I don't know *what* to make of this." He carried a camera on his left forearm. "Maggie, are you there?" he asked through the commlink. "Can you see this?"

"Maggie's coming," said Andi, who was watch officer.

He struggled to get closer.

"What do you have, George?" It was Maggie. He knew she'd be straining to see the object on the big screen.

"Don't know." He was in now, and stood over the device. Metal bars and plates were connected to a system of springs and pulleys. Everything was heavily corroded.

"Shine the lamp to your left," Maggie said. "Look, there's a tray." There were small objects that looked like stones in the tray. "See if they're loose," she said.

He took one out, dabbed at it carefully, and held it close to the camera. There was a dark smudge on it.

Maggie was silent for several moments. Then her voice went very soft. "Goddammit, George, I think you've found us a printing press!"

"Well, good," said George.

"Yes." Her voice was ecstatic, and he heard her clap. "Show me the frame."

He did.

"Closer," she urged. And then: "It's got some sort of typesetting arrangement. It's filled with type."

"What language?" said Andi. "Can you tell?"

"Not yet. But we might be able to restore enough of it." He listened to her breathe. "It might be the jackpot."

"How do you mean?"

"Place like this would need multilingual prayer-cards. Or whatever. If there's a Rosetta stone here, this could be *it*. George, haul it out."

Henry was napping in the community room when his commlink chimed. He came immediately awake. Henry lived these days in constant fear of disaster. He knew he was violating safety procedures, risking his people, risking his career. Not good, but he knew that history was watching him. It was not a time for caution. "What is it, Andi?"

"Kosmik on the line. You want to listen? Or take the call?"

"I'm busy," he said. "You do the talking. If necessary, tell them you'll check with me and get back. And, Andi?"

"Yes?"

"Don't give them any trouble. Okay?" He shook the last of the sleep out of his brain, got up, and walked wearily downstairs to Operations.

Henry loved Quraqua. He loved its quiet mountain ranges, and its long wandering rivers; its vast silences and its abandoned cities. The ancient walls and towers rose out of deep forests, bordered great plains, embraced harbors. Many of the more recent ruins remained in good condition: one could not stroll through them without anticipating that the dusty fountains would one day flow again, the lights come on, and the avenues fill with traffic. Quraqua was a place, in Richard Wald's memorable phrase, "on the shore of time."

He had been here sixteen years, had married two of his wives here, one of them atop the Golden Stair at Eskiya. He had gone back to Earth only when necessary, to fight with the Second Floor about funding, or to take on those who wanted to rearrange his priorities. He was a blue-collar archeologist, an excavator, a detail man, tough, competent, good to work for. Not brilliant, in the way that Richard was brilliant. But solid. Methodical. If one could say that Richard Wald was curious about the inscription at Oz, it was equally arguable that Henry was driven by it. And not because of some deeper mystery behind the arcane symbols, but because he understood he was locked away from fundamental truth, essential to understanding this thing he loved so much.

Andi was waiting for him. As he arrived, she pressed Transmit. "This is the Temple. Go ahead, Kosmik."

The monitor glowed, and Harvey Sill's image appeared. "Dr. Jacobi, please. Director Truscott wishes to speak with him."

"Dr. Jacobi is not available. Director Truscott may speak with me if she wants. I'll be happy to relay her message. Or if you prefer, I can have Dr. Jacobi return the call."

"Oh, for God's sake." Melanie Truscott replaced Sill. "We don't have time for bureaucratic nonsense, young lady." She paused, and lifted her eyes above Andi, as if she were searching the room. "Henry, I know you're there. Please talk to me. We have an emergency."

Henry sighed, and walked around in front of the screen. "Hello, Melanie," he said wearily. "What seems to be the problem?"

"We've had an accident."

Henry glanced sharply at Andi, a gesture delivered primarily for Truscott's benefit. "What happened? Do you need help?"

"No. But *you* might be in some danger."

"What do you mean?"

"We lost control of one of the snowballs. An orbiting piece of ice. It fell into the Yakata three minutes ago."

He smothered his anger. "Where?"

"Roughly sixteen hundred kilometers south of you. It impacted at seventy-two point five south, one-fifteen point two west."

Andi brought up a map of the region, and marked the location.

Truscott's eyes fastened on Henry. "A tsunami has formed," she said.

"Melanie, you are a *bitch*."

"I'm sorry you think so, Henry. But I hardly think that's the issue." She *looked* guilty. She tried to stare him down, but the fire had gone out of her eyes.

"How big is the wave?"

"We don't have a measurement yet."

"Please let me know when you do."

"I will. And, Henry—I'm sorry about this. If we can help—"

"Yes. Of course. Temple out." He broke the link. "We'll need to evacuate the Temple. How fast do tidal waves travel?"

Andi was already consulting the data banks:

TSUNAMI. (SEA WAVE, SEISMIC WAVE, TIDAL
WAVE.) AN OCEAN WAVE RESULTING FROM
AN UNDERSEA EARTHQUAKE, VOLCANIC ERUP-
TION, OR OTHER SUBMARINE DISTURBANCE.
THE TSUNAMI MAY REACH OVERWHELMING
DIMENSIONS, AND HAS BEEN KNOWN TO TRAV-
EL ENTIRELY AROUND THE EARTH. (Cf., THE
ARGENTINEAN PLATE SLIPPAGE, 2011.) IT PRO-
CEEDS AS AN ORDINARY GRAVITY WAVE. THE
WATER FORMING TSUNAMIS TENDS TO BUNCH
UP BEHIND THE WAVE WHILE IT IS TRAVEL-
ING THROUGH DEEP WATER. ON APPROACH-
ING SHALLOW AREAS, VELOCITY DECREASES,
BUT THE WAVE WILL INCREASE SHARPLY IN
HEIGHT. LOW-LYING AREAS MAY BE ENGULFED.
TSUNAMIS DO NOT RESULT IN ANY WAY FROM
TIDAL ACTION. THE POPULAR TERM "TIDAL
WAVE" IS A MISNOMER.

She scanned ahead.

VELOCITY OF THE WAVE EQUALS THE SQUARE
ROOT OF GRAVITATIONAL ACCELERATION
TIMES THE DEPTH OF THE WATER.

"Do we have the sea depths south of here?" Henry asked.
Andi shook her head. "I don't think they've been mea-
sured very exactly." Her fingers danced across the keyboard.
"Best guess is that it will be traveling at five or six hundred
kilometers per hour. But it's only a guess."
"Son of a bitch." She listened to Henry's harsh breathing.

Hutch was riding her cart, carrying six containers toward
the sub bay when Henry broke in on the common channel.
"We've got an emergency," he said softly.
She turned a corner and saw Eddie Juliana coming out of
one of the storerooms. He was scribbling on a lightpad.
Henry outlined the situation briefly. Hutch thought it was
probably a false alarm, a maneuver in a war of nerves. But
Eddie was staring at her, eyes wide.

"We don't know yet how fast it's coming," Henry continued, "or where it is, or how big it is. But it could be here in a couple of hours. Everyone is to leave the Temple. Return immediately to Seapoint."

"My God," said Eddie, "we'll lose it all."

George broke in: "Henry, we're in the middle of something."

"*Now*, George. I want everybody back here within thirty minutes. Please acknowledge to Andi. Don't worry about securing equipment. Frank, what's the status on the sub?"

Carson was enraged. "It's loaded. We were just getting ready to head for the pier."

"Forget it. Is Tommy with you?"

"Yes."

Eddie climbed onto the cart. "Get going," he said to Hutch.

"Tommy." Henry sounded calm. "Take the sub and head straight out to sea. Go as far as you can."

"Why not leave it where it is?" asked Carson.

"Because it's safer in deep water. We don't know what'll happen here. Frank, I need you and Hutch to find the wave. I want to know where it is, how big it is, and how fast it's coming."

Carson acknowledged.

"One more thing. It's going to be hard to see. Tidal waves are small when they're in deep water. Maybe only a meter or two high. But it's *long*. There might be a kilometer or two between the crest and the trough."

Hutch and Eddie rolled into the sub bay.

"I'm not sure what constitutes safe cover for something like this," Henry continued. "If we have time, I'm going to get everybody ashore, out of the way of this goddam thing."

"Then you'll need the sub," Carson said.

"It'll take too long. We'd need time to unload it, and then a couple of trips to get everyone out. And then another three quarters of an hour to get to high ground. No, we'll use the jetpacks if there's time. *You* find out what the situation is. Where is it? How bad? When will it get here?"

"Don't forget," Andi added, "to get both shuttles away from the dock."

Eddie jumped off the side of the cart as Carson closed the cargo hatch. "What are you doing?" he asked.

Carson blinked at the question. "Getting underway."

"You've got room for more." He was trying to direct Hutch to pull closer to the sub.

"Forget it, Ed."

"Anyway," added Hutch, "the sub's going out to meet a tidal wave. Last thing you want is a lot of ballast. It's probably already overloaded."

That brought a worried reaction from Tommy. "Maybe we should unload some of this stuff."

"Listen," said Eddie, "this place might get wrecked. We've got to save what we can."

"Seapoint'll be fine," said Carson, but he threw a worried glance toward Hutch. "Let's get going."

Before they were clear of the base, Hutch had used her remote to start *Alpha* inland. Five minutes later, she and Carson rode the Temple shuttle into a dripping sky.

Below, Tommy, frightened and alone, headed out to sea.

George, deep in the Lower Temple, was also reluctant to adjust his priorities. "Henry," he pleaded, "we can have it out of here in an hour."

Maggie, wherever she was, joined in: "Henry, this is *critical*. We can't take a chance on losing it."

They were on the common channel. Hutch had been distracted, hadn't heard enough to know what *it* was. "We may not *have* an hour," Henry said. "Don't argue with me; I've got too much to do. George, get back here."

Hutch stared at the ocean. It looked peaceful enough. "This kind of screw-up," she said to Carson, "intentional or not, should cost her her career."

"Who?"

"Truscott."

"That's a joke. We're politically unpopular right now. They'll give her a medal."

Scanners are specialized. Those mounted on the Temple shuttle, intended for archeology, were designed to penetrate subsurface objects and provide detail at short range. What Hutch needed was the broad sweep of her own instruments. "We took the wrong shuttle," she said.

"Too late now. It'll have to do."

It was still snowing.

Hutch looked at her screens. "The wave might be only a meter or so high. I'm not sure that's going to show up."

Carson frowned. "What if we go lower?"

She responded by taking it down on the deck. But she kept air speed at three hundred until Carson grumbled. "We've got to make better time than this."

"We won't find it at all if we aren't careful. There are a lot of waves out there."

Carson shook his head. "This drives me right up the wall. Tidal waves are supposed to be *easy* to see. You sure Henry knows what he's talking about?"

"He's *your* boss. What do *you* think?"

Richard was helping Janet pack rations. The rest of the Academy team trooped in, in twos and threes. Henry plowed back and forth through the community room, head bent, hands locked behind his back.

Carson's voice came over the link. "We're at one hundred kilometers. Nothing yet."

Tri and George came in. That made thirteen people present. All accounted for.

"Okay, people," Henry said. "Now that we're all here, I think you should know what we intend to do. Let me say first that I think Seapoint will be safe. But there's no way to be sure. If we have sufficient time, we'll evacuate. Karl has brought up some light cable. We'll form a human chain, and use the jets to go ashore. Once there we'll head immediately up the pass. There's accessible high ground there, and we should be able to get well out of harm's way within a half hour or so after we get to the beach."

"How long," asked Andi, "is 'sufficient time'?"

"Two hours," he said. "If we don't get two hours to clear out, we'll stay here."

Art Gibbs stood. He looked uncertain and nervous. "Maybe we should put this to a vote, Henry."

Henry's eyes hardened. "No," he said. "No votes. I won't have anyone killed over democratic principles."

"Maybe there is no wave," said Carson. "Maybe it's a gag."

"Could be," Hutch said.

Henry's voice broke through the gloom. "Nothing yet, Frank?"

Carson looked pained. "Negative, Henry. Everything's calm out here."

"I don't think we're going about this right," said Henry. "You're moving too slowly. If it's in close it won't matter if you find it because we'll ride it out here anyway. What we need to know is whether it's far enough away to allow us time to get to shore. Why not take it up to top speed? If you find it far enough out, we're in business. If not, nothing lost."

"No," said Hutch. "I don't know much about tsunamis, but I *do* know they come in packs. Even if we hustled out and found a wave, we couldn't be sure there weren't others in close. We're not looking for *one* wave. We're looking for the nearest."

At two hundred kilometers, they ran out from under the storm. The sea was choppy, moonlit, restless. Icebergs drifted everywhere.

They flew on and watched the screens and the ocean. They began to sense that Henry had also begun to hope it was a false alarm.

In the glow of their navigation lights, an enormous black fluke rose out of the water. "Whale?" she asked.

"No whales on Quraqua." Carson looked down. "It has to be a fish. But I don't know that much about local wildlife." Then, without changing his tone, he said, "There's the wave."

It was long and straight, a ripple extending unbroken toward the horizon. It was not high, perhaps two meters. And not at all ominous. Just a surge of water trailing a black, polished wake. "You sure?" she asked.

"Yeah. That's it."

"Henry, this is Hutch. We've got it."

"Where?"

"Four hundred kilometers. It's moving at five-fifty."

"Okay," he said. "We'll stay here."

"Yeah. For what it's worth, it doesn't look bad."

Tommy Loughery was running on the surface. He had heard them pass overhead, outbound, although he'd seen nothing in the clouds.

"Tommy." Andi's voice.

"Go ahead, Andi."

"You heard everything?"

"Sure did."

"When it gets near, go deep. It should be easy to get below the turbulence."

"I will," he said. "Good luck."

"You too. But I think we'll be okay."

He agreed. He'd seen the pictures transmitted from the shuttle, and it now seemed to him like a needless panic. His scanners were watching for the wave. If it grew enough to become a hazard, he would have plenty of time to get down. Truth was, he was grateful to spend a few hours in the storm, watching the snow come down, listening to the sounds of the ocean. The Temple had become claustrophobic, and oppressive, and grim. He wouldn't have admitted it to anyone, but he was almost glad that Kosmik had pushed them off. He'd been here only a semester, and he was scheduled for another. It had begun to seem endless. Better to get back to a world filled with women and lights and old friends and good restaurants. It would not have helped his career to break his contract and leave early. But now, he could return to D.C., and take advantage of his field experience to land a teaching job. In the future he'd leave the long-distance travel to others.

Because the craft was designed to lie low in the water, Tommy's sensors gave him good range only when he topped the crest of a wave. But that happened often enough to keep him aware of anything coming his way.

He drifted, watching the sea and thinking about better days. After a while, he heard the shuttle return, and a few minutes later his sensors gave him an unusual blip at sea level. Range twenty-two kilometers. Decreasing *very* rapidly. "Andi."

"Go ahead, Tommy."

"I see it. Estimate speed five hundred. It just looks like a long wave."

"Thanks, Tom. Take the sub down."

"I'm forty kilometers out. And diving." But he waited on the surface. It did not appear dangerous. He'd seen bigger along the Carolina coast. He maneuvered the sub until he had the prow pointed directly at the surge, and then he moved slowly forward.

The blue line on his screens grew.

Lightning flickered silently overhead.

He turned on his spotlights, but he could see nothing except rain. The prow tilted abruptly, and he rode *up*. For a breathless moment, he thought he was going to be flipped. The sub pitched and righted itself and moved again through smooth water. "No sweat," he said, under his breath.

• • •

"Look at that son of a bitch," murmured Carson.

The wave raced in graceful silence through the night. In their lights, it was black and clean and elegant. "It's slowing down," said Hutch. "It's under four hundred now." It was also expanding: it was still a solid front, without a crest, but it had begun to uncoil. To grow.

"Shallow water, Hutch." They were both looking at the data displays. "They lose velocity as they approach beaches. Thank God for small favors."

"Frank, how deep is Seapoint?"

"At high tide, which we are approaching, it's thirteen meters. Should be enough."

Carson reported to Andi. She sounded frightened.

The shuttle was running before the wave, close down on the water to facilitate measurement. "I just thought of something," said Hutch.

"What's that?"

"The monkeys. Are they on the beach at night?"

"They're going to have to worry about themselves, Hutch. But no, they aren't. Usually. Some come down, occasionally, after dark, just to watch the sea. When a study was done of them several years ago, it was one of the characteristics the researchers found most interesting."

The Towers came up on the monitor.

Behind them, the wave was a whisper barely audible over the roar of the sea.

They wheeled through the Towers. The tide was out. Hutch remembered that big waves were supposed to do that, suck coastlines dry and then deliver the water back in.

The wave rose, and mounted, and entered the shallows. It was not breaking; rather, the sea seemed to be hurling itself, dark and glittering and marble-smooth, against the ancient Towers and the rocky coastline beyond.

Seapoint. Wednesday; 0320 hours.

Radio and laserburst transmissions were relayed to Seapoint through a communications package mounted on a buoy which floated serenely on the surface directly above the cluster of sea domes. It was now forwarding the shuttle's images of the oncoming wave. Those images were displayed below on eleven monitors, in five different locations. But the one that had everybody's attention was located at the main diving port, a room of substantial size, with a large pool in its center. This was the chamber through which heavy equipment could be moved into the sea. It was advantageous under the present circumstances because there was no loose gear nearby, no cabinets, nothing that could injure anyone. Moreover, the pool was bordered by a handrail, to which they could attach themselves when the time came. There had been considerable discussion as to whether they wouldn't be safer seated in chairs with their backs to walls that faced the oncoming wave. But the sense that there might be a need to get out quickly overcame all other considerations.

They had sealed off the pool by closing the sea doors, after testing once to determine that the weakest among them (thought to be Maggie Tufu, who thereby became irate) could open them manually.

The atmosphere then became almost that of a picnic. The images of the oncoming wave revealed a disturbance so essentially moderate and quiescent that none could take it seriously. The men, for the most part, made it their business to look bored throughout the exercise, while the soft laughter of the women echoed across the pool.

Nevertheless, Richard saw that neither the boredom, nor the laughter, was real. Stiff, somewhat unnerved himself, he strolled among them, trading uneasy banter. And, when it seemed appropriate, giving assurance he did not feel. "I've seen worse at Amity Island," he told Linda Thomas. It was a lie, but it made them both feel better.

With several minutes remaining, the sub checked in. "No problem here," Tommy reported. He could not resist admitting that he had ridden over the top of the surge. If the sub had survived *that*, the wave couldn't be too serious.

As it approached, all eyes followed it on the screen. The images were the standard shaded blues of nightlight, and there was no audio, which combined to dampen the effect that Hutch and Carson were experiencing from the shuttle. Maybe it was just as well.

One by one, they took their places along the guardrail, used belts and lines to secure themselves to it, activated their energy shields, and began breathing from their airpacks. Richard watched the wave shut off the sky. Someone, Andi, noticed that the water level at the Towers had dropped.

The wave charged across the last kilometer. White water showed along its crest.

They could feel its approach in the bulkheads. They braced themselves, knelt on the deck, gripped the rail. Then the chamber shook, the lights dipped and went out, and the voice of the beast filled the night. The pool erupted and the screen went blank.

Someone whimpered, and there was awed profanity. A second blow fell, heavy, immense, delivered by an enormous mallet.

Richard was thrown against his belt and banged his ribs. Beside him, Linda cried out. Tri was somehow torn loose and flung into the water.

But nobody was seriously hurt. The shocks continued, with generally decreasing fury, for several minutes. The lights came back. They were startled that it had been so severe after all, but relieved that they were all alive, and they started to laugh. It was nervous, tentative laughter. And Henry released his death grip on the guardrail, and gave them all a thumbs-up. "Ladies and gentlemen," he said. "Congratulations."

LIBRARY ENTRY

They came in the spring of the year to tell me you
  were dead.
They spoke of war and pride, and how you'd laughed
  at fear,
And called my name.
All the while the sea grew black and still.
Now you lie in a distant land, far from the summer day
When we left our tracks on the foamy sand—
Yet in the deeps of the night
You call my name, your voice in the roar of the tide.

—Fragment from *Knothic Hours*
Translated by Margaret Tufu
Cambridge University Press, 2202

10.

On board Alpha. *Wednesday; 0610 hours.*

During the course of an hour, three sea waves struck the Temple site. The first carried away the rear wall of the Temple, blew off the roof, and destroyed the colonnade; the second, which was the largest of the three, demolished two of the Knothic Towers, and buried the Lower Temple; and the third ripped one of Seapoint's domes from its moorings and deposited it two kilometers inland. Several sets of living quarters and a holographic display center went with it. Perhaps worst of all (since the Temple and the Towers were down to their last few days anyhow), an avalanche of sand and loose rock blocked shafts and passageways throughout the excavation site. The military chapel disappeared in the debris.

But they hadn't lost anyone. There were contusions and bruises to go around, and more discouragement. But they were *alive*. And Karl Pickens summed up one point of view when he suggested they would do well to take the hint and abandon the operation.

Hutch, listening in the shuttle, agreed. She and Carson were coming in from another sweep of the area. They'd been all the way out to the impact site. The sea was covered with ice, but there were no more tsunamis coming. Carson sat wrapped in alternating moods of gloom and outrage. Henry sounded tired and washed out on the circuit, as if it didn't matter anymore.

The floatpier was gone, of course. And Priscilla Hutchins flew above the last of the Towers.

Melanie Truscott's message had been delivered.

Art Gibbs and George Hackett met them with the sub, and they spent the next hour transferring cargo. Without the pier, the task was considerably more difficult. Midway through the operation they dropped a case, and watched it sink slowly out of sight. It was, of course, not beyond recovery, but there was no time to go after it. All in all, it was an awkward, slow business.

George was surreptitiously watching Hutch, and she enjoyed his mild confusion when she talked to him. Amid the gloom generated by Henry's people, he alone managed to retain his good humor. "You do what you can do," he told her, "and forget the rest. No point getting ulcers over things you can't control."

But there were moments when he seemed distracted, and he eventually confessed that he would have liked to see things end under better circumstances. "We're always going to wonder what's down there," he said. "These people lived here for thousands of years. It's a pity to just bury them."

Hutch was silent.

"We'll protest," said Art. "And that's all. And that's the problem with this outfit. Nobody here has any guts."

"What would you suggest?" asked George.

Art stared back at the young giant. "I don't know," he said wistfully. "I don't know. But if I were Henry I'd find something."

"Don't get personally involved," said Carson. "It's a management problem."

"I think we should find a good lawyer and sue the bastards," Art continued. "They were negligent. At least. I don't know about anybody else, but I think I hurt my back." He grimaced in mock pain.

"It wouldn't do any good," Carson said. He and George were doing the bulk of the work. They'd tied the two vehicles together, but there was still a lot of bumping and rolling. George was in the sub, passing containers to Carson. It was a hit-and-miss proposition at best, and Hutch was surprised they lost only the one.

"Why not?" he asked. "It would show the world how Caseway and Truscott operate."

"Nothing would come of it," said Carson. "They'd just blame some pilot way down the chain of command, and throw him to the wolves. Nobody at the top would get hurt."

"But we've been mugged," said Hutch.

"That's true," said George, who was tying down a container. "And we know who did the mugging."

"There should be a way to get at them," said Art. He looked out of place in the role of avenger. He was tentative, self-effacing, cautious—completely unlike the energetic egos one usually found in these remote corners of known space. It was almost as if he'd got on a bus one day in downtown Chicago, and had ended at the Temple.

Hutch was thinking about the gang member Truscott had disarmed and killed in Newark. *She* wouldn't sit idly by and accept this kind of treatment.

Other than the missing dome, the complex had suffered no major damage. Hutch knew that some leaks had sprung, that one of the smaller modules, housing the compartments used by Andi and Linda, had burst and filled with water. And she could see a couple of people dredging near the sub bay.

She'd begun to wonder whether the drop had been a direct result of her conversation with Truscott. It was hard to draw any other conclusion.

Damn.

Henry's voice broke in on the common channel. "George? We need you at the site."

George acknowledged. "Guess you guys will have to finish without me."

Hutch felt a chill. "They aren't going to start mining again?"

"Probably."

"It's getting a little late," she said.

Art looked at his watch. "Forty-three hours, and change."

They reloaded the sub and returned to the surface. This time, they went a little farther from shore, seeking smoother water. Hutch recalled *Alpha* from its mountaintop, and guided it in alongside.

Watching Eddie pass cargo across to Art was a funny scene. Neither was strong or adept, and there was a lot of whooping and finger-pointing and suggestions on how the other could improve his performance. Hutch had installed a Teflon deckplate from *Wink* in the shuttle hold, to ease the operation. Just put the container down inside the hatch, and slide it wherever you want. It worked well, and she was delighted.

They finished up and were on their way back to Seapoint for more when Henry broke in again. "As you're aware," he said, "we've been cutting the evacuation pretty close. Good sense suggests we clear out now.

"But most of you know we've found an object in the Lower Temple that appears to be a rotary printing press. It uses movable metal type, and the typeface are in place. Maggie was able to identify several Casumel C characters before the wave hit. Unfortunately, it is still in the Lower Temple. It won't be easy to get back to it in the time we have. But, *if* we can recover it, we might have an entire *page* of C text. I need not tell you what that means.

"We are currently doing everything we can to reach the artifact. At the same time, I want to start moving people up."

"Just a moment, Henry." It was a woman's voice. And she sounded unhappy. Hutch looked questioningly at Art.

"Sandy Gonzalez," said Art. "She did most of the work for us on Oz."

"What is it, Sandy?" Henry asked.

"Mining under these conditions is too dangerous. Let's give it up and get out."

"You won't be involved in it, Sandy."

Wrong response, Hutch thought. Henry was supposed to be smart. Maybe he wasn't getting enough sleep. "I'm not just trying to save my own skin, Henry," Sandy snapped. "What I'm saying is, enough is enough. Call it off before somebody gets killed."

"Okay." Henry showed no emotion. "Anybody else want to say something?"

Another woman spoke up. The voice was familiar, but Hutch couldn't place it. "I wouldn't want to spend the rest of my life wondering what the hell that city on the moon is about, and knowing I might have been close enough to find out, and didn't try."

"Linda Thomas," said Art. "She's very good. And very young. I wish I had her future."

One by one, the others spoke. Even, finally, Frank Carson, from the shuttle. Hutch was surprised to hear him vote to cut their losses and leave. But the team was hopelessly divided, with some individuals arguing both sides of the question. Karl Pickens wanted to stay because he refused to be forced off, *run out of town*, but thought the Temple had been too severely weakened to go back in. "*I* wouldn't want to go down there. And I don't think we should allow anyone to. Even if anybody's crazy enough to volunteer."

That brought an irritated stir.

Janet, who had already voted to stay, said, "I hope our watchword isn't *safety first*."

"Richard?" said Henry. "What do you think?" Hutch wondered whether they could see each other.

"Not my call," Richard said in his most objective monotone. "Whatever you and your people decide, I'll support."

No, goddammit, Hutch thought. Tell him to clear out. This down-to-the-wire approach leaves no room for error.

They did not ask *her*.

"Okay," said Henry, "for now, we'll play it by ear. George, take no chances." Hutch didn't like that very much. It was a non-decision, and they needed a little forceful leadership. "Meantime, we'll start moving the others out. If we don't make good progress in the chapel, we'll break it off in plenty of time." He was breathing heavily. "Eddie, how are we doing with the artifacts?"

Eddie's voice was cold. "We're going to lose most of them. Maybe we should concentrate on saving what we have, instead of running around—"

Since what they could save depended solely on the number of flights the two shuttles could make, and they were already operating at full capacity, Hutch failed to see how "concentrating" would help. If Henry understood that, he chose to say nothing. "We will save what we can," he said smoothly. "Hutch, we're going to start hauling people as well. How many can you carry? Other than yourself?"

"Four in *Alpha*. And you can put three passengers in the Temple shuttle."

There were sixteen people, counting Richard and Hutch. "When's your next flight?"

"In about two hours. As soon as we get loaded."

"Okay. Take Maggie with you. And Phil." Those were the philologists. They could work as easily on *Winckelmann* as in the dome. "And Karl and Janet. I'll figure out the rest—"

"I object," said Pickens. "I didn't say I wouldn't help. I just said it was *crazy*. That doesn't mean I want to duck out."

Janet also demurred, and the "meeting" dissolved in confusion.

Richard was waiting when they returned to the sub bay. He looked troubled, and drew Hutch aside. "We may have a problem," he said.

"Tell me something I don't know. These people are going to kill themselves. I thought *you* were a fanatic."

"Hutch, it's more than just the rush for this one last artifact. Henry and his people have built their careers around this place. And now, as they approach the payoff, someone wants to yank it away. You want the truth?"

"Of course."

"Henry's right. They should stay and get the printing press. Anything less is a betrayal."

She was silent.

He smiled gently. "I need you to do something for me. Do you know David Emory?"

She knew *of* him. Had even met him once at a wedding. A rather prissy African with an Oxford accent. Emory's specialty had something to do with extraterrestrial religions. He wrote books on the subject. "Yes," she said. "I know him."

"He's on Nok. I'd like you to get a message to him."

"Sure."

"About the discontinuities. I'd like to know whether these are random events, or whether there's a pattern of some sort. Maybe there's a planetary or social mechanism. Something biological, possibly. Something that activates periodically." He bit his lip, savoring his inability to get hold of the puzzle. "I'd like to know whether he's seen any evidence of a similar type of event on Nok."

"Why don't you ask him yourself? Seapoint has an interstellar link."

"No privacy. I'd rather keep it to ourselves for now."

"Okay. I'll get it out from *Wink*."

"Thanks. And ask for a prompt response."

Her voice dropped to a conspiratorial whisper. "Now I need to ask *you* something."

"Sure."

"Melanie Truscott."

"What about her?"

"What happens to *her* when this is over?"

He got uncomfortable. "She gets promoted." His eyes drifted away from her. "I know how you feel, Hutch. But we'll lodge a protest. Kosmik will produce a report, send us a copy, apologize, and that'll be the end of it." He shrugged. "Maybe if someone had been killed—"

Janet Allegri was pleased that Henry hadn't given up on tunneling back into the Lower Temple, but annoyed at being among the first to be evacuated.

Nevertheless, she did not complain. She returned to her quarters to pack. She had brought few personal possessions with her three years ago, but she'd managed to accumulate several artifacts. That wasn't legal, of course. Everything was supposed to be turned over to the Academy. But the Academy already had enough to fill a warehouse, and everybody else had taken a souvenir or two. It was more or less traditional.

One, her favorite, was a sun medallion, so-called because of the rising solar disk and the inscription, *Live for the light*. She liked it because it sounded so *human*. She also had an inscribed urn, from the Late Mesatic Period, whose symbols no one could read; and a coin with a Quraquat image on one side, and a *Colin* bush on the other. Years from now, these mementoes would be among her most prized possessions. Something to remind her of two lost worlds: the Quraquat, and her own youth.

She folded them carefully in her clothes, took her three bags out of the closet, and laid them inside.

The sheets would stay. And the towels.

She took framed photos from her walls, pictures of her brother, Joel, and his family in their living room at Christmas, of six members of the Temple team walking the beach, of the Zeta Fragment (which Janet had found, and which had provided Maggie's first insights into the Casumel languages). She'd lived a substantial portion of her adult life here. Had established herself professionally. Had experienced several romances. It hurt to know that these spaces would soon be filled with mud and water.

She dragged her bags into the passageway, and bumped into Richard.

He gave her a startled look, and she understood his mind had been elsewhere. "May I help?" he asked, after a moment to collect himself.

She'd had little opportunity to speak with him since his arrival. His reputation rendered him a daunting figure, and she felt intimidated. "Thank you, yes. Please."

He gazed at her thoughtfully. "Are you all right?"

"I'm fine. Why do you ask?"

"You look pale." He glanced at the bags. "It's okay," he said. "There'll be other places."

They carried the luggage through the community room, down to the lower level, and into the bay. Later, Janet would recall that they had talked during the short walk; she would not remember what he had said. Incidentals, no doubt, the sort of perfunctory remarks to which people freshly acquainted are inevitably limited. But she would always remember that he had seemed kind.

Maggie Tufu was the Academy's ranking exophilologist. She had a high opinion of herself, but she might have been *that* good. She'd made her reputation on Nok, where she'd deciphered ancient and modern languages. Unlike most of the outstanding field performers, Maggie was also a gifted instructor. She was a legend at the University of Pennsylvania.

She'd succeeded at everything in her life that really mattered, with two exceptions: her marriage, and her inability to do anything with the few inscriptions that had survived on Pinnacle.

Now she faced a third potential failure. No one with the Jacobi team had grasped more quickly than she the importance of deciphering Linear C. Like Richard, she believed it might lead eventually to the Monument-Makers, and to the secret behind Oz. Maggie was one of the few who believed there *was* a secret. Her colleagues by and large shared Frank Carson's view that the lunar artifact was simply alien, and that once one recognized that, there was not much else to say.

Consequently, when the numbing news arrived that the Academy was abandoning Quraqua, that its archeological treasures were being sacrificed to create a habitable world, she had thrown aside all other projects, and devoted herself exclusively to the Linear C problem.

They had recovered roughly five hundred writing samples of the target language, mostly from a dozen major sites. Generally, they consisted of only a few clusters of symbols. Context tended to be limited to the knowledge (or assertion) that the sample had been taken from a government building, or a library, or a statue of an animal.

The Lower Temple had major potential. Maggie possessed several tablets of varying degrees of completeness, transcribed in one or another of the Casumel family. These were probably inspirational tales, because they were accompanied by pictographs that translated to rainstorms, the sea, military valor, the moon. And so she could make a guess here, and take a stab there. She had reconstructed a primary alphabet, and several alternates, and had started a vocabulary. But she desperately needed more samples.

The printing press was the answer. That should give her two or three thousand characters of text. *A magnificent find.* If she could get her hands on it.

This morning, she was lingering over a tablet which had come in almost two years before from an excavation site several hundred kilometers inland. She had scanned and indexed it, but had not sent it back to the Academy with her regular annual shipment.

The piece was an oblong, as wide as her hand, about twenty centimeters long. It depicted the Quraquat hero Malinar as a child, with a dish in his hand, feeding a ferocious ursine animal with tusks and huge eyes, while an infant watched. She knew the myth: the animal was a horgon, a demon beast capable of seeing all things. The horgon was one of the classic monstrosities of local mythology, a creature suggestive of divinity gone wrong, not unlike Satan. No one could hide from it. No one could defeat it. But it traditionally spared children, because *this* child had fearlessly approached it with a plate of food to divert attention from his sister. The horgon rewarded Malinar's valor, and never after was known to attack the young. The *valor* ideograph, which consisted of three arrows within a circle, appeared atop the engraving. And there were six lines of text. She believed she had identified several terms: the verbs *to see* and *to offer*, and the nouns *Malinar* and *horgon*.

In addition, the text supported some of her syntactical notions.

She had not sent the tablet on to D.C., because she had recognized the character group for *horgon* from somewhere else: *it was part of the Oz inscription.*

• • •

Andi was in the process of powering down nonessential electronics when Karl passed through Ops with his luggage. On the lower level, he saw Art Gibbs and Sandy Gonzalez tarping a digger. Other equipment, pumps, generators, jetsleds, had been brought in, and were now being laid in storage. There was a tendency to behave as if Seapoint were simply being mothballed, as if someone would return and pick up where this expedition was leaving off.

The Academy would ordinarily have salvaged its equipment, the diggers, the sub, Seapoint itself. But the decision to evacuate had been made suddenly, without including Henry in the process. And consequently too little time had been allowed, and it had become necessary for the Temple team (and their managers back on the Second Floor in D.C.) to choose between bringing out expensive gear or rescuing artifacts of unknown value. The artifacts, of course, had taken precedence. Karl had been on duty when the Second Floor had directed Henry to leave personal luggage at Seapoint, to make extra room aboard the shuttles for storage. Henry had been around long enough to know better than to disagree. But he forgot to implement.

Karl entered the sub bay. It was empty. He strode along the walkway that bordered the docking pool and dropped his bags beside Janet's, along the boarding ramp. "I'm ready," he said to her. The place was filled with Eddie's containers. There were more than a hundred. "Do we really have to haul all these up to the ship?"

"There are more coming." Janet smiled wearily. "Karl, what are you going to do when you get home?"

"I have a position at the Institut von Archäologié." He tried to make it sound casual. But they both knew it was a prestigious appointment.

"Congratulations." She kissed him. "I have no idea what I'm going to do." There had been a list of vacancy announcements around for about a month. The Academy would keep a few of the team on the payroll, and it would try to assist the others. Most, like Karl, would be going back to the classroom. "I want to stay in the field," she said. "But the waiting list for Pinnacle and Nok are both long."

"Two years, last I heard," Karl said. Allegri was a damned good archeologist. With experience. But it would be like the

Academy to waste her, to offer her a job teaching undergraduates. "Maybe they'll make an exception for people here." The approach lamps came on. "Get Henry to put in a word for you."

The water began to churn. "Pity about all this," she said. "Henry deserves better."

"He may not be done yet," said Karl. "He wants Linear C. And I'm not entirely sure he won't get it."

LIBRARY ENTRY

Like most mythic heroes, Malinar may have had a remote historical basis. If so, the reality is hopelessly entangled with fable. This hero appears in epochs thousands of years apart. This is no doubt due to the extreme length of Quraquat history, and to the lack of technological progress after the exhaustion of the world's nonrenewable natural resources, resulting in a telescoping effect upon earlier eras, all of which come to resemble one another.

Although Malinar's time predates the construction of the Knothic Towers by almost ten thousand years, he is nevertheless said to have visited the holy site to consult an aspect of the Deity. The Temple then stood on a rock shelf well above the sea. We possess a tablet thought to depict the event.

Unfortunately, most of the Malinar cycle is missing. We know neither the reason for the consultation, nor its result. We know only that the Quraquat could not bear the thought that their great hero had not at some point visited the imposing shrine on the north shore.

—Linda Thomas, *At the Temple of the Winds*
Harvard University, 2211

11.

Seapoint. Wednesday; 1418 hours.

"I'm sorry we found the thing, Hutch." George Hackett was weary, but he managed to look upbeat anyhow. "If I had my way, we'd call the whole business off. I'm ready to go home."

"How long have you been here?"

"Four years."

"Long time."

"Seems like forever." They were alone in the community room, enjoying coffee and toast. The sea moved against the view panels. "I don't think I'll do any more field trips."

Hutch enjoyed being with him. She loved the glow of his eyes, and his gentleness. Old passions were reviving. When they were together, she had a tendency to babble. But she curbed it, and maintained a discrete distance, waiting for him to make a move. When he did, if he did, she would have to put him on hold until they got home. Anything else would be unprofessional. She knew from long experience that it was impossible to keep secrets on shipboard. "Why not, George?" she asked, in a detached tone. "Your career is in the field, isn't it?"

He shook his head. "I'm not an archeologist. I'm an engineer. I only came out here because the opportunity surfaced, and I thought it was a chance to travel." He laughed.

"Well," she said, "you've certainly traveled."

"Yeah. That I have." He looked at her wistfully. "You know, Hutch," he said, "you're lovely. It's been worth the trip just to meet you."

She, in her turn, glowed. "That's nice of you," she said.

"I mean it."

144

She could see that he did. "What will you do when you get home?" she asked.

He stared at her. "I'm going to find a place where there are green parks and lots of summer days. And where all the women look like *you*." He reached out and stroked her cheek.

Eddie Juliana kept working, kept packing containers. "We'll get everything up," he said. "One way or another, we'll save it all." He urged Hutch to work harder. "These," he said. "These go first. Just in case. Forget the stuff that's down in the bay. In case Truscott decides to drop any more bombs on us." He stared at the ceiling as if observing her attitude on the space station. "Yes," he said, "load these." He indicated a line of red-tags. "I'll get the others." He nodded to himself. "Most definitely."

Hutch worried about him.

"By the door," he said, as they entered his workshop, oblivious of her concern. He was indicating three containers. "These are weapons. From the lower level outpost." He went after the first, signaling Hutch to bring over a cart. "Whatever else happens, we don't want to lose them. They're invaluable." Ordinarily she would have grumbled or gone on strike. But she felt sorry for Eddie, and did what she could. "There's another red-tag next door," he said.

But the container wasn't sealed. She looked in. "It needs a dash of poly-6," she said.

"Take care of it." He arrowed off toward the washroom.

She picked up the gun, aimed it into the container, and pulled the trigger. A thick white stream gushed over the plastene-wrapped artifacts, and the room filled with a faintly acrid aroma. She watched the foam rise, and shut it off. The poly-6 began to inflate, and Hutch hefted the gun and aimed it at an imaginary Melanie Truscott. Eddie reappeared and looked at her impatiently. She pointed the nozzle toward him, and her index finger tightened slightly on the trigger. "Pow," she said.

Pow.

He was in no mood for games. He capped the container, and rolled it onto the cart.

And Hutch had the beginning of an idea. "Eddie, how much of this stuff do we have?"

"Poly-6? Plenty. Why do you ask?"

"How does it work?"

"I don't know the chemistry," he said. "You make it with two barrels." They were in plain sight, labeled "A" and "B." "They're separate compounds. The stuff is inert until it gets mixed. That's what the gun does. When they combine, the urethane expands and hardens. It's been around for centuries. And it's ideal for safeguarding artifacts in shipment."

"Do you have an extra dispenser? A gun?"

"Sure." He frowned. "Why?"

She was calculating storage space on *Alpha*. "Listen, we may have to cut down the size of this next shipment a little."

"*What?*" He sounded wounded. "Why?" he asked again.

"Because I'm going to take two barrels of poly-6 with me."

Eddie was horrified. "There isn't room."

"We'll make room."

"What on earth for?"

"I'm going to use it to say hello to Melanie Truscott."

An hour later, *Alpha* climbed toward orbit, carrying Hutch, Janet, Maggie, Karl, and Maggie's number one analyst, Phil Marcotti. Also on board were twenty-nine containers filled with artifacts, and two barrels of poly-6 components.

Maggie Tufu turned out to be younger than Hutch had expected. She'd heard so much about the woman's accomplishments, that she was startled to discover Maggie was probably still in her twenties. She was tall, taller in fact than either of the men. Her black hair was full and luxuriant, worn in a twist that was probably designed to make her look older. Her eyes were also black, and her features retained much of the Micronesian cast of her forebears. If she'd been able to loosen up, to smile occasionally, she would have been lovely.

She tended to set herself apart from the others. Hutch did not sense arrogance, but rather simply a preoccupation with work. Maggie found people, and maybe everything except mathematics and philological theory and practice, boring.

Her colleague, Phil Marcotti, was a beefy, easygoing extrovert. About forty, he enjoyed his work, and was among those who would have preferred to stay until they'd recovered what everyone was now referring to as "George's printing press." He confided to Hutch that, if he'd had his way, nothing short of armed force would have moved the Academy team. Curiously, this amiable, happy man was the most militant among Henry's true believers.

Maggie took Hutch's right-hand seat. During the ascent she tied into the auxiliary computer and busied herself with rows of alphanumerics. "In one way, we're very lucky," she told Hutch. "We don't get as many Linear C samples as we'd like to. Of course, you never have enough samples of anything. The language is just too old. But a fair amount of what we *do* get comes with illustrations. We have the beginning of a vocabulary."

"Really," said Hutch, interested. "Can you show me some examples?"

"Sure. This"—a cluster of characters appeared on the screen—"is 'sun.' They were letters, not ideograms. And *that*"—another group—"is 'moon.' " She smiled, not at Hutch, but at the display. "This is 'hoe.' "

"*Hoe*," said Hutch. "How did you arrive at that?"

"The group was used to illustrate an epigram about reaping what you plant. I think."

Karl stared moodily out at the clouds. His eyes were distant, and Hutch wondered whether he was thinking about his future.

Janet fell asleep within minutes after their departure. She was still out when the shuttle nosed into its bay on *Wink*.

Hutch calibrated the B ring spin to point one gee. They unloaded the artifacts, now only a tenth of their planetary weight, and carried them through double doors into Main Cargo. Here, Hutch passed out footwear that would grip the Teflon deck. The storage area was wide and high, spacious enough to play basketball. They crossed to the far bulkhead, and secured the containers beside the two earlier shipments.

Main Cargo had been designed to stow heavy excavation equipment, large quantities of supplies, and whatever the Academy teams deemed worth bringing back. Except for the shuttle bay, it occupied the entire ring. It was compartmented into four sections, each equipped with outside loading doors.

When they'd finished, Hutch conducted a brief tour. She took her passengers to A Deck, pointed out their cabins, showed them the lounge and rec facilities, demonstrated how the food dispensers worked, and joined them for dinner. They drank to their new home. And they seemed to brighten somewhat.

After they'd finished, she took Janet aside. "Are you interested in a little payback?" she asked.

Janet looked at her curiously. "What are we talking about?" Then she smiled. "You mean Truscott?"

"I mean Truscott."

She nodded. "I'm willing to listen."

"There'll be a risk."

"Tell me what you have in mind. I'd love to see her get hers."

"I think we can arrange it."

She led the way back to B ring. Full ship's gravity, which was a modicum over point five, had been restored. The outside loading doors were located in the deck. In each of the four cargo sections, they were of different dimensions. She'd picked the No. 2 hold, where they were biggest, large enough, in fact, to accommodate an object twice the diameter of the shuttle.

Hutch inspected the doors, satisfied herself they were adequate to the task, and explained her idea. Janet listened skeptically at first, and then with mounting enthusiasm. By the time Hutch had finished, she was grinning broadly. "I don't think I'd want you mad at me," she said.

"If we get caught at it, we'll both wind up out on Massachusetts Avenue with tin cups."

"Will they be able to figure out who did it?"

"Maybe. Listen, I owe you. And I wouldn't want to be responsible for your getting into trouble. I'll understand if you want to keep clear."

"But you can't do this alone."

"No. I can't."

"I wouldn't miss it. The only real problem I can see is that we won't be able to brag about it afterward."

Hutch was feeling pretty good. "It's a small price to send Melanie Truscott a message from the downtrodden."

"Can we really do it?"

"Let's find out."

She cut gravity, and they went to the shuttle and retrieved the two barrels of poly-6. They hauled them back to No. 2 hold and put them in the middle of the deck, which is to say, centered over the cargo doors. Next Hutch went back for the connector hose and gun.

Now that she was committed, Janet showed no hesitation, had no second thoughts. Good woman to have at your back, Hutch thought.

"We have to have something to start with," Janet said.

Hutch had the ideal answer. "Sit tight," she said. She went up to A ring, to the rec locker, and got one of the medicine balls.

Janet broke into a wide smile when she saw it. "The very thing," she said. She had connected the hose to each of the barrels and to the gun.

Hutch put the ball down and stepped back. She eyed the dispenser. "Would you like to do the honors?"

"Delighted." Janet pointed the instrument at the medicine ball. "Just what the doctor ordered," she said wickedly, and pulled the trigger.

White foam spurted out, coating the deck and the ball. The ball rolled away. "This might take a while," she said.

"Not once we get started."

The ball lost its roundness quickly, and became an uneven, white chunk of hissing foam.

The object expanded as a natural result of mixing the polymer content in one barrel with a water-activated isocyanate in the other. It was designed, once it had set, to resist extreme temperature changes.

They took turns, and learned to back off occasionally to let the chemical dry.

It got bigger. Even when they weren't drenching it with fresh spray, it grew.

It grew to the size of a small car. And then to the size of a garage. And they kept pouring it on.

It got so big they could not reach the top, and they brought over a container to stand on. The thing had gone lopsided, long and wide rather than high. Bloated at one end. "It looks like a dead whale," said Janet.

Hutch fired again. "Born to the poly gun," she said, laughing.

"The thing's a monster!"

When the stream finally sputtered and faltered, pride illuminated their features. "It's magnificent," said Janet, ceremonially flinging the gun away.

"I wouldn't want to have to deal with it."

"Exactly what I was thinking."

Hutch spoke softly: *"Never monkey with the Pimpernel."* They shook hands. "Okay. Phase two. You stay here. I'm going up to the bridge."

Quraqua floated overhead, hazy in the sunlight. There was no moon.

Melanie Truscott and her space station were on the far side of their orbit. Hutch scanned for Kosmik's two tugs. She found one. The other was probably down among the snowballs, where it would be hard to distinguish. It wouldn't matter: even if it *was* in the neighborhood of the space station, things were going to happen too fast.

Truscott had no means of independent propulsion. No starship was docked.

Hutch fed the station's orbital data into the navigation console, scanned the "torpedo"—how that word tripped across the tongue—computed its mass, and requested an intercept vector. The numbers came back. With a minor correction, the torpedo could be targeted to complete seven orbits and hit the station on its eighth. In twenty-one hours.

She sat back to consider potential consequences. Last chance for a no-go. Once the thing was launched, she would not be able to change her mind without giving away the show. How might things go wrong? Lawsuit? Heart failure on someone's part?

She saw again the wave surging in, black and cold. And the last Tower. And Karl and Janet, trailing bags like refugees.

She opened the ship's intercom. "Ladies and gentlemen, we're going to be making a minor course correction in three minutes. You'll want to strap down. Please acknowledge."

"Karl here. Okay."

She locked in the new course.

"I need a little time." That was Marcotti.

"Phil, we're going in three minutes, ready or not." She checked her power levels.

"This is Maggie. Ready when you are."

She opened a private channel to Janet. "All set?"

"Yes." The word had a slight echo; Janet was inside her Flickinger field. "How fast will it be going when it hits them?"

"Seven thousand, relative to the station. Impact will occur at seventeen minutes past eight, Temple time, tomorrow evening."

"Seven thousand klicks is pretty fast. Maybe even a chunk of foam will do some serious damage."

"It'll bend a few things," she said, "and pop some rivets. But they'll see it coming, and they'll either get off the station or button up. They'll be fine."

"Okay. What next?"

"Course change." She switched channels. "Phil?"

"Almost ready," he said.

"Good. Please strap down."

Moments later he was back. "Okay," he said. "I'm all set."

She activated the intercom. "Movement in one minute." She engaged the "Execute" function, and watched the seconds drain away.

"Where are we going?" asked Maggie.

"Nowhere," said Hutch uncomfortably. "It's just a routine maneuver." She was a poor liar.

Thrusters kicked in, and the *Winckelmann* rose to a higher orbit, and changed its heading by a few degrees. When it was over, Hutch issued the stand-down. Then she switched back to Janet's channel. "Everything all right?"

"So far. It rolled a little, but it's still over the doors."

"Going to zero-gee on your deck."

"Okay. I've begun to depressurize."

The B ring slowed. And stopped.

Hutch watched the monitor. The torpedo rose.

"Good show," she said. She already knew that she'd break their agreement to say nothing. She would tell Richard. This was just too good to keep to herself. He'd be angry, but eventually it would become a joke between them. And years from now it would be the bright shining moment in this period of general despair. If the Academy was being forced out, it would go down with all flags flying.

"It's still over the doors. I'm going to open up now."

"At your leisure."

"Doors are opening."

"Hutch?" A new voice. Karl's.

"Yes, Karl?"

"Can I get access to a twelve-by?"

A wall-length monitor. "Yes. In Three A." That was the auxiliary bridge. "But stay put for a couple of minutes. Okay? We're doing routine maintenance."

"Doors are open," said Janet. She was inaudible to the others.

"Okay," said Karl.

"I'll tell you when." Hutch broke away to Janet: "Clearance?"

"Looks good."

"All right. Here we go."

Because ring rotation simulated gravity, the decks were at right angles to the ship's axis. The cargo doors, therefore, opened off the side of the ship. The torpedo's exit would be to starboard. Inside Main Cargo, it was already on course. All they needed to do was remove the ship.

Hutch aimed the thrusters to take the *Wink* to port, and fired a light burst. And again. "Maneuver complete," she told Janet.

"Doing fine. The torpedo has begun to descend." From her point of view, it was leaving through the deck.

"Still have clearance?"

"Enough. It'll be outside in about thirty seconds."

"Make sure you don't go out with it."

"Hutch," she said, "I believe we've just had a baby."

Priscilla Hutchins, *Journal*

Tonight, for the first time in my career, I have omitted a significant item from a ship's log. It is an offense that, if detected, would result in the loss of my license.

This whole business was probably a bit off the deep end. But I couldn't resist lobbing something back at them. If in the end I am disgraced and run off, it will have been for a good cause.

Wednesday, June 9, 2202

Thursday. 0854 hours.

The descent into the Lower Temple was filled with silt and rock. George Hackett, whose specialty was submarine excavation, had examined scans of the area, and vetoed proposals to dig a parallel shaft. "Safer," he'd admitted, "but too time-consuming."

So they'd braced everything they could, sucked out the loose sand, and cut through the stone. They got down to the side tunnel in good order, but it too had collapsed. Richard Wald, doing his tour as operations officer, was watching when he got a call from Janet on board *Wink*.

"I have something for Henry," she said.

"He's in the Temple. You want me to patch you through?"

"Please. You should listen in."

The mission director was a murky image wielding a particle beam projector. That was another aspect of this effort that scared the hell out of Richard: the experience level of the volunteer help. Sending Karl up to *Wink* with the first group had been a mistake. Karl, Richard had heard, was a master at tunneling.

Henry's homely features appeared. "What is it, Janet?"

"The Field Report is in. Have you by any chance seen it?"

"No. Truth is, I've been a little busy." He sounded annoyed.

"Okay. You're going to want to take a look at the extraplanetary survey from Nok. Section four delta."

The Field Report was issued monthly by the Academy. It was an update on current missions and future projects. Richard had found it and was bringing it up on his screen.

"Janet, please get to the point."

"They've discovered four rock *cubes*. In orbit."

Richard saw it. *My God.* "It's all connected," he blurted out. *This was wonderful.* Inakademeri—Nok—was itself a moon, circling the ringed gas giant Shola. The cubes were in the same orbital plain as Shola's rings and the rest of the bodies orbiting the central world. *Early analysis suggests they once occupied equidistant positions. They are of identical dimensions, each roughly 2.147 kilometers on a side.* And the Noks, like the Quraquat, had never been in space. *What in hell was going on?*

"What do you think, Richard?" Henry asked. The sound of his name startled him.

What *did* he think? Right angles again. That's what he thought.

Later, Maggie told him about the horgon. "Maybe," he said, "we can get by without reading the inscription."

"In what way?" Maggie was speaking from one of the terminals on *Wink's* bridge.

"All those squares and rectangles. And two round towers."

"With slanted roofs."

"Yes. My point, exactly. Oz *has* to be a direction finder."

"We've thought of that too."

"How sure are you that *horgon* is actually in the inscription?"

"Reasonably sure, Richard. I wish I could give you more. But I just have no way to check it."

"The round towers are unique. Their roofs are not flat, like every other roof in Oz. They incline, directly away from the center of the city. They're aimed at the stars. What could their purpose be other than to serve as markers, to designate lines of sight? Draw a line across each of those rooftops, from the lowest point to the highest—which is to say, from the precise mathematical center of Oz—and extend them into space. At the angle of the roof's inclination."

"You're thinking that there might have been a star associated with the horgon—"

"Like the Dog Star."

"Yes. But if it's true, *I* don't know about it. And I don't know who would."

"Dave Emory might."

"Maybe." She still looked puzzled. "If it's that simple, why build all the rest of it? Why not just make the towers?"

"I suppose," said Richard, "you could argue they wanted to be sure the towers weren't overlooked."

"But you think there's more—"

"Oh, yes. There's *more*." No doubt about that. Unfortunately.

Thursday, June 10, 2202

Dear Dick,
    . . . The discovery of the cube moons has had an unsettling effect. Yesterday, we were of two minds about recovering George's printing press. Today, with the link between Quraqua and Nok established beyond doubt, everybody wants to take whatever risk is necessary to get the damned thing. That kind of unanimity makes me uneasy. Even though I agree.

The refusal of the bureaucrats at Kosmik to budge on the matter of time is nothing less than criminal. I've been in touch with the commissioner, but he tells me nothing can be done. He points out, quite rightly, that no one, including me, has been able to get Caseway to listen to reason.

History will damn us all. . . .

Richard

—Richard Wald to his cousin Dick
Received in Portland, Oregon June 30

12.

Hutch took Andi, Tri, and Art and another load of artifacts to the ship; and Carson carried Linda Thomas and Tommy Loughery. It was Carson's last delivery. On his return to the Temple, Henry preempted him for the tunneling effort. Eddie dissolved in apoplexy, but nothing mattered anymore except the printing press.

There was now a lot of help on *Wink*. Hutch could unload quickly, but the time saved was negated when she had to replace a fused pumpboard. A good engineer might have handled the problem in twenty minutes, but for Hutch it was a struggle. In-transit maintenance and repair was a skill pilots seldom needed, and it had never been her strength.

She started back down in *Alpha* as soon as she finished. But she'd lost her window by then, and faced a long flight. By the time she glided in over the Temple site, the torpedo was homing in for the last stage of its run against Kosmik Station.

The difficulty and danger of loading without the floatpier had by now forced them to find a harbor. Eddie had located a rock shelf, sheltered from the tide, but at a considerable distance from Seapoint. The water was deep enough for the sub, and the currents were relatively tranquil.

Hutch was watching a telescopic view of the space station relayed from *Wink*, and she was monitoring their communications. Traffic patterns showed nothing unusual. No sudden bursts to the tugs, no change in routine, no upgraded precedence. They had not seen it.

Below, Eddie and the sub were waiting. Eddie had no help because everyone else was either on the tunnel operation or on *Wink*. Several dozen containers were stacked on the shelf, and Hutch suspected Eddie had done it all. She blinked her lights at him. Poor bastard. In the crunch, they had left him alone.

How could Truscott's people not yet have picked up the torpedo? Answer: they're not looking. She detected no short-range sensor activity. They were ignoring the regulations. Damn. If the thing came in unnoticed, the whole point would be lost.

Janet, speaking from *Wink*, asked if everything was okay.

"Yes. Descending on Eddie's harbor." They carefully avoided discussing, on an open circuit, what was really on their minds. They'd debated making up a code, but discarded the idea as too dangerous.

Their eyes met, and Janet's excitement threatened to bubble to the surface. "Everything quiet here," she said. Translation: she saw no activity either.

Three minutes later, *Alpha* set down precisely as Janet, on their agreed-upon schedule, opened a channel to the orbiter, and patched Hutch through.

Harvey Sill's beefy frown formed on the screen. "What is it, *Winckelmann*?"

"This is Hutchins. Sorry to bother you, but you might have a problem."

He angled his head so he could look at her through half-open lids. "What sort of problem?"

"Are you scanning short range?"

"Of course we are." He looked up, away from her. Did something to his console. Spoke to someone.

"One of your snowballs may have got loose. Check to the northeast, out at about twenty-five hundred kilometers."

"Hang on, *Winckelmann*." He sighed. There was a fair amount of pleasure in listening to his contempt change, through not so subtle variations, to concern, and then to dismay.

"I'm surprised you don't maintain a search," she said innocently. "It's a violation."

"Son of a bitch." His voice went up an octave. "Where the hell'd that come from?"

She shrugged. But he wasn't watching her any longer. He reached forward, past the screen. "Goddammit, Louise." He punched keys, and jabbed an index finger at someone. "*There*," he said. "Over *there*." He glanced at Hutch. "Thanks, lady—" The screen blanked.

"Let me know," said Hutch, in the silence of her cockpit, "if I can help."

Truscott made it to the operations center from her quarters in less than a minute. The alarms were still sounding, and voices filled the circuits. "No mistake?" She stared at the object, repeated across the bank of twelve situation screens.

Harvey Sill wiped his lips with the back of his fat hand. "No, it's closing straight and true. A goddam bomb."

"Where did it come from?"

Helplessly, Sill turned up his hands. "Somebody screwed up."

"How much time do we have?"

"Seventeen minutes."

"Where's it going to hit?"

"It's coming in from above. Eight-degree angle. It looks as if it'll go right into Engineering." That was the hub. "There's a chance it might hit the rim. But it won't make much difference. That thing will go through us like a hot knife."

"Which part of the rim is exposed?"

"Blue."

Someone shut the alarms off. "Get everyone out of there. Harvey, prepare to evacuate. Jeff, get off an SOS to the *Winckelmann*. Ask them to come running." She opened a channel to Engineering. "Will?"

Pause. "I'm here, Melanie. What's going on?"

"Collision coming. Big one. Button up and get out of there."

"*Collision?* With what?"

"Runaway snowball. Don't leave anybody behind."

She heard him swear. "On our way. It'll take a while to shut down."

"Be here in five minutes. You need help?"

"Negative." More profanity. "Listen, how big is this thing? We could lose life support and power all over the station."

"No kidding," growled Sill.

Three crewmen moved smartly into the operations center, took seats at the auxiliary boards, and plugged in. The CRT group: Command Response Team. They would coordinate communications and evacuation efforts throughout the emergency.

Jeff Christopher, the watch officer, looked up from his

screen. "I make it about thirteen hundred tons."

"We're lucky," said Sill. "A small one."

"Coming at seven-kay klicks." He tapped his earphone, listened, and nodded. "Melanie," he said, "*Winckelmann* says they don't have a pilot aboard. Nobody knows how to run the damned thing."

Truscott stared out into the dark.

Sill exhaled and sank back in his chair. "We're not going to be able to get everyone off."

"I know. What have we got nearby?"

"Nothing close enough to help."

"Okay." She opened the common channel. "This is Truscott," she said evenly. "We have a snowball bearing down on us. Collision in thirteen minutes. Abandon the station."

"We've got two APVs and a shuttle," said Sill. "We can get three passengers, plus the pilot, into each APV. That's one more than they're designed for, but we can do it. We can put twelve more in the shuttle."

"Make it fourteen."

"Goddammit, Melanie, it won't accommodate fourteen."

"Find little people. *Do* it. That leaves how many?"

"Four," said Sill. "You and me. And two others."

She thought of ordering him off, but paid him the compliment of saying nothing.

Voices rippled through the heavy air:

"I read A deck secured."

"Terri, we haven't heard from Dave. Check his quarters."

"No, Harold. Don't come up here. You're scheduled on the boat. With Julie and Klaus—Yes, I'm serious. Now move."

"Well, he's got to be somewhere."

Nine minutes. "Ask for two volunteers. Jeff, close out and go. We don't need you anymore." Before Christopher could comply, she added, "But first get me some cushions."

"How many?"

"As many as you can. Make it quick."

Sill was struggling with his assignment. "Why not ask your staff to stay on? The senior people?"

She looked at him, and felt a wave of affection. "They're as scared as everybody else," she said. "I won't order anyone to stay. Harvey, we may die here. I want to have good company." She was watching her technicians moving reluctantly toward the exits. *They knew there wasn't room for everyone, and their eyes glided over her. She read embarrassment. And fear.* A couple of them approached, Max Sizemore, who touched her shoulder in an uncharacteristically personal gesture; and Tira Corday, who mouthed the word "thanks" and was gone.

Sill spoke to Ian Helm with the Antarctic group. He was trying to arrange a quick rescue for the people in the APVs, who would have only an eight-hour air supply. Danielle Lima, the station's logistics manager, was bent over her commlink giving instructions to someone, but her dark eyes never moved from Truscott. Her features were immobile. She was a lean young brunette, bright, ambitious, a good worker, a woman at the beginning of her life. All the color had drained out of that lovely face. She signed off, but her eyes continued to cling to the director. "I'll stay," she said, and turned quickly away.

Truscott stared at her back. "Thanks," she said. But Danielle appeared not to hear.

Blue section was 70 degrees around the arc from Operations, opposite the direction of rotation. Which meant they were probably as safe here as they could hope to be. They'd be well out of the way of the thing both coming and going. What the hell—maybe they had a chance at that.

Danielle spoke into her commlink: "Okay, Hans. Get over here as quickly as you can." She smiled up at Truscott. "Stallworth will stay."

Truscott was trying to think, do what she could to give them a chance. "Get back to him. Tell him to stop by Supply on his way and pick up four Flickingers."

She surveyed her operating team: Marion Edwards, who had never worked for anyone else in Kosmik; Chuck White, a young climber who hoped to be an executive one day (and probably would); and Penny Kinowa, innocent, quiet, bookish. Penny read too much, and desperately needed to become more aggressive. But she was one hell of a systems coordinator. Edwards was removing the base crystal from the mainframe. "I'll see that this gets off the ship safely," he said uncomfortably. Unstated, of course, was his intention to carry it off personally. However this turned out, things would never be the same among this crew.

The crystal contained their records and logs. Wouldn't do to lose that, even if they were all killed. That would be

Norman Caseway's first response to the disaster: did they save the data? Reassured on that point, he would want to know who was responsible for the catastrophe. It wasn't enough that she would be dead; they would also destroy her reputation.

"Okay," said Harvey. "CR team out. You three are on board the remaining APV. *Go.*"

Penny and Danielle traded glances. There was a world of meaning in that final exchange. The two were friends. That also might end, if they survived.

Sill was directing the final shutdown of the station. Truscott watched him. He would make a good manager, but he had a little too much integrity to survive in a top job. After a promising start, he'd made enemies and had wound up here. He'd go no higher, no matter how things turned out.

Edwards closed off his position. "All nonessential systems shut down," he said. "Hatches are closed, and the station is as secure as we can make it."

Chuck White was trying to look as if he were considering staying. "If you need me—"

Truscott wondered how he would respond if she accepted the offer. "Get moving. They're waiting for you. And thanks."

"Six minutes," said Sill.

The snowball, gouged, lopsided, ominous, grew in the screens.

Christopher appeared with two crewmen. They had a pile of cushions and pillows, which they dumped on the deck.

"That's good," said Truscott. "Thanks." She waved them out. They were now alone.

The shadows and the surface features didn't seem to change. "It isn't *rotating*," said Sill.

She nodded. "We'll think about it later, Harvey."

"*Everything* rotates." Sill stared. Maybe it was simply very slow.

Hans Stallworth came in, arms full of harnesses. He was tall, intense, formal. His specialty was electronics, and he always seemed uncomfortable in Truscott's presence. She thought of him as being superficial, and had been surprised when he offered to stay. "Hello," he said, with as much elan as he could muster.

Sill shook his hand. "Good to have you here, Hans."

He set the harnesses down, and no one needed to be told to put one on. Truscott removed her belt. "Find something you can use to tie yourself down. We don't want anyone flying around in here."

"Pity we don't have a serious set of deflectors on this thing," said Danielle.

Sill laughed. "It would be like drawing the blinds. Look at that son of a bitch."

It filled the screens.

"Harvey, let's depressurize the station. All of it."

Sill nodded.

"I wonder," said Stallworth, "whether we wouldn't be better off outside."

"No." Truscott secured her harness and activated the field. "Let's keep as much protection as we can get."

Danielle and Stallworth, who had had little experience with the Flickingers, helped each other. Sill swung his harness lazily over his head and dropped it across his shoulders. "Other shuttle's on the way," he said.

"ETA?"

"About three hours. They should be in plenty of time to pick up survivors." He inspected their harnesses, announced his approval. "Activate the homers," he said, and demonstrated how. "If you're thrown clear, and you're unconscious, they'll still get to you." His fingers moved across the command console. "Commencing depressurization."

Stallworth was looking out through a viewport, shading his eyes. "I see it," he said.

Truscott followed his gaze but could see nothing. "Confirming original projection," said Sill, not without a trace of pride. "It'll hit Blue on the way in, and then impact directly with the hub."

Danielle had posted herself at the comm console. "Both APVs are away. Shuttle's about to launch."

"They get everybody?"

"They've got twenty-two. We make twenty-six." All accounted for.

"They may not get far enough away," said Danielle. "We may be safer in here."

"Two minutes," said Sill.

"Shuttle?"

Danielle checked the board. "Negative."

"What's holding them up?"

The officer spoke into a side channel. "They thought somebody else was coming. Ginger says they have room for one more."

"Doesn't matter now," Truscott said. "Tell her to clear out." She looked toward Sill. "Seal it up. Close off everything. Power down. Except the lights. Let's keep the lights on."

Electronics died throughout the wheel. Computers went to maintenance modes, monitors blanked, food processors gurgled to a halt, water heaters died.

"Shuttle away," said Danielle.

A star had appeared. Truscott watched it brighten and take shape. It developed ridges and chinks. No craters. Irregular, almost rectangular surface. Club-shaped, she thought.

Not spinning.

"Okay," she said. "Everybody down. The main shock will come through the deck. Lie flat. Use the pillows to protect all vulnerable parts. Tie yourself to something solid."

They watched it come.

Forty seconds.

It sailed through the sky, bright and lovely in the sunlight. It moved across the viewport, corresponding to the rotation of the outer rim, and disappeared finally to the left.

Truscott reached deep inside for the old arrogance, her lifelong conviction that things always turn out well if you stay cool and do the things that need to be done. She hoped she looked arrogant. That was what they needed now. That and divine intervention. "Face away from the impact," she said, pointing where she meant.

"They need to build these bastards with seat belts." It was Stallworth. He sounded calm.

And in that moment, it hit.

The station shook.

Someone screamed. They were thrown against pillows and deck.

But there was no hammer blow. Klaxons did not scream, and the steel bulkheads did not rip. A few alarms sounded: minor damage. And that was all.

"What happened?" asked Danielle, still holding tight to her chair.

Sill said: "Damned if I know."

"Everybody stay down." Truscott was taking no chances.

And, in her earphones, there was a voice from one of the ships: "Where *is* the goddam thing?"

Truscott, dazed, was also puzzled by the sound of the strike.

Bonk.

13.

_____

Seapoint. Thursday; 2005 hours.

"The space station is having a problem." This was how Janet alerted the people on *Wink* and at the Temple site to the approach of the torpedo. She broadcast a running description of events and relayed the frantic plain-language calls among the orbiter, the ground stations, and the tugs. To Henry and Sandy Gonzalez, who were in the Seapoint operations center, she also transmitted telescopic views of the object closing on the orbiter. The station, its twin outer wheels rotating placidly, looked flimsy. It was a tense moment. One would have had to pay close attention to detect the overlay of satisfaction in Janet's voice.

All work stopped. They watched with morbid fascination.

"No estimate on mass. But it is closing very fast."

"Serves the bastards right," said Henry.

And Carson: "Not very competent, are they? Plunked by one of their own rocks."

Sandy stood at Henry's side. "Maybe we've got our extension after all," she said.

"Is everybody off?"

"Don't know."

"Can't be. They're still talking on the station."

Despite their animosity for the terraformers, nobody wanted to see them dead.

"Is it actually going to *hit*?" Henry asked Janet.

"Yes," she said. "No question."

Henry's next thought was that the *Wink* should be riding to the rescue. "Where's Hutch?"

"With *you*. She's on the surface."

He noted, and then dismissed, an impression that her reaction was wrong. Not pleased. Not fearful. But *righteous*.

165

"Okay. Contact somebody over there. Explain our situation, and tell them we stand by to assist any way we can. I'll turn Hutch around and send her back up if it'll help."

Janet hesitated. "Okay. But I doubt they'll want any help from us."

"Offer, anyway."

She took a long breath. "I'll get right on it."

Moments later, he had audio contact with Hutch. "What can I do?" she asked innocently.

"Stand by. We might have a rescue mission for you." And, to the tunnelers: "It's closing fast. Just seconds now."

Henry watched it race across those last few kilometers, a shining white bullet. It blasted into the space station, and both vanished in an eruption of white spray. "Impact," he said.

Sandy let out her breath.

The picture slowly cleared, while excited voices asked for details. Incredibly, the orbiter was still intact. It had developed a wobble, but it was still turning at the same unhurried pace.

Ten minutes later, Janet reported back. "They said thanks. But they're doing fine."

Below the sea floor, George and Carson worked with a particle beam to extend their tunnel. They were beneath the outer wall of the military chapel, attempting to chart the best route to the printing press. George was nothing if not conservative, and no amount of urging by Henry or anyone else could persuade him to embrace unnecessary risks. Consequently, they installed braces and proceeded with all possible caution. "I'd like to get back down there as much as anybody," he told Henry. "But common sense is the first priority."

George knew the general direction of the printing press. He employed the particle beam with increasing impatience, and he was tired. Shortly they would go back, George to rest, and Carson to relieve Henry at the monitor. Sandy and Richard would take over the digging, and Henry would man the pumps. In fact, he could already see the flash of lights in the tunnel.

And something else. A reflection, on the silt. Carson picked it up. It was a piece of smooth rock, a tablet, about eight centimeters across, flat on both sides. "It's got writing on it," he said. He brushed it, examined it in the lamplight. "Something on the back. An image of some kind. A spear, maybe."

He held it up for the camera, and they transmitted pictures back to Seapoint.

"Hell." Henry got excited. "Look at it. It's Linear C."

"Bingo," said George. "Jackpot." He turned it over and squinted. "What is it?"

The reverse pictured what appeared to be a long, tapered rod, spade-shaped at one end, heavy and thick at the other. "It's a sex organ," said Sandy, with an oblique laugh. "Fully distended and ready for battle."

Maggie's voice came from the ship: "Funny how some things seem to be universals."

"Damndest chapel decorations I've ever seen," said Carson. Maybe there was a brothel in the area. "Did the Quraquat have brothels?"

"Yes," said Sandy. "And the Noks as well. Seems to be a fixture of the advanced male, regardless of species."

The important consideration was that they had another sample of Linear C. And there might be more. While Richard and Sandy took over the tunneling, Carson and George began a search. George had little enthusiasm for the hunt, but Carson seemed tireless. Within an hour, they had recovered a small trove of tablets, and other, mostly undefinable, objects.

Five of the tablets, including the original, were sexually explicit. Others contained arboreal and sea images, and one depicted a sailing vessel. Several lines of text were engraved on each. They were too worn to make out, but restoration might be possible. One by one, George displayed them to the camera.

He was about halfway through when Maggie's voice came on-line. "These are superb, Henry."

"Yes," said Henry. "They are quite good."

"Can we go back to that last one?" she asked. The tablet depicted a disembodied, fully erect male member protruding through a wreath. There was also a line of symbols curved around the perimeter. "We know some of these," she said. "Marvelous." Nobody made a joke of it.

George showed them another one. "Good," breathed Maggie.

And another.

"Let's see that again," Maggie said. Another sexual theme, straightforward this time: a simple coupling. "We didn't get a very good picture of the text. Both sides, George. Give us more light."

There was a single term atop the amorous pair.

"What *are* these things?" asked Carson.

"Probably decorations," said Maggie. "Doesn't matter, for now." Then she started. "Henry, can you see that? The title term?"

The word at the top of the tablet was from the inscription at Oz.

"Damn!" Henry was ecstatic. "Richard, are you there?"

"I'm a little tied up at the moment." He was on the beam projector.

"George, show that one to Dr. Wald."

"No question about it." Maggie bubbled with excitement. "It's not identical, though. The Oz inscription has an additional character, and the letters are differently formed. But that's purely stylistic. I'll be more certain when we can get it cleaned up. Six of the symbols match perfectly. If we don't have the same word, we should have the same root."

"You're right," said Richard. "It's *lovely*."

"I think," said Sandy, "this building is distinct from the chapel. Frank's probably right about the brothel. Sex may have been part of the rituals."

"Okay." Richard was speaking to Maggie, and examining the tablet. "What does the word mean?"

"Sex," said Maggie. "Or ecstasy."

"Where does that leave us?" asked Henry. "*This way to a hot time?* Is that what the Oz inscription says?"

Richard shook his head. "It need not have a sexual connotation," he said.

"I agree," said Sandy. "The word could mean love. Or fulfillment. Or release."

"Or," suggested George, "ships that pass in the night."

Kosmik Station. Friday; 0030 hours.

Truscott looked up at the sound. "Come."

Sill entered. His eyes were fierce, his lips drawn into a scowl.

She pushed back from her desk, and swung round to face him. "What have you got?"

"It wasn't a snowball."

"We already know that."

"We've retrieved some of it. It was a polymer."

She nodded. "It was *manufactured*," she said.

"I don't see what other conclusion we can draw. And since there's no one here except the Academy people—"

Truscott laughed. Not her usual measured chuckle. Her heart was in this one. And, when he only looked on in surprise, she reproached him. "Come on, Sill," she said, "where's your sense of humor?"

He reddened. "I don't see what's funny, Melanie. They've created a lot of trouble. People could have been killed."

"Yes." Her eyes fell away from him. "They've paid us in our own coin, haven't they?"

Temple of the Winds. Friday; 0200 hours.

The tunnel resisted their best efforts. The mud was tougher to deal with than the rock. However much they sucked out, it kept coming back in. Carson, on Richard's private channel, confessed that it was useless.

Detonation was eight hours away.

Too close.

The base was quiet. Eddie was gone now, banished to *Wink*, ostensibly because his services were no longer needed, but really because he kept asking Henry to give it up, and to reassign Carson to help move artifacts. Hutch was off again and would rendezvous with the starship in another hour. When she returned, they were all to be waiting at the inlet, bags packed, ready to go. No matter what.

Richard sat in the operations center. The monitor was a montage of blurred light, slow-moving shadows, tunnel walls. Grunts and epithets and profanity rolled out of the commlink.

The room was damp and chilly. Technically, he was supposed to stay awake, but conditions had changed: the watch officer was no longer coordinating a wide range of operations. And you had to sleep sometime.

On impulse, he called *Wink's* bridge, where he woke Tommy Loughery. "Is Maggie available?" he asked.

"She's right here."

He'd expected it. They'd sent up the new tablets—there were thirteen of them—on board *Alpha*. And she would be waiting for their arrival.

"Good morning, Richard," she said. "When are we going to break through down there?"

"You mean to the press?"

"What else? It's getting late."

"It's what I wanted to talk to you about. We may not make it."

"That's not what Henry thinks."

"Henry is optimistic. He wants this one, Maggie."

"So do I."

"You already have a substantial number of samples. With more coming. You've seen the new set. What happens if we have to leave with nothing else? Will it be enough?"

"Maybe." She looked drained. "The analysis will take time. I just don't know." Her dark eyes reflected worry. "It would be a lot easier with the printing press."

"If that's in fact what it is."

"That's what it is."

Richard stared at her. "Can you estimate the odds?" And, when she looked puzzled, he explained. "Of being able to decipher the inscription? With no more samples."

"We *are* pushy tonight, aren't we?"

"I'm sorry. This may become, in the morning, life and death."

Shadows worked in the corners of her eyes and in the hollows of her temples. "Richard, *get* the whatever-it-is. Okay? If you really want to help, *get it out of there* and bring it to me."

0600 hours.

"It's imminent now. We're almost there."

Richard was exasperated. "Call it off, Henry. Let's clear out."

"She won't be back for two hours. What's the point of standing around out on that rock? We've still got time. Let's use it. Have faith."

0711 hours.

Hutch, gliding through the morning light, was not happy. The commlink echoed with the low-powered hum of particle beams, the burble and banging of vacuum pumps. Voices leaked through the clatter:

This is where it was supposed to be.

But it isn't. It's not here.

Neither is the wall. The whole goddam chamber dropped. Or rose.

Why didn't you take a picture?

We did. It was here two days ago.

We thought we could see it. It was the plank. We were looking at the damned plank!

Maybe we just missed it. Is that possible?

No.

And the words that stung her, enraged her, spoken by Henry: *Get the scanner over here. Take another look. Let's find out where it is.*

She activated Richard's private channel. "You're out of time."

"I know. Just give us a few minutes. Till we find out where the goddamned thing went."

"Richard, the creek is about to rise."

"Hutch, you have to understand. This isn't my call. These people *know* the risk. This is just too important to turn around and walk out on. Come on, you can tough it out."

"You're beginning to sound as crazy as they do," she snapped. And she broke the link without letting him reply. She switched to Carson, who was waiting in his shuttle at the inlet. "Frank, you got any control over this?"

"Not much."

"Henry's going to get them all killed."

"No. He won't do that. Whatever else happens, he'll be out in time. You can trust him."

Okay, I recognize this.

You sure, George?

Yeah. Yeah, no question about it.

All right, let's go. Where the hell's the goddam projector?

"Hutch," said Carson. "Another hour here may be worth years of research at home. Be patient."

"Another *hour*?"

"That's my guess. But it still gets us out of here with time to spare."

"Hutch." George's voice. "Do you have a winch on board?"

"Yes. I can activate a winch."

"Okay. Plan is that after we free the printing press, we'll lift it into the Upper Temple. We've got everything in place to do that. You drop the line. As soon as the press is clear of the shaft, we'll connect it, and you can haul it in. The rest of us should be on board a few minutes after that."

She shook her head. "This is crazy, George. You haven't even *found* the press yet."

"We're working on it."

Richard came back. "It's okay," he said soothingly. "We'll make it. And we'll have the printing press with us."

She watched the shoreline unroll below. It was a brilliant, sun-washed day, white and cold, filled with icebergs and needle peaks and rocky islands. Long thick waves slid across snow-covered beaches. Beach monkeys walked and played at the edge of the surf.

The inlet came into view, and she started down. The Temple shuttle, resplendently blue and gold in the sunlight, waited on the shelf.

Hutch landed clumsily. As if her haste would change anything. Carson stood on the rock. He was too courteous, or too distracted, to comment on her technique.

0837 hours.

The particle beam cast an eerie blue-white glow through the chamber. Water bubbled and hissed. George was firing blind. He was cutting through that most dangerous of obstacles, loose rock and sand.

The digging strategy was to pick an area that looked stable, if you could find one, divide it into individual targets, and attack each separately. You sliced a hole, and stopped. If nothing happened, you enlarged the hole. Then you braced everything and moved on. "The problem," he told Henry, "is that the tunnel will have to be widened further to get the printing press out."

George was pleased with himself. In the field, engineers tend to exist in a somewhat lower social stratum than pure archeologists. Not that anyone mistreated him. The Temple team had always been a close-knit crew. But he was taken less seriously as a professional. His was a support role, and consequently he was something of a hanger-on. When celebrations broke out, they never drank to George.

But this time, *he* had made the discovery. *George's Printing Press.* And *he* was leading the assault on the Lower Temple. It was a good feeling. A good way to wrap up his efforts here. It was a little scary, maybe. But he felt immortal, as young men invariably do, and he did not believe that Kosmik would actually pull the trigger if there were still people down here.

Moreover, the timing was perfect. He was entranced by Hutch, infected with her brilliant eyes and her vaguely distant smile. His own tides ran strong when she was nearby, and *she* was now watching him in action. How could he possibly fail to stay the course? And during those dark, claustrophobic moments when an appreciation of the risk seeped through, he drove it away by imagining the hero's reward that waited.

Maggie's voice cut in. "We have a preliminary reading from the 'sex' tablet." She was referring to the character group that appeared atop the wedge, and in the Oz inscription. "We don't think it's a sexual term."

"What is it?" asked Richard.

"We've located parts of the same cluster of symbols elsewhere. We've got the root, which suggests *duration*, maybe infinite duration."

"You're right," said Sandy. "That does it for sex."

"There's a positive connotation. It's linked with sunlight, for example. And ships in peaceful circumstances. I would be inclined to translate it along the lines of good fortune rather than pleasure."

"You sure?" That sounded like Tri.

"Of course I'm not *sure*," she snapped. "But there's a fair degree of probability."

"So," said Richard, "we have *good fortune* and a mythical beast. What's the connection?"

Ahead, George turned off the projector, and waited for the water to clear. "I think we're through," he said. "We have a tunnel."

Henry and Sandy moved forward to insert the braces. George poked at the roof. Gravel and silt floated down. "No guarantees," he said.

Henry shrugged and plunged ahead. "George," he called back, "do what you can to widen it."

"Not while you're in there."

"Do it," said Henry. "My authority."

Your authority's not worth much if you're dead. Suppose George started cutting and the roof fell in? He shouldn't even allow Henry to proceed before he conducted a safety inspection. But things were happening too fast.

Obediently, he activated the particle beam, and chipped away at the sides of the tunnel.

The chamber had partially collapsed. Henry crawled between broken slabs and decayed timbers. His lamp blurred. "Up ahead somewhere," he told his throat mike. The printing press should have been close enough to show on the sensors. But he was getting no reading.

He came to a wall.

He floated to a stop and laid his head against it. That's it, he thought. He hated this place the way it was now: squeeze past rock, dig through mud, grope in the dark.

Richard moved up behind him, held his lamp up. "Over there," he said. "It's open to your right. Look."

He pointed and Henry saw that it was so. But he knew it was getting desperately late and that he had a responsibility to get his people out. While he hesitated, Richard pushed past. His lamp moved in the dark.

"I think I can *see* it," he said softly.

Sandy's hand gripped his shoulder. "We ought to wait for George," she said.

"Attaboy, Richard," said Maggie. She was ecstatic.

Henry followed the light, turned a corner, and swam down into the small room that he remembered from his previous visit. "We've got it," Richard was saying. He knelt two meters away, blurred in the smoky light.

The frame was half-buried. They scrounged around, digging with their fingers, trying to work it free. They found a rectangular chase. A gearbox lay beneath loose rock. "It's the press bed," said Maggie.

A second chase was wedged under a cut slab.

Sandy's scanner revealed something in the floor. She dug it up. At one time, it had been a compartmented drawer or case.

Henry poked at the chases. "There *is* type set in these things," he said.

"Good!" Maggie egged them on. "It's enough. Let's go. Get it out of there."

The frame was stuck tight. "We need the pulser," said Henry.

Richard touched his arm. "I don't think we want a beam anywhere near it."

It was large, almost two meters long, maybe half as wide. Sandy and Richard tried to pry it loose.

It did not give.

"This is not going to work," Sandy said. "Even if we get it out, it's too big to take back up the tunnel." She looked at it in the lamplight. "How about just taking the chases?"

"Why the chases?"

Maggie's voice crackled. "Because that's where the type is set."

Hutch broke in. "It's about to get wet up here. If you're planning on leaving, this would be a good time."

Henry measured the chases with his hands. "We'll still need to widen the exit," he said.

"How about just taking a good set of holos?" George suggested.

"No help," said Maggie. "We need the chases. And we need the type. We're going to have to do a major restoration if we're ever going to read those."

Henry was playing his light around the room. "Should be some type trays around somewhere."

"Forget it." Richard tugged at the chases. "Sandy's right. Let's make do with what we've got."

"If there's more type down there," said Maggie, "it would be nice to have it. The type in the chases will be pretty far gone."

"Goddammit, Maggie," Hutch exploded. "You want the type, go down and get it yourself."

The common channel went silent.

"Okay, let's do it," said Henry. "Cut it. We've no time to be particular." The particle beam ignited.

George cut with a will. He broke the press apart and dragged the chases free.

"Sandy," said Henry, "get to the top of the shaft and be ready to haul when we're clear of the tunnel. Richard, why don't you go up and give Hutch a hand? No point in your hanging around."

"You'll need help with these things," he said. "I'll wait."

Henry nodded. "Okay." He checked the time. "We can manage it."

"Hurry up," said Maggie. Henry remembered an incident years before when a football had rolled onto an ice-covered lake and the older boys had sent him out to recover it. *Hurry up and throw it in*, they'd cried, *before you fall through.*

0935 hours.
The tide sucked at the Tower. There were a couple of icebergs on the horizon. The coastal peaks glittered in the sunlight.

Hutch, angry, close to tears, swung the winch out, hooked a ten-pound ring weight to the cable, and punched the button. The ring fell into the sea, followed by fifteen meters of line. The shuttles lay side by side in the water. Carson stood on *Alpha's* wing, rocking gently with the motion of the waves. "This is crazy," he said. "I can't believe this is happening."

It was a gorgeous day, clear and gold. The hour before the end of the world.

Four of Quraqua's flying creatures, animals that resembled manta rays, flowed in formation through the sky, headed north.

"Maybe," he said, "we should talk to Kosmik."

Hutch stared at the cable.

Inside the military chapel, George, Richard, and Henry had completed their work and started down the tunnel at last.

Kosmik Station. 0945 hours.
Truscott stood behind Harvey Sill with her arms folded. Her face was dark with anger. "Any progress yet?" she demanded.

"Negative." Harvey pressed his earphones tight. "They're still on the surface."

"Can you tell what's happening?"

"They're in the tunnels. That pilot, what's-her-name, is pretty upset. She's got something going for her, that one. But I don't know what it's about. It's even possible this stuff is all prerecorded to drive us nuts."

"You've gotten paranoid, Harvey. Have you asked them what their situation is?"

Sill shook his head. "No."

"Why not?"

"Because I thought it would encourage them if they thought we were worried."

Truscott was beginning to feel old. "Harvey, get them on the line."

"Might not have to. Incoming from the *Wink* shuttle." He put it on visual. "Go ahead, *Alpha*."

The woman pilot looked down at him. "We've got an emergency, Kosmik. Please let me speak with Dr. Truscott."

The director stepped forward. "I'm here. What's the problem?"

"We still have people in the tunnels. They aren't going to make it out before the deadline."

"Why not?" Truscott bit off the words, like pieces of ice.

"They were trying to finish up. Sorry. I don't have control over this. Can you delay the firing?"

Truscott let her hang a moment. "How long?"

"An hour," Hutch said. She sounded desperate. "One hour."

"You have any idea how much trouble this makes for us? What it costs?"

"Please," said Hutch. Her eyes were wet and red. "If you go ahead, you'll kill them."

She let the pilot see her contempt. "One hour," she said, finally. "And that's it."

Hutch nodded, and looked relieved. "Thanks."

When the link had been broken, Sill said evenly, "That's a mistake."

"We'll argue about it later. Get the word out. Tell everyone to stand down. One hour."

Kosmik Ground Control South, Aloft. Friday; 0954 hours.
The first white lamp lit. The nuclear weapon at Delta Point had just armed.

Ian Helm sat in the right-hand seat of his shuttle. No clouds obscured his view. The south polar ice sheet spread out below him, from the ridges along the Koranda Border, which masked the line of the northernmost volcanoes, to Dillman Harbor, where they'd set up the first base camp two years ago. He remembered standing in that great silence, cold even through the Flickinger field because his heating unit had malfunctioned, warmed rather by the exhilaration of the moment, by the knowledge that he would one day annihilate this ice continent, melt its mountains and its foothills, fill its valleys and rills with steam and rain. In a single glorious sequence, he would convert this wasteland into the stuff of regeneration. No one would ever really give him credit, of course. Caseway and Truscott would take all of that. And they deserved it; he didn't begrudge them their due. He was satisfied that the design was his. And the finger on the detonator.

"Ian." A green light flashed on the instrument panel. "Sill's on the circuit. Wants to talk."

The blue and white glare from icecap and ocean hurt his eyes. Helm looked at his pilot. "Jane," he said, "do we have a disconnect?"

She frowned. "Just pull the plug."

He yanked it out. "Let everybody know that we're worried about the possibility of bogus instructions. Set up a code word. No one is to accept a transmission without it."

"What code word?"

He thought briefly. "Fidelity." Jane looked troubled. "I'll put it in writing."

"Truscott won't be happy."

"I'm saving her from herself," he said.

Two more lamps blinked on. One at Little Kiska close to the pole, and the other at Slash Basil inside a volcano.

"Eventually, she'll thank me."

LIBRARY ENTRIES

The velocity of a tsunami equals the square root of gravitational acceleration times the depth of the water. Depths in the ocean surrounding the southern icecap on Quraqua are relatively modest; the velocity of the wave could be expected to diminish in the narrow confines of the Yakata. Calculation shows that a major tsunami, traveling at the unlikely average speed of 850 kilometers per hour, could not reach the Temple within four hours. At 1000 hours, Jacobi was correct in believing he still had a substantial safety margin from waves originating at the ice pack.

However, in their concern about tsunamis, the Academy team overlooked a more immediate danger: shock waves triggered by the collapse of the ice pack would travel at 7.1 kilometers per second, arriving at the Temple area in about six minutes.

A major fault, running east to west across the Yakata, would react to the shock waves by triggering a seismic response. This secondary earthquake would almost certainly generate sea waves. It was these waves which struck the coastline approximately eleven minutes after the initial detonation.

—Barnhard Golding,
God on Quraqua: The Temple Mission (2213)
Eberhardt & Hickam, Chicago

Let your courage shine before you, fear nothing, take no thought for your well-being. Live by the law, and know that, in your darkest hour, I am at your side.

—Fragment from *Knothic Hours*
(Translated by Margaret Tufu)*

*Original hard copy includes notation "Let us hope so" in translator's handwriting, dated Friday, June 11, 2202.

14.

Temple of the Winds. Friday; 0943 hours.

The two chases constituted the essence of the find. Rescue these, with their text relatively intact, and they would have all they could reasonably hope for. Therefore, despite the urgency, Richard moved with caution. He and Henry took the time they needed to extricate the artifacts from their tomb and start them up the tunnel. George moved ahead of them, removing obstacles and where necessary widening the passage.

They reached the vertical shaft at four minutes to ten.

Henry shone a light upward. "What do you think? Wait it out here until after zero hour? If there's a quake while we're in the shaft, the chases could get damaged."

Richard could not help but admire Henry's singlemindedness. A quake in the shaft would damage more than the chases. On the other hand, he couldn't see that they were any safer staying put. "Let's keep moving," he said.

A line stretched up into the dark. George passed it to Henry, and they secured it around the first of the artifacts.

"Melanie, we have a problem."

She had known there *would* be problems. There were always problems when you tried to shut down an operation this size. "What is it, Harvey?"

He looked unhappy. "Helm won't answer up."

They were inside two minutes. "Forget him. Call the control posts direct."

"I tried. Signals are locked out. We need a password."

"Hutch." Truscott's voice.

"Go ahead, Kosmik."

The director's face was red with anger. "I've been unable to get through to our stations. Detonation will proceed as scheduled."

"But we've still got people down there," Hutch protested.

"I'm sorry. We'll assist any way we can. Keep us informed."

Ten o'clock.

The southern sky brightened. A second sun might have ignited just below the horizon. Hutch looked away. "Richard."

"Okay."

"It's started. I can see it from here."

"All right. Keep cool. We're coming. We've got time."

The sea was calm.

"Ready here," said George. He was at the top of the shaft.

"Look okay?" Henry asked Richard.

"Yes. Let's do it."

George took in the slack, and they lifted the chase into the shaft, and commenced to haul. Henry swam up with it, guiding it.

Richard stayed with the second unit. He brushed silt from it; ridges of individual characters passed under his fingertips. What a treasure it was.

But he was alone in the tunnel, and he felt the weight of the sea. The walls were bleak and claustrophobic. Tiny fish swam past his eyes.

The cable came back. He secured it quickly around the chase, creating a harness.

Above, George pulled the first one out of the shaft. They grappled with it for a few moments, casting shadows down the walls, and then it disappeared. George turned back. "All set," he said.

"Go," said Richard. "Haul away."

At that moment, the water moved. Just the barest tremor, but a school of fish that had been watching darted away.

"Coming up," said George. Richard pushed the chase into the shaft. It dropped a half meter, and then began to rise. He opened a channel to Hutch. "You're not sitting on the surface, are you?"

"Of course I am. How else did you expect to get aboard?"

"Maybe not a good idea." He floated up behind the artifact.

"We're getting shock waves. Keep an eye open."

"I will."

Richard delivered some final cliché, some plastic reassurance that could not have helped her state of mind.

On *Wink*, Janet Allegri strode onto the bridge, walked up to Maggie Tufu, and, without saying a word, knocked her flat.

Melanie Truscott had watched with helpless fury as the white lamps blinked on. Seconds before detonation, she noted that one unit, at Point Theta, had not armed. Locking mechanism had failed. A ten-buck part.

"What do you want to do?" asked Sill.

Goddam Helm. Some of the Academy people would likely die. Worse, if they blew off one icecap and not the other, they might induce a wobble, and possibly cause a complete reorientation of planetary spin. Quraqua could be unstable for centuries. "Tell Harding to cancel the hold. Proceed as planned."

Sill nodded.

"When you get Helm, I want to speak to him."

The design did not call for simultaneous explosions of all devices. The patterns of ice faults, the geometry of the underlying land (where it existed), the presence of volcanoes, the distribution of mass: these and other factors determined the sequence and timing of individual events. It is sufficient to note that all but one of the fifty-eight southern weapons detonated within a period of four minutes, eleven seconds. Blasts ranged from two to thirty-five megatons.

At the icecap, approximately eight percent of the total mass was vaporized. Formations that had stood for tens of thousands of years were blown away. Enormous sheets, like the one at Kalaga, fractured and slid into the sea. Millions of tons of water, thrown out by the blasts, rushed back and turned to steam. Mountainous waves rolled out of the white fury and started a long journey across the circular sea.

During the third minute after the initial detonation, a volcano buried deep in the ice pack exploded. Ironically, it was not one of those whose throat had been laced with a bomb. But it was the first to go. The others erupted according to plan.

Hot rain began to fall.

Shock waves rippled out at five to seven kilometers per second, triggering earthquakes in their wake.

Hutch stood in the hold while the cable came up. The spacecraft floated beside the Temple shuttle. Carson stayed in his cockpit, as a precaution against the unexpected. The jolt that Richard had felt moments earlier in his tunnel had been indiscernible on the surface, nothing more than a ripple and an air current. But a second, more severe shock wave now arrived. Hutch was pitched forward.

Alpha filled with voices from the Temple.

"That was a big one."

"Everybody okay?"

"Damn, I think we lost part of it."

"Let it go, Richard."

"Only take a minute."

"Hutch, you've got a package." It was Henry. "Haul it in."

She winched it up and the first chase broke the surface. An impossibly corroded box. But Hutch knew first-hand the miracles of enhancement. *I hope it's worth your lives.*

She pulled it aboard. Water poured out of it. She disconnected, and heaved the line back over the side.

"Okay, Richard, let go." That was George. "I've got it."

The sea had turned rough. Water boiled and churned.

Sandy appeared to port. She swam swiftly to the shuttle, and Hutch pulled her in. "By God," said Sandy, "we did it."

"Not yet. Where *is* everybody?"

"Coming. A couple of minutes."

"Okay. Listen, we're going to get a little crowded here. Things'll go quicker if you're in the other shuttle."

"Whatever you think," Sandy said.

Carson tossed a line, and she dived back into the sea.

"Frank," Hutch said, "I'll pick up the rest of them." She hesitated. "It might be a good idea if you got some altitude." She cast a worried glance toward a troubled horizon. "Watch for waves."

Most of the undersea lamps had gone out. Only the red trailmarkers still burned bravely within the murky recesses of the wrecked Temple.

They carried the second chase out into the clear water of

what used to be the nave, where the cable from the shuttle was waiting. Richard's hair was in his eyes, and he was exhausted. He felt the drag of the sea. Undertow.

Odd that it would be so strong on the bottom.

"Negative, Hutch," Frank told her. "Nothing yet."

"Okay. What scares me is that I can see the top of the Temple."

"What? That's under five meters of water. At low tide."

"Yeah? Well, I'm looking at it." She switched channels. "Hey, guys, move it. We got another tidal wave coming."

"How close?" Henry's voice.

"Probably a couple of minutes."

Richard broke in: "We're coming as fast as we can." He sounded exasperated. And maybe resigned.

"Hutchins?" It was Truscott. "What's happening down there?"

"I'm a little busy right now." There was a visual signal, but she did not put it on the display.

"I've ordered two of our CATs to assist. But they're four hours away."

In a less stressful moment, Hutch would have recognized the concern in Truscott's voice. But not today. "That'll be a little late, thanks." She broke the link. Looked again through her scopes. Sea still calm.

"Hutch?" Carson again. "I see it."

Cold chill. "Where?"

"Twenty-five kilometers out. Coming at, uh, five fifty. You've got three minutes."

"You guys hear that?"

"Yes—" George's voice.

"Forget the chase. Get up here." She trained her scopes on the horizon. Still nothing. "Frank, how big is it? Can you tell?"

"Negative. Looks like the other one. Small. You wouldn't notice it if you weren't looking for it."

"Okay." She watched a stone wall break the surface. "Water's still going down."

George pulled in several meters of slack. The others held the chase while he secured it. Twice around. Loop crosswise. Reconnect with the cable. Don't lose it now. When he finished, Henry pointed toward the surface. "Let's go."

"You can take it aboard, Hutch." George let go the line and started up.

The currents dragged Richard along the sea bottom. Above, the shuttle hull was dark, and *close*, in sunlit water.

Henry was also drifting. "Heads up," he said. "The tide's a bitch." His voice was shrill.

"Hang on, Henry," said George. "I'll get you."

Hutch was frantic: "Let's go!"

Richard got a hand on the cable. He was still on the bottom, and his arms were weary.

"George," cried Hutch. "Come back. We'll get him with the shuttle. Richard, where are *you*?"

"With the chase."

"On the cable?"

"Yes."

"Okay. We're out of time. Hang onto the line. Got that? Don't let go, no matter what."

There was a loose end on one side of the artifact. He got it around his waist and knotted it. Then, wearily, he stopped struggling.

"There he is." Hutch's voice again. Richard wasn't sure who she meant. He thought, *She's always been there when I need her*. He felt strange. Disconnected.

"Relax, Henry," said George. "We've got you."

"Goddammit," Hutch said, "the son of a bitch is on top of us." Over the voices, he heard a murmur, like a wind stirring.

"You still there, Richard?"

"I'm still here."

"Can you secure yourself to the cable?"

"I already have."

"Okay. About thirty seconds and we're going for a ride."

"Don't lose the chase, Hutch," he said.

George: "Here, take him." They must be talking about Henry.

And Carson: "Get out of there, Hutch."

"Okay, I got him. Hang on, Richard—"

His line jerked and the sea brightened. He rose a meter, moved horizontally, and started to settle. There was a second tug, stronger this time.

The water rushed past him.

• • •

The wave was *not* like the others. This was a *mountain* of water, a liquid behemoth roaring toward her across the open sea, breathing, white-flecked, green, *alive*. It crested five kilometers out, and broke, and built again. And Hutch had waited until she could wait no longer.

There would be no lone Tower standing after this one.

George had finally got Henry on board. "Go," he told her, and Carson was frantic. *Eleven hundred meters high. You're not going to get out, Hutch—*

The last of the Knothic Towers awaited the onrush. The sea had withdrawn and its base was mired in muck. The angel-creature on its pinnacle knelt placidly.

The ruined Temple glittered in the sunlight. She saw no sign of the beach monkeys.

Henry's voice came out of the hold, demanding to know what was being done for Richard. *Little late to think about that.* Hutch was ten meters off the surface now, watching the line, watching for some indication he was still there.

The chase came out of the sea first. Richard dangled beneath it. Reassured, she began to climb. "This'll hurt," she warned him. And she poured the juice to the magnets.

He cried out. But she could hear his breathing.

The shuttle rose, fleeing inland, fleeing toward the defile, running before the wall of water. This was not a *wave*, in the sense that the earlier tsunami had been a wave. The entire ocean was rushing inshore, hurling itself forward, mounting the sky, blocking off the sun. Bright daylight turned wet and furious, and the thing kept growing. White water boiled at its crest.

Hurricane-force winds ripped at the spacecraft, hammered it, drove it back toward the surface.

Too slow. She was moving too deliberately, trying to protect Richard, but in the shadow of the monster her instincts took over: she cut in her jets, quarter speed, the most she dared. The shuttle leaped forward, climbed, and the ancient river valley opened to receive her. Spray coated her wings and hull. The roar filled her ears; George, trying to be stoic, bit down on a whimper.

The tail was thrown violently to one side, and she almost lost the controls. *Alpha* pitched and yawed; her stabilizers blew.

Then they broke out, wobbled, and looked down on the crest. Hutch, for the moment, ignored the half-dozen bleeps and flashing lights on her board. "Richard," she cried into the link, "you okay?"

No answer.

"Richard?"

She listened to his carrier wave.

DOWNLINK HOLO

"Hello, Richard. Greetings from Nok." David Emory squares his shoulders. He is an intense man, with intense eyes, and quick birdlike gestures. His skin is very dark; his hair at this period has just begun to gray. He wears an open-necked short-sleeved brown shirt with huge pockets and flaps, of the style made popular by the dashing simmy adventurer, Jack Hancock.

He is seated on a small boulder, overlooking a river valley. Behind him, white and red sails are visible on the river. Docks, a winding road, and a pair of ferry stations line the banks. The countryside is cut into agricultural squares. The setting is quite terrestrial. Save for the enormous ringed planet which hangs like a Chinese lantern in the sky, one might think he was in Wisconsin.

This is Inakademeri. Nok. The only known world, other than Earth, which is currently home to a living civilization.

The colors are slanted toward purple, a bright but nonetheless gloomy twilight.

He waits, allowing time for his correspondent to take in the view. Then: "I've heard about your problems on Quraqua and I can't say I'm surprised. Vision is in short supply. Here the natives are waging a global war, and we'll be lucky if we don't all get blown up. Bombs falling day and night. World War I without gasoline.

"To answer your question: we do have what you describe as a discontinuity. Around A.D. 400. Religious background, sinful world, vengeful deity. Sodom and Gomorrah on a global scale. According to the sacred texts, it happened in a single night. We don't take that too seriously, but we cannot account for the general destruction. Bill Reed thinks some sort of virus might have got loose and done the damage. The truth is probably more mundane: major *wars, combined with plague and famine.*

"You asked about the age of civilization here. Common wisdom puts it at six thousand years, roughly the same as ours. Also like us, they have an Atlantis legend, a place called Orikon. Except that this one really existed, Richard. Don't know how old it is, but it would go back a long way."

He gestures toward the river valley. "Incidentally, you will be interested in knowing that tradition places Orikon in this area. Come see it, before they blow up the neighborhood. Cheers."

—David Emory, Response CKT144799/16
(Received on *Winckelmann*, June 16, 2202)

INTERLUDE

PASSAGE

The flight home lasted twenty-seven days, eleven hours. This brought the *Winckelmann* in approximately two days behind schedule, well within the inexactitudes imposed by transdimensional travel.

During the voyage, the members of the Academy team went through a period of mourning. Those who had argued to press their luck at the Temple found that their exhilaration over having recovered the foundations of a Linear C vocabulary was diluted by a shared portion of guilt. Henry, particularly, sank into dark moods. He spent time with his people, but they could see that the life had gone out of his eyes.

They responded to all this, for the most part, by losing themselves in examining their trove of artifacts and data, and beginning the decades-long process of analysis and interpretation. No such retreat was available to Hutch.

Almost none understood the ties between Richard Wald and his longtime pilot. They regarded his death as their own loss, and tended to reserve their sympathies for members of the Temple team. The ship's captain was left to her navigation.

For Hutch, the moment when an emotional link with George might have developed came and went. George kept a discreet distance, she thought, while he awaited an encouraging signal from her. But the time was not right for even an implied promise of future possibility. Maybe it was her need to mourn, or the general gloom that weighed on her during this period. Or maybe even her fear that George might come to associate her with disaster. Whatever her motivation, she began a policy of treating him with polite neutrality, and found that it locked quickly into place.

When they docked finally at the Wheel, they held a farewell dinner in the Radisson Lounge. Everybody said a few words, and there were some tears. And the steaks were very good.

In the morning, the first contingents rode shuttles to Atlanta, Berlin, and London.

PART THREE
BETA PAC

15.

The Academy of Science and Technology (HV Simulation Section), Washington, D.C. Tuesday, October 19, 2202; 1700 EDT.

Hutch stood at the edge of the cliff and looked down at the stars and at Shola's shimmering rings. The gas giant itself was behind her, low in the sky.

It was unsettling. This was not like climbing around the hull of a ship. She smiled at her reaction, and knelt, partly to examine the lip of the cliff, partly to regain her balance.

It was not the jagged, irregular rim one would expect, but the precision cut of a jewel.

This was a truly *alien* place, a place without purpose, a place that made neither aesthetic nor functional sense. But certainly, after Oz, a place with an echo. A stone plain, polished and chiseled, spread out behind her. It was pool-table flat, marred only by a few craters and a spread of fissure lines. The limits of the plain were not horizons; rather, at fairly close range, the smooth rock simply stopped, and one knew instinctively that beyond those abrupt summits, the cliff side fell away forever. The sky surrounded her, came at her from all angles. It was full of fire and light and crescents. A great clockwork, its spheres and stars clicked steadily through their rhythms while she watched.

It oppressed her. It was ominous. Frightening in a way she could not quite grasp.

Four of these objects circled the big world the Noks called the Companion. Identical size. Once equidistant. Two of them were badly charred.

Charred. Again, like Oz.

What were they?

193

There were no cryptic symbols here, as there were in the round tower. But there was a message nevertheless, an *outcry*, perhaps, in this spartan geometry.

She removed the helmet, and the lights came on. She laid it on the table beside her, and looked out at the Arlington skyline.

Déjà vu.

                              Cumberland, Maryland
                                    10/19/02

Dear Henry,

I have a translation: Farewell and good fortune. Seek us by the light of the horgon's eye. *A horgon is a mythical Quraquat monster. But don't ask me what it all means.*

                                    Maggie

On the anniversary of the publication of Richard Wald's landmark study, *Memory and Myth*, his family and friends conducted a celebration of his life. They chose a hilltop in Arlington, a site from which the Academy was visible, and erected a small pavilion. It was a bleak day shortly before Thanksgiving, gray, threatening rain, with the kind of chill that no clothing can deflect.

Hutch received an invitation and considered staying away. She was not one to be taken in by the façade of affirming life when she knew damned well what was *really* on everyone's mind. It was all still too painful, too close to the bone. Maybe next year she could sit comfortably and reminisce about him, but for now all she could recall was the limp figure dangling below the shuttle.

When the day came, however, wearing the talisman he had given her, she was there. The event's sponsors had set up a small platform atop a low hill, and laid out a table beneath a stand of spruce trees. They filled the table with souvenirs and artifacts and photos. There were copies of Richard's books and tablets from Pinnacle and crossbows from Quraqua and representations of the Monuments. The Academy's seal and colors were centrally displayed.

Refreshments were in liberal supply. People spotted old friends, and clustered in animated conversations. Hutch stood off to one side, ill at ease and dispirited. At noon, a tall man who looked like a younger Richard climbed onto the platform and waited for the crowd noise to subside.

"Hello," he said. "I know some of you, but not all. My name's Dick Wald. I'm—I *was*—Richard's cousin. He'd have been pleased to see how many of you came out here today. And he'd have wanted me to say thanks." He paused, and looked over the crowd. "He often said he was happy with his life, and fortunate in his friends. We used to make a lot of 'dead' jokes about him. And there are so many archeologists here today that I know you've had to put up with them too. You know how they go, about how everybody he knows has been dead at least eight hundred years. About how he only speaks dead languages. Well, there's a lot about death in an archeologist's field of interest, and it seems painful that it should come eventually to the archeologist himself." He paused, and the wind moved in the trees behind him. "I'd like to invite Bill Winfield to say a few words. Bill taught Sumerian 101 to Richard."

In turn, people got up and spoke about him. They thanked him for launching their careers, and for helping them with money or advice or encouragement. For setting the example. Several quoted favorite passages from his books, or idle remarks tossed off on windswept evenings:

The difference between history and archeology is the difference between public policy and a coffee table. One is theory and analysis and sometimes even spectacle. The other is a piece of life.

There is a kind of archeology of the mind in which we unearth old injuries and resentments, pore over them, and keep them close to our hearts. Eventually, like thousand-year-old air encountered in a tomb, they poison us. It gives me to wonder whether the value of history is not overrated.

I have always felt a kinship with the gravediggers in Ham-let. They are the first recorded archeologists.

History has nothing to do with reality. It is a point of view, an attempt to impose order on events that are essentially chaotic.

And an observation from an essay on Pinnacle which Hutch wished he had himself taken seriously: *The universe has a sense of humor. Two years ago, a man in Chicago was driving to his wedding when a meteor totaled his car. The prospective bridegroom took the hint and left town. When*

*conditions prevent a prudent excavation, archeologists would
do well, also, to take the hint.*

When the last of those who wished to speak had finished,
Dick Wald asked if there were anyone else. Instinctively,
Hutch shied away from public appearances. But she could
not do that today. Not knowing what she would say, she
strode to the platform, and turned to face the crowd. Many
knew her, and she heard a smattering of applause.

She groped for the right words. "I'd just like to say," she
said, "that he was always good to work for." She paused.
The sky was clear and blue and very far away. "He died
doing what he believed in. He died, I think, the way he
would have wanted." She looked around desperately, and
wished for divine intervention. Her mind had gone blank.
Reflexively, she took hold of the talisman, and drew it out
into the sunlight. "Love and prosperity," she said. "He gave
me this. Its inscription, in one of the Quraquat languages, says
love and prosperity will be mine while I wear it. Actually,
they were mine as long as I knew *him*."

Later, she said hello to Dick. He told her Richard had
spoken of her often. Up close, his resemblance to Richard
was striking. And there was a trick of speech, a tendency to
draw out r's in the manner of Bostonians, that they shared.
She could have closed her eyes and believed he was back.

The Academy was out in force. Henry showed up, an act
that must have taken considerable courage because a lot of
people, including Hutch, blamed him for Richard's death. He
had aged during the few months since their return. His face
was gray in the dull light, and he walked uncertainly.

"How are you?" Hutch asked, offering her hand.

He took it, but his grasp was perfunctory. "Good," he said.
"It's nice to see you, Hutch." His eyes traveled between her
and the speakers' platform, which was now empty. "I would
have preferred better circumstances."

An awkward silence followed. Hutch knew a reprimand
was in the works for Henry. The whole world knew it. He
had announced his retirement, and he faced the prospect of
becoming the central figure in a landmark legal dispute over
the issue of court jurisdiction beyond the solar system.

"I didn't thank you, by the way," he said, "for everything
you did."

"I was glad to help," she said.

"I wish things could have turned out better." He was backing away from her, anxious to be gone.

"Me, too," she said weakly.

Princeton
Saturday, Nov. 27, 2202

Dear Priscilla,

Just a word to let you know that Cal Hartlett got married today. I know we've had this conversation before, and I hope you won't take this the wrong way, but there's another good one you could have had. That boy idolized you. I've met the bride and she's pretty, but she isn't in your league.

Please think about the future. We're not getting any younger.

Mom

Hutch put her feet up on the hassock, sipped her coffee, and stared out over the rock plain. She was well away from the edge this time, and Shola was off to the right. Although the gas giant dominated the sky, its light was dim. Overhead, there were no stars. She was looking directly into the Void. Look hard enough, long enough, and one could see the other side, the distant flicker of the Sagittarius Arm.

The coffee tasted good.

Portland, Oregon
Monday, Nov. 29, 2202

Dear Ms. Hutchins,

The enclosed holo arrived here several weeks ago, before you got back from Quraqua. In fact, it came before I'd heard about Richard's death. I haven't been certain who to send it to, and I thought you would know. I thought somebody at the Academy might have some interest in it.

Best wishes.

Dick Wald

(ENCLOSURE)

DOWNLINK HOLO
Leader marked "PERSONAL FOR RICHARD WALD"

David Emory in a field office. "Richard," *he says,* "It's ironic that you would have been asking about this just a few days ago. We have found Orikon. I thought you'd like to hear what we have, but please keep it to yourself until we publish.

"We've known for some time that the ruins were located under a modern city, where they were not accessible to direct investigation. Or, more accurately, I've known, but since we couldn't get an actual physical piece for dating purposes, there was no way to prove anything.

"The scanners showed a metal circumference around the ruins, with lines jutting off. Theory was that it was a defensive structure of one kind or another." *He takes a chair, and crosses his arms over his chest, quite satisfied with the direction events have taken.* "This world is subject to enormous tides, because of its proximity to the Companion. There are sea walls here now, to restrain the ocean. But these structures are recent.

"Orikon was located on a cluster of islands which are now hilltops. At low tide, they looked out over swamps. So the question always was: how, under such circumstances, could the inhabitants travel from one section of the city to another? This is no small feat, by the way. We are talking about islands spread over twelve hundred square kilometers. Furthermore, how did they maintain access to an ocean when they had to travel over ground that was sometimes a sea and sometimes a swamp?

"The solution: they had a monorail. This is mountainous country, and we went looking on some of the peaks for evidence. Yesterday we found it: a piece of concrete bolted into the side of a precipice. We now have other evidence as well. They seem to have thrived between 18,000 and 16,000 B.C. So it turns out civilization is three times older here than we thought.

"Orikon lives, Richard."

Henry removed the helmet. Sunlight warmed the room. Hutch looked out at the Morning Pool, the Ivers Museum, elta Park, and, in the distance, the Washington Monument.

"Good of you to bring it by," he said. "May I make a copy?"

"Of course." She waited for a sign that he agreed with her assessment of its significance.

"Well." He folded his arms and pushed back comfortably. "How is everything with you?"

"Fine," she said.

"Is something wrong?" he asked. "You seem tense."

"Henry, you don't seem surprised."

His leathery face did not change. "What surprises *you*, Hutch?"

"We've got a second discontinuity on Nok. Two on each world. That makes a trend."

Henry studied her across the broad expanse of his desk. The office was big, crowded with mementoes of his career. "You're assuming that Orikon suffered one of these events."

"Of course. How else would you explain the disappearance of a civilization capable of building a monorail?"

"We aren't talking about established facts, Hutch. We are fully aware of events on Nok. *You* should be aware that Emory has a tendency to jump to conclusions. However, there *is* a curious coincidence. He says the most recent artifacts are from about 16,000 B.C." He looked at her expectantly.

She didn't see the point.

"The events on Quraqua," Henry said, "were divided by eight thousand years."

"—And on Nok by *sixteen* thousand. Twice as long. But what does that suggest?"

He shrugged. "Multiples of eight. For whatever significance that might have." He looked old; his movements were stiff and seemed to require conscious effort.

"Multiples of eight? Would we know if there'd been an event on Nok around 8000 B.C.?"

"Probably not. The current cycle of civilization got started three thousand years later." He studied the top of his desk. "I have no problems with a coincidence. *One* coincidence."

"What's the other?"

"The resemblance between Oz and the cube moons."

"So what do we do now?"

"*I* retire," he said. "And hope I have some money left after the lawyers get finished with me."

"Henry, you can't just walk out—"

"I sure as hell *can* just walk out. Listen—" His face reddened and he leaned across the desk. "Do you have any idea what all this means to me? I'm about to be drummed out. Blamed for the death of an old friend." His lip quivered. "And God help me, maybe they're right."

"But we need you."

"And I needed *you*. We went through hell out there, and I made a decision that I'm going to have to live with the rest of my life. You're taking an accusing tone with me now. Where were *you* when we were trying to get a few answers? All you could contribute was to hang on the other end of that damned commlink and try to panic everybody. Did you really think we didn't know what was coming? We went down there with our eyes open, Hutch. *All* of us."

And you didn't all make it back. But she said nothing. He glared at her, and then the energy seemed to go out of him, and he sank back into his chair.

"I'm sorry you feel that way," she said. "I did what I had to."

"As did I."

They looked at one another across a gulf. Finally, Hutch said, "You *will* follow up on this. Right?"

"*You* follow up on it. If you find something, I'll be in Chicago."

Henry's anger hurt. Had the others felt the same way? My God, had *Richard* gone to his death disappointed in her? A cold wind blew through her soul.

She could not go back to her apartment that night.

She wandered among some of her old hangouts, ending eventually at the Silver Dancer, which was a favorite nightspot for airline types, and which had probably never seen an archeologist. She drank a series of rum-and-cokes that had no effect on her. Somewhere around midnight, she encouraged a shy young flight attendant with good eyes and went home with him.

She gave him the night of his life.

Hutch wanted to let it rest, to put it behind her. But she could not. So, on a crisp, clear evening a week after her conversation with Henry, she met Frank Carson for dinner at an

Italian restaurant along the Arlington waterfront.

"I wouldn't worry about it," he said. "Henry tends to get upset, and he's been through a lot. He told me, by the way, that he'd talked to you."

Carson was a good guy. He tended to take a paternal line with her, but she could forgive that. She came very close to approving. "He resents me," she said.

He asked her to explain. When she'd finished, he tried to wave it away. "I did the same thing," he said. "I was on the circuit to Henry, and I kept pushing them the whole time. It's not to your discredit that you wanted them out of there. In your place, Henry would have done the same. He's upset with me, too."

It was just after sunset. They were drinking Chianti, and watching a boat discharge passengers from Alexandria onto the dock. "What do *you* think?" she asked. "About the discontinuities?"

He didn't hesitate. "I don't think anything's established yet. If it turns out there *was* an event on Nok eighteen or twenty thousand years ago, I still don't think it would mean very much."

"What about 'the engines of God'?"

"Beg pardon?"

" 'He will come who treads the dawn, Tramples the sun beneath his feet, And judges the souls of men. He will stride across the rooftops, And he will fire the engines of God.' It's from a Quraquat prayer book. Art thought it might have been a prediction of the Second Discontinuity on Quraqua. The timing was right."

"There are always predictions," he said.

Their dinners arrived, spaghetti and meatballs for both.

"Feel better?" Carson asked, after she'd made inroads.

"Yes," she said. "I guess so."

"Good. I've got some news for you: we've tracked down the horgon."

She looked up from her plate, delighted. "Good," she said. "What have you got?"

"Well, it's kind of interesting. You know the thing was a mythical monster. It was all claws and teeth, it had fiery eyes, it was armored, and it stood on two feet. It had a built-in flame thrower." He paused. *"And it could see three hundred sixty degrees."*

Hutch did a double take. "The horgon's eye," she whispered.

"Yes." Delighted, Carson drew out the aspirate. "That's what *we* thought. The beast is associated with the child-hero Malinar, and with Urik, who was a kind of Quraquat Hercules. Malinar rescued his sister when she was threatened by the creature by diverting its attention with a plate of food. The thing pitied the child and spared him. And the girl. We know there was a cycle of Malinar myths, but the horgon story is the only one we have.

"Urik is perhaps the best known of all Quraquat mythical figures. The important point is that he would certainly have been known to the Quraquat of the Linear C era."

"So we get a fit," said Hutch.

"Yes." He speared a meatball and tasted it. "Good," he said. "Anyway, Urik lived at the beginning of *their* civilization, in a world filled with enchantment and dark spells and divine retribution for anyone who got out of line. Only one god in this scenario, the usual male deity, with the standard short temper and no-nonsense code of conduct. Monotheistic systems, by the way, were common on Quraqua during that period. There is residual evidence of polytheistic religions, but over thousands of years the original tales must have been rewritten to reflect correct views. And there's *another* universal tendency."

"What's that?"

"Monotheistic religious systems are usually intolerant." He smiled warmly at her, and his tone softened. "This is actually quite nice," he said. "Having dinner with the loveliest woman in Arlington, Virginia."

Appreciative, Hutch reached across the table and squeezed his hand.

Back to business, he said: "Somebody was having trouble with a horgon. It was terrorizing the countryside and generally raising hell. So they called in Urik."

"Okay."

"The only way to kill it was to put a sword into its heart."

"Seems straightforward," said Hutch.

"It's an old story," he said. "Hermes and Argos."

"Beg pardon?"

"Greek myth. It's a hunter's tale. You are trying to bring down the ultimate prey, a creature that's exceedingly deadly, and you can't hide in the bushes. And you can't take it head-on. So you have to devise a trick.

"In the Urik story, a series of heroes, over the course of a generation or so, have tried to kill the monster. They used all sorts of imaginative schemes to get close to it. They tried to blind it with sunlight reflected from a polished shield; they tried to sneak up on it disguised as a female horgon; they tried to put it to sleep with a magic trombone."

Hutch smiled. *"A magic trombone?"*

"Well, not really. But it *was* a mystical instrument, a pipe of some sort. In any case, things always went wrong. The hero put the pipe down to get a good grip on his sword, the horgon woke up, and the hero got barbecued. That was the technique that Hermes used, by the way. It worked for him.

"There was also an attempt by a female. Her name was Haska, and she brought along an army of pages to keep dousing her with water. The horgon cooked the pages, but Haska was fortunate enough to escape with her life. She was the only hero to do so, until Urik.

"Now—and here's the point—Urik got involved in all this because his lover, Lisandra, was carried off by demons, and he was advised by a neighborhood sage that he could find her only with the assistance of a *horgon's eye*."

"Bingo."

"Yes. It would seem that whoever carved the inscription was familiar with Quraquat mythology. Incidentally, the various sources aren't consistent as to the number of eyes the creature actually had. Anyhow, Urik's boyhood friend Calipon went with him, and the two planned to distract the horgon by giving it a meal."

"A cow?"

"The horgon's diet was apparently limited to people."

"Oh."

"Or the hero's imagination was. Calipon volunteered. The strategy they settled on was that *he* would deliver a frontal attack. Urik was to stay back until the attack failed, and the creature was half-gorged."

Hutch tilted her head. "Did this seem like strange behavior to the Quraquat? They weren't suicidal, were they?"

"Keep in mind, Hutch, that you're talking as if there were only a single culture. The Quraquat, like us, had a wide range of codes of behavior. Some embraced suicide as a reasonable action. But we know almost nothing about the period that gave rise to the Urik tales. For that matter, we don't know much about the later civilization that built the Temple of the Winds. So I can't really answer your question. Calipon, incidentally, was a hero in his own right, but he achieved his immortality through his sacrifice. Eventually, a nation was named for him."

Her eyebrows rose. "The second-banana hero."

"Yes. And selfless. Still another universal, Hutch. You see it everywhere. Nok has several variations. So do we. Patroclus, for example."

"Why didn't the other guy, what's his name, Urik, offer to be the main course? After all, it's *his* girlfriend they're after."

"Well, it wouldn't be decent to rescue the lady by throwing her lover to the wolves. No, Calipon is in the narrative for the specific purpose of serving as the sacrifice. And doing it willingly. That's what gives meaning to the tale. It's the point of the story. Everyone has an obligation to the greater good."

"It worked, of course, right?"

"Yes, Hutch. It worked. Calipon died, Urik finished off the horgon, and retrieved one of its eyes. Eventually, with the help of a sacred sea bird, a *diver*, he also retrieved the lovely Lisandra. In celebration of the manner of her freedom, she placed the eye on a gold chain and wore it ever after at her throat. And, in representations, she is said always to have been accompanied by a diver." He propped his chin on his hand and studied her. "So the question is, where does all this leave us?"

"That's *it*?" she asked.

"That's *it*." Carson lifted his glass. The electric candles glittered in the Chianti.

"He rescued her, and they lived happily ever after," she said.

"No." He shook his head. "That isn't the end. It never is. Not for epic heroes. There has to be a final validation of the myth, a recognition by a divinity, and by the community, of the significance of the heroic acts. And it has to be set up. The setup is that, while the hero is away on a quest, raiders attack his home. Lisandra dies protecting their son.

Urik catches up with the bandits, and does them in, although he is mortally wounded in the encounter. And the gods have their opportunity to bestow divine honors. The reward for Urik—Calipon is not mentioned—is to be accepted into the company of God's warriors, a deathless squadron to be called on in time of great need. The members were memorialized *by being placed in the sky.*"

"That's interesting," said Hutch. *"Seek us by the light of the horgon's eye.* Are the Monument-Makers showing us where they live?"

"Maybe."

"If so, the horgon's eye is a star. Possibly the *home* star."

"That's exactly what I thought," said Carson.

Hutch disposed of some spaghetti. "Could we be looking for a constellation?"

"I would think so."

"Which one? Do we know the Quraquat constellations?"

"Not from that era."

She sighed. "We're still at sea. How do we find one that looks like a big Quraquat with a spear? And then, how do we narrow it down to an individual star?"

"I don't think we're looking for Urik. He's not the one who's associated with the horgon's eye. It's Lisandra. *She* carried it."

"Whatever," said Hutch. "Did Lisandra get a constellation, too?"

"Urik and Lisandra were lovers. In mythical systems, lovers, if they are of sufficient stature, are never separated beyond the physical realm. These two would be closely associated throughout the mythic cycle, and so we should expect to find them together in the heavens."

"It's still hopeless." Hutch threw up her hands. "Have you ever been able to make pictures out of the stars? How would we ever recognize her?"

"Good question. If you have a suggestion, I'd be happy to hear it."

"I have no idea."

"Maybe it's not *that* hopeless. We've got a hole card: the horgon's eye is red."

LIBRARY ENTRY

They drink my deeds in the halls of the Ka,
And bless their arms with my name.
Yet I, riding through deep snow,
In the dark of the moon,
Do not pause.

Where, now, is Calipon my comrade?

The pennants ripple atop Haster's outpost,
Brave colors, gray and blue, rock and sea,
My colors,
Bright still in the fading light;
I nod, but do not stop.

And where, at last, Lisandra?

—from *Urik at Sunset*
(Translated by Philip Marcotti)

16.

The Academy of Science and Technology, Washington, D.C.
Friday, December 10, 2202; 1545 EST.

Professor Emeritus Eric Kofton of Georgetown was visiting
the Quraquat display at the Ivers Museum when he noticed a
zodiac carved in a three-legged table. It didn't take him long
to learn he had made a discovery, but he had no idea of its
importance. The Academy awarded him a certificate.

The images were idealizations, giving no hint what the
constellations might look like. But there were inscriptions
identifying the figures. "I don't know whether it'll help us,"
said Carson, unrolling a poster reproduction. "The table is
from the same part of the world as the Casumel culture.
Unfortunately, it's only a few hundred years old. So maybe
it's the same zodiac, and maybe it isn't. But look at this."
He pointed at a snouted Quraquat with spear, shield, and war
helmet. "It's *called* the Warrior."

"Urik, do you think?"

Carson looked hopeful. "We need to stay objective. But he
comes complete with a female."

"The female's a separate constellation? Or part of the same
one?"

"Separate. Its name doesn't have an English equivalent, but
it would translate to the 'Beautiful Woman Virgin-Mother.' "

Hutch grinned. "That's Lisandra. I'd recognize her anywhere."

He looked down at a notebook. "The constellations are
listed by occupation. Or function. There's a woodsman. A
fisherman with a net. A soronghilia plant."

"A what?"

"The Tree of Life. Symbol of immortality. There's an axe.
Even a strider."

"We could have used a few pictures of the constellations."

"They would help." They were in Carson's office on the fifth floor. It was filled with memorabilia from both his military and archeological careers. She counted three models of combat aircraft, and the Temple shuttle. Awards and photos covered the walls. A young Carson in Air Force gray posed beside a black Labrador retriever. An older version stood beside a striking brunette.

"Who is she?" Hutch asked.

"Just a friend." His face clouded briefly. "Used to be."

Fearing she had intruded, Hutch retreated to the subject at hand. "What are the other constellations?"

"A bucket, a shield, a couple of animals—"

"No horgon's eye?"

"No. And something we think was a scales."

"It's interesting. But it's hard to see that we've made any progress."

In answer, he handed her a simmy helmet. She put it on, and a starfield blazed into existence. "View from Oz," he said. "Circa 9000 B.C." The stars lay across half a sky, the campfires of a distant army. Beyond lay the black heart of the Void. Two crosshairs appeared left and right. "They represent the two towers, Hutch. You're standing directly in the center of the city. Each crosshair is targeted on a straight line from your position to the corresponding round tower, and angled up parallel to the rooftop."

The sky rotated, and one of the crosshairs locked on a red star. "That's from the tower with the inscription," Carson said. "The star is Orchinda. The Orchid. It's a red giant, only about nine light years from Quraqua. More violet than red, not that it matters."

If they had guessed right, when the horgon's eye appeared in one sight, the target sun would appear in the other. The target—she glanced at the other crosshair—was dim.

"I don't recall its numerical designation. We've never been there. It's a class G. Sixty light-years from Quraqua, a hundred fifteen from here."

"Is that *it*?" Hutch was prepared to respond with an appropriate outburst, but Carson was too reserved. It wasn't going to be this easy.

"Maybe," he said. "There are seventeen red stars that appear in one or the other of the crosshairs. Sixteen of those give us a star in, or very near, the opposite sight. The problem is that we have to assume the towers have slipped over the millennia, been affected by quakes, meteor strikes, whatever. So we're looking at everything within four degrees of the target area."

"How did you arrive at that figure?"

"By throwing darts."

"How many suspect stars did we wind up with?"

"About eighty."

She sighed.

"Hutch, we need to go back and do a complete survey at Oz. Establish the extent to which there's been ground movement."

"How long would that take?"

"Years. Right now, nobody at the Academy wants to hear anything about either Quraqua or Oz. And I don't think there'd be much enthusiasm for sending out *eighty* expeditions either. Especially when we have no idea whether our margin for error is too conservative. Which it probably is." He looked discouraged. "At least, we've had some movement."

Hutch was looking at the black Lab in the photo.

"Her name was Spike," he said.

"Odd name for a female."

"My nephew named her." He followed her gaze to the picture. "Something wrong?"

"Animals," she said.

"Beg pardon?"

"You said there were animals. How about a *diver*?"

"I'm sorry?"

"A diver. The sea bird that was connected with Lisandra."

"Damn. I never thought of that."

The sky moved again. "It had a long beak," she said.

"You think that'll help?"

"It's the diver's primary characteristic. I looked it up. Like Hercules' club, or the dipper's handle. It would be a row of stars. Three or more. Maybe even prominent, if we're lucky."

"*That's* optimistic. More like two stars, I'd think. Maybe one. You know how constellations are."

"No," she said. "Two won't work. You can draw a straight line between any two stars in the sky. If we don't have three, we're wasting our time."

"Okay," he said. "What's to lose? The horgon's eye, the diver, and the virgin should all be in the same neighborhood. We'll line up every red star that gets close to either crosshair, and look for the beak."

This was not the sort of search that was likely to produce a sudden, blinding result. They worked through the afternoon, recording those stars which might possibly have served as the all-seeing eye: Olphinax, forty light-years farther along the shore of the Void; Tulikar, with its dense companion; Kampatta Prime, centerpiece of the Quraquat Pleiades. They added Anapaka to the list, and Hasan and Alpha Qui and three stars whose only designations were their catalog numbers. Each was accompanied by a nearby line of stars that might, by imaginative observers, be classified as a beak. "How do we know," asked Carson, "that it isn't curved?"

"Beg pardon?" said Hutch.

"The beak. How do we know it's supposed to be straight? It could look like a pelican."

"No," said Hutch. "I saw a picture of one. It's straight."

It was all too inexact. Their margin for error resulted sometimes in multiple hits: a single horgon's eye candidate produced two, three, and in one case six, targets in the other crosshairs.

The search for the beak proved fruitless. They discovered a basic universal truth: Almost anywhere one looks in the sky, stars line up in threes and fours. Eventually, they cataloged more than fifty candidates and began the process of elimination. All stars that were not class G or M, or that were not at least three billion years old, were excluded. ("A bit arbitrary there," said Carson. "But Rome wasn't built in a day.") Multiple star systems, which are probably too unstable to permit life to develop, were also disregarded. Stars which had already been surveyed were removed.

By the end of the afternoon, the number of candidates was down to thirteen.

"We've done pretty well," she said.

"We've done a lot of guesswork. I liked the old days when we could just order up a survey. This isn't nearly good enough. We have to pin it down, isolate it. And *then* we have to persuade Ed Horner."

Hutch felt desperate.

"Let's quit," Carson said. "Day's over."

It turned into a gloomy, rainswept evening. She wondered whether Carson had already given up, whether he was hoping she would see the futility of continuing, of risking their careers for a cause that most of the Academy people considered ludicrous. And *that*, it suddenly struck her, was the *point*. From his perspective, she had nothing to lose. She was a pilot, with no professional career at risk. Whatever happened, no one would laugh at *her*. It was Carson who was taking the risk, *his* colleagues who smiled tolerantly, *his* judgment at issue.

They went to dinner again, in Georgetown. But it was a mistake because they reinforced one another's discouragement. Afterward, Hutch was glad to get home. She climbed into a simmy and sat with it until she fell asleep.

Somewhere around two, she jerked fully awake. There *was* another test they could try. The obvious one.

Carson would have to go to the commissioner, and they'd have to pull some strings. But it could be made to work.

The Tindle Array, Farside, Luna. Monday, January 24, 2203; 1130 GMT.

Alexander Coldfield walked into his office, peered through his tinted windows across the vast expanse of Mare Muscoviense, and slid into his seat. Off to his left, a coffee machine perked noisily. The thick columns and spidery dishes of the Tindle Array marched across the lunar plain.

Coldfield loved places that were isolated and hostile. He'd grown up in the Bronx, and had escaped to North Dakota at his first opportunity. He discovered an affinity for fireplaces and barren plains, for good wine and heavy snow. Solitude became his watchword. His affection for a landscape grew in direct proportion to its inconvenience for natives and inaccessibility to travelers.

He was a career government employee. He had worked in outposts from Manitoba to New Brunswick. The break of his life had come when, at thirty-two, he'd been appointed observer and technician at the one-man weather station on uninhabited Kaui Island, two thousand miles west of Hawaii. When he went there, he expected to remain forever, and would have, had not the lunar assignment come up.

The Tindle Array, located in the Tsiolkovsky area, had required a technician/operator. The tour was designed to last one year, and he could take his family if he wished. Of course, Coldfield had no family. That had been a problem at first. One of the busybodies in OHR had wondered about his psychological well-being. But Coldfield was solid if anybody was, and he'd made his case convincingly. The analysts agreed.

The appeal of the assignment was enhanced by the fact that Tsiolkovsky was located on the far side of the Moon. The Earth would never rise over the Array.

None of this should be construed to suggest that Coldfield was a misanthropist. He most definitely was not. In fact he liked people, felt he had been fortunate in his acquaintances over the years, and made good use of the relay circuits to a dozen points on Earth to talk with old friends. The truth about him was complicated. It involved a degree of self-doubt, of discomfort with strangers, and a thoroughgoing dislike for crowds, combined with a genuine love for remote places and a strong meditative inclination. (He would never have admitted to the latter.)

The Tindle was to have consisted of one hundred eleven fully steerable antennas, each sixteen meters in diameter. They would occupy an area forty kilometers across, and be set on individual tracks ranging from eight to sixty meters long. The project was only two-thirds constructed, but the government had run out of money. No one seriously believed that it would ever be finished. But it added up to tens of thousands of moving parts, which had to be kept operational under extreme conditions. It would not have been correct to say there was always work, but repairs were needed often enough to justify Coldfield's presence.

The tasks were simple enough. When something went down, the systems isolated the problem for him, and usually all he had to do was trek out to the offending unit and substitute a microboard or a crystal.

He had even become involved in the operational side of the Tindle. Harvard-Smithsonian had requested his help in entering values directly into the machines, and had asked him in some cases to execute programs manually. Coldfield understood, despite his operators' denials, that they wanted to increase his contact with other people. He was the first person to come alone to the Array, and they were watching him closely.

He had passed the evening with a biography of Evelyn

Lister, who was enormously popular in her time, but who was now widely perceived as the architect of the catastrophic conditions which had overtaken and ultimately leveled the old United States. The biography showed no mercy, and it warmed Coldfield to read the attacks. He objected on principle to the powerful. Even when they were dead.

The Array was listening to OQ 172, a quasar ten billion light years out. Coldfield took his work seriously, and had acquired some rudimentary astronomy. But he did not understand the peculiar significance of quasars, nor could he make much out of the analytical readouts. Still, he knew it had something to do with creation. And he was curious about that. He had grown up in a family of religious skeptics. But, on the back side of the Moon, the supernatural seemed very possible.

The brief chime of the commlink startled him. He swung away from the windows, stabbed the receiver. "Coldfield."

Michael Surina's image blinked on. "Hello, Alex. How are you doing?" Surina was the project coordinator. He made it a point to call once a day. His concern for the Big Array's lone inhabitant both warmed and touched its subject.

"Fine," Coldfield said.

"No problems?"

There was a coupling that needed replacing on No. 17, and the plumbing in one of the bathrooms was backing up. (He had three.) But there was nothing that could be described as a problem. "Negative, Mike. Everything's quiet."

"Okay. We're changing the program, so don't be surprised when things start to happen."

"What's going on?"

"We want to listen to a new target. A *series* of new targets."

"When?"

"We'll wrap up the quasar exercise in a little over six hours. At 1922 Zulu. Then we're going to adjust the entire schedule. The operation will take several days."

"Several days! There'll be hell to pay."

"Doesn't matter. We'll do it."

"What are we going to tell McHale and Abrams and the rest of them? They've been waiting a year and a half for their time."

"We're taking care of it. You won't have to deal with them at all."

"Damn right I won't." Surina was young, but would probably irritate too many people to move up. Now he sat watching Coldfield, and his expression implied that he understood, but that Alex knew how bureaucracies were. It's no concern of ours if they screw up, his eyes said. Naturally, on an open link he wouldn't make those sentiments overt. "This is a hell of a way to run an operation, Mike," said Coldfield.

Surina shrugged. "Somebody at the Academy is pulling strings, and favors are owed."

Naturally. Surina could say what he liked, but Abrams and the others would bitch at him. "What kind of targets?"

"Short range. Local stars. You're going to do a search for patterned radio signals."

That was unusual. The Tindle had never, to his knowledge, examined anything closer than the galactic core. "Why?" he said. "What are we looking for?"

"LGMs."

"Beg pardon?"

"LGMs. Little green men."

THE WORLD REVIEW

COMMENTARY

The European Commonwealth is informally floating a proposal that we announce our presence to the inhabitants of the earthlike world Inakademeri, and begin negotiations with a view to assisting the natives technologically, and to securing territory which would serve as a homeland for populations of undeveloped nations.

This may be an idea whose time has come. Inakademeri is sparsely populated, wracked by global war, depleted of natural resources. The "Noks" need help. In fact, there are groups among them who claim to know of our presence, who say they have seen our aircraft and shuttles. Whether in fact they have is of no consequence. What is significant is that these unfortunate creatures, who think we may exist, literally pray for our intervention.

There would be some inconveniences. Settlers would have to become accustomed to an eleven-hour day/night cycle. The climate on the whole tends to be wetter than ours. But it is livable.

Biosystems on Nok are sufficiently like our own that
we could subsist quite well on that world's food supply.
It may well be that we have a second Earth available,
that we need not wait decades for Quraqua to develop.

The World Council should give careful consideration
to this proposal. If no more serious objections exist than
those already advanced, it should be approved, and action
taken within the shortest possible time.

—"The Observer"
Wednesday, January 26, 2203

Carson called her in on her birthday, February 1. "It's Beta
Pacifica," he said.

NEWSDESK

BAHRAINIS SHELL BORDER TOWNS
Council Threatens Military Action

CORE CASES INCREASE IN AFRICA, MIDDLE EAST
Bone Loss Syndrome May Worsen
Fear Spreads to West
Foxworth Assures Nation: "No Need to Panic"

SIX DIE IN BLAST IN MANHATTAN BAR
El Corazon Admits Responsibility
Demands Repeal of Immigration Ban

EGYPTIAN FERRY CAPSIZES
110 Dead; 300 Missing

FOXWORTH PROMISES TAX EQUITY FOR MUL-
TIPLE-CHILD FAMILIES

CHINA MAY BE BUILDING NUCLEAR WEAPON
Hiao Denies USE Charge
Will Resist Inspection "by Force of Arms"

INDIAN FAMINE MAY HAVE KILLED MILLIONS
World Council Pledges Aid;
Demands Cessation of Hostilities

PRICES CONTINUE TO CLIMB
CPI Hits Annual Rate of 11%
Sloan: "Foxworth Neglects Economy"

POPE VISITS BRAZIL
Decries "Modern Life Styles"

BEWARE CHRISTMAS CON ARTISTS
Elderly at Risk
"Real" Trees, Gift Subscription Funds Lead List of Scams

ATLANTIC CLUB PREDICTS GRIM FUTURE
"Great Famine May Have Been Only Prelude"

NEW E-SAT GOES ON-LINE
Network Near Completion
Will Provide Near-Unlimited Clean
Energy for Africa, Middle East

**LEGION TRADES BOOM-BOOM FOR 4 PLAYERS,
5 DRAFT CHOICES**

Chicago. Sunday, February 6; 2100 hours.
"You owe it to yourself."

From his balcony on the thirty-fourth floor of the Tiara
Marriott, Henry Jacobi looked out across a breathtaking view
of Chicago and the lakefront. The crosstown glidetrain moved
through the sea of light. "I don't think so," he said, without
turning.

Carson had thought he knew the older man. Consequently
he had come with full confidence that when presented with
the facts, and the possibilities, Henry would relent, would cast
his personal demons overboard. Would accept his responsibility to take command of what might become *the* epochal
mission.

"No," Jacobi said into the silence that drew out between
them. "You'll have to do this one without me."

"Why, Henry?"

"My God, Carson, don't you know what's been going on
at the Academy? You put my name on this mission and it's
dead." He turned, came away from the railing. "I appreciate
your coming. And God knows I appreciate the offer. But not

this time. The Institute has a good job for me here. I'll be doing what I like, and it's low profile."

The air off the lake was cool. Carson lifted his glass. The ice cubes clinked. "Good Scotch," he said.

Henry sat down, grunting with the effort. "It's not what you think. I can live with the events. But I want to see you succeed. That at least will give the events at the Temple some meaning." His eyes were dark. "Have you picked your crew yet?"

"Yes," said Carson. "I'd like to run it by you."

"No." He pulled his sweater tight. "It's *your* call. You'll have to live with it. How many are you taking?"

"We'll have five. Counting me."

"And Ed has approved it?"

"Yes."

"Good. He needs something spectacular, or *he's* going to be out here, in the adjoining lecture hall." The broad, friendly-mutt features lit up. "Good luck, Frank. Give 'em hell."

Arlington. Monday, February 7; 1000 hours.

"I was hoping you'd ask."

"How could you think we might not, Hutch?"

"I wasn't really sure you'd want me." She managed her game smile. "Thanks."

Beta Pacifica was two hundred twenty-five light-years from Earth. Again, on the edge of the Void. Fifty-five light-years from Quraqua. "What's the radio signal like?" she asked. They had been very secretive. Had in fact sworn her to say nothing of the pending mission.

"Continuous repetitive patterns. Every few seconds, sometimes. No long segment ever completely repeats, but there are patterns that seem to be variations of each other. Coming from a single transmitter."

"A *single* transmitter?"

"Yes. As far as we can tell, the sender never gets a response."

"That seems odd. Maybe we just can't hear it."

"Probably. Ed thinks it's a beacon. Incidentally, the source of the transmission is probably not on a planetary surface."

"What makes you think that?"

"It's several AUs from the star, and it's in a polar orbit. A *polar* orbit, Hutch."

They hugged. "It was *put* there," she said, squeezing hard.

• • •

Langley Park, Maryland. Monday, February 7; 1930 hours.

The entry bell sounded, the display blinked on, and Maggie looked at Frank Carson. He knew, of course, that he was on camera, but he still could not entirely conceal his impatience. Carson never changed: he liked things to happen according to schedule, disliked even the slightest delay. He wore a yellow wool pullover and cuffed dark-blue skims. She thought of him as a good detail man, somebody who ensured that equipment was maintained and supplies arrived on time. But the price of that kind of talent seemed to be a kind of overwhelming grayness. Carson was impossibly *dull*. He was well-meaning, even indispensable. But he was dreary company. She keyed the downstairs lock.

"Door's open, Frank," she said. She pushed back from her notepads and sketches, blanked the monitor, which resumed its wall-panel appearance. She'd lost track of time. It was too late to do a cleanup now, but the room was cluttered rather than dusty. She could live with that. Maggie had no idea why Carson had asked to see her. It couldn't be social, and it wouldn't be connected with the Oz inscription; she had already solved that for them. What was left?

Possibly, they were planning some sort of formal expression of appreciation for her. If that were so, she'd be happy to accept. And they might have sent Carson to arrange it, try to get her to show up at the appropriate place without giving away the game.

Maggie was still luxuriating in the afterglow of having deciphered the horgon lines. (That she had found the final elements of the solution among texts already present in the data banks, that the last-minute material sent up by Henry and Richard had *helped*, but might not have been necessary, she had told no one. The fact tarnished her achievement slightly, and left her vaguely resentful, but against whom or what she was not entirely certain.) She had been working on her notebooks since their return, and was now in the process of deciding what she would do next. Academy policy was to rotate field and home assignments, and she had offers from Oxford, Harvard, CIT, and the Institute for Advanced Studies.

The door opened to reveal Carson. "Hello, Maggie," he said.

She extended her hand. "Hi, Frank. Good to see you."

Conversation had always been difficult between them, and she felt the thickness in the air already. Carson was a master of the inconsequential; *she* had no use for small talk.

"I'm sorry to bother you at home."

"It's okay." There was an odd sense of worlds coming together. Carson belonged light-years away. She indicated a chair, and sat beside him. "Frank, what can I get you?"

"Nothing, thanks."

"You're sure?"

"Yes," he said. "Nice apartment."

"Thank you." She *was* proud of it. Tasteful furniture, walls lined with technical texts and novels, framed ideographs and poetry from the *Knothic Hours*, in the original.

"D.C. changed while we were away." He went on for some minutes in a superficial vein, commenting on the unseasonal warmth; the likelihood of rain; the local outbreak of CORE, the African virus that induced a kind of super rickets.

Maggie sighed and waited. When she saw her chance, she asked what was happening. Translation: Why are you here?

His gaze intensified. "Maggie," he said, "we're going out again."

That surprised her. "Who is?" she asked. "Out where?"

"The inscription points to Beta Pacifica. It's in the same area, along the edge of the Arm."

Maggie had not really believed they would pin down a candidate. At least not so quickly. She'd expected the effort would take years. "Why not let a survey ship take a look at it?"

"Because we think they're still there." He paused for effect. "Maggie, we've picked up radio transmissions." His eyes were big and round and very full. Maggie Tufu had never been given to emotional demonstrations. Particularly not with Frank Carson. But now she jabbed a fist in the air. "Magnificent," she said. "Am I invited?"

The Academy. Wednesday, February 16; 1345 hours.

Ed Horner looked up as Carson entered. "Good to see you, Frank," he said. "Is everything ready?"

Carson nodded. "Yes. We're all set."

"Very good." He rose, came around the edge of the desk. He looked hard at Carson, as if he were trying to see past him, to calculate odds. "Since there *is* a signal, we are going to find *something*. But I want to impress on you that your task is limited to establishing whether there is anything there that warrants a full mission. *If they actually exist*, I do not want details. Do you understand? I want you to make the determination and come back with a recommendation. If they're there, keep in mind we know nothing about them. Don't stop to chitchat. Don't let them see you. Get in and get out—"

"We will," said Carson.

"Incidentally, your departure time has been moved up. You've got forty-eight hours."

Carson opened his mouth to protest.

"You'll need to let your people know," the commissioner continued. "I know this puts you on a short schedule, but we're under pressure. Hard questions are being asked in high places. I'm not sure how long we can hold the lid on this operation."

Carson's mouth clamped firmly on whatever it was he was going to say. "Thank you," he said, finally.

"Don't bother." Horner held out his hand. "Just come back to us."

Hutch and Carson left Atlanta Launch at sunset. The shuttle was filled with passengers, mostly wealthy sightseers who would be outward bound tomorrow on the *Estrata*. Interstellar tourism was developing into a growth industry. Those wealthy enough to pay for the privilege could sail past neutron stars; watch from short range the deadly dance between Delta Aquilae and its massive companion; cruise past the Great Maelstrom on Beta Carinis IV; navigate the smoking marble flatlands of Lesser Culhagne, the Cold Star. And end the voyage with dinner in the shadow of Holtzmyer's Rock on Pinnacle.

They were mostly couples, middle-aged and older, well-dressed, excited by the views of Earth and Moon. There were a few children, some station personnel, and two men who turned out to be theoretical physicists working on artificial gravity.

One was a tall, garrulous black with a gray beard and knife-sharp features. His colleague was a taciturn Japanese who watched Hutch with eyes that were full of suggestion.

The black man's name was Laconda, and he reminded Hutch of her old high-school algebra teacher.

She commented that she'd always understood that artificial gravity was impossible, and Laconda responded with talk about high-energy particles, guide paths controlled by magnetic fields, and local space warps. Hutch got lost quickly, but she understood enough to ask whether the method, if it worked, could not also be used to produce anti-gravity?

Laconda smiled, pleased by the aptness of his student. "Yes," he said. "That should follow. And the critical point is that very little energy would be needed."

"Cheap anti-gravity?" Carson's eyebrows rose. "Makes you wonder where it will all end."

The physicist glowed with satisfaction. "The future is coming very quickly," he said, glancing toward Hutch to gauge her reaction, "and we need to be prepared for it." He oiled through the phrase with smooth precision.

Hutch was still considering the possibilities when they began their approach to the Wheel. True anti-gravity. Not the parlor magic stuff of superconductivity, but a real low-cost system that would negate mass and resistance. The power needs of the world would plummet. "You could," she told Carson, "move a sofa with the flick of a wrist. Sail over New York without an aircraft. We'd no longer be tied to the ground, and our individual strength would go to infinite." She grew thoughtful. "It would be a new kind of life."

"It's science fiction," said Carson. "It'll never happen."

The Japanese looked up from his computer, glanced around to assure himself that Laconda was out of earshot, and said quietly: "Your friend is right, young lady. It's a crock. The thing's a government grant, it'll never work, and Laconda knows it."

Hutch was glad to see the *Winckelmann* again. She strode down the access tunnel, entered the main port, which was at the top of the ship, crossed the bridge (a technician was running queries on the navigation systems), dumped her bags on the deck, and began an inspection tour. She was not so pressed for time that she could not have gone to her station quarters, but she enjoyed the sense of security and comfort within the familiar bulkheads.

There was a framed picture of Cal on her worktable, taken two years ago. Shortly after they'd met. He was wearing the outsize green golfer's hat that she'd once thought so charming. Still did, actually. She picked the picture up and slipped it face down into the upper right-hand drawer. Long past time—

Maintenance people were wandering through the ship. Hutch went down to C ring to check supplies. The inventory showed food and water for six people for eight months. She conducted a physical check, and signed off.

Two hours later, she met Carson in Vega South. He was every bit as anxious as she was to be away. "I would hate to get shut down now," he said.

"Relax. We'll be fine."

They sat at a corner table sipping drinks. "This is all happening pretty fast," he said. "We need to think a little about how this expedition should be run, what we want to accomplish, where things might go wrong. For example, what do we do if there actually *is* a functioning supercivilization?"

"We get out as quickly as we can, and come back and report. I thought you said Horner made that clear."

"But we can report *without* physically coming back. Are we really sending a team of researchers all that way just to push an alarm?"

"I assume he doesn't want another disaster."

"But how do you *avoid* risk? Look: if we come back and say somebody's out there, and it's somebody who had star flight twenty thousand years ago, how is *anyone* going to approach them safely? No. What he really wants is some hard data. But he can't tell us that flat out. He has to assume we'll be smart enough to understand. If they're there, we bring back enough details to make it possible to plan a follow-up mission. But how much is *enough*?"

Earth glowed softly in sunlight.

"Is this the same conversation you told me about?"

"You've got to read between the lines a little, Hutch. He doesn't want us losing the ship, or letting them know we're around." He looked better than she'd ever seen him. He had lost weight, his energy level was up, and he was grinning like a big kid. "But he needs more than a go/no-go."

Well, whatever, she thought. In any case, she expected to enjoy herself. It was, after all, the flight that Richard had always hoped to make.

• • •

Janet Allegri and George Hackett arrived shortly after 0715. They came together, arm in arm. Janet looked fresh and enterprising, ready to go. She wore a blue and white jumpsuit with a Quraqua mission patch. Her blond hair was cut short, military style, and she moved with her customary flounce. Hutch was surprised by a jealous twinge.

George walked easily at her side, one stride for every two of hers. A sweater was knotted round his neck, and he swung an imitation leather athletic bag. They might have been headed for an outing in the park.

Hutch met them at the top of the exit ramp. Both had been out of the D.C. area since their return from the Temple, and she had seen neither. They embraced and exchanged greetings. "You said you weren't going to do any more field trips," she told George. "Get tired of the home front that quickly?"

He grinned. "No," he said. "Frank asked me to come, so I came." He hesitated. "I also knew *you'd* be along."

Hutch caught Janet's Oho,-what-have-we-here? expression. "Thank you," she said, enjoying the moment. It was good to know she wasn't completely overshadowed.

She led them into the *Wink*, showed them where to stow their bags, and distributed mission patches and mugs. They featured an eighteenth-century four-master under full sail through an ocean of clouds, beneath a prominent star. The legends *Beta Pacifica* appeared at the top, and *Onward* at the bottom.

When they were settled, they wandered casually through the ship, talking about what they'd been doing, and about the mission. Hutch explained how they'd tracked down Beta Pac, and put a diagram of the signal on a monitor. "Hard to see a pattern anywhere," said Janet.

"It's *there*," Hutch said.

George watched for a while. "Who else knows?" he asked.

"We've kept it quiet," Hutch said. "Hardly anybody, other than the commissioner."

"And he's letting us go after it?"

"I think he feels that since *we* tracked it down, it's ours."

"More likely," said Janet, "he figures it's a long shot, and he wants the results in hand before he mentions it to anybody. No point looking foolish again."

Flight luggage arrived. They all went down to get it and were dragging it back to their quarters when Carson charged through the main airlock. "Hello, George," he said, shaking hands. "Is Maggie here yet? We need Maggie."

"We haven't seen her," said Hutch. "What's the problem?"

He looked flustered. "The results from the Tindle were routinely passed to higher authority."

Hutch shrugged. "That doesn't surprise me."

"No. But apparently somebody actually *read* them. It looks as if they figured out what the implications are. Horner's people learned that they are about to be told Beta Pac is off limits until further notice. If that happens, he'll have no choice but to stop the mission."

"How'd you find out?" asked Janet.

"The commissioner's private secretary." He was looking at his watch and an empty approach tunnel. "He wants us out and gone."

Hutch was trying to think it through. "They can't communicate with us in hyper. How much time have we got?"

"Don't know. We'd better assume it could come at any time."

"The ship's ready to go. I'll only need a few minutes to run through the checklist. If we can get clearance from Flight Ops."

"See if you can reach Maggie," said Carson.

Janet pointed to the monitor. "No need," she said. Maggie Tufu was outside carrying an overnight case.

Hutch called Flight Ops. While she was getting departure information, Maggie made her entrance. Stern and striking, she was an intimidating presence. She greeted them, and her dark eyes glanced perfunctorily around the room, hesitating momentarily when they encountered Janet. She did not seem to notice Hutch.

The Traffic Controller gave Hutch a choice. "If you can get out at 0810, it's a go." That gave them fifteen minutes. "Otherwise, we don't have another post until 1630 hours." That wouldn't be much better than the original departure time.

"We'll be ready," she said. "Put us on the log."

Maggie turned toward Hutch. "Have my bags arrived yet?" She saw no activity in the luggage chute. "No."

"You may have to leave them," said Carson.

"You're kidding." Maggie's expression changed, but it did not grow dour, as Hutch had expected. Instead, it took on an impish quality. "I'll be a little short of clothes." She showed them the overnight case.

"We've got plenty of coveralls on board," said Hutch. "Several sizes."

Maggie did not object, but looked ruefully at the overnighter. "I didn't realize we were in *that* much of a hurry. Don't we have several hours yet?"

"They're trying to cancel the mission," said Carson.

"Hutchins," she said, "can you determine when my luggage will get here?"

Not this side of Christmas, honey, I hope. "It's still in the sorter," she reported gravely. Too bad. Have to do without.

Maggie looked for sympathy. "Any possibility we can wait?"

"First contact in the nude," Janet said, grinning.

"It's in the pipe," said Hutch. "There isn't anything we can do to hurry it along."

Carson looked uncomfortable. "How long?" he asked Hutch.

"Maybe a half hour."

"Have to do without, then," said Carson.

The console chimed. "Preflights check out." Hutch said. "We have permission to depart."

Maggie took a long deep breath. "Let's go," she said, turning toward Janet. "You're close to my size. A little hefty, maybe. But if we take your stuff in a bit, we should do fine. Right?"

17.

_____

On board NCA Winckelmann. *Friday, February 18; 1025 GMT.*

They rode outward from the sun. *Winckelmann's* twin Hazeltine engines were fully charged, and she could have made the insertion into transdimensional space at any time, but regulations set minimum standards to avoid backwash. Her flight plan called for a jump in twenty hours.

Carson sat with Hutch on the bridge. He was an odd mix that day: delighted that they were finally on their way, fearful that the recall might come, uneasy about the nature of the mission itself. "It's hard to plan for," he said. "I hate going into a situation blind."

"That's what makes it interesting," said Hutch. The atmosphere was thick. They had both been glancing frequently at the communications console. "Maybe we ought to take out some insurance against getting canceled."

"How can we do that?"

"We should probably have a communication malfunction." She checked the time. "We're due to file a movement report in a few minutes. I'll garble it. That'll establish the problem for official purposes. After that, we don't respond to anything. Once we're in hyper they can't talk to us in any event. When we get to Beta Pac, we can effect repairs, or not, depending on events."

"Do it," he said.

"Okay. Now I have a question for *you*. If we get positive results from this trip, is it likely to help get Henry off the hook?"

Carson didn't think so. "It can't hurt. But the Academy is in a corner. If they don't act against him, then they're in effect condoning his action. They can't afford to do that. No.

226

Maybe history will do right by him. The Academy won't. And the media won't." He looked at her, and she could read the pain in his eyes. "And maybe they're right. He *is* responsible."

He fell silent, took out his notepad, and drifted away from her. After a while, he began writing. Hutch had detected a change in Frank Carson since the Temple. Like Henry, he seemed to have aged. He was more reflective, less optimistic. Despite the bravado talk about going beyond the mission parameters, she sensed he would be more cautious than he might have been a few months earlier.

She caught a glimpse of a title in his notebook, and smiled: CARSON AT BETA PAC. It sounded like Napoleon in Egypt, Schliemann at Troy, Costikan at Pinnacle. *I hope you make it, Frank.*

She turned her attention to the movement report, brought it up on her screen, and garbled the back half of it. No way they could misunderstand: *Wink* has a communications problem. She hit the Transmit button.

The response was almost immediate.

WINCKELMANN: SAY AGAIN YOUR MR08.

Okay, she thought. *We're in business.*

A few hours later, while Hutch was making final enhancements for the transdimensional insertion, the message board chimed again. Hutch assumed it would be another request for a communication status check. But this was altogether different:

WINCKELMANN FROM ACADEMY: ABORT MISSION AND RETURN. ABORT REPEAT ABORT. PLS ACKNOWLEDGE. HORNER.

She cleared the screen and switched on the ship's intercom. "We'll be making our jump in eleven minutes. Everybody belt down. Please respond to the bridge."

She showed the message to Carson. "We never received it," he said.

Still, they both felt better when the stars went out and the fog closed around the ship.

That evening, after dinner, Carson held a general briefing. The first question: What was known about Beta Pac? "Not much," he admitted. "No survey ship has visited it, or been anywhere close for that matter. Class G star, about three billion years older than the Sun. Located along the edge of the Void."

"So we have no idea," said Janet, "what's waiting for us?"

"None," said Carson.

Maggie pressed her fingers together. "This signal," she asked, "started on its way at about the beginning of the twentieth century. Have we made any attempt to find out whether the source is still active? Did we check with any other stations?"

Carson nodded. "We asked Nok to try to get a reading for us, and the *Ashley Tee*, which is our closest survey ship. Neither heard anything, but that could be because they're out of effective range for their receivers. The signal the Tindle picked up wasn't much more than a whisper."

"Three centuries is not a long time," said George, "if these are the people who built Oz eleven thousand years ago."

"So what's the plan?" asked Janet. "What do we do when we get there?"

Carson was all business. "We're homing on the signal. We're going to make the jump back into standard space as close to the source as we can. It's hard to formulate a strategy beyond that. We've been directed not to make contact, if they're there. And not to allow ourselves to be seen. But we want to find out who's home. And bring back whatever details we can. To that end, by the way, we will make no transmissions while we are in the Beta Pac system."

Maggie leaned forward attentively. They were gathered around a table. "Let me play devil's advocate for a moment. We may be talking about a civilization with twenty thousand years of development. Possibly a lot more. Does anyone really believe we can sneak in, take a look, and leave undetected?"

"We don't know they've had twenty thousand years of development," said Janet. "They could be frozen in place. Or in a dark age."

Carson agreed. "We can imagine all kinds of possibilities. Let's just take normal precautions. And play the rest by ear."

Maggie looked annoyed. "Why would an advanced race care whether we wandered in or not? That seems a trifle arrogant to me. I suggest we sail right up to the front door, and show the flag. No pussyfooting around. That might get their respect right off the bat."

"You could be right, but that's a direct violation of my instructions. We won't do it that way."

Hutch was not officially a member of the expedition, and consequently not entitled to express an opinion. Still, she was responsible for the safety of the ship. "I think," she said, "we should take the possibility of hostile response seriously."

"They won't be a threat," insisted Maggie.

Janet peered at her over the top of a teacup. "Why not?"

"If they're advanced, they're rational. Unprovoked hostility is *ir*rational. And if they're not advanced, we don't have to worry about their hostility." Her tone was that of a harried instructor.

George listened quietly through most of the discussion. Eventually, he asked about the Academy's view. "Who does Horner expect us to find? Is there a real chance these are the Monument-Makers?"

"Ed doesn't know any more than we do," Carson said.

"I'll give you a straight answer," Maggie told George. "If there's anyone at Beta Pac, it won't be the Monument-Makers."

Hutch was surprised and irritated by the conviction in her voice. "How can you be so sure?" she asked.

"It might be the same *race*," Maggie explained. "But the Monument-Makers are gone. Just as the classical Greeks are gone. I mean, no one seems to be running around making Monuments anymore. Haven't for thousands of years. But the Monuments *do* imply that a long-lived, stable civilization once existed. Anybody want to speculate what happens to a culture that survives for twenty thousand years? Does it become highly advanced? Or moribund? Does it develop in some oblique way?"

"Check out China," said Janet. "Or Egypt. Or India. *Our* experience is that durability is not necessarily *good*."

Later, Hutch took Carson aside. "Let's talk worst-case scenario for a moment. What happens if we arrive and are promptly attacked?"

"Why do you ask?"

"Give me an answer first."

"We clear out."

"Okay. But you should be aware, for planning purposes, that after we jump into Beta Pac space, we will need a minimum of fourteen hours to recharge the engines. We are not going to be able to clear out on a moment's notice. No matter what."

He nodded. "Okay. Let's hope we don't have a problem."

Hutch had not forgotten Maggie's willingness to sacrifice her comrades. She didn't like harboring grudges, and her professional responsibilities militated against allowing her feelings to show. She made a pact with herself, to accept Maggie Tufu, with the reservation that, in a crisis, she would not trust the woman's judgment.

Of her four passengers, Maggie was the only one who still qualified as a stranger. Hutch had not had an opportunity to spend any time with her at the Temple, or on the flight from Quraqua.

She was polite enough. But the woman saw everything as simplistic or ironic, and seemed to take nothing seriously other than the professional issues raised by her work.

Despite her presence, this group, unlike others Hutch had carried, showed no tendency to fragment. No one hung back, no one spent inordinate amounts of time in a compartment, no one got buried in the cybernet to the exclusion of all else. Even Maggie came around after a few days, shedding much of her arrogance. She took time to engage in occasional small talk, although it was clear she found it not particularly stimulating. She also revealed an uncommon skill at poker. Gradually, Carson discovered that she had an interest in military affairs. George commented that she was much more sociable here than she had ever been on Quraqua, and Hutch wondered whether they were being driven together by the approach of the unknown.

They gathered every evening after dinner, and the conversations ranged over a world of topics. Somehow, out here, terrestrial problems seemed more clinical, more amenable to solution. Plans were brought forward to combat starvation and reduce population, to stop wars and perhaps end international rivalry once and for all, to deal with teenage sexuality, and improve the public schools. They agreed that all the plans, however, had something of a fascist ring. There was a tendency, between the stars, to lose patience with disorder.

They debated whether it was really possible for a social structure to survive intact for tens of thousands of years. Janet argued that that kind of stability would necessarily imply "damn near absolute rigidity. The place would be a literal hell."

They talked about the Monument-Makers, and about the discontinuities. And eventually they began to talk about the things that really mattered to them. Hutch learned that the woman in Carson's photo had run off with a securities dealer, that Maggie was morbidly afraid of death, that Janet had trouble attracting reasonable men. "I don't know why," she confessed, and Hutch suspected it was true. Most men she had known would have felt threatened by Janet Allegri, would never have felt comfortable in her presence.

George, she decided, wanted to excel so that a young woman who had walked off years ago would regret her choice.

And Hutch? She wasn't sure what she gave away. She was careful not to mention Cal, and she didn't talk about Richard. But Janet told her years later that she had first come to understand Hutch when she described her fear and humiliation while Janet took on the strider. "I promised myself I would never stand by again," Janet quoted her as saying. And she added, herself: "I liked that."

As for the mission, one series of questions was central: if these were, indeed, the Monument-Makers, would they remember their visit to the solar system? Would they remember their own great days?

"Oz," said George, when asked to produce a question for the aliens. "I want to know why they built Oz."

The evening gatherings quickly took on a ceremonial aspect. They toasted one another and the commissioner and Beta Pac. Mission symbols and patches, worn on Academy blue, became *de rigueur*. Whatever reserve was left drained away, and they relaxed in each other's company. They joked, and laughed, and required everyone to produce entertainments. There were magic tricks and monologues and sing-alongs. Maggie, reluctant at first to join in, demonstrated an ability to impersonate the voices and mannerisms of everyone on board. She'd captured Carson's military demeanor and George's back-country accent; she caught Hutch's trick of tilting her head when puzzled, and Janet's slightly voluptuous stance.

They staged a dance (ties for gentlemen, skirts for ladies), and they began running an improvisational comedy, *Great Excavations*, in which a group of misfits at a mythical dig took turns trying to fleece and bed one another.

Hutch enjoyed the fun and games, which always seemed to work well within the closed belly of a starship where human companionship counted for so much. Night after night, they talked into the early hours, and Hutch felt the bonds among them strengthening.

Near the end of the third week, Maggie took her aside. "I wanted you to know," she said, "that I'm sorry about Richard."

"Thank you," Hutch responded, surprised.

"I didn't know you were so close, or I would have said something earlier. I think I was a little stupid."

"It's okay." Hutch felt a wave of regret. Not sure why.

Maggie looked uncertain. "I know a lot of people think Henry is getting a bad deal. They think *I'm* responsible for what happened." Her dark eyes found Hutch, and held her. "I think they're right." Her voice caught. "I'm sorry," she said again. "We did the right thing. Richard knew that. That's why he was there. But I wish it could have turned out differently."

Hutch nodded. Maggie hesitated, opened her arms, and they embraced. Maggie's cheek was warm and wet.

Hutch lived by her rule; she maintained a cautious demeanor toward George. She had been delighted at his inclusion in the mission, but she also recognized that his presence necessarily created a difficult situation. His eyes lingered on her through the long evenings, darting quickly away when she looked back. They brightened when she spoke to him, became animated when she asked his opinion about the topic of the hour. His voice softened noticeably in her presence, and his breathing downshifted.

She would have liked to talk frankly with George, explain why she was not responding. She did not, after all, want to discourage him. But she could say nothing until he provided the opportunity by making an overt move.

When it came, she blew it.

They had fallen into the habit of pronouncing each session formally closed with a midnight toast, and marking off another day on the mission calendar which Carson had constructed and placed on a bulkhead in the lounge. (The everpresent four-master loomed above the five weeks and two days allotted for the outbound flight.) On the twenty-sixth evening, George had seemed especially vulnerable. He had seated himself across from her, where he could demonstrate monumental unconcern. But color went to his cheeks early in the session, and stayed there.

When the group broke up, he approached her. "Hutch," he said in his most serious manner, "can we walk?"

Her pulse fluttered. "Of course."

They descended into the lower reaches of the ship. The configuration had changed for this mission. She was still carrying three rings, but they were smaller. The vast cargo areas had been removed; the living quarters were reduced. There was still ample space to store artifacts, should the need arise, but Hutch no longer felt she was walking into an aircraft hangar. This *Wink* would present a considerably smaller target to scanners.

"Hutch," he said almost timidly, "you're one of the loveliest women I've ever seen."

"Thank you," she said.

"When we get back, I'd like to have an evening with you. Just us."

Yes. "We can do that."

He was very near, not quite touching her, his breath warm and uneven. She steered them toward a viewport. Outside, the mist of the interdimensional world drifted slowly past. They might have been in an old house on the edge of a moor.

"It's like *you*," he said, watching the fog. "You can't see into it, you can't quite get hold of it, and it keeps moving."

She laughed. They both did. And she made the first move. It was subtle enough, and would not have been noticeable to a bystander: she *leaned* in his direction, a mere centimeter or so. A signal passed between them, and she sensed his body make its own decision.

"Hutch—"

He reached out, tentatively, and touched her hair. His lips were very close.

Hutch felt her tides begin to run. Fingertips touched. Flanks brushed. His eyes held her. His hands curled around her shoulders, and her cheek touched his. It was warm. She was up on her toes, lips parted, open, waiting.

The moment expanded. Her breathing, her heartbeat, melted to his. Breasts, protected only by the flimsy material of her work uniform, touched him. He bent to her, met her mouth with his own, not pressing her. She accepted him, let him explore the thrust of her lips. Her heart hammered, and she lost her breath. When finally he broke away, she caught the nape of his neck, softly, firmly, and drew him back.

She had one final moment of clarity, of reluctance, and then folded herself against him, inviting him, becoming part of him. She had to get up on her toes to reach him, but she loved it. His fingers brushed her right breast, lingered, drew away.

She'd been on flights which featured people padding between rooms in the middle of the night. She didn't want any part of that. "Come with me," she said.

He moved silently behind her.

"Only tonight," she said.

His hand settled on her shoulder, touched her throat. And then he stopped. "Hutch," he said, "do you *really* want to do this?"

Yes, you fool.

She led him into the shuttle bay. The *Alpha* lay in its cradle, shadowy, silent, potent. The cockpit windows glittered in the uncertain light. (They had replaced the damaged tread, bent by the tsunami.)

He swung her easily off the floor, strode across the deck, and paused at the shuttle cargo door. He jabbed at the release mechanism, but nothing happened.

She did it for him; there was a maintenance seal that had to be removed.

He ducked inside with her, found a blanket, and spread it out.

"You didn't answer my question," he said as he bent to her again. "Because I don't want to spoil anything. I love you, Hutch."

She kissed his cheek. Drew his head down. "Be careful what you say. I might hold you to it."

"Now and forever," he said. The response was sufficiently artificial that she almost laughed. But he added, solemnly, "I mean it, Hutch."

What waited at Beta Pac? Maybe they were being invited to join the Galactic League. Or to receive a history and detailed atlas of the Milky Way, with its civilizations and its points of interest and its rest stops. Carson sprawled comfortably in his chair, feet propped up. "How do you suppose an individual in such a culture would define fulfillment?" he asked. "What would they want out of their lives?"

"Same as us," said Janet.

George sipped dark wine. "What would that be?" he asked.

"Power," she said. "And love."

"It's impossible to know," said Carson. "That's why they're *alien*."

Hutch sat with a book open on her lap. "But we *are* able to understand alien mythologies, at least the ones we've encountered so far. Which means we are motivated by the same drives." She thought once again about the footprints across the ridge on Iapetus. "I would guess they'd live, as we do, for achievement. To *do* something. And to want others to know what they've done. That's the whole point of the Monuments."

The wall panels were open, and the internal lights played off the fog. There was always a sense of something just beyond the limits of vision. Hutch remembered an old story that pilots who had gone outside during transdimensional flight occasionally heard voices.

George kept their bargain and stayed at a distance. She was pleased that he understood the need for discretion, and that he refrained from demonstrating the possessiveness which was so often the immediate downside of a sexual encounter. There was no second event. Both had been around long enough to recognize the damage that pairing up does to a small team on an extended mission. So they strove for the same pleasant amiability with each other that they displayed toward each of their colleagues. In Hutch's case, at least, it required no small effort.

Unlike her personal life, *Wink* glided placidly through the veils. It never trembled, never quivered, never accelerated. No inner systems quickened, and of course it received no messages from outside.

Hutch enjoyed doing simmies with this crew. She portrayed a series of love interests attached to cynical antiheroes, like Margo Colby in *Blue Light* and Ilsa in *Casablanca*. George charmed her as Antoine in the one, and Carson was appropriately vulnerable as Rick in the other. (It showed her a side of his personality that she had not anticipated. And she was

moved almost to tears when George/Antoine left her behind
and rode to his death near Moscow.)

Carson had a taste for open-air historical spectaculars. He
looked dashing, if a little beefy, as Antony at Actium, astride
a white charger, the sun glittering against his horsehair helmet. Maggie was, they agreed, sensational as Cleopatra.

When it was her turn to choose, Maggie inevitably went for
the MacIver Thomson cliffhangers, in which she excelled as
the quintessential damsel in distress. (It struck Hutch as odd
that their most intellectual member would opt for thrillers.)
And, by God, she was good: she screamed her way through
Now the Dawn, hunted by the members of a bloodthirsty
cult; fled the maniacal clown Napoleon through the deserted
amusement park in *Laugh by Night*; and fought off Brother
Thaddeus, the murderous monk, in *Things That Are Caesar's*,
while her would-be rescuer, the globe-trotting adventurer Jack
Hancock (George), tried to recover from a vicious whack
on the head and an attack in the rook tower by a pair of
eagles.

Janet specialized in women gone wrong. She portrayed
Lady Macbeth with such pleasure and malevolence that Janet
herself, seated beside Hutch, was chilled. (Watching acquaintances in the classic roles added an extra dimension to the
experience, provided they were good. It all depended on
the energy level and passion that one could provide to the
mix.) Janet was also the scheming Mary Parker in *Roads
to Rome*, and Katherine in *Bovalinda*. "You have a taste for
power," Carson remarked while she was seizing control of a
metals consortium and simultaneously plotting to murder an
uncooperative husband.

"Yeah." Her face glowed. "Damn right."

Hutch discovered something about herself during the evening they watched *Things That Are Caesar's*. There is an
all-out, no-holds-barred love scene in a rock pool within
an abandoned monastery. And it was with an uncomfortable
stirring in her breast that Hutch saw George, *her* George,
close in on Maggie for a long aquatic grapple. It wasn't
really George, of course, any more than it was really Maggie.
It wasn't even their bodies: the subjects had supplied only
fully clothed images and personality ranges; the computer
had generated the rest. But Hutch felt a rising heat all the

same, and she could not avoid a sidewise glance at Maggie, who was enjoying herself. As was George, sitting with a silly smirk.

Beta Pacifica was somewhat smaller than Sol, and slightly cooler. The radio source was located fifteen AUs from the star. "We should materialize within fifty thousand kilometers of the target," said Hutch as they began waiting for Navigation to signal that a jump was imminent.

"We won't hit it, will we?" asked Janet.

"Chances are thin." Hutch grinned. "Fifty thousand kilometers is a lot of space. There's a better chance that both Hazeltines will fail."

"That's not necessarily reassuring," said Janet. "You're assuming it's a station. What if the source is on a planet?"

"There's no appreciable probability of that," said Carson. "Anyhow, the mass detectors would pick up any significant gravity well and cancel the jump. Right?" He looked toward Hutch.

"Right," she agreed.

Carson brought up a star chart. "We're back in our old stomping ground," he said. That was approximately true: Pinnacle, Quraqua, Nok, and the Beta Pac system were all located along the rim of the Orion Arm.

"Party time's over," said Janet as they closed to within a few hours of their ETA. "Time to go to work."

LIBRARY ENTRY

(Scene 221 from Things That Are Caesar's: Ann Holloway is carried by the giant monk, Brother Thaddeus, through an underground passage into a rock chamber. She is stunned, and only begins to recover consciousness as he sets her down. She is wearing an evening dress, but it has been partially ripped away, exposing a shoulder and the upper curve of one breast. Brother Thaddeus, in obedience to his vows, shows no interest. He removes his sash and uses it to tie her wrists. When he has finished, he drags her across the stone floor toward an iron ring in the wall.)

THADDEUS
(Starting to secure her to the ring)
    No need to pretend, little one. I know
you are awake.

ANN
(Stirring, confused, most of the fight now out of her)
    Please don't.
            (Looks around wildly.)
Jack? Where are you?

THADDEUS
He is past helping you, child. He is
past helping anyone.
        *(Opens a panel in the wall,
    revealing a switch. Zoom on switch.)*

ANN
        (Tries to cover herself)
Let me go. Let me go, and I'll tell no
one.

THADDEUS
I'm not afraid of what you can tell,
Ann Holloway.

ANN
Then why kill me?

THADDEUS
*(Pulls the switch. We hear the sound of running water.
A stream begins to gush into the chamber from above.)*
    I have no intention of killing you. It
is your past that condemns you. Your
long nights of illicit pleasure cry out
for atonement.

ANN
No! It's not true. You're crazy.

THADDEUS
(Sounding genuinely sorry; water gushes over her.)

Have courage, child. God's cleansing
waves will save you yet. It is your
only path to paradise.

ANN
*(Strains at the chain. The torn blouse falls open, revealing
still more, but she is well past worrying about it. Camera
in close as she struggles.)*
Jack—

THADDEUS
*(Pauses at the entrance to the chamber, prepared to
close the heavy stone door.)*
Pray, my dear. It will ease your
passage.

*(She screams. He begins to close the door. Water pours
into the chamber.)*
The peace of the Lord be with you.
*(Bows his head. Camera in close. He hears something
behind him, turns. Camera looks past him, down the
passageway. Jack stands silhouetted in flickering torch-
light.)*

JACK
Where is she, you madman?

THADDEUS
(Surprised to see him.)
Hancock? Do you really still live?

ANN
(Desperate)
Jack! I'm in here.

THADDEUS
You should have accepted the grace the
Lord gave you, and stayed away.

JACK
(Advancing)
Hang on, Ann.

THADDEUS

*(Closes the door behind him, sealing off Ann, and blocking
the passageway.)*
> You cannot help her. Best prepare for
> your own judgment, which is very close.

*(Touches the crucifix which hangs on a thin chain about
his neck.)*
> The wicked are like the chaff which the
> wind drives away. The wicked shall not
> stand.

*(Moves forward. They close in combat, and Thaddeus'
greater size gives him an immediate advantage. He quickly
forces Jack back, removes a cord from his robes, and loops
it around Jack's neck. Meantime, cutaway shows water
rising rapidly in the chamber. Ann struggles, etc. Holding
Jack temporarily helpless, Thaddeus hauls him back along
the corridor until he reaches the torch. Here, there is a
lever in the wall. He pulls it, and a pit opens at their
feet. A few rocks drop into the dark, and it is a long
time before we hear them land. He drags Jack toward
the edge of the pit. Jack breaks free, and the struggle
rages while the water rises around Ann.)*

THADDEUS

> For you, O God, delight not in
> wickedness; no evil man remains with
> you; the arrogant may not stand in your
> sight.

*(The water passes Ann's waist. She is thoroughly
drenched, of course, and thoroughly revealed. Outside,
Jack seizes the torch and uses it to break away. The men
struggle at the edge of the pit. Ann's shoulders go under,
and her screams fill the chamber. Jack is down on one
knee, forced relentlessly into the pit.)*

THADDEUS

> Ask forgiveness, Hancock. This is your
> last chance to save your immortal soul.

JACK

> You crazy son of a bitch.

THADDEUS
Then I ask pardon in your name. The
Lord forgive you.
*(Secure in the knowledge he has won, Thaddeus releases
the pressure on Hancock's windpipe, and clutches his
crucifix. The water is now cutting off Ann's screams.
Jack sees his chance, and seizes the crucifix, ripping it
free. He jams it into Thaddeus' groin, and the giant
folds up in agony. He seizes Jack and both fall into the
pit. We hear a long scream, and then we see a hand
rise over the edge of the shaft. Jack climbs painfully out,
unbars the door, and casts the bar aside. Theme swells as
water pours out of the chamber, and he moves quickly to
rescue Ann. He turns off the water, cuts her bonds, and
lifts her, choking and gasping, into his arms.)*

ANN
Jack, thank God you got here. He said he
killed you.

JACK
I think he missed. You okay?

ANN
Sure. Dragged up a few flights of
stairs. Punched out a bit. Half
drowned. Otherwise, I'm fine.

JACK
Good. Because the evening's young.

"How long?" Carson watched the mist drift past. He pushed
back in his chair, trying to look calm, dispassionate, but he
was excited. Damned near ecstatic.

All gauges on the jump-status indicator had gone to a bright
amber. "Coming up on three minutes." Hutch began to divert
power to the fusion plant. "The jump should be smooth. But
buckle down anyhow."

Systems lamps went green. The power levels of the
Hazeltines were beginning to rise. Real-space mass was
showing zero.

Maggie, closeted with George and Janet in the passengers' cabin, said, "Please, God, let them be here."

Red lamp. Unsecured hatch in one of the rear storage areas. Hutch opened it, closed it again. The light went green.

Janet said, "This is going to be a terrible disappointment if Beta Pac is a radio star, and the analysts were wrong. They've been wrong before."

"Two minutes," said Hutch. The comments around her receded to background noise. Only George's voice got through. But no one really had anything new to say. They were talking to create a web of security, impose a sense of familiarity on a condition they'd experienced before but which was nevertheless potentially quite different.

They floated forward.

"One minute."

Lights dimmed.

The real-space navigational systems, which had been in a power-saving mode, activated. The fusion plant went to ready status. External sensors came on line. Shields powered up.

Someone wished her luck.

Navigation came to life.

And, with scarcely a bump, they slid out into the dark. Stars flowered in the deeps, and she felt a brief flash of vertigo, not unusual during transition. They sailed beneath an open sky.

"I'm always glad to be out of there," said Carson, releasing his restraints.

"Maybe not," said Hutch. She jabbed a finger at the main navigation screen. An enormous black disk lay dead ahead. "Everybody stay belted in, please."

Fusion was about to ignite. She stopped it.

"What's wrong?" Maggie hadn't missed the strain in Hutch's voice.

Hutch gave them the image. "Talk later. I'm going to throw on the brakes."

"What is it?" George asked.

"Not sure." She went to full mag. It looked like a *world*. "That can't be right. Mass detectors show zero." She reset, but nothing changed. "Don't know what it is. Hold on."

Carson stared out the forward screen. "Son of a bitch—"

"Braking," said Hutch softly, "*now*." She engaged the

retros, didn't ease into them as she normally would, but hit them hard.

"It's just an area with no stars," said Janet. "Like the Void. Maybe it *is* the Void."

"If it is, it's in the wrong place."

The thing ahead reflected no light.

"Hutch?" Maggie's voice had risen a notch. "Are we going *into* that thing?"

"It's getting bigger," said George.

"It can't really be there." Hutch's fingers moved across keys. "Self test okay."

"It's not a sphere," said Carson. His beefy features had hardened, and the eager-to-please archeologist had been replaced by the old colonel. Military bearing front and center. In an odd way, it was reassuring.

"What else could it be?"

Carson was squinting at the images. "It looks like a *football*," he said.

Worried sounds were coming out of the passenger cabin.

"Hang on," said Hutch. "We're going sharp to port." She punched in a new set of values, maybe more thrust than they could stand, and hit the button. Again, they were thrown against the webbing.

A haze had risen before her eyes, and it was hard to talk against the push of the thrusters. "*Collision*," she said. "Imminent." The words hung in the frantic air.

Carson took time to breathe, steady his voice. "How long?"

Hutch felt cold and empty. "Seven minutes. And change."

The object filled the sky. To their eternal credit, the three in the cabin kept their heads, and did not distract her. She even heard them trying to laugh about their situation. She opened a channel. "You can see what's happening," she said, speaking as though she were describing an interesting view. "We have a problem."

"How serious?" asked Janet. "Is it as bad as it looks?"

Hutch hesitated. "Yes," she said. "I think so."

She eased off on the thrusters, and killed the course change. "What are you doing?" asked Carson.

They were in free fall again. "No point torturing everybody."

"What do you mean?" said Maggie. "We aren't going to give up, are we? Just like that?"

Hutch didn't respond. Didn't know how to.

"How about jumping back?" George suggested.

"Can't."

"Try it."

"There's no point."

"Try it. What's to lose?"

The black football was growing. Carson said, "Not good." In the passenger cabin, someone laughed. Janet.

"I'll try to reinsert when we get closer," Hutch said. "Give the engines a chance to breathe. But don't expect anything."

Maggie whimpered.

Carson, strain finally locking his voice somewhat, asked, "How fast will we be going when we hit?"

Hutch was tempted to dodge the question. Throw back some facile response like *fast enough.* But they deserved better. "Almost fifty thousand."

What *was* the damned thing? She decided they weren't quite dead-on after all. They would hit a glancing shot. Not that it mattered.

"Goddammit, Hutch," said George, "we ought to be able to do *something.*"

"Tell me what." Hutch had become deadly calm.

No way out. The object was vast and dark and overwhelming. An impossible *thing*, a disk without light, a world without rock.

"No moons," said Carson.

"What?"

"It has no moons."

"Hardly seems to matter," someone said; Hutch wasn't sure who.

Four minutes.

A terrible silence took the ship as her passengers settled into their own thoughts. Janet looked subdued and frightened, but managed a resigned smile; Maggie, tougher than Hutch would have expected, caught her looking, wiped her eyes and nodded, seeming to say, *not your fault.* George's glance turned inward and Hutch was glad she hadn't waited. And Carson: he wore the expression of someone who had absorbed a prank, and was taking it all quite philosophically. "Bad luck," he told her. And, after a long pause: "It happens."

"Did we get a message off?" Janet asked.

"Working on it."

"How big is it?" asked Maggie. "This *thing*?"

Hutch checked her board. "Forty-three hundred kilometers across. Half again as wide as the Moon."

It crowded out the stars.

Hutch saw a blip on her status board. "It's putting out a signal," she said.

"Same one they got at the Tindle?" asked Maggie, breathless.

"I think so. It's fifteen-ten. That's the right frequency. Computer's doing a match now."

"That's a pretty fair piece of navigation," said Carson. "We hit it right on the button." They laughed. And in that moment Hutch loved them all.

"Transmission's away. They'll get a full set of pictures. And it *is* the same signal."

"What now?"

"Time to try the jump. On a count of ten." She set up, and shook her head at the energy level for the Hazeltines, which was around six percent of minimum requirements. "Okay." She hit the "Go" button.

The engines whined.

And shuddered.

Whined again.

She shut it down. "That's it."

They were beginning to see features in the thing. Ribs. The void became a surface: blue-black, polished like plastene, or an ocean. "You know what's crazy about this?" said Carson. "We're still not getting gravity readings. What *is* this thing? Anything that big *has* to have a gravity field."

"Detectors have a glitch," said George.

Under a minute. Hutch stopped watching the clocks. In the cabin, she heard the sound of a restraint opening. "Stay belted down."

"Why? Why bother?" It was Janet.

"Just do it. It's the way a well-run ship does things." She wiped her mouth with the back of her hand. Her training screamed at her to hit the retros. But she only shut down the screens, locking out the terrifying perspective.

She closed her eyes. "Damn," she said, not quite able to stop the tears. She felt oddly secure in the sealed bridge, as if the long plunge had somehow been arrested. She loved the soft leather texture of the pilot's chair, the green radiance of the gauges, the electronic murmur of *Wink's* systems.

"Hutch?" Carson's voice was calm.

"Yes?"

"You're a hell of a woman."

In the dark behind her eyelids, she smiled.

18.

On board NCA Winckelmann. *Thursday, March 24; 1103 hours.*

Hutch listened to the familiar sounds of the bridge. To Carson's tense breathing, to whispers from the passenger cabin, prayers maybe, wishes, things undone.

She felt terrified and helpless and humiliated, but for all that, she did not want it to be over—God, she did not want it to be over—

She squeezed her eyes shut. Squeezed the rest of the world down to her heartbeat and the soft curve of the chair. And the countdown that some inner voice maintained—

Three. Two . . .

A hammerblow struck the hull.

The ship shuddered. Alarms exploded. The electrostatic hum of power in the bulkheads changed subtly, deepened as it sometimes did when the vehicle was responding to crisis. Carson shouted something unintelligible.

But she was still *alive*.

They had problems. The navigation board was on fire; black smoke poured into the air. Warning lamps blazed across the banks of consoles. Two of the monitors died. Computer voices spilled from the commlinks. Deep within the ship, systems sighed and shut down.

But oblivion did not come.

She looked at the gauges and could not believe what she saw. Their altitude was a hundred forty kilometers. And *rising.*

Rising.

She silenced the klaxons and stared at her status board. The power plant was going unstable. She shut it down, and switched to auxiliary.

Then she let out her breath.

"What happened?" asked Carson in a tentative voice.

"Damned if I know. Everybody okay?"

They were rattled. But *okay*.

"Is it over?" Janet asked.

Someone began to laugh.

In the passenger cabin, a cheer broke out.

"We seem to have gone *through* it," Hutch said. "Don't know how—"

"Son of a bitch, Hutch," said Maggie. "That was beautiful!"

Hutch's hands trembled.

"What did you do?"

"Damned if I know."

She killed the fire, and sent out a distress call. Carson reached over and clapped her on the back. "I don't think I want to do *that* again," he said.

They passed through three hundred kilometers.

"Hutch," said George, "that's the finest piece of piloting I've ever seen."

They were all laughing now. She joined in, and if the celebration had a hysterical edge to it, she didn't care. No one cared.

The ground was receding. It glowed softly. The illumination might have been internal. Or possibly reflected starlight.

"Maybe," said Maggie, laughing and crying simultaneously, "it was just smoke."

The sky had developed a distinct roll. "We're tumbling," Hutch said. "That's all right. We can fix *that*."

"Are we okay?" asked George. His voice trembled.

"Yeah. We're fine." Hutch was running through her checklist. Seconds after impact, the fusion plant had sent a blast of energy through the ship. There were systems in place to guard against the effects of a surge, but they were not, could not be, entirely effective. Who knew what might have burned out? She would need a walk-through to assess damage. "We're in good shape," she said. "We've got some power problems, but nothing we can't handle." Their situation was uncomfortable, but she saw no reason for alarm.

Auxiliary power consisted of a net of batteries and solar collectors. Several of these were also down. *Not good.* "We can maintain life support. And spin. But we can't fire the main engines, and the Hazeltines can't recharge, so we have no stardrive. We are dead in the water." Navigation readouts implied altitude adjustment systems were out of line. Water pressure had dropped precipitously, but was now holding steady. That meant a tank had burst. The Hazeltine flux detection system was putting out a flat line. Even if she had power to go hyper, she'd have no real way to control their point of re-entry. But we could be worse, she thought. Damned lucky. Her hands were trembling.

They were getting far enough away now that the object was regaining its ovoid shape. "Could it be water?" asked Maggie.

"Even *that* would've wrecked us," said Carson. "Unless it was just a couple of centimeters deep."

"Hey." Janet sounded surprised. "Why do I keep trying to fall out of my chair?"

"Because we're tumbling," said Hutch. "Our gravity's off center."

Carson was preoccupied with the ovoid. "It's thin. Micro-thin. Has to be."

"Can we straighten out?" Maggie looked unhappy. "I'm getting sick."

"Trying."

The number four thruster showed negative. She disabled it, and set up a bypass firing sequence. "Heads up," she said. "We're going to have a little movement."

"We have power to spare?" asked Carson.

"Enough. We're going to be here a while, and we don't want to have to deal with all this rolling—" She executed, and felt the satisfying push of the rockets, felt the ship respond.

The firing sequence was long and complicated, but the stellar dance slowed, changed direction, changed again, and almost stopped. *Almost*. There was still a mild lateral motion.

"Best I can do," she said. "You can stand up now. But be careful, we have a wobble."

"You want to try it again?" said George.

"No. Too much drain. We'll live with this."

"What do we do next?" asked Janet.

"Take a look at the damage to the fusion plant," Hutch replied.

Carson shook her hand. "Thanks," he said.

"Not my doing. We were lucky."

"I suppose. Thanks, anyway."

The others crowded onto the bridge. The exhilaration was subsiding. "*Can* we restore power?" asked Janet.

"I'm running the diagnostics," said Hutch. "But I can tell you the answer. Fusion plant repair is not something you do on the run. We should proceed on the assumption that we will not have it available. Which means we are stuck here." She released her restraints.

"Then we need to get help." Maggie took a long deep breath. "Somebody's going to have to come and bail us out. First thing to do, I guess, is get off a distress call."

"We've already done that."

Maggie had arrived on the bridge, and was walking unsteadily across the deck, testing her balance. "Nobody's going to want to do any drinking," she said. "The floor runs uphill."

"Where would rescuers have to come from?" said George. "Nok?"

"Probably." Hutch was looking at flight schedules. "There isn't much else in the region. Unless you want to ride with Kosmik. They've got a ship at Quraqua."

"We're going to be laughingstocks," said Janet. "We go out looking for an artifact, and crash into it."

"The *Valkyrie's* at Nok. Just got in, if we can believe the schedule. They normally stay about four days. We're two days away, transmission time. So it'll still be there when our SOS arrives."

"It *does* mean," said Maggie, "that we lose the mission. Everybody'll want in now; we'll be squeezed out, and the credit will go elsewhere." She looked desperately at Hutch. "Do you have any ideas?"

"No, Maggie. All we can do is wait to be rescued."

"How long will it take?" asked Janet. "The trip from Nok, I mean."

"The packets are fast. If they leave as soon as they hear the distress call, the *Valkyrie* will be here in eleven days."

"We can live with that," said George. "Maybe in the mean-time we can figure out what that *thing* back there is."

The real problem surfaced five hours later.

Hutch was still trying to reroute and reprogram her status board when Janet strolled in, blowing conspicuously on her hands. "It's getting cold in here."

It *was* chilly. Hutch's board showed 103° Celsius. Hot enough to boil water. She ran a diagnostic, and got a Negative. No problems. She shook her head, got up, and walked over to one of the ducts. "It's pumping cool air."

"It's not really *cold*," Janet said. "But it isn't room temperature either."

"We better go down and take a look. The programming is probably scrambled. But I can't get at it from up here."

They collected George in the passenger lounge, and crossed over to C ring, Life Support and General Maintenance. They walked halfway round the long outer passageway, picked up a repair harness, and entered Engineering. The bulkheads were lined with housings, casings, cabinets. The metal was cold.

"We should have brought sweaters," said Janet. "Let's make this quick."

Moving about was difficult because of the tumble. There was a tendency to lurch anti-spinward. As they moved toward the spine of the ship, it translated into an affinity for strolling into left-hand walls, and falling down easily. They stumbled past the fusion power unit, a set of teardrop cylinders framed within a series of tori. A yellow status lamp and the pale light from the control panel provided the only illumination.

"You sure you don't want to try to fix this?" asked George.

"Yes," she said. Fusion units were strictly dockyard work. Not to be touched by operating personnel. Hutch's training was clear on the point: switch to auxiliary systems, cut back wherever possible on power usage, and go home. By the shortest route. Here, of course, with the Hazeltines exhausted, they weren't going anywhere. In that case, send for help.

They inspected the series of tanks and drums which housed the ventilation system. Nothing obvious suggested itself. Hutch brought the air flow schematic up on the control terminal.

Four recyclers, operating in series, maintained the appropriate carbon dioxide/nitrogen/oxygen mix. These were large cylinders from which air was pumped into three enormous pressurized tanks, where it was stored until needed. The recyclers and tanks were interconnected. Prior to re-entering the ventilation system, air passed through a series of four convectors, which heated (or cooled) it to the proper temperature. The four convectors all showed "Nonfunctional."

They removed one of the hatch covers and looked at a

charred ruin. "So we replace them. Right?" asked George hopefully.

"We can replace *one* of them."

"You only have one spare?" Janet sounded skeptical.

"One spare," said Hutch. "These things don't give out. And this sort of damage is not supposed to happen."

"Right" said Janet.

"How much good does one spare do us?" asked George.

"I don't know. We'll have to figure it out. But it should mean that we'll freeze a little more slowly."

"I'll tell you what I think it is." Maggie, wrapped in a blanket, jabbed a finger at the ovoid. It was blown up, and spread across a wall-length screen in the lounge. It looked somewhat like a spider web, half-seen on a moonless night. They could make out a fine network of lines, a sense of fragile beauty. "It's the ultimate Monument, and if this is not the home system of the Monument-Makers, at least it suggests we're on their track."

Carson was wearing a sweater and had a spread draped over his legs. "Are we agreed we went through it?"

"Had to," said Maggie. "Say—" She brightened. "Maybe we've got some samples aboard."

Carson's eyes met hers. "On the hull."

"Could be."

He looked up at one of the air ducts, walked over to it, and held his hand in front of it. "It's colder," he said.

A door at the rear of the compartment opened. Janet came in, followed closely by Hutch and George. All had acquired jackets, and they looked discouraged.

"Not so good, huh?" said Carson.

Hutch described what they had done. The new convector was in. "We'll get a *little* heat," she said.

"How about diverting the air flow?" said Maggie. "Put the air from the working conductor in *here*."

George shook his head. "It doesn't work that way. The air passes over all four conductors and *then* exits into the individual ducts."

"Then cut off the other spaces altogether," suggested Carson. "I'd think a smaller volume of air will cool down more slowly because less of it is exposed to the outer bulkheads."

Hutch nodded. "We thought so too. But we're limited as

to where we can cut down. Anything that freezes over, we lose. Data banks in B ring, for example; food and water and life support in C."

"How cold will it get?" asked Maggie.

Hutch took a deep breath. "*Cold*." She patted Carson's wool-clad shoulder. "You're going to need more than that. Let me see if I can get my systems back on-line, and maybe we can figure out some options." She passed through the cabin, headed for the forward door.

"Before you leave," said Carson. "I've got a question on a different matter. We keep getting further away from that *thing*. Is there any chance of turning around and going back? To get a closer look?"

"It wouldn't be a bad idea," said Janet. "It would give us something to do while we're waiting for help to arrive. And we wouldn't look quite so silly when this is over."

Hutch shook her head. "We don't even have the power to stop our forward motion, Frank, let alone reverse it. No, *Wink* isn't going anywhere except straight ahead for a while. Sorry—" And she was gone.

The obloid floated on a wall-sized screen. George frowned, turned his head sidewise, used his hands to frame a picture, frowned again. "Anybody mind if I reduce this?" It was at five mag. Nobody objected, and he took it down, stage by stage. He played with it awhile, back and forth, and turned suddenly to Maggie. "You know what I think? It's a *bowl*. Look at it: it's a big, curved, planet-sized bowl." He cupped his hands, and tilted them so they could see. "You come in at the right angle, the football looks like a bowl. See?"

"You're right," said Carson. "So what is it?"

Maggie sank deeper into her blanket. "We know it puts out radio signals. It's apparently a big *dish*. A relay station, maybe. Certainly a beacon of some kind."

"Why would you want a beacon that big?" asked Janet.

"Maybe they never developed the TD band," said Carson. "Is that possible? That they could have FTL travel, but not FTL communications?"

"I guess it's *possible*," said Maggie. "But it makes no sense. Why would anyone with a stardrive want to send a message that would need decades, or centuries, to get to its destination?" Her nose was cold. She rubbed it. "You know," she said, "this place is starting to get downright drafty."

ARCHIVE

ZZ 03/241611
XX EMERGENCY EMERGENCY EMERGENCY
TO: GENERAL DISTRIBUTION
FROM: NCA *WINCKELMANN*
SUBJECT: GENERAL DISTRESS
GENERAL DISTRESS CALL ALL SHIPS/STATIONS. UP-
DATE 01. REQUIRE IMMEDIATE ASSISTANCE—LIFE
THREATENING SIT/BETA PAC. LIFE SUPPORT FAILURE.
WILL MAINTAIN ALL-CHANNEL SIGNAL, STANDARD
SET. THIS IS A FIVE ALPHA EMERGENCY, EXTREME
DANGER, EXTREME NEED FOR HASTE. MESSAGE WILL
REPEAT AT EIGHT-MINUTE INTERVALS.

On the bridge, Hutch faced the bad news. The lone convector would prevent the temperature from falling below -36°C.
That in itself would not be comfortable, but it was survivable.
The problem was that the system that supported the convector
would start to freeze up at twenty below. It was then likely
the convector would fail. If that happened, it was going to
get very cold.

How long would it take?

She was unable to measure current heat loss. It appeared to
be somewhat more than a degree per hour. At that rate, they
could expect to hit zero sometime tomorrow. There would
be other hazards as it got colder: air pumps would fail, food
dispensers would cease to work, the power system might give
way altogether, trapping them in a frigid, dark shell.

She had six Flickinger belts to fall back on, but there were
only twenty-four hours of air for each. Once the power went,
there would be no way to refill the breathers.

My God. She sat and stared at her instruments.

She needed an idea. And no reasonable possibility presented
itself. A sense of her culpability began to take hold. Not that
she had erred in any way that a board of inquiry could bring
a finding against her; but she was ultimately responsible for
the safe delivery of her passengers. Whatever that took. At
the moment, she was not sure what it might take—

When she felt she'd postponed the confrontation as long
as she could, she pushed away from the console, took a deep
breath, and returned to the cabin.

Carson was absorbed in his notebooks when she entered. The others were talking, a conversation that immediately faded.

"Okay," she said, "here's where we are." She outlined their situation, trying not to seem alarmed, speaking as if these were merely complications, trivial inconveniences. But the inevitable conclusion was that they would freeze before help could come. Carson watched her without putting down his pen, as though prepared to take notes. Janet remained impassive, blue gaze fixed on the deck; George and Maggie exchanged glances freighted with meaning.

When she finished, they were quiet. Maggie tapped an index finger thoughtfully against her lip. Hutch sensed disbelief. "What do we do?" asked George.

Janet looked up. "Can we build a fire? Keep it going in here?"

"There's nothing to burn," Hutch said. Even their clothes were fire-resistant.

George looked around as if he expected to find a stack of logs. "Got to be some stuff somewhere."

"If there is, I don't know what."

"And we can't expect help earlier than eleven days?"

"At best." Everyone looked at the calendar. Rescue might arrive sometime April 4.

"It'll be pretty cold by then," said Maggie.

Carson was writing again. He didn't look up. "How about abandoning ship? Take the shuttle? Is there any place we can reach from here?"

"No," said Hutch. "We've got about a week's air supply in the shuttle. There's an oxygen world in the biozone, but we couldn't get close in the time we have."

"Do *you* have any suggestions?" asked Maggie.

The crunch. "I'll think better in the morning. But yes: maybe we can reconfigure the micro-ovens that cook our food to put some additional heat in here. Actually, we can probably manage that fairly easily. It won't be much, but it'll be something. The problem is that the rest of the ship will freeze."

"Which means?"

"The recyclers will stop, for one thing. That'll be the end of the air supply." She looked at them. "Listen, we're all exhausted. I'm sure we can work out something. But we need to sleep on it."

"Yes," said Carson. "Let's give it a rest. We'll come up with some ideas tomorrow."

Hutch huddled under three blankets during the night. She rolled and tossed and stared into the dark. Where else could she get *heat*? The first priority was to keep the convector going, but she could see no way to do that.

By first light, she was still awake, and exhausted. But it was time to stop beating herself up. She wrapped a blanket around her shoulders, grabbed fresh clothes (she had not undressed), and padded across the cold floor to the bathroom. They still had hot water. One of the first tasks this morning would be to salvage a water supply from C ring.

She closed the door behind her, and opened the faucets. When she judged the room was warm enough, she dropped the blanket, stepped out of her clothes and into the shower. It felt good, and she soaped herself down thoroughly. But she was cataloging places where they could find containers. Damn, this was a nightmare.

George was in the main cabin, brewing coffee. He was wrapped in a thick robe. "How we doing?" he asked, holding out a cup for her. His usual optimism had vanished, and she knew that he too had lain awake much of the night.

She took the cup. The coffee was good, and imposed a sense of routine. "Okay, I guess." Her nose and ears were *cold*.

He looked glad to have company. "This is scary," he admitted.

"I know."

Hesitantly, he asked: "Any ideas?"

The reluctant criticism stung. "Not yet."

Deep in the ship, a hatch closed.

George's gaze met hers. "Who's wandering around back there?"

She checked her board. "Lower level. One of the supply rooms."

"Maybe somebody else can't sleep."

Hutch opened a channel. "Hellooo?"

Nothing.

"Ghosts," he said.

"I think we're hearing a computer glitch."

He could not entirely keep the emotion out of his voice.

"Hutch, you know the ship pretty well. What are our chances?"

She took a minute to drink him in. Despite his size, there was something of the eternal child in George. He was boyishly good-looking, enthusiastic, careful of her feelings in a situation which he understood must be especially painful to her. And he was striving manfully to hide his fears. Somehow, it was for George she was most anxious. "We'll find a way," she promised.

"I've got something else to tell you."

Hutch didn't think she wanted any more news. "What's that?"

"I've been up on the bridge. I hope you don't mind."

"No," she said. "Why would I?"

He nodded. "There's no radio noise out here anywhere. Except what comes off the star. And the signal we followed."

"None at all?"

"None. No electronic radiation of any kind." In the press of events, the reason they'd come to Beta Pac, on the track of an artificial radio broadcast, had got lost.

"But we're still picking up the signal from the Football?"

"Yes. It's still there. But that's all there is. Hutch, I don't think anyone's here." His eyes looked away. "I've got a question."

"Go ahead."

"We'd all like to find out what it is. The Football, I mean. We can't turn the ship around, but what about going back with the shuttle?"

"No," she said quietly. "We could *do* it. But we wouldn't be able to get back to the ship." She finished off the last of her coffee.

He studied her for a long moment. "Does it matter? Whether we can get back?"

The question jolted Hutch. "Yes," she said. "It *matters*."

Someone was coming.

It matters.

Janet appeared in the doorway, shivering. "Cold," she said. "Hutch, we need some ideas."

Hutch was still thinking about the shuttle. "Maybe you're right," she said. They had no place to go. But that didn't mean they shouldn't use *Alpha*.

• • •

Hutch woke Maggie. "Let's go."

She pulled her blankets more tightly around her and did not look up. "Go? Where?"

"The shuttle. It has a heating system. Get whatever you need."

Hutch hurried to her own quarters, grabbed clothes, towel, toothbrush, comb, whatever she could carry. She'd come back later for the rest. Now, with the prospect of warmth imminent, the temperature seemed to plummet. Her teeth were chattering when she entered the shuttle bay. Carson arrived at the same time.

She opened the hatch with her remote and they climbed in. The pilot's seat was stiff and cold. She switched on the heater and waited. George appeared, hauling a suitcase. "Good idea," he said.

He threw the bag into the rear. The blowers kicked on, and warm air flowed into the cockpit. "Hallelujah!" he said. The others arrived, and hurried inside.

"Shut the hatch," said Janet, trying to find room. "Keep it warm."

"Why didn't we do this last night?" Maggie grumbled from a rear seat. "Or didn't we think of it?"

Janet blew on her hands. "It feels good. I'm not leaving here until help comes."

"Cargo area in back will be warm in a few minutes," said Hutch. "We can set up living quarters in there."

They passed clothes and overnight bags back and then crowded into the cockpit and shut all the doors. Hutch handed out coffee.

She felt better now than she had since they'd come out of hyper. She wasn't sure yet they were safe, hadn't taken time to think it through, but for the moment at least, life was good again. The hold was gray and cramped and utilitarian. It would provide little privacy. But it already looked like the best accommodation she'd ever had.

"What's our situation exactly?" asked Carson. "We're getting our power from *Wink*, right? That's not a very reliable source."

She nodded. "We should have all the power we need. We can switch to internal if we have to, but we won't be using much other than heating and lights. The shuttle's batteries are designed for a much heavier workload. I suspect we'd be okay for six months or more on internal alone. Not that we'll be here that long," she added hurriedly.

"How about air?" asked Janet. "How much air do we have?"

"For five people?" Air was their potential problem. "If we used only the shuttle tanks, we'd be limited to about a week. But we're getting our air from *Wink*. We'll continue to do that as long as it's available. When it freezes out there, we'll switch to our own system. But we should be fine. There are a lot of things we need to do though, and we have to get to them before it gets too cold outside."

"Food," said Janet.

Hutch nodded. "That'll be your job, okay? We'll assume rescue will be late."

"Where do we put the food?" asked George. "Space is limited in here. We know where to get more if we need it. Why not leave it outside? It's not as if anything will spoil."

"I'm not so sure," said Hutch. "We're talking *cold*. Better we have it in here where we can control temperatures. I don't want to leave anything to chance."

"Okay," said Carson. "What else?"

"Water. Frank, you take care of that." She told him where to find containers, and then turned to Maggie. "Cargo area divides into three sections. There's a washroom at the rear. We'll expand that, and use the other two sections as living quarters. See what you can do in the way of furnishings. Oh, and if you can get us a supply of towels, soap, dishes, that would help." She glanced around the cabin. "I'll be back in a little while."

"Where are you going?" asked Carson.

"The bridge. We have to tie into the ship's communication system. Back here, we won't know what's going on."

"We'll need the Flickinger belts, too," said Carson.

"Right. We've got six in storage. I'll bring them back. You guys should take a few minutes and make a list of what we need. Try not to miss anything." She opened the hatch and climbed out. The air seemed less cold than it had.

She went only a few steps before she smelled something burning. "We've got a fire somewhere," she told the link. That brought everyone boiling out of the shuttle.

It was coming from one of the ducts. They traced it to the food processors, and minutes later they were all on the scene.

One of the units had overheated and burned out its wiring. They tried to shut it down, but the override didn't work, and they ended by disconnecting it.

The temperature was now near freezing, and no one had anything heavier than a light jacket. They were thoroughly chilled when they returned to *Alpha*.

"I'll go with you to the bridge," said Carson. "I don't think anybody should go anywhere alone anymore."

That made sense to Hutch, but before she could reply, Janet held up her watch, and pointed out the window. "It's still dark," she said.

It was by then almost 7:00 A.M., GMT. Ship's time. The lights should have brightened in their simulation of the day-night cycle.

Hutch took care of her technical chores first, ensuring that she had full control of *Winckelmann*'s communication systems. For good measure, she also connected routine shipboard controls. She wondered how long her circuits would last after the starship froze over. It occurred to her that *Wink* might suffer a complete communications blackout. Maybe, if that happened, she could launch *Alpha* at noon April fourth, on the assumption that *Valkyrie* would be in the area. But that was risky: if the rescuers failed to arrive, there would be no guarantee they could reconnect with the ship's air supply. Furthermore, she wondered whether the shuttle bay doors would respond when the time came.

She consulted the computer:

Q. AT CURRENT RATE OF HEAT LOSS, AT WHAT TEMPERATURE, AND AT WHAT TIME, WILL SHUTTLE LAUNCH DOORS BECOME INOPERABLE?

A. AT 284 DEGREES CENTIGRADE. 031903Z.

"Uh-oh," said Janet. "The nineteenth? Wasn't that last week?"

"I think we can write off the computer," said Hutch.

Daylight arrived at 1010 sharp. It snapped on, bright, intense, noon at sea. They were spread out through the ship, foraging what they could, and they greeted the sudden illumination with cynical cheers.

They set themselves up as comfortably as conditions allowed. They disengaged chairs and tables from the main cabin, found three divans, and anchored them in their living quarters. They even mounted a few prints. Maggie put a crystal dolphin on one of the tables, and Janet tried to rescue the occasional plants that were scattered around the ship. But it was much too late for *them*.

As a safety precaution, Hutch shut down all unnecessary systems. The rings no longer turned, and their simulated gravity ceased. Everything had to be bolted down. Drinks were taken through straws, and the shower was an adventure.

On Monday the 28th, the fourth day after the collision, they received a reply from Nok. Hutch read it, and then handed it around:

RECEIVED YOUR 03/241541Z and 03/241611Z. UNFORTUNATELY WE HAVE NO SHIP TO SEND. HAVE PLACED YOUR REQUEST ON GENL BROADCAST TO NEAREST VESSEL, SURVEY SHIP ASHLEY TEE, CURRENTLY IN HYPER. ESTIMATED ARRIVAL TIME BETA PAC APR 11 RPT APR 11. GOOD LUCK.

"My God," said Janet, "that's two weeks. What happened to the *Valkyrie*?"

Hutch slumped into her seat. "Maybe they canceled the run. They do that if there's no reason for a flight. Maybe it needs maintenance. Who knows? What difference does it make?"

LIBRARY ENTRY

During my entire career, which has embraced a number of notable successes (if I may be allowed the indulgence), along with some spectacular failures, I know of no single event that has so frustrated me as being sealed inside Winckelmann *and its shuttle craft, within a few million kilometers of an archeological puzzle of overwhelming dimension. And being able to do absolutely nothing about it.*

My companions share my concern, although they are distracted by life and death issues. I'm scared too. But I'd still like to get a look at the Football. What is that thing? Incidentally, I should record here that I'm glad we have Hutchins along. She is something of a jerk. But I know she'll pull us out of this. If it can be done.

—Margaret Tufu's *Journals*, dated March 29, 2203
Published posthumously by
Hartley & Co., London (2219)
(Edited and annotated by Janet Allegri)

19.

On board NCA Winckelmann. *Tuesday, March 29; 1218 hours.*

"We're going to have to come up with something else."

Ship's temperature had dropped to -30°C. Electronics systems had begun to fail. Water lines had long since frozen. Hutch, concerned that a hatch somewhere might freeze and cut them off from other parts of the ship, left everything open.

Janet found an auto-kitchen on C deck and carried it back to *Alpha*. It was capable of making sandwiches, coffee, and snacks. They also commandeered a refrigerator.

The day after the bad news had come from Nok, *Wink's* lights went out. Hutch thought she could restore them, but saw no point in making the effort. So they huddled in their warm, illuminated cocoon, in the belly of the dark ship.

And they worried about the air supply. They were still breathing from the ship's tanks, and tapping the ship's power. But the loss of the lights had shown them the future. Any time now, the voltage that drove the recyclers would fail, or the pumps would freeze, or any other of a dozen misfortunes would shut down the oxygen supply. *Then* they would have to switch to the onboard tanks, and from that time they would have one week left. Plus roughly twenty-four hours with the Flickinger belts. The *Ashley Tee* was due, at best, in thirteen days. Which meant that if the ship's air supply failed any time within the next five days, they would not make it.

A green light glowed on her status board, confirming the flow of air from the *Wink* into the shuttle. If it stopped, *when* it stopped, the lamp would blink off and an alarm would sound.

She looked out into the darkness. Illumination from the shuttle windows etched the decks. "Not much fun, is it?" asked George, breaking a long silence.

She shook her head. "Not much."

"We'll be okay." He squeezed her shoulder. "It's always hard when you can't do anything except sit and wait."

Several minutes later, the remaining convector quietly died.

The Football was no longer easy to see at zero mag. It was a small patch of night with indefinite boundaries, an empty place among the stars. A well in a city of light. Its radio pulse played across a monitor that Maggie had set up. Carson sat watching it intently. A second screen displayed telemetry. He was absentmindedly scooping cereal out of a bowl in his lap. Beside him, Maggie dozed.

Hutch and George played chess, the board balanced on a water container. Janet was dividing her attention between a book and the game. (She would play the winner.) George munched a chocolate cookie. They had adjusted reasonably well to the lack of amenities. The shuttle had almost come to feel like home.

Exercise was of course feasible only outside in the bay. They could still walk through the ship protected by the Flickinger energy fields, but that would stop when they lost the external air hookup, because it would then become impossible to refill the breathers without draining the shuttle's supply.

They didn't talk much about the dangers of the situation. But in the pointedly irrelevant conversations that had become the order of the day, Hutch noted a tendency to lower the voice and speak in hushed tones, the way one does in church. The fiction that escape was only a matter of time was maintained.

And they continued to speculate about the Football. They had tracked the signal source to the center of the object.

"It *has* to be an antenna," said George, stabbing the air with a rook. "And a standard radio transmission would have to be intended for someone in this system." He set the piece down to support the queen's bishop pawn, which was under pressure. It was early yet, but the game was turning against him already. As usual. "I wonder whether anyone's listening?"

"*Someone* must be," said Janet. "Somebody would have to come out here once in a while to do the maintenance."

"Maybe it doesn't need maintenance," said Hutch. She sailed into a line of pawns with a black bishop. Sacrifice. George could not see the point. "Don't underestimate an unknown technology," she continued.

Carson picked up the cereal bowl and tilted it so that it lay at the same angle as the Football. "Hutch," he said. "Was there a blip of any kind when we went through the object? Did it seem to notice we were there?"

"Don't know. I wasn't recording the signal. I couldn't see any reason to at the time."

Janet grinned politely at George, and shook her head. "Resign," she said.

"Why is it so *big*?" asked Hutch.

"Maybe it's more than a relay," George suggested.

"What else *could* it be?"

"A telescope, maybe. Something like the Tindle. But bigger."

"A *lot* bigger," said Carson. "With a telescope that size, you could see someone strike a match across the Void."

"Your move," said Hutch, smiling.

George pushed back from the board, shrugged, and pushed over his king.

"If it *were* a telescope," said Janet, "it would have to be solid, right? We were doing, what? Fifty thousand klicks? We'd have disintegrated."

"Depends," said Carson, "on how it's made."

Janet set up the pieces, and turned the board to give Hutch black. "Something else," she said. "Assume you had a bowl that big. How would you turn it?"

"What?"

"If it's a telescope, how would you turn it? I would think that any attempt to move it would wreck it."

"Maybe you don't turn it," said George. "Maybe it was preset to observe something that doesn't move much. Very little apparent motion."

"I can't imagine how the thing would hold together." The voice was Maggie's.

"I thought you were asleep." Carson's smile was almost paternal. "*If* it's a telescope, and if it's permanently aimed, what do you suppose it's looking at?" He cleared his screen, and directed the question to the computer.

Maggie got up and stretched.

Janet, who was a decent match for Hutch, opened as she always did, with c4, the English Game. Hutch wondered how it happened that a woman who was so aggressive, so careless of her own safety, would become enamored of an opening that was deliberate, methodical, and cautious.

"*Nothing*," said Carson. "There's nothing at all in its line of sight."

"It's been there a long time," said Maggie. "Back it up to about 10,000 B.C. and take a look."

George picked up Janet's book. It was a historical novel, set immediately after the collapse of the U.S. He paged through.

Carson got a result, and smiled. "The Lesser Magellanic Cloud. That's interesting."

"Why?" asked George.

"Closest extragalactic object," said Hutch.

"Hard to believe," said Janet, "that anyone would build that kind of monster to look at *one* astronomical target. It seems like overkill."

George frowned. "I thought the nearest galaxy was Andromeda."

"Andromeda's the nearest *big* one," said Hutch. "It's two million light-years out. But the Magellanic Clouds—there are two of them—are only about a tenth as far."

Maggie rubbed her eyes. "I'm more interested in what's at *this* end. You said there's an oxygen world in the biozone. What does it look like?"

"We don't have much detail," said Hutch. "The sensors are pretty badly skewed. Temperatures are earthlike. There are water oceans. It's got life. But it's putting out no ECM. And that's about all we know for certain."

Janet opened her mouth to say something, but the lights in the room dimmed. They did not quite go out.

Hutch peered into the cockpit. The warm green glow of the oxygen lamp still burned. "We're okay," she said.

Moments later, they came back up.

No one was sleeping well. Everyone tossed and turned, and made pointless trips to the washroom, and read late into the night. They had three divans to stretch out in. That created problems. At first the men had insisted they would sleep on the deck. Hutch, feeling the weight of tradition, refused the divan, and declared her intention of sleeping up front in the pilot's chair; Janet and Maggie announced they would accept no special consideration. Eventually, they agreed to a schedule. Everybody would get a divan three nights out of five, and spend the other two in the cockpit.

Despite the limited fare, there was a tendency to overeat. They stayed closer to the shuttle now, rarely going out for walks. The long unlit passageways of the starship had an unsettling effect.

Hutch learned that Janet had been a peace activist during the Arab Wars, had picketed the World Council regularly, and had been jailed in New York and Baghdad. "In New York, we whitewashed the cells," she said, "and the cops got irritated. We had good P.R. NewsNet was always there next morning to take pictures. Eventually, they had to do something. Didn't look good having all these straight A types getting locked up. People got excited a lot easier in those days."

Hutch came to realize that Frank Carson, for all his bravado, and his considerable accomplishments, was unsure of himself. He needed the approval of those around him, and he was not entirely comfortable in his role as mission director. She sensed that he was relieved that the crisis had come on shipboard, in Hutch's area of responsibility. For that reason, perhaps, he was especially sympathetic to her, whom he perceived as having, to some degree, failed. Hutch found it difficult to mask her annoyance. She questioned her own competence, but didn't care to have others participating in the exercise. Furthermore, her tolerance for sympathy was low.

George was drawing closer to her. Periodically, while he joked about the lack of privacy or the advantages of celibacy ("Keeps the mind clear"), Hutch detected passion in his eyes. Her own emotions churned. She loved being near him, but it was frustrating that they could be alone only if they took walks together. Which was to say, advertised that there was something going on.

Maggie made no secret of her reservations regarding male intellectual capacities. "They're okay when they're alone," she might say, "but put a woman in the room and their IQ drops thirty points." She masked these comments as light banter, but everyone suspected there was a wound that had not healed. No one took offense.

At 1106 GMT, Thursday, March 31, precisely one week after the collision, the alarm sounded. Hutch unbuckled, but Carson pushed her back. "Relax. I've got it." And he floated forward to the instrument panel.

No one said anything. They could hear him up there, could hear the play of electronics. "Air pressure's down," he said. "We're not getting much."

"Let's go take a look," said Hutch.

The line that connected *Alpha* with the starship's pumps had cracked. A stream of vapor fountained out, turned to crystals, and floated away.

"I would have thought," said Carson, "that everything in a shuttle bay would be impervious to the cold."

"There are limits," Hutch told him. "This place isn't supposed to be constantly frozen." The decks, and the equipment, were covered with frost. When she flashed her light around, the beam filled with fine white particles. Hutch examined the line. "We've got a couple of spares. We'll replace it."

It was now -77°C.

They got up a bridge game that night, taking turns sitting out. It lasted longer than usual, and when it was over no one wanted to sleep.

Hutch had one of the divans. It was more comfortable than the web-chair up front, but she still had to tie herself down to avoid floating off.

"Eventually," George said, "we'll all sit around at the Mogambo and reminisce about this." He didn't explain what the Mogambo was.

"I hope so," she said. The lights were out.

"Wait and see," he said. "The day will come when you'd do anything to be able to come back here and relive this night."

The remark surprised her. It was out of character. "I don't think so," she said. She thought he wanted to say more, but was leaving her to fill in the blanks. Their third occupant was Maggie. No dummy she: Hutch knew she would have liked to shrink into her blankets. Damn. "Goodnight, George," she said, and whispered, too low for anyone to hear, "maybe."

• • •

The line to the pumps gave way again the following morning just as she was getting up. Carson was in the cockpit waiting for her.

They went out into the bay, carrying lamps, and removed the line a second time, with a view to putting in another replacement. While they were working on it, Hutch became uneasy. "Something else is wrong," she said.

"What?" asked Carson.

It took a minute. "Power's off."

The electronic murmur that normally filled the starship was gone.

"Hey." George's voice came from the shuttle. "We got red lights in here."

"On my way," said Hutch. And to Carson: "That's it for the pumps. We'll have to switch to internal air."

"It's too soon," said Carson.

"I know."

"Okay," said Maggie. "As things stand now, we will use up the last of the shuttle's air April eighth. Give or take a few hours. The breathers will carry us over to the ninth. The cavalry gets here two days later."

At best.

Ship's communications had switched over to a backup power cell. Beyond that, the vessel was dead.

"*Wink's* tanks are full," said George.

Hutch nodded. "That doesn't help us without a working pump."

George, perhaps for the first time, saw things going terribly wrong. He looked pale. "Can we go manual?"

She shook her head.

"I'll tell you one thing," said Janet. "If we're not going to survive this, I don't want to die in here. Why don't we launch, and get away from this mausoleum?"

"We could," said Hutch. "But if help comes, *Wink* will be a lot easier to find than the shuttle."

She too looked rattled.

George's eyes locked on Hutch. "There's *got* to be a way."

"How about Kosmik?" said Maggie. "Quraqua's closer than Nok."

Hutch pulled her knees up under her chin. "I requested help from them ten minutes after we got the response from Nok. They *should* have seen the original distress calls. And they've probably also seen Nok's reply. Assuming best outcome, that they realized we were in trouble, that a ship was available, and that they dispatched it immediately after Nok backed off, they will probably arrive a little earlier than the *Ashley Tee*. But not by much. Travel time on the jump is eight days. They'll need another day to find us after they get here. At least."

"We'd still be dead," said George.

Maggie had been drawing arcane symbols on her lightpad. "I'm not anxious to suggest anything radical." She pronounced each syllable precisely, as if she were reading lines. "But we have a total of forty days of air to divide any way we please."

Carson's eyes came into sudden, sharp focus.

"I'm not recommending anything," she said again. "But it's something to think about."

Four people could last ten days. There would be a chance.

She must have read Hutch's expression. "I'm sorry. We don't seem to be having any luck this time out," she said.

"There's a possibility we haven't tried yet," said Carson. "The Monument-Makers. We know their address. Maybe we haven't been asking the right people for help."

The antenna clusters did not respond. Hutch and Carson went out onto the hull and found what they had expected: the units had been scraped off in the collision. They jury-rigged repairs and installed a guidance system stripped from the bridge. They had brought out a portable transmitter and a booster, and tied everything together. The signal was pre-recorded. It would be a simple SOS on the multichannel, centering on frequencies used by the Football. If there *were* aliens abroad in the system, they might not be able to read the signal, but it would clearly be artificial, and it would have to arouse their curiosity. And, maybe, bring them running. These were desperate measures, and no one had any real hope they would succeed. But it was all they had left.

They looked out across the same schizoid sky that one found all along the edge of the Orion Arm: a tapestry of stars to port, and a black river to starboard. Across the river, they could see the glow of the far shore.

"Ready?"

Carson's voice shook her out of her reverie. She activated the transmitter.

Carson nodded. "Okay. I hear it." Above them, light from the open shuttle bay hatch illuminated the underside of the A ring.

She tucked her equipment into a pouch. Carson had straightened, and stood watching the constellations rise and set around the curve of the ship. Silhouetted against the moving stars, he should have been a heroic figure. But he wore a white pullover with a little sail on the breast pocket, and a pair of fatigues. Despite his surroundings, he looked like a man out for a stroll.

Through the entire operation, her mind was on Maggie's arithmetic. *Four people might make it.*

That evening, Hutch sat up front watching the communication lamps on the main console. Distracted, discouraged, frightened, she felt overwhelmed, and was unaware she wasn't alone until she smelled coffee beside her.

Maggie.

"You okay?" Maggie's voice was controlled. Deliberately calm.

"I've been better."

"Me, too." She had something to say, but Hutch knew she'd get around to it in her own good time.

They stared out into the dark bay. "The Monument-Makers know about us by now. If they exist." Maggie held her cup to her lips.

"That's true."

"You know this is the first *functional* artifact we've found. Anywhere."

"I know."

"This is a historic trip." Another pull from the coffee. Maggie was nervous. "People will be reading about us for a long time to come."

Hutch didn't think *she* would look so good. She would rank right in there with the captains of the *Titanic* and the *Regal*.

"You ever been in serious trouble before?" asked Maggie. "Like this?"

"Not like this."

"Me, neither." Pause. "I don't think we're going to come out of it."

Hutch said nothing.

Maggie's eyes shaded away from her. "I can understand this has been harder on you than on the rest of us."

"It hasn't been very easy on anybody."

"Yeah." Her face was masked in the shadows. "Listen. I know you're blaming yourself."

"I'm okay." Hutch's voice shook. Tears were coming. She wanted to tell Maggie to go away.

"It isn't *anybody's* fault."

Maggie's hand brushed her cheek, and it was more than Hutch could stand. "I feel so helpless," she said.

"I know," said Maggie.

Janet Allegri, Diary

April 2, 2203

This is an odd time to start a diary. I've never done it before, never even considered it, and I may be down to my last few days. Still, I watch Maggie writing into her lightpad every evening, and she always looks calmer when she's finished, and God knows I'm scared silly and I need to tell somebody.

I feel as if I should be doing something. Writing a will, maybe. I've neglected that, but I can't bring myself to begin it. Not now. Maybe it's too much of an admission.

I should probably make some recordings. There are people I need to say goodbye to. In case. But I'm not ready for that yet either.

I've been thinking a lot about my life the last few days, and I have to say that it doesn't seem to have had much point. I've done well professionally, and I've had a pretty good time. Maybe that's all you can reasonably ask. But tonight I keep thinking about things not done. Things not attempted because I was afraid of failing. Things not got around to. Thank God I had the chance to help Hutch throw her foamball. I hope it gets out. It's something I'd like to be remembered for.

(No second entry to the "Diary" is known to exist.)

• • •

We will have to pitch somebody over the side.

Hutch had one of the divans that night, but she remained awake. If it had to be done, *then 'twere well it were done quickly*. And, though she shrunk from the necessity, though tears rolled down her cheeks, and cold fear paralyzed her, she understood well enough the ancient tradition: save her passengers, at whatever cost to herself.

Without her, they had a chance.

Every moment she continued to breathe, she lengthened the odds against them.

Midway through the night, she found herself back in the pilot's seat, unsure how she had got there. Outside, the bay was black. Silent. Dimmed lights from the cockpit threw a glow across one of the cradle bars. Snowflakes drifted through the illumination.

The ship's air supply was freezing.

Do it now. Get it over with. End it with dignity.

Alpha had two air tanks. One was full, the other had already dropped off by an eighth.

Maybe she should wait until morning. Until her head was clear. Maybe then, somebody would find a way to talk her out of it. Maybe someone else would volunteer.

She shook the idea away.

Do it.

A pulser bolt would end it quickly.

She got up, opened the storage compartment behind the rear seats. Two pulsers gleamed in the half-light. They had orange barrels and white stocks, and they were not too heavy even for a woman of Hutch's size. They were used primarily as tools, but had been designed so they could double as weapons.

She picked one up, almost casually. She charged it, and when it was done, and the little amber light pinged to green, she set it on her lap. Bright metal and black handgrips. She raised it, not intending to do it *now*, just to see how it felt, and pressed the muzzle beneath her left breast. Her index finger curled round the trigger. And again the tears came.

Do it.

The drifting snow blurred. Be careful. If you make a mess of it, you could slice a hole through the shuttle. Kill everyone else too.

She realized suddenly that would happen anyway. The

weapon had no setting low enough to ensure the vessel's safety. She would have to go outside into the bay to do it right.

George, where are you?

She put the weapon down.

They had talked about their options before the lights went out. By now everyone understood that *four* people had a good chance at survival. And five had *none*. Hutch had said little. Carson took the moral high ground: *I don't want to be rescued at the expense of seeing someone else die.* No one disagreed, but she knew what they were really thinking. Really *hoping*.

Maybe they would get lucky: maybe the SOS would bring the Monument-Makers; maybe they could sleep a lot and use less oxygen. If anyone harbored resentment against Hutch, there was no hint. But she felt the weight of their eyes, of the occasional unguarded inflection.

Janet suggested a lottery. *Write everybody's name on a piece of paper, put the pieces in a box, and draw one.*

They looked guiltily at each other. And George's eyes had found Hutch, and she'd read what was in his mind: *Don't worry. It won't come to this.*

And Maggie: *If we're going to do it, we need to get to it. This is a window that's going to close fast. And then two of us will have to go.*

In the end, they postponed the discussion until morning.

But there was no way Hutch could face that tribunal. She pushed herself from her chair, picked up one of the Flickinger harnesses, sealed off the inner cabin, cycled the air out, and opened up.

Snow flakes floated before her eyes. Not snow flakes, really. Frozen atmosphere. The temperature had dived further, faster, than they had expected.

Holding the pulser, clasping it close, she stepped out of the shuttle. The deck crunched beneath her magnetic boots; some of the flakes clung to metal surfaces. It would have been easy to imagine she was back home, beneath a heavy sky, the white ground cover extending off into the dark.

She used her remote to seal the cockpit. Lights blinked on and off, signaling the return of heat and air.

Goodbye.

She crossed the bay. Behind one of the storage containers

would be best. Somewhere out of the way. Good form. Don't want to be lying out in plain view. She managed a grin.

Equipment lockers and overhead struts and consoles retreated into the dark swirl. She turned on her wrist lamp, and kept its beam low. Her imagination carried her into the Pennsylvania woods where she had played twenty years before.

There were no stars, and the storm pressed down on the trees, heavy, and wet, and quiet.

She moved slowly across the deck, and stopped behind a row of storage cabinets. *Here.*

Just pull the trigger.

Don't damage the Flickinger harness. Or the air tank. Stay away from the chest. Head is best. Maybe she should kill the energy field. It wouldn't stop the pulser beam, but it might deflect it.

The snow drifted through the lamplight.

She looked at her wrist controls and raised the weapon.

Push the button, pull the trigger.

Snow.

Snow!

The idea washed over her. *Yes.* She held both hands out to the flakes. They swirled and danced. Some landed on her palm. They did not melt, of course, but remained white and soft against pink flesh.

Yes!

A few hours later, Hutch and George came outside and opened the shuttle bay doors. (Whenever they touched, their fields flashed.) Since all other partitions and hatches and doors throughout *Wink* were already open, whatever remained of the starship's heat escaped quickly into space.

It was a glorious day, and Hutch loved everybody. She did a pirouette as they walked back toward *Alpha*, bringing Carson's admonition that she be careful, zero gravity, magnetic boots, and all that.

George noticed her tracks of the morning, prints that seemed to go nowhere. He frowned and looked at her darkly, but asked no questions.

And while Hutch, in later years, often described herself as having been monumentally obtuse on the Beta Pac flight, she never told anyone she had been outside the shuttle. In her own mind, she was never sure whether she would actually have pulled the trigger.

Three days later, when the shuttle's starboard air tank had been exhausted, Hutch brought the port tank on line. Everyone except Maggie (they had by now established a policy that someone stay with the shuttle at all times) picked up whatever empty containers were available, and advanced on *Wink's* maintenance section. They used buckets and bowls and plastene housings. They took frames off consoles and uprooted lockers and hauled everything back and set it down before the three main starship air tanks.

Hutch chose the middle one, and dwarfed by the installation, took up a position at its forward end, where the connection valve to the recyclers was located. "Everybody stand back," she said. "There'll be some pressure here." She took a pulser out of her tool belt and aimed at the base of the connection, in close to the tank. With a sense of considerable satisfaction, she pulled the trigger. A yellow beam ignited, and sliced through the metal. White mist spouted and formed a pale cloud.

"That it?" asked Carson.

"Let's hope so." Hutch walked around to the side of the tank and pressed the firing stud again.

George eased in beside her. "Hold it a second," he said. "If we didn't get rid of all the pressure, this thing could explode in your face."

She nodded. "We should be all right."

He reached for the device, but she held it away from him. "Let me do it," he said. "You stand over by the door."

"Forget it. Back off, George." She pulled the trigger.

The beam touched the plastene, which bubbled and began to peel away. Hutch watched with equanimity. It was going to work.

She refocused the pulser, and fired again. The tank hissed, and a long split appeared. She cut it wider, and someone put a light to it, *into* it.

It was filled with heaps of snow. Frozen atmosphere. The snow was blue-white, and it sparkled and glowed.

They filled their containers and returned to the shuttle bay and passed them into the *Alpha* through the cockpit. They dumped the snow into their empty starboard tank. When they had measured out enough, they closed the tank. Several containers remained on the outside deck.

Then they had a party.

And when it was over, and they thought everyone else was asleep, George and Hutch went up to the cockpit and took one another for the second time.

Of course, everybody knew.

LIBRARY ENTRY

I sailed up a river with a pleasant wind,
New lands, new people, and new thoughts to find;
Many fair lands and headlands appeared,
And many dangers were there to be feared;
But when I remember where I have been,
And the fair landscapes that I have seen,
Thou seemest the only permanent shore,
The cape never rounded, nor wandered o'er.
                —Henry Thoreau

from *A Week on the Concord and Merrimack Rivers*
(Copied into his notes by George Hackett, April 5, 2203.)

20.

In the vicinity of Beta Pacifica. Friday, April 8; 2110 hours.

Melanie Truscott came to the rescue on the fifteenth day after the collision. She arrived in the *Catherine Perth*, a sleek new transport, and dispatched a shuttle to pick them up.

The transfer craft was one of the new Trimmer types, designed primarily for hauling heavy equipment. Because it was too big to enter *Wink*'s bay, the pilot brought it alongside the main door, where they rigged up a cable. No one was sorry to leave. Maggie, on her way out, commented that it was a good thing they hadn't had to depend on the locals.

The shuttle pilot was a weathered, middle-aged man, jaunty in Kosmik green. He waited in the cargo hatch, grinning and shaking hands with each of them as they came aboard. "Good to see you. You folks okay?" His voice had a vaguely Midwestern accent. "Jake Dickenson. Let me know if I can do anything to help. Coffee up front."

When they were all in and belted down, he asked their names, and recorded them on a lightpad. "Only a short flight," he said, tucking the pad under one arm, and retreating to the cockpit. Hutch was trying to pick the *Perth* out of the starfield, and having no luck, when they pulled away from *Winckelmann*.

They disembarked a half-hour later, and found Harvey Sill waiting. Sill wore an open-necked white shirt two sizes too small. He looked not quite as tall as he had on Hutch's overhead monitor. But in every other way, he was *bigger*. There was something of the rhino, both body and soul, about him. His voice was big, and he oozed authority. He made no effort to hide his disgust at being called out to rescue incompetents.

277

He delivered a perfunctory greeting to Carson and Janet, whom he knew, frowned at Hutch as if he recalled having seen her but couldn't remember where, and ignored the others. "Please come with me," he growled, and strode off.

The *Perth* was returning about a hundred members of the Project Hope crew, and their equipment, to Earth. It dwarfed the scaled-down *Winckelmann*, and had the feel of a small city. Its cabins and lounges were filled with people. "You were lucky," Sill said. "Ordinarily, we wouldn't have had a ship available." He sounded as if they deserved a less happy conclusion.

"No justice anywhere," said Hutch, drawing a frown.

They followed him into a board room. The decor was far more luxurious than the Spartan furnishings of Academy vessels. The bulkheads were tastefully paneled in stained walnut. Portraits of stiff-looking elderly men and women ringed the room. The Kosmik seal was mounted between a pair of corporate flags. A carved door was set in the bulkhead on the other side of a broad conference table. Sill waved them into seats around the table. "Wait here," he said. "The director wants to talk with you, and then we'll assign you quarters."

He spun on his heel and left.

"I'm not sure," said Janet, "I wouldn't prefer to go back to the *Wink*."

Minutes later, the carved door opened, and Melanie Truscott came in. She wore a Kosmik worksuit, without ornamentation. She faced Carson, smiled politely, and offered her hand. "Good to see you again, Frank," she said.

Carson's expression was masked, but Hutch knew he was embarrassed. "We appreciate your assistance, Melanie."

Her gaze flicked across the others. "I know you had a difficult time. I'm glad we were able to help." She moved on to Janet. "Do I know you?"

"Dr. Janet Allegri. I don't think so. I was with the Temple group."

"Welcome aboard the *Perth*, Dr. Allegri." She gave the name just enough of a twist to suggest that the formality was amusing.

Maggie was next. "I've seen *you* somewhere. Maggie—"

"—Tufu."

"You're the cryptologist."

"Exophilologist."

"Same thing." Truscott's eyes narrowed. "You were the reason they stayed too long."

To Hutch, it seemed as if everyone stopped breathing. But the statement was delivered as if it were a simple, obvious fact rather than a judgment.

"Yes," said Maggie. "That's probably true."

Truscott took a seat, not at the head of the table, which they had unconsciously left empty, but between George and Janet. "Things don't always work out as we'd like," she said. And, looking across at Hutch: "And you are the pilot."

"I am."

"I know you, too. Hutchins, I believe."

"Yes. You have a good memory, Dr. Truscott."

"My job is largely political." She peered into Hutch's eyes. "What happened to your ship? To the *Wink*?"

"We jumped in at the wrong place." She glanced at Carson. *Do we want to tell her any more?*

"How do you mean?"

Carson encouraged her. "There's an object out there that registers no mass," she said. "We showed up in front of it."

Truscott nodded. "That would be one of the telescopes."

"One?" asked Maggie.

"Oh, yes. There are eight in all, we believe, although we've only located five so far. It's an array." If she had said she'd encountered a flight of wild turkeys, Hutch could not have been more surprised. It had never occurred to her that the monster was anything other than unique.

"Where are the others?" asked Hutch.

The light shadowed and softened Truscott's features. She must have been breathtaking when young. "All in the same orbit." A steward entered with a tray heaped with sandwiches, wine, and fruit drinks. "A remarkable engineering project. Certainly well beyond *our* capabilities. Wouldn't you agree, Frank?"

"Yes," said Carson. "Have you seen one up close?"

"No. You were our first priority."

"Thank you for that. They must be very thin." Carson let his curiosity show. "I wonder how they hold together?"

She regarded him with interest. "Tell me, Frank, how did you know something like this was here?"

"An accident," he said. "We're on a routine survey."

Truscott's eyes glazed. Of course. "If you like. Do you

want to see the object you hit?"

"Yes, we would. Very much."

"I'll give the word to the captain. The *Perth* was about to leave for home when we heard your distress call. We came this way with every intention of continuing that journey after we ensured your safety. But the damage you've sustained can't be repaired out here." She swung her attention to Hutch. "Do you concur?"

"Yes," said Hutch.

Truscott smiled at her, as if they shared a secret. "When is the Academy vessel due?"

"About three days."

"You understand we cannot wait. I intend to examine the artifact, and then we will proceed home. Ah, you don't approve."

And leave the Monument-Makers to others? Damn real.

"We need to talk," said Carson.

"I'll be happy to listen."

"Frank—" Hutch used a warning tone. If there were discoveries of a technical nature to be made at Beta Pac, they did not want to allow Kosmik any claim to them.

Carson's hesitation was evident. The room fell silent for several beats. Then he said "We have reason to believe there are ruins in this system. We would like very much to be put down near them." Hutch smiled to herself. He was making it up as he went along.

"What is the nature of the ruins?"

"We don't really know yet, Melanie. Relatively primitive."

"Of course."

"Can you take time to do that?" asked Carson. "Give us a pod and some supplies, and we'll wait for the *Ashley Tee* on our own."

She shook her head. "I won't risk your lives." She seemed to be watching Hutch closely, gauging her reaction.

Carson sat back in his chair and tried not to look uneasy. "Let me reassure you that we would not be at risk. The *Ashley Tee* will be here within a few days. At most. You could land us and be gone within twenty-four hours. And we'd be fine."

Truscott's tone softened. "Travel delays are expensive. I don't see how we could manage an extra day. In any case, my passengers are anxious to get home." She tented her fingers, and appeared to dismiss the idea. "I am neither inclined, nor at liberty, to leave you."

Hutch decided to try her luck. "Dr. Truscott," she said. "This might be a major find. You have a chance to make a contribution."

She looked curiously at Hutch. "Would I, really?"

"Like the old days. You haven't given all that up, have you?"

Truscott registered surprise, and her eyes stayed on Hutch for a long moment. "No, young lady, I haven't." She got up, went to the door, and opened it. "Let's see what the telescope *looks* like. Then maybe we can talk some more." She rose. "We'll see. Please help yourselves to the food." And she left the way she had come.

Hutch climbed out of her clothes, showered, and collapsed on the bed without bothering to dress. Gravity felt good. She was asleep within minutes.

She was still asleep several hours later when someone knocked.

"Just a minute," she said. Her robe was still packed in her luggage. She grabbed a pair of slacks, pulled on a blouse, and opened the door. Melanie Truscott stood in the passageway.

"Hello," said Hutch.

"Hello, Ms. Hutchins." Truscott's voice was level. "I hope you're comfortable."

"Yes, thank you." Hutch made way. "Won't you come in?" She used the remote to clear the bed out of the room, and turned on a table lamp. The apartment still looked moderately untidy, but the director didn't seem to notice.

She smiled, and found a seat. "I've been talking with Dr. Carson. You had a close call."

"Yes," she said. "We were lucky to come out of it."

Truscott's hair was swept back, her brows neatly arrowed. She spoke, and moved, with graceful economy. "You *were* lucky. There's no question about that. But you did pretty well," she said.

Hutch thought she'd performed poorly. Moving into the shuttle, and transferring the snow, had both been good ideas. But she'd been slow coming up with them. "Thanks," she said.

Truscott shrugged. "I'd fly with you any time." She looked quite placid, a neighbor who had strolled in for a friendly visit. "I came by because I thought you and I should talk."

"Really? Why?"

"Clear the air." Her tone changed. "You sent over the foamball."

It wasn't a question. And the directness of the statement took Hutch unaware. "Foamball?" She met the older woman's eyes. Oddly, she saw no rancor in them. She would not ordinarily have hesitated to own up, take this woman on. But there was the question of Academy liability. Furthermore, Truscott seemed likable, and her manner suggested that Hutch's deed was ill-mannered. Rude. Perhaps even irresponsible. "That's true," she said. "But I'll deny it if you quote me. How did you know?"

The smile came again. "Obvious. No one else had the opportunity. And I'm a decent judge of character."

Hutch shrugged. "You deserved it. You were playing hardball."

"I know." She looked *pleased*. "I assume you'll be happy to know that no permanent damage was done. You gave me some bad moments. Made me look silly. But after a while, my people noticed that I stayed. That I got as many off as I could. I think they compared me to some of the other management types they've known. I gather I came away looking pretty good. Anyway, I wanted to say hello to you properly, and let you know there are no hard feelings."

Hutch thought of Richard clinging to the end of his lifeline while the wave took him. "Easy for you to forgive," she said.

Truscott nodded. "I know. And I'm sorry. But you knew it was coming. Why the hell didn't you get him out?"

"Don't you think I would if I could have?"

Hutch stared angrily at the older woman, and Truscott said quietly, "There's some brandy in the cabinet beside the monitor. Will you have a drink with me?"

Hutch hesitated.

"If you refuse, I understand. And I would be very sorry." She got the bottle, and filled two glasses. "If it helps, Corporate feels the same way you do. They're blaming me for Wald's death. I'm to be fed to the court of public opinion."

Hutch didn't care much for brandy. "I'm not sure whose

fault it was," she said, reaching for a glass. "At this point, it hardly matters."

Truscott looked somber. "Nobody wanted it to happen."

"Of course not." She couldn't quite keep the sting out of her voice. "We're all well-meaning."

The director nodded. "To Richard Wald," she said.

They drank, and Truscott refilled their glasses.

"So what happens now? With you and Kosmik?"

"Board of inquiry. They'll find culpability on my part if I let it go that far."

"Can you stop it?"

"I can make a public apology. Take the blame. I don't mind doing that. It happened on my watch, and I can't really evade responsibility. Did I tell you I was directed to see that no one was hurt?"

"No—" Hutch felt a new surge of resentment.

"It's true. I thought I'd arranged things pretty well. But I blundered."

"How?"

"Doesn't matter."

"What will happen to you?"

"They'll get my resignation, I'll drop out of sight for six months, and then I'll start a new career. I'll be fine. I have friends."

Hutch was silent for a long time. Finally she said, "Losing him was such a waste."

"I know. I've been reading his books." She sighed. "Hutch, you have a job with me any time you want it."

They drank to that. They drank to *Perth*, and to *Alpha*.

Then, amused, Truscott proposed a toast to Norman Caseway. "God bless him," she said. "We couldn't have got here without him. And you'd still be waiting for the *Ashley Tee*."

"How do you mean?"

"The *Perth* brought out the people who are going to implement phase two of Project Hope. It also brought the directive for me to go back and face the music. Caseway did not send my recall on ahead. Instead, he arranged to have it handed to me by the ship's captain. An insult. But, as a result they had to wait around a few days while I finished with loose ends. If that hadn't happened, the *Perth* would have been on its way home when your SOS came through.

There would have been no ship to send after you."

Hutch drained her glass, refilled it, and refilled Truscott's. "One more," she said. Hutch did not have a lot of tolerance for alcohol. It didn't take much to loosen her inhibitions, and she knew she should not propose this new toast. But she couldn't help herself.

"To whom?" asked Truscott.

"Not a *whom*, Melanie. You don't object if I call you Melanie? Good. Not a *whom*, Melanie. A *what*. I give you, the foamball."

Hutch raised her glass.

Truscott's aristocratic features darkened. She looked hard at Hutch, and the cloud lifted. "What the hell," she said. "Why not?"

It was clearly a *bowl*. Carson's team gathered in an observation lounge during the approach, where they had access to a wide-screen display and communication with the ship's operations center. Harvey Sill joined them, announcing that he had been assigned to assist. "Don't hesitate to ask for anything you need," he said, with marked lack of enthusiasm.

Perth moved in on the open side of the object. It broadened, and mutated into an inverted world, a world whose landscape sank, and whose horizons rose. They glided below the rim, and their perspective shifted again: the surface flattened, became a blue-black plain, stretching to infinity. The horizon rose, and the lower sky went black. They passed beneath an enormous arch, one of a network tied in to strong points across the face of the object. "This is the only one of the telescopes," Sill said, "that's still transmitting."

"Have you tried to translate the signal?" asked Carson.

"We don't really have the means to attempt it. But we can tell you that they were aimed at the Lesser Magellanic."

There was a young male crewman with them, wearing earphones. He reported precise physical specifications as they came in—diameter, angle of curvature, declination. "And thin," he said. "It's very thin."

"How thin?" asked Carson.

"At the rim, they're saying a little under six-tenths of a centimeter."

"That's still thick enough to have ripped us up," said Hutch. "How did we get *through*?"

"There's an antenna at dead center," said the crewman. "And it looks as if that's where the transmitter is." He listened to his earphones and nodded. "Operations reports it *is* rotating around its axis. They say one complete rotation in seventeen days, eleven hours, twenty minutes."

"What holds it together?" asked Maggie. "It seems too fragile."

"It's not metal or plastic. We're getting odd readings: potassium, sodium, calcium. Heavy concentrations of calcium at the center construct."

"Do we have a picture of it yet?" asked Sill. "The center?"

"Coming up now." The crewman glanced at the screens. The bulkhead opposite the window changed colors, went dark, and revealed a cluster of black globes, a group of small dish antennas, a few domes. "The signal source," said the crewman.

Carson glanced at Sill. "We'd like to get a good look at it," he said.

"We'll take you in close."

"Is there a way we can date this thing?" asked Hutch.

"Maybe if we had a sample," said Janet.

"I don't think we want to do that." Carson looked uncertain *what* he wanted to do. "How about scrapings? Can we do it with scrapings?"

Janet thought about it. "Maybe."

"It's even thinner away from the rim," said the crewman. "Scanners indicate that thickness in this area is less than two millimeters. There's a latticework of thicker material, providing support. But for the most part, the object is micro-thin."

Nobody noticed Truscott until she spoke. "Now we see why *Wink* survived," she said.

She was accompanied by a narrow, uniformed man whom she introduced as Captain Morris. His eyes were the color of water, and his hair was black and cut close in a military fashion. He acknowledged their names and shook hands with an irritating air of self-importance.

They were approaching the cluster of antennas.

"Historic moment," Truscott said. "We are getting a look at the first piece of alien high tech. We'll try to do an analysis, see if we can figure out precisely what we're looking at. How about you, Frank? Do you have an expert along who can give us some answers?"

Carson looked at his colleagues. He received no encouragement. "We're a little short on experts," he said.

Perth glided over the featureless blue-black terrain. Her lights played on the surface, producing muted yellow blurs. The ship might have been moving across a burnished marble floor.

"How does it get power?" asked Janet. "Solar?"

"Probably," said George.

Truscott looked at Carson. "Do you want a sample?"

"Yes," said Maggie.

Carson nodded. "Try not to damage anything."

The captain showed irritation. "We'll take care of it," he said coldly. He spoke into his commlink, listened, and looked puzzled. "Melanie, we can't find the collision site."

"Were we looking for it?" asked Carson.

Morris nodded. "We tracked your course backward, as a navigation exercise for my junior officers. There's no hole anywhere in the impact area large enough to run a starship through. Or anywhere else for that matter."

"Your junior officers flunked," said Carson.

Morris responded with a superior smile. "My junior officers are quite good. And we've checked the numbers. There is no error." He looked at Hutch. "You did not change course, I understand."

"That's correct," she replied. "But we did take some damage. I had to adjust for a tumble, and it's possible that when I terminated the burn the thrusters didn't shut down simultaneously. That could have resulted in a new heading."

Morris shook his head. "There *is* a hole in the impact area. But it's not big enough to accommodate a *shuttle*, let alone *Wink*."

"That's odd," said Truscott.

"That's all there is," said the captain.

"Why don't we take a look?" Hutch suggested. "At the hole we *did* find."

The site was plowed up, exploded outward. They floated above it, in Flickinger belts, looking down through the open space at stars on the other side.

"It's less than seven meters across at its widest point," said the Ops officer, a young woman named Creighton.

"Well, we certainly didn't come through here," said Hutch. "There *must* be another one somewhere."

"No." Morris spoke from the bridge. "There *is* no other hole. We've looked everywhere."

"There *has* to be," Carson insisted.

Lights played across the damage.

"This is strange." George was holding his hand over the hole. He pushed it through, and withdrew it. And pushed it through again. "There isn't clear passage here," he said.

Janet, who'd been examining the membranous material of which the Bowl was constructed, directed her lamp into the hole. "He's right," she said. "There are threads or thin fabric or something in it—"

"Filaments," said Maggie.

ARCHIVE

"Yes, director?"

"Do you have anything yet on the sample?"

"We've just begun."

"What do you know so far?"

"It's organic."

"Are you certain?"

"Yes. I can give you more details in a few hours. But it looks like a spider's web."

Commlog, Ship's Laboratory, NCK Catherine Perth
Dated April 10, 2203

Melanie Truscott, Diary

I have not been able to sleep tonight. We have withdrawn from the immediate neighborhood of that telescope, construct, creature—God help me, I don't even know how to think of it. Now we begin the business of trying to learn who put it there. And why.

There is no evidence of artificially generated electromagnetic radiation anywhere else in the system. Even the other telescopes are quiet. (I wonder, does that mean that their transmitting equipment has given out? Or that the telescopes are dead?)

The third and fourth worlds are both in the biozone, but only the third has life.

April 10, 2203

21.

Melanie Truscott, Diary

Even the transmitter seems to be organic!

How old is this thing? Allegri says that dating the scrapings will require more elaborate techniques than we have at our disposal. She told me privately that she doubts whether they can be dated at all.

The technology level that produced this is unthinkable. I cannot imagine that, if the builders exist, we could enter this system unobserved. If they are here, they made no effort to assist people who were in desperate trouble. And I find that disquieting.

April 11, 2203

On board NCK Catherine Perth. *Monday, April 11; 0510 hours.*

Beta Pacifica III floated in the windows and viewscreens of the *Catherine Perth*. It was a terrestrial world, with a global ocean and broad white clouds. There was a single land mass, a long slender hook, seldom more than two hundred kilometers across. The hook was often broken by channels, and occasionally by substantial patches of ocean, so that it was in fact a series of narrow islands strung together. The coastline was highly irregular: there were thousands of harbors and peninsulas. It extended literally from the top of the planet to the bottom, sliding beneath both icecaps. In the south, it curved back up almost to the equator.

There were ribbons of forest, desert, and jungle, usually stretching from sea to sea. Plains crowded with tall, pulpy stalks dominated the equatorial area. Snowstorms were active in both hemispheres, and it was raining along the flanks of a long mountain range in the south.

Four moons orbited the world. They were airless, cratered rocks, ranging in size from a fifteen-kilometer-wide boulder to a giant a third larger than Luna.

After the discoveries at the Bowl, Truscott had found it easy to persuade her passengers that they were aboard an epochal cruise, and that they would not want to pass up a stop at Beta Pac III. To encourage their cooperation, she broke into the special stores, provided sumptuous meals, and passed out free liquor. Captain Morris objected to all this, and Harvey Sill sternly disapproved, but the passengers were happy enough. And that was all she cared about.

It was dusk over the westernmost arc of the continent. They had approached the world from sunward with a high degree of enthusiasm and were now on their first flyby. Among the members of the Academy team hopes were high, although no one would say precisely what he was hoping for, nor even admit to any degree of optimism. In this sense, Hutch was like the others, playing the hardheaded pessimist, but overwhelmed by the possibilities.

The passengers tried to stay close to them. When history happened, which Truscott's campaigning had induced everyone to expect, they wanted to be able to say they'd been on the spot. Consequently, Carson and Janet had been pressed into giving seminars, and they'd all signed autographs.

As *Perth* approached its rendezvous with destiny, the team retreated to their observation lounge, where Beta Pac III floated on the wall screen. Other monitors carried pictures of the moons, the Bowl, a schematic of the planetary system, comparisons between Beta Pac III and Earth, and rows of telemetry from probes.

Telescopes had been trained for days on the expanding world. They had not yet seen indications of intelligent activity: neither engineering works nor signs of environmental management were visible. But it was possible that an advanced society—this was Maggie's argument—would have learned to live in communion with the natural order. So they watched the continent slide past the terminator. And hoped for lights.

But no soft yellow glow punctuated the gathering darkness. The night swallowed everything.

Collectively, they let out their breath.

"Pity," said George.

Carson nodded. "Nobody home, I think."

Hutch had been sitting quietly, contemplating the image, but she was thinking about Richard, who should have been here for this moment, whatever the outcome. "Too soon to know," she said.

Captain Morris, seated on the bridge at the command console, looked up into the camera, straight into their eyes, and opened a channel. "Still negative EMR," he said. "If there's anyone down there, they aren't generating power." He smiled condescendingly, pleased (Hutch suspected) at the general disappointment. He was mean-spirited, one of those unfortunate creatures who enjoys seeing others fail. Hutch had eaten dinner with him the previous evening, and his position seemed to be that, yes, highly developed species probably existed in the Milky Way. But *here*? Where *we* are? *That* was too incredible.

The numbers on the atmospheric lower levels appeared: 74% nitrogen, 25% oxygen, a goodly fraction of a percent of argon, a miniscule amount of carbon dioxide, and traces of neon, helium, methane, krypton, hydrogen, nitrous oxide, and xenon. Very Earthlike.

Snacks arrived. Snacks appeared constantly, adding to the generally festive atmosphere aboard ship. Coffee, cheese, pastries, fruit juices, beer, rolled in an unending stream out of the galley. Hutch ate more than she would ordinarily have allowed herself, and refused to give in to disappointment. The fact that they were here at all was cause to celebrate. If there was to be no welcome from the Monument-Makers, they had still achieved much. "What do you think?" she asked Carson.

He smiled encouragingly. "If they're not there, maybe they left something behind."

"I'd like to find *something*," said Truscott, who was standing beside Maggie Tufu, looking out at the darkness. "I truly would."

"You've gone well out of your way for this," said Hutch. "We appreciate it."

"You didn't leave me a lot of choice," she said. "It was a chance to be on the *Santa Maria*. I wouldn't have wanted to tell my grandkids that I could have ridden with Columbus, and passed it up."

Janet, who had been up all night watching the approach, retired to a corner chair and fell asleep. In a sense, it signaled the death of their wilder hopes.

Monitors displayed planetary characteristics:

ORBIT

SIDEREAL PERIOD:	1.41 Standard Yr
PERIHELION:	1.32 AUs
APHELION:	1.35 AUs

GLOBE

EQUATORIAL DIAMETER:	15,300 km
OBLATENESS:	0.004
MASS (EARTH = 1):	1.06
DENSITY (WATER = 1):	5.3
ALBEDO:	0.44
AXIS TILT (DEG):	18.7
ROTATIONAL PERIOD (D/H/M):	1/1/17

OTHER

ELECTROMAGNETIC RADIATION (ARTIFICIAL):	None Noted
MEAN EQUATORIAL NOON TEMPERATURE (EST):	28°C

"Hey!" Carson pointed at one of the moons. The one designated Three-B.

At the same moment, they heard the captain's voice, raised a notch above his usual monotone: "Director, we have an anomaly on Three-B."

"We see it," said Truscott. Three-B was the largest of the satellites. It was heavily scored, covered with lava seas. In the northern hemisphere, they could make out, on the western arm of a broad plain, *something*. A mark. An eruption. A *speck*.

"What is it?" said Carson. "Can you give us a better picture?"

The image got bigger. And clearer. "We don't know yet," said the Captain. "It's the same color as the surrounding rock."

"It looks like a square," said Janet, awake again.

Morris had become almost frenetic. It was amusing to see him nonplused. "It *does* appear symmetrical," he said.

"It's an Oz," said Hutch.

"Roughly two hundred kilometers on a side," continued the captain. "*Big*."

"She's right," said Carson. "It's the same damned thing they've got at Quraqua."

Maggie raised a triumphant fist. "Except bigger. A *lot* bigger."

Truscott looked at Carson. "Do we want to inspect it up close?"

Carson glanced at each of his people in turn. "No," he said. "We know what it is."

Truscott nodded. "Obviously," she said. "It *is* Oz, isn't it? Why do I have the feeling you've been holding back on me. What's the connection with Quraqua?"

Carson shrugged. "No big secret," he began.

After the continent had drifted into the world's night, the Academy team reviewed the pictures. They looked for likely city-building sites: harbors, river junctions, mountain passes. And for roads. For any evidence of habitation.

George was looking at a site about 30 degrees north, where the land mass narrowed to less than half a kilometer. Lush red and yellow forest rolled downhill from a promontory and spilled into the ocean on both sides. It was the kind of area that, on Earth, would have been natural high-roller real estate. Good place to spend a weekend with Hutch. His mind drifted and his tides began to rise when he noticed a sharp angle in the trees. A shadow. A *wall*, maybe.

Or a place where a wall had once existed.

He could find nothing more definite, and was about to show Hutch, when Janet said quietly, "I think I've got something."

They were only dark pocks on a river. But they were regularly spaced.

"I think they're bridge supports," said Janet, her voice rising. "Son of a bitch, they are!" She threw up her hands. "Ladies and gentlemen, we have a *bridge*!"

Well, they didn't really have a bridge. They had the remnants. But it didn't matter. Cheers broke out. The assembled passengers surged forward, spilling coffee, pounding one another, calling to others outside to come see. There were handshakes all around and Hutch got squeezed and kissed and squeezed again. But she didn't mind. Goddam, she did not care.

"Congratulations," said Truscott.

"How much time," said Carson, "can you give us?"

"Frank," she said patiently, "I am already well behind schedule. We had an agreement."

"But we *have* found something."

"Yes, we have. The Academy has a new archeological site to explore." She took a deep breath. "I'm sorry. I even think I know how much it means to you. But we have to get moving. I'm glad we got something out of this, but I'm going to authorize departure. Morris is raising a storm. And he has grounds for complaint. You'll have to come back with your own people."

Hutch thought she knew what it would mean. Somebody would figure out that this world had been home to a starfaring society. There'd be a lot at stake, and consequently the mission would be taken away from the Academy. There'd been momentum in that direction before they left home. Carson and his friends might one day return, but it would take a while, and they would be subordinate parts of a much larger operation.

Damn.

Truscott left, and they sat listlessly around the lounge, commiserating with one another, crashed from the emotional high of a half hour before. Hutch stood all she could for fifteen minutes, and got up to go somewhere else. As she did, the commlink chimed, and Sill's image appeared. "Dr. Carson," he said, "would you come up to the bridge, please? Bring your colleagues with you."

"We have an object in orbit."

Melanie Truscott, with the captain in tow, steered her five passengers to the main navigation display. It was mostly starfield, with a muted planetary arm across the bottom. One of the stars was extremely bright. "*That* one," she said.

Hutch felt a ripple of exhilaration. "What kind of object?"

The captain answered. "We don't know. You're looking at mag five. But it isn't a natural satellite. Its RI is way too high for its range."

"An RI is a reflectivity index," said Truscott. "It's *big*.

Bigger than our station at Quraqua."

Hutch and Carson silently shook hands.

"John." Truscott was addressing the captain. "Are we prepared to make a quick exit if we have to?"

"Yes, Director." He motioned to one of his crewmen, a quick jab with his index finger, and the crewman spoke into a mike. Hutch suspected they were warning all passengers to tie down.

"Is there any indication of onboard power?" asked Hutch.

"Negative." Morris bent over one of the consoles. "Nothing." He looked sternly at Truscott. "Melanie, we have a ship full of people. I think we should leave the area."

The bridge was immense by Hutch's standards. There were four officers on duty, not counting the captain. One, a young woman seated at the navigation console, touched his shoulder and directed his attention to a display. "We've got lights down on the surface," she said. "Low power. *Very* low. Probably not electrical."

"Reflections?" asked Truscott.

"Possibly," she said.

Truscott turned to Carson. "Someone's made your point for you, Frank. What do you want to look at first?"

When had Hutch ever seen Carson look more pleased? "The orbiter," he said.

"Very good." She folded her arms. "I believe we are about to commit history."

They pursued the white star down the curve of the world.

It took a hauntingly familiar form on the scopes: a double-ring rotating wheel, not unlike the home station, or Kosmik's orbiter at Quraqua. The architectural style was less utilitarian. This orbiter possessed a degree of elegance and panache, of blurred lines and eclectic curves. It looked fully capable of harboring winding staircases and secret rooms. It was a station with a gothic flavor, maybe the kind of station Poe would have designed.

Windows were everywhere. But they were dark.

Hutch loved it. She watched it drift closer, felt a cool stirring within her, a chill that was simultaneously pleasurable and disquieting.

"Negative EMR," said one of the officers. "It's tumbling." And, moments later: "Wheels not rotating."

Pity, thought Hutch. We're too late again.

She knew Carson well enough to read his discouragement. There was no denying the signs: the Bowls in disrepair, no lights on the surface, a collapsed bridge, and a dead orbiter. The Monument-Makers were gone.

"We'll want to board," said Truscott.

Carson nodded *Yes*, as if he had anticipated a struggle.

The captain's features hardened. "I advise against it, Director."

There was something wrong about it. More than its strangeness, because strangeness was at the heart of the thing, designed into it, underscored by all those unlighted windows. Something else was wrong.

"I understand, John. But we can't really sail away and just leave this." Truscott's face glowed with excitement. "And I wouldn't miss it for anything." She looked at Carson. "I assume you would like to come?"

Hutch saw a shade of disapproval cross Carson's features. In view of the long history of accidental damage caused to artifacts by untrained personnel, he would have preferred to limit the landing party to the Academy group. But he was prudent enough to hold his tongue. "Of course," he said.

"Any others from your team?"

"I expect," said Carson, "everybody."

"Very good. We can manage it." She turned to Sill. "How about you, Harvey?"

"If *you're* going."

She swung back to Morris. "Seven for the shuttle, Captain."

Hutch went to her compartment to change. She was still uneasy. There was something that shouldn't be there. Or something missing. It was at the edge of vision, a memory that one can't quite grasp.

She switched on her monitor. The orbiter was coming into sunlight. Its twin wheels would once have rotated counter to each other. Now the entire artifact simply rolled slowly over as she watched.

What might its design reveal about its builders? It was the sort of question Richard would have asked. What do the esthetics tell us? There were symbols on the hull, black, angled strokes and tapered loops. Two groups of characters, she thought. Two words. What had they been?

Details appeared: blisters and antennas and connecting coils and hatches and maintenance pods (at least she assumed that was what the teardrop bulges above and below the rim, distributed at equal intervals, had to be) and loading bays and equipment whose purpose would have to await closer inspection.

A long cable trailed behind the thing.

And hatches were open.

She wrapped her arms around her knees and stared hard at the object, trying to imagine how it might have been when it was active, and exotic ships circled it. And the antennas received signals from the Great Array.

How long ago?

She got up, padded across the floor, and into the washroom. She started the flow of water in the shower, adjusted the temperature of the stream, and stepped in. It was cool and brought a sting of pleasure.

Gravity was generated on all starships the same way: by rotating the living spaces, whether they were located within a permanent hull, as was the case on *Perth*, or within the ring-shaped modules of the *Winckelmann*. Consequently, the shower stream bent slightly counter to the direction of spin. Not enough to be noticeable, but the same crosswise pressure sent the water swirling across her toes and down a drain located at the side of the stall. Hutch enjoyed the sensation; it was one of the many effects of shifting gravities that she relished, that lent her wings and granted a sense of freedom from terrestrial shackles.

And today, while she closed her eyes and let the cool spray wash over her, it occurred to her that the space station had also been designed to spin. To create the same effects.

And *that* was what was wrong.

She finished quickly, dried off, slipped into a *Wink* work uniform, and hurried up to the Academy observation lounge. Carson was still there, and Maggie. The others had gone, presumably to prepare for the boarding.

"Everything okay?" Carson asked as she burst into the room.

"Why was it built to rotate?" she demanded.

"Why was *what* built to rotate?"

"The space station, damn it."

Maggie stared at her, astonished at the question.

"Why is it so much like *our* stations, Frank? The Monument-Makers are supposed to have had anti-gravity. So we always assumed they had artificial gravity as well. But then why build rotating wheels?"

"Maybe we were wrong," said Maggie. "Either we still haven't found the Monument-Makers, or—"

Frank finished her statement. "—this was built *before* the Monument-Makers came to Iapetus."

"That," said Maggie, "would mean this thing's been up here more than twenty thousand years. I don't think that's possible."

Carson did not want to talk about more complications. "Maybe it's a Monument from their early days. So they kept it in place. Let's not worry about it now."

"Another Monument?" Hutch didn't believe that for a minute. She opened a channel to the bridge. The captain was not there, but she spoke to the command duty officer. "I wonder if you would do me a favor?"

"What do you need?" The CDO was a middle-aged, graying, no-nonsense woman.

"The space station," she said. "How stable is its orbit? How long would you say it's been here?"

The CDO looked uncomfortable. "We're navigators, Ms. Hutchins. You'd need a physicist to come up with that. I'd like to help, but we just don't have the expertise."

"Do what you can," said Hutch, using a tone that implied full confidence.

The CDO allowed herself a pleased smile. "We'll try."

John F. Morris, was a man with narrow shoulders, narrow tastes, and narrow vision. He had achieved the highest position to which he could aspire, and he had done it by unrelenting loyalty to the company, taking care not to offend the wrong people, and good old nose-to-the-grindstone attention to detail. He was not a man to be overwhelmed by other people's histrionics, but he could recognize a career danger. His great strength, and his great weakness, was an unblinking, clear view of the downside. He knew that Melanie Truscott was in difficulty, and that she was taking liberties with his ship. The fact that she had every right to do so (within certain specifically-provided-for parameters), that she had full authority to direct his movements, might not help him if someone decided to take offense at the misuse of company property. Or if something went seriously awry. It was for these reasons that the captain had remained aloof and cool during the approach to Beta Pac III. He was not prepared to defy Melanie Truscott, because he knew very well that one did not advance one's career by offending the powerful, even when the powerful were in trouble. People at her level had a way of resurrecting themselves. But he was not a good enough actor to conceal his displeasure.

He felt compromised, and he resented it. His resentment extended in no small way to the Academy refugees whom he'd pulled from their wreck. Especially Carson, who pretended to know everything.

Satisfied that the shuttle would be ready for its rendezvous with the station when promised, the captain went looking for Truscott. He found her in the forward lounge, deep in conversation with Sill. She looked up when he entered, noted his grave appearance, and smiled in her most reassuring manner.

"I'm not comfortable about going any further with this," he said.

"Oh?" Truscott's gaze sharpened. "What is it that bothers you?"

"Several things." His voice shook. He did not like opposing a superior, even to the extent of adhering to his duty to provide sound advice. But now that he was fairly begun, he would maintain a steady course. "First, the transfer of personnel to a derelict of unknown nature is a violation of the regs. However you try to cut it. And if there's any kind of emergency, we aren't well-equipped to deal with it. Our medical department is limited. We have only one shuttle. If you get into trouble over there, we cannot come to your rescue. At least, not very easily. And certainly not quickly. Furthermore, I have collaborated in this fiction about a maintenance stand-down, but that won't protect us if we have to answer difficult questions. Should a problem arise, should we sustain any sort of major equipment loss, damage to the ship, or, God forbid, lose someone, I think Corporate would be extremely short with both of us." He paused to let the seriousness of their situation sink in. "There are other potential problems. For example, the artifact is probably priceless. If we damage it, might we not be held liable?"

Truscott nodded, in that infuriating manner that suggested she had already considered all these things. "And what do you suggest we do, John?"

"That's easy. Set course for home. Report the finding, and let people who are trained in these things, and properly equipped, deal with them." He straightened his shoulders.

"You're probably right," she said. "But I can no more turn away from this than you could walk out the airlock. John, don't you have any curiosity? Don't you want to know what's over there? Or what's down on the surface?"

"Not when it interferes with my duty."

"I understand. We'll have to disagree on this one. Please continue the preparations."

He bowed. "As you wish. The shuttle is ready."

"Thank you. And, John?"

He turned, standing in the doorway.

"Log your objections."

"Thank you, Director."

He walked back through the quiet passageways of the *Catherine Perth*, toward the bridge, and he knew that if things went wrong, she would do what she could for him. But it wouldn't help much: they'd all go down together.

The comm watch officer chimed Carson. "Response to your question, sir."

Frank was walking with Maggie toward the shuttle bay. "Go ahead."

"Telescopic examination of the anomaly on Three-B *does* reveal charring. Over perhaps thirty percent of the structure."

Carson watched his team file into the shuttle ready room. George looked happy and anxious; Maggie was intense and full of electricity. He had grown close to Maggie during this mission, had found her far more human than he would have believed. And less detached than she would have wanted to reveal. Today, standing on the edge of history, she anticipated photos. And had dressed the part.

Janet was playing her usual casual role, unflappable, talking quietly to Hutch. But she was a little more erect than usual, her eyes brighter, and he sensed her eagerness to get about the day's business.

And Hutch herself. He'd learned to read her moods. Today she was distracted, preoccupied, thoughtful. He understood that their objective was more personal for her than for the professionals. The archeologists had uncovered their grail, and maybe far more. But Priscilla Hutchins had never learned to let go; she was carrying a lot of baggage with her to the derelict.

"Safety first when we get over there," he said. "Take care of yourself, and don't break anything." They would split into three groups: Janet and himself, George and Maggie, and Hutch with Truscott and Sill. "I'd have preferred that we didn't have to carry Dr. Truscott and her pet bulldog along, but since they own the shuttle, there's not much we can do. Hutch, I want you to keep an eye on them. Don't let them get hurt; don't let them wander off.

"We'll keep in contact, check in with each other every ten minutes. Try not to get involved with the details of what we see. We need a map and a general survey. Once we've got those, we'll set up a plan of action and try to go about this systematically."

"How long will we be staying?" asked Maggie.

"Four hours. That allows us a reasonable safety margin. We'll carry a couple of extra Flickinger harnesses and air tanks on the shuttle. Just in case. Hutch?"

"Will there be someone with the shuttle throughout the operation?"

"Jake is our pilot. He'll stand by. We're going in through an open hatch. It's one of several. Apparently, when the owners left, they never bothered to close the doors."

Sill came in. "We'll be ready in a few minutes," he said.

George was studying a lightpad. "The station has at least six airlocks," he said, "or apertures that look like airlocks. The outer hatches on three of them are open." He looked at the faces around him, inviting an explanation.

"They left in a hurry," suggested Janet.

"Don't know," said Sill.

"I think," said Maggie, "we're going to discover the artifact has been stripped of everything valuable. The last visitors were looters. Which would explain why they didn't bother to close the doors." She put a finger to her lips. "I wonder why there are no other stations? The later ones? There should be more advanced orbiters."

"Who can say?" said Carson. "Maybe they all went down." He looked at each of them. "Okay, what else? What have we missed?"

Hutch looked up. "Pulsers?"

"We'll have one with each group," said Carson.

"Why do we need them?" Maggie asked.

"To get through doors that won't open."

But Maggie looked uncomfortable. "What's wrong?" asked Janet. "That's not unreasonable."

"Don't know," she said. "The place is a little spooky, and I'm not sure it's a good idea to be walking around in there with weapons. In case somebody gets nervous."

"If nothing else," said Carson, "we might need it to cut through the inner door of the airlock."

Truscott and Sill arrived. "Sorry to be late," she said. "Our people have been doing a structural analysis of the station."

"What have they concluded?" asked Carson.

Truscott passed to Sill. "Primitive," he said. "It isn't up to our technology at all. And by the way, we have an answer to Hutchins's question about the orbit. As far as we can tell, it's stable. This thing may have been here a long time. Possibly for thousands of years."

"One other thing," said Truscott. "We've found some more ruins. A lot of them."

Melanie Truscott, <u>Diary</u>

"As for man, his days are as grass; as a flower of the field, so he flourisheth. For the wind passeth over it, and it is gone; and the place thereof shall know it no more."

—Psalms 103: 15–16
April 11, 2203

22.

*Approaching the space station at Beta Pac III. Monday,
April 11; 2140 hours.*

They looked through large oval windows at long passageways, and wide sunlit rooms filled with oversized chairs and
carved tables and broad carpets.

"They knew how to live," Hutch told Truscott. The two
women had been talking like old school friends. Everyone
was a trifle garrulous on this flight, except maybe Sill, who
simply stared warily out the window.

Their pilot, Jake Dickenson, was elaborately uneasy, and
full of advice. "Don't assume there's no power," he warned.
"Be careful what you touch." And: "Keep in mind there's
always a chance the thing might be booby-trapped. We don't
know what the circumstances were when these people left."

They drew alongside, and the air in the shuttle thickened.
The station was brick-red. It looked like a run-down fac-
tory, cluttered with struts and joists and supports and turrets.
There was no attempt here to create a smooth outer skin:
the hull supported a wide array of pods and antennas and
beams. There were also parapets, dormers, crests, and brack-
ets whose only *raison d'etre* appeared to be decorative. The
turrets might have housed living quarters, with wrap-around
windows.

"Shuttle bay to port," said Jake. Two cradles were visible
through a pair of windows. A small, blunt-winged craft lay
in one of them.

They passed above an antenna field. Sill poked an index
finger against the window. "Here's what I mean about primitive technology. Look at these. These are conical antennas.
They are *light-years* behind the biosystem apparatus they
were *growing* on the Bowl. This station is probably limited

302

to radio. And their technology for *that* isn't very good. Look at the antenna booms."

"What's wrong with them?" asked Carson.

"Ungodly long. We've been doing better than that since the twentieth century. And it uses oversized solar panels. They're inefficient. This thing wasn't built by the same people who designed the telescope."

Hutch described her own conclusion that the shape of the station suggested a technology more primitive than the one associated with the Iapetus visitors.

"How long ago was that?" asked Sill.

"Twenty thousand years."

"Which means what? That this thing is older than that?" He squinted out the window. "I don't believe it."

"Why not?" said Carson. "You've already said this thing is *old.*"

"But not *that* old," replied Sill.

Hutch didn't believe it either. But she was tired thinking about it. They needed to wait until they had more information.

The shuttle glided past long rows of empty windows. She glanced at George, entranced by the view. "What are you thinking?" she asked.

He seemed far away. "How lucky I've been," he said. "I got an assignment with Henry right out of the box. Most of the guys in my class wound up working on reclamation projects in Peru and North Africa. But I got to see the Temple. I was there when most of the major discoveries were made. Now I'm here—"

Jake's voice broke in: "Coming up on the front door."

Truscott surveyed her passengers. "Let's go," she said.

They'd picked out an open hatch more or less at random. The station's red skin moved slowly past the viewpanels. Hutch had just begun to check her equipment when Jake gasped.

"What's wrong?" Sill asked.

"The inner door to the airlock," he said. "It's open, too."

"No seal," said Maggie. *The station was exposed to vacuum.*

"Can we get a picture?" demanded Sill. "That doesn't make sense. Airlocks are always designed to prevent anyone from being able to open both doors at once. Because if you do, you die. Maybe *everyone* dies."

"Someone must have overridden the safety mechanism," said Hutch. She looked toward Carson. "I wonder if all the open hatches are like this?"

The shuttle nosed into lockdown position. Meter-long extensors, equipped with magnetic couplers, had been added for this flight. Now Jake extended them. When he was satisfied both were in contact, he activated the power. A mild jar ran through the craft. "We're in business," he said.

He sealed off the cockpit while his passengers buckled on Flickinger harnesses, stepped into magnetic boots, and checked breathers. When they were ready, he depressurized their cabin and the cargo bay. Sill opened the door at the rear of the cabin and led the way into the cargo section, where he distributed portable scanners and collected two pulsers.

He strapped one to his side in an easy, familiar motion, and held the other out to Carson. Carson took it, checked it expertly, and put it on.

Sill produced about thirty meters of cable. "We'll string a tether out to the station's hatch. Lock onto it when you go. Everything's turning, so if you get thrown off, we might not get you back." He glanced around to assure himself that energy fields were all active. "Director," he said, "would you like to do the honors?"

Truscott declined, and looked at Carson. "Frank—?"

And Carson, in the spirit of the proceeding, turned it over to Maggie. "She got us here," he said.

Maggie nodded appreciatively. "Thanks," she said. They opened the doors, and the derelict's surface curved past within arm's length. It was pocked and scarred. Maggie reached out, and *touched* it. First contact.

"If you like," Hutch told Carson, "I'll set up the line."

He nodded, and she pushed through the door.

"Careful," whispered Sill.

Hutch's momentum carried her across to the station's hull. She put both boots down on its metal skin, and looked for the hatch.

Above. About ten meters.

Sill clipped the cable to a magnetic clamp, secured the clamp to the hull of the shuttle. Then he passed the line and a second clamp to Hutch. She snapped the line to her belt and started toward the hatch. Her perspective shifted: the deck of the cargo hold, which had been "down," rotated 90 degrees. Her stomach lurched, and she closed her eyes to let the feeling pass. The trick now was to focus on the derelict. Steady it. Make herself believe it was stationary. Forget the shuttle, which was now vertical. The sky moved around her, but she concentrated on the hatch.

The airlock was big enough to accommodate a small truck. The inner door was indeed open, but she could see nothing beyond except metal deck and bulkhead. She attached the clamp and waved to Maggie, who promptly drifted out of the shuttle.

Hutch warned her about keeping her eyes on the hull. She nodded, and tied onto the cable. But she had difficulty from the start, and Hutch had to go get her. When they got back to the airlock, she helped her inside, where the environment was less upsetting. "You okay?" she asked.

Maggie crumpled into a ball. In a weak voice she reassured her rescuer.

"I hope this is worth it," Hutch said.

"It is," Maggie said feebly.

They came over one by one. The sunlight was strong, and everyone used filters. They climbed rapidly into the lock, anxious to gain the security of an enclosed space.

The inner passageway beckoned. Maggie recovered quickly and claimed her privilege, stepping through into a bare, high-ceilinged chamber. Bilious orange walls were lined with empty bins. One was cluttered with debris, pinned by the motion of the station. There were instruments, and a giant boot, and plastic sheets and semiflexible material that might once have been clothing.

"Maybe they left the airlock open," said George, "to preserve the interior. If they really wanted to maintain this as a memorial, I don't know a better way. Let the vacuum in, and nothing will deteriorate."

Janet was fascinated by the boot. "They were *big*, weren't they?"

Carpeting still covered the deck. Passageways that dwarfed even George opened off either end of the chamber. They were lined by windows on one side and closed doors on the other. The doors were quite large, possibly four by two meters.

When Hutch, who was the last one through the airlock, caught up with them, they were examining the equipment. George thought he recognized some of it—"this is a recharger, no question"—and Maggie had already begun to collect symbols. Carson picked a passageway at random and moved into it.

None of the doors yielded to gentle pressure, and they would not of course break in, short of necessity. The outer bulkhead consisted mostly of windows. Outside, they could see the sun and the shuttle. One of the windows had been punctured, and they found a corresponding hole a couple of centimeters wide in the opposite deck. "Meteor," said George.

They clicked along awkwardly in their magnetic shoes, staying together, not talking much, moving like a troop of children through strange territory. Hutch noted a vibration in the bulkhead. "Something's going on," she said.

It was like a slow pulse.

"Power?" asked Truscott.

George shook his head. "I don't think so."

More deliberately now, they advanced. The sun moved past the windows and out of sight. The corridor darkened.

Sill produced a lamp and switched it on.

The heartbeat persisted. Grew stronger.

The planet rose and flooded the passageway with reflected light. Its oceans were bright and cool beneath broad clouds.

Ahead, around the curve, something *moved*.

Rose. And fell.

A *door*. It was twisted on a lower hinge, but still connected to the jamb. As they watched, it struck the wall in time to the vibration, moved slowly down and bounced off the deck.

They looked through the doorway into another, smaller chamber. A crosspiece set at eye level resolved itself into a rectangular table, surrounded by eight chairs of gargantuan dimensions. The chairs were padded (or had been: everything was rock-hard now). Hutch entered, feeling like a four year old. She stood on tiptoe and directed her lamplight across the tabletop. It was bare.

George had a better angle. "There are insets," he said. He tried to open one, but it stayed fast. "Don't know," he said.

The furniture was locked in place. "It looks like a conference room," said Janet.

Cabinets lined the bulkheads. The doors would not open. But, more importantly, they were inscribed with symbols. Maggie made for them like a moth to a flame. "If it *is* the

Monument-Makers," she said, after a few moments, "they aren't like any of the other characters we've seen." She was wearing a headband TV camera, which was relaying everything back to the shuttle. "God, I love this," she added.

There was another doorway at the rear of the room, and a second, identical suite beyond.

Hutch turned off the common channel, and retreated into her own thoughts. She watched the shifting shadows thrown by the lamps, and remembered the lonely ridge on Iapetus, and the single set of tracks. Who *were* these people? What had it been like when they gathered in this room? What had they talked about? What mattered to them?

Later, they found more open doors. They looked into a laboratory, and an area that had provided support functions to the station. There was a kitchen. And a room filled with basins and a long trough that might have had an excretory use. The trough was about as high as the table. They saw what might have been the remains of a showering facility.

Daylight came again. Forty minutes after it had passed out of the windows, the sun was back. At about the same time, they came to an up-ramp which split off the passageway.

"Okay," said Carson. "Looks like time to divide. Everybody be careful." He looked at Maggie. "Do you have a preference where you want to go?"

"I'll stay down here," she said.

He started up. "We'll meet back here in an hour. Or sooner, if anybody finds anything interesting." Truscott and Sill fell in behind him, and the plan to have Hutch watch them collapsed. Carson grinned, and signaled for her to forget it. Hutch, delighted to be rid of what had promised to be onerous duty, rejoined George and Maggie.

They continued along the lower level, and almost immediately found a room filled with displays and consoles half-hidden by lush, high-back chairs. "Computers," breathed Maggie.

There were photos on the walls. Faded. But maybe still discernible.

Maggie was trying to get a look at a keyboard, but the consoles were too high. She glowed with pleasure. "You don't think they'd still work, do you—?" she wondered.

"Not after a few thousand years," said Hutch. "If it's really been that long."

"Well, even if they don't, the keyboard will give us their alphanumerics. That alone is priceless."

Then George got excited. He'd found a picture of the vehicle they'd seen in the shuttle bay. It was in flight, and the space station was in the background. "Glory days," he said.

A second photo depicted Beta Pac III, blue and white and very terrestrial.

Eager to have a look at the consoles, Maggie moved in front of a chair and pulled off one of her magnetic shoes, planning to float up onto the equipment. But she became suddenly aware of something *in* the chair. She half-turned, and screamed. Had she been successful in removing both shoes, she would probably have launched. As it was, one foot remained locked in place, and the rest of her anatomy careened off at a sharp angle. She pitched over, and crashed into the deck.

The chair was *occupied*.

Carson's voice erupted from the commlink. "What's happening? Hutch—?"

Maggie stared up at the thing in the seat, color draining from her face.

"We've got a corpse," Hutch said into the common channel.

"On our way," said Carson.

The occupant of the chair was a glowering, mummified *thing*.

"This one, too," said George, trying to steady his voice, and indicating the next chair.

Two of them.

Maggie, embarrassed, stared up at the corpse. Hutch walked over and stood beside her. "You okay?"

"Yeah," she said. "It just startled me. I wasn't expecting it."

Its eyes were closed. The skin had shriveled to dry parchment. The skull was dust-brown, lean, narrow. Ridged. Long arms ended in large hands that retained a taloned appearance. The gray-black remains of a garment hung around its waist and clung to its legs.

"There must have been air here for a while," said George. "Or the bodies wouldn't have decomposed."

"I don't think that's so," said Maggie. "Organisms are full of chemicals. They'd cause a general breakdown whether the corpse is in a vacuum or not. It would just take longer."

It was belted into its chair.

Had been belted in when the airlocks were opened.

Its dying agony was still imprinted on its face.

What had happened here?

Maggie gingerly touched its knee.

Hutch stood in front of it, and knew the thing. Recognized it.

Carson and the others filed in.

They spread around the room, moving quietly. "Is it them?" Truscott asked. "The creatures from Iapetus?"

"Yes," said Carson. He looked around. "Anybody disagree?"

No one did.

"Sad," Maggie said. "This is *not* the way we should have met."

Sill was just tall enough to be able to see the work stations. "It's their operations center, I think," he said.

George turned back to the photos. They were encased and mounted within the bulkhead. Most were too blurred to make out. But he saw a cluster of buildings in one. He found another that appeared to be a seascape. "That could be Maine," said Sill, looking over his shoulder.

Hutch could not look away from the corpses.

Strapped down.

Had they been murdered? Unlikely. The restraining belt did not look capable of holding anyone who didn't want to be held. Rather, they had stayed here while someone opened the airlocks and let the void in.

The station was a mausoleum.

They found more corpses in spaces that seemed to have been living quarters on the upper level. They counted thirty-six before they stopped. There would undoubtedly be more. The bodies, without exception, were belted down. They understood the implication almost from the start, and it chilled them. *It was a mass suicide. They didn't want to get thrown around or sucked out by decompression, so they overrode whatever safety features they had, tied themselves in, and opened the doors.*

"But *why*?" asked Truscott. Carson knew the director to be tough and unyielding. But she was shaken by this.

Maggie also seemed daunted. "Maybe suicide was implicit in their culture. Maybe they did something wrong on this station, and took the appropriate way out."

In the aftermath of their discovery, they roamed aimlessly through the station. Adhering to the spirit of Carson's safety concerns, or maybe for other reasons, no one traveled alone.

Maggie commandeered Sill and stayed close to the operations area. They prowled among the computers, and took some of the hardware apart, with a view to salvaging data banks, if they still existed.

George and Hutch went looking for more photos. They found them in the living quarters. They were faded almost to oblivion, but they could make out figures wearing robes and cloaks. And more structures: exotic upswept buildings that reminded Carson of churches. And there were two photos that might have been scenes from a launch site, a circle that resembled a radio dish and something else that looked like a gantry. And a group photo. "No question about *that* one," said George. "They're posing."

Carson laughed.

"What's funny?" asked George.

"I'm not sure." He had to think about it before he recognized consciously the absurdity of such intimidating creatures lining up for a team picture.

In another photo, two of them stood beside something that might have been a car, and waved.

Carson was moved. "How long ago, do you think?" he asked.

George looked at the picture. "A long time."

Yet the place did not evoke the weight of centuries, the way the Temple of the Winds had. The operations spaces might have been occupied yesterday. Things were a little dusty, but the station was full of sunlight. It was hard to believe that the sound of footsteps had not echoed recently through the long corridors. But there was an easy explanation for that: the elements had not been able to work their will.

George found a photo of the four moons strung out in a straight line. "Spectacular," he said.

"Maybe more than that," said Carson. "It *might* give us the age of this place."

• • •

Maggie found the central processing unit. It appeared to be intact. "Maybe," she said.

Sill folded his arms. "Not a chance."

Well, they would see. Stranger things had happened. She would remove it, if she could figure out how to do it, and send it back to the Academy. They *might* get lucky.

Three hours after their entry, they regrouped and started back to the shuttle. Maggie had her CPU, and they carried the photo of the four moons. They also had taken a couple of computers.

Hutch was preoccupied. She watched the shifting light and said little as they clicked back through the passageways.

"What's wrong?" Carson asked at last.

"Why did they kill themselves?"

"I don't know."

"Can you even *imagine* how it might happen?"

"Maybe they got stuck up here. Things went to hell planetside."

"But there's a shuttle on board."

"It might not have been working."

"So you'd have to have a situation in which, simultaneously, your external support broke down, and the onboard shuttle also broke down. That sound likely to you?"

"No."

"Me, neither."

Priscilla Hutchins, *Journal*

Tonight, I feel as if someone took an axe to the Ice Lady. The Monument-Makers seem to have vanished, to be replaced by pathetic creatures who build primitive space stations and kill themselves when things go wrong. Where are the beings who built the Great Monuments? They are not here.

I wonder if they ever were.

0115, April 12, 2203

23.

Beta Pacifica III. Tuesday, April 12; 0830 GMT.

The shuttle glided through the still afternoon above a rolling plain. The windows were drawn halfway back, and fresh air flowed freely through the vehicle. The smell of the prairie and the nearby sea stirred memories of Earth. Strange, really: Carson had spent all those years on Quraqua, on the southern coastline, and he'd never once felt the sting of salt air in his nostrils. This was also the first time he'd ever ridden a shuttle without being sealed off from the outside environment.

First time with my face out the window.

There were occasional signs of former habitation below: crumbling walls, punctured dams, collapsed dock facilities. They were down low, close to the ground, moving at a hundred fifty klicks. The sky was filled with birds.

They came up on a river. It was broad, and mud-colored, with sandy banks, and giant shrubs pushing above the surface close to shore. Lizardlike creatures lay in the sun.

And more ruins: stone buildings in the water, worn smooth; a discolored track through forest, marking an ancient road.

"They've been gone a long time," said George.

"Want to go down and take a closer look?" asked Jake, their pilot.

"No," Carson said. Hutch could see that he wanted to do precisely that, but Truscott had given them thirty-six hours. "Mark the place so we can find it again."

The prairie rolled on. They listened to the rush of air against the shuttle, watched the golden grass ripple in the wind.

"Something ahead," said Maggie.

It was little more than a twisted pile of corroded metal. Carson thought it might once have been a vehicle, or a machine. Impossible to tell from the air.

They left the river and flew over a patch of desert, passing over walls, and occasional storage tanks sinking into the dunes like abandoned ships.

Prairie came again, the land rose and narrowed, and ocean closed in on both sides. In this area, rock walls were everywhere, like pieces of an enormous jigsaw puzzle.

They picked up another river, and followed it south into forest. Mountains framed the land, and the river disappeared occasionally underground, surfacing again to roll through picturesque valleys.

Carson had a map on his display. "Seems to me," he said, "that the towns are located in the wrong places."

"What do you mean?" asked Hutch.

"Look at this one." He tapped the screen. A set of ruins were well out on the plain, several kilometers from the ocean, and fifteen from a river junction. "It *should* be here, at the confluence."

"Probably was, at one time," said Maggie. "But rivers move. In fact, if we can figure out when the city was *on* the confluence, we might get a date for all this."

"They shared the human taste for living by water," said Hutch.

Carson nodded. "Or they relied heavily on water transportation." He shook his head. "Not very rational, for a civilization that had anti-gravity thousands of years ago. What happened? Did they have it, and then *lose* it?"

"Why don't we go down and look?" suggested Janet.

Ahead, the river drained into a bay. "Up there," Carson said. "Looks like a city. And a natural harbor. We'll land there."

The forest took on a jumbled, confused appearance. Mounds and towers and walls broke through the foliage. It was possible, with a little imagination, to make out the shape of streets and thoroughfares.

Was the entire continent like this? One vast wreck?

Jake touched his earphones. "Ops says the *Ashley Tee* has arrived. Rendezvous in about forty hours."

"Marvelous!" said Maggie. Maybe they would be able to stay now, and inspect this world of the Monument-Makers at their leisure.

Jake congratulated them, but Hutch saw that he was not

pleased. When she asked, he said that he did not want to get pulled out now.

The forest overflowed a wide, sun-dappled harbor. Great broad-leafed trees crowded the shoreline. The shuttle sailed out over the open sea, and curved back. A narrow, grassy island divided the harbor mouth into twin channels. Both were partially blocked by a collapsed bridge.

Hutch saw truncated squares in the water, massive concrete foundations (she thought), and piles of rubble.

"There used to be *big* buildings down there," said Janet. "Maybe something on the order of skyscrapers."

"There are more in the woods," said George.

"Anybody got a suggestion," asked Carson, "where we should set down?"

"Don't get too close to the shoreline," advised Hutch. "If there are predators, that's where they're most likely to be."

They picked out a clearing about a half-kilometer from the harbor. Jake took them down and they landed among wet leaves and bright green thickets.

Hutch heard the cockpit hatch open. "Hold it a minute," said Carson. "We need to talk a little before we go out there." Good, she thought. For all their experience on the Quraqua mission, these were not people who necessarily understood the potential for danger on a new world. The old fear of contamination by extraterrestrial disease had been discarded: microorganisms tended not to attack creatures evolved from alien biosystems. But that didn't mean they might not attract local predators. Hutch had gotten an object lesson on that subject.

Carson assumed his best military tone. "We don't really know anything about this place, so we'll stay together. Everybody take a pulser. But please make sure you've got a clear field of fire if you feel you have to use it."

They would not need energy shields here; but they would wear heavy clothing and thick boots to afford some protection against bristles, poison plants, stinging insects, and whatever other surprises the forest might have for them. "Which way do we go?" asked Maggie, zipping her jacket.

Carson looked around. "There are heavy ruins to the north. Let's try that way first." He turned to Jake. "We'll be back before sundown."

"Okay," said the pilot.

"Stay inside, okay? Let's play it safe."

"Sure," he said. "I'm not interested in going anywhere."

The air was cool and sweet and smelled of mint. They gathered at the foot of the ladder and looked around in silent appreciation. Bushes swayed in a light breeze off the sea; insects burbled and birds fluttered overhead. To Hutch, it felt like the lost Pennsylvania, the one you read about in old books.

The grass was high. It came almost to her knees. They got out, checked their weapons, and picked out an opening in the trees. Carson moved into the lead, and George drifted to the rear. They crossed the clearing and plunged into the woods.

They immediately faced an uphill climb. The vegetation was thick. They picked their way between trees and spiked bushes, and occasionally used the pulsers to clear obstacles.

They topped a ridge and paused. Tall shrubbery blocked their view. Janet was trying to look back the way they'd come. "I think it's a mound," she said. "There's something buried here." She tried using her scanner, but she was too close, literally on top of the hill, to make out anything. "*Something*," she said again. "Part of a structure. It goes *deep*."

George produced a lightpad, and started a map.

They worked their way down the other side, past an array of thick walls. They ranged in height up to treetop level, and were often broken, or leveled. "This is not high-tech stuff," said George. "They've used some plastics, and some stuff I don't recognize, but most of this is just concrete and steel. That fits with the space station, but not with the telescope."

"It doesn't follow," said Janet. "The more advanced stuff should be on the surface. A low-tech city should be long-buried."

Animals chittered and leaped through the foliage. Insects sang, and green light filtered through the overhead canopy. The trees were predominantly gnarled hardwoods, with branches concentrated at the top. Lower trunks were bare. They were quite tall, topping out at about five stories. The effect was to create a vast leafy cathedral.

They forded a brook, walked beside a buckled stone wall, and started up another mound. The area was thick with flowering bushes. "Thorns," warned Maggie. "The same defenses evolve everywhere."

The similarity of life forms on various worlds had been

one of the great discoveries that followed the development of FTL. There were exotic creatures, to be sure; but it was now clear, if there had ever been much doubt, that nature takes the simplest way. The wing, the thorn, and the fin could be found wherever there were living creatures.

They explored without real purpose or direction, following whims. They poked into a concrete cylinder that might once have been a storage bin or an elevator shaft. And paused before a complex of plastic beams, too light to have supported anything. "Sculpture," suggested Maggie.

Carson asked Janet whether she would be able to date the city.

"If we still had *Wink*," she said.

"Okay. Good." He was thinking that they could send the *Ashley Tee* to find the ship, and recover what she needed.

At the end of the first hour, Carson checked in with Jake. Everything was quiet at the shuttle. "Here too," he said.

"Glad to hear it. You haven't gone very far." Jake seemed intrigued. "What's out there?"

"Treasure," said Carson.

Jake signed off. He had never before been first down on an unknown world. It was a little scary. But he was glad he'd come.

Jake had been piloting Kosmik shuttles for the better part of his life. It was a prestigious job, and it paid well. It hadn't turned out to be as exciting as he'd thought, but all jobs become dull in time. He flew from skydock to ground station to starship. And back. He did it over and over, and he transported people whose interests were limited to their jobs, who never looked out through the shuttle ports. This bunch was different.

He liked them. He'd enjoyed following their trek through the space station, although he'd been careful to keep his interest to himself. It was more his nature to play the hard-headed cynic. And *this*: he knew about the Monument-Makers, knew they too had roamed the stars. Now he was in one of their cities.

The heavy green foliage at the edge of the clearing gleamed in the bright midday sun. He leaned back and clasped his hands behind his head. And saw something. A glimmer of light in the trees.

It looked like a reflection.

He poked his head through the hatch and leaned forward and watched it for several minutes. Something white. A piece of marble, maybe. The warm harbor air washed over him.

They stopped by a crystal stream and gazed at the fish. The filtered sunlight lent an air of unreality and innocence to the forest. There *were* paths, animal trails, but they were narrow and not always passable. Occasionally, they had to back away from a dead end, or a steep descent, or a bristling thicket. Carson wore out his pulser and borrowed Maggie's.

The stream ran beneath a tapered blue-gray arch. The arch was old, and the elements had had their way with it. Symbols had been carved into the stone, but they were long past deciphering. Maggie tried to read with her fingertips what lay beyond the capability of her eyes.

She was preoccupied, and did not hear a sudden burst of clicking, like the sound of castanets. The others didn't miss it, however, and looked toward a patch of thick briar in time to see a small crablike creature pull swiftly back out of sight.

Beyond the arch, they found a statue of one of the natives. It was tipped over, and half-buried, but they took time to dig it up. Erect, it would have been twice George's height. They tried to clean it with water from a nearby stream, and were impressed with the abilities of the sculptor: they thought they could read character in the stone features. Nobility. And intelligence.

They measured and mapped and paced. George seemed more interested in what they couldn't see. In what lay hidden in the forest floor. He wondered aloud how long it would take to mount a full-scale mission.

There was no easy answer to that question. If it were up to the commissioner, they would be here in a few months. But it would not be that simple. This world, after all, could be settled immediately. And there would be the possibility of technological advantage. Hutch thought it would be *years* before anyone would be allowed near the place, other than the NAU military.

Jake climbed out onto the shuttle's wing, dropped to the ground, and peered into the trees. He could still see it.

The clearing was lined with flowering bushes, whose lush

milky blooms swung rhythmically in a crisp wind off the harbor. They were bright and moist in the sunlight. Jake's experience with forests was limited to the belt of trees in his suburban Kansas City neighborhood, where he had played as a kid. You could never get in so deep that you couldn't see out onto Rolway Road on one side, or the Pike on the other.

He understood that despite its peaceful appearance, the woodland was potentially dangerous. But he wore a pulser, and he knew the weapon could burn a hole in anything that tried to get close.

The day was marked by a sky so blue and lovely that it hurt his eyes. White clouds floated over the harbor. And sea birds wheeled overhead, screaming.

He touched the stock of his weapon to reassure himself, and walked toward the edge of the clearing.

They were fairy-tale trees, of the sort often portrayed in children's books with grimaces and smiles. They looked very old. Some grew out of the mounds, enveloped the mounds in their root systems, as if clutching whatever secrets might be left. The city had been dead a long time.

"Hundreds of years," said Maggie.

The underbrush now was sparse, and the trees were far apart. It was a forest cast in summer sunlight, a vista that seemed to lose itself far away among the living columns.

They came over the crest of a hill and caught their collective breath.

The land dropped gradually away into a wooded gully, and then rose toward another ridge. Ahead, a wall emerged from the downslope, from thick, tangled brush, and soared out over the ravine. It was wide and heavy, like a dam. Like a rampart. It extended somewhat more than halfway across the valley. And then it stopped. Five stories high, it simply came to an end. Hutch could see metal ribs and cables. A skeletal stairway rose above the wall, ending in midair. There had been crosswalls, but only the connections remained. The top was rocky and covered with vegetation.

"Let's take a break," said Carson. "This is a good place to eat lunch." They broke out sandwiches and fruit juice and got comfortable.

Everyone talked. They talked about what the valley had looked like when the city was here, and what might have happened, and how everything they had gone through had been worth it to get to this hillside.

Carson opened a channel to the shuttle. "Jake?"

"I'm here."

"Everything's quiet."

"Here, too."

"Good." Pause. "Jake, this place is spectacular."

"Yeah. I thought you'd think that. It looked pretty good from the air. Are you still coming back at sundown?"

Carson would have liked to stay out overnight, but that would be taking advantage of Truscott. And maybe foolish, as well. Now, with the *Ashley Tee* within range, he was sure she could be persuaded to wait for the rendezvous. Which meant they had plenty of time to poke around. No need to push. "Yes," he said. "We'll be there."

"I read."

Carson signed off, and turned to Hutch. "How long will the *Ashley Tee* be able to stay in the neighborhood?"

"Hard to say. They'll have a two-man crew. They stay out for roughly a year at a time. So it depends on how much food and water they have left."

"I'm sure we can scrounge some from Melanie," Carson said. (Hutch did not miss the new familiarity.) "I tell you what I'd like," he continued. "I'd like to be here when the Academy mission arrives, say hello, and shake their hands as they come in. By God, that's the stuff legends are made of. Maybe we can find a way."

Jake could see a white surface, buried in the foliage.

He stopped at the edge of the trees, slid the pulser out of his pocket, and thumbed the safety release. The shuttle waited silently in the middle of the field, its prow pointed toward him. Its green and white colors blended with the forest. He should make it a point to get some pictures of the occasion. Jake's shuttle.

The *Perth* name and device, an old Athena rocket within a ring of stars, was stenciled on the hull. The ship was named for the early space-age heroine who had elected to stay aboard a shattered vessel rather than doom her comrades by depleting their already-thin air supply. Stuff like that doesn't happen anymore, Jake thought. Life has become mundane.

He poked his head into the foliage. It was marble. He could

see that now. It was clean and cold in the daylight. But the shrubbery around it was thick and he could find no path. He used the pulser to make one.

He was careful to keep the weapon away from the structure. But he got tangled among the bushes and almost caught himself with the beam. That threw a scare into him.

It looked like a table.

An *altar*, maybe.

It was set beneath a parabola. A line of markings was carved across the rim. It looked old.

Damn. He should have brought the camera. He'd have to go back and get one.

He activated the common channel. "Frank?"

"Here." Carson was eating.

"There's something out here that looks like an altar," said Jake.

"Where?" He caught an edge in Carson's voice.

"Just south of the clearing." He described what he had seen.

"Damn it. You're supposed to stay with the shuttle."

"I *am* with the shuttle. I can see it from here."

"Listen, Jake. We'll take a look when we get back. Okay? Meantime, you get inside the cockpit, and stay there."

Jake signed off. "You're welcome," he said.

The altar was not designed for anything of human size. When he stood in front of it, the table-piece was above eye level. The workmanship was good: the stone was beveled and precisely cut.

He was enjoying himself thoroughly. He struck a heroic stance, hands on hips. He looked up at the parabola. He touched the symbols on the front of the altar.

I wonder what it says?

He walked back into the clearing. Maybe he had actually discovered something. Directly ahead, the shuttle gleamed beneath the bright blue sky.

The grass rippled in the wind.

He felt movement atop his right shoe. Reflexively, he shook his foot, and it exploded in pure agony. He screamed and went down. Something sliced into his ribs, slashed at his face. The last thing he knew was the smell of the grass.

The wall came in from their right off the valley. It was wide enough to accommodate eight people walking side by side, so that after it had plunged through heavy shrubbery into the glade, it came to resemble a roadway. At its point of entry, it was about shoulder high to Hutch. But midway across the clearing, it was broken, and the entire left-hand side had sunk or been removed. Or never existed. It was hard to know which, but the structure dropped in a single vertical step to about the level of their knees, and slipped into the hillside.

They inspected the structure, which was concrete reinforced with iron. Hutch climbed atop the upper section, and pushed through the foliage. The forest floor fell away rapidly.

The stairway lay two-thirds of the way out. "It goes all the way to the bottom," she said. That was not strictly accurate: a lower flight was missing. It picked up again further down and appeared not to stop at ground level, but rather to sink into the earth. How much lay buried in the forest floor? She called for the scanner. "There are at least eight stories in the ground," she said thoughtfully. "It could be a lot more." They would need an airborne unit to get decent images.

She returned to the glade. "Later," Carson told her, looking at his watch. "We'll get a better look later."

Overhead, the swaying, sun-filled branches that blocked off the sky looked as if they had been there forever.

They passed beyond the valley, moving at a leisurely pace, and came to a dome. Janet scanned it and announced that it was a sphere, and that it was probably a storage tank. "It was painted at one time," she added. "God knows what color."

Carson looked at the sun in the trees. "Time to start back."

George opened a channel to call the shuttle. After a moment, he frowned at his commlink. "I'm not getting an answer," he said.

Carson switched on his own unit. "Jake, answer up, please."

They looked at one another.

"Jake?" George went to status mode. The lamp blinked yellow. "We're not getting a signal. He's off the air."

Hutch tried calling the shuttle directly. "Still nothing," she said.

"Damn it," Carson muttered, irritated that his pilot would simply ignore his instructions. He missed his military days, when you could count on people to do what they were told.

"Okay, we'll try again in a few minutes." The daylight had reddened.

They took a group picture in front of the dome. Then they began to retrace their steps.

"Mechanical problem," George suggested. But they were uneasy.

Janet moved with her usual strong gait. Alone among her comrades, she was confident everything was okay at the shuttle. Her mind was too crowded with the triumph of the moment to allow any temporary uncertainty to spoil things. She was accustomed to being present at major discoveries (major discoveries were so common during this era), but she knew nevertheless that when she looked back on her career, *this* would be the defining moment. First-down in the city by the harbor. It was a glorious feeling.

Fifteen minutes later, they had re-entered the valley of the wall, and were headed uphill in single file. Janet had drifted to the rear. She was thinking that she would not live long enough to see this place yield all its secrets, when she noticed movement out of the corner of her eye, just beyond the beaten grass. She looked, saw nothing, and dismissed it.

Her thoughts switched back to the ruin underfoot—

Almost simultaneously, Hutch shouted *Look out*! and a hot, sharp needle drove into her ankle. She screamed with pain and went down. *Something* clung to, scratched at, her boot. She thought she glimpsed a spider and rolled over and tried to get at it. The thing was grass-colored and now it looked like a crab. Maggie ran toward her. Pulsers flared. Around her, the rest of the party were struggling. The agony filled the world.

Carson's reflexes were still good. Janet's scream had scarcely begun before he'd sighted and killed one of their attackers: it was a brachyid, a crablike creature not unlike the one they'd seen earlier in the day. But pandemonium was breaking out around him.

Janet was on the ground. Maggie bent over her, hammering at the thick grass with a rock.

Carson's left ankle exploded with pain. He crashed into a tree and went down.

Hutch dropped to a kneeling position beside him, pulser in hand.

Crabs.

He heard shouts and cries for help.

Maggie reached back and called *Pulser!* and Hutch slapped one into her hand. The brachyid was clamped to Janet's boot. Carson watched it rock madly back and forth in a sawing motion. Blood ran off into the grass. Maggie shoved the weapon against the shell and pulled the trigger. The thing shrieked.

"Stay out of the grass!" cried George. "They're in the deep grass!"

A black spot appeared on the carapace, and began to smoke. Short legs thrust out from under the shell and scratched furiously against Janet's boot. Then it spasmed, shuddered, and let go. Maggie drew it out.

Hutch spotted another brachyid. It was in front of them, watching with stalked eyes. A thin, curved claw scissored rhythmically. She bathed it in the hot white light from her pulser. Legs and eyes blackened and shriveled, and it wheeled off to one side, and set the grass afire. Hutch, taking no chances, sprayed the entire area, burning trees, rocks, bushes, whatever was nearby.

It occurred to her that they might be venomous.

"More coming," said George. "Ahead of us."

Hutch moved out in front, saw several of them ranged across the path. More moved in the grass to either side. "Maybe we should go back," she said.

"No," said Carson. "That might be the whole point of the maneuver."

"*Maneuver?*" George said anxiously. "You don't think they're *trying* to box us in?"

The brachyids charged, churning forward with a frantic sidewise motion that was simultaneously comic and revolting. Their shells reminded Hutch of old-time army helmets. Something like a scalpel flashed and quivered from an organ in the carapace situated near the mouth. Claws twitched as they approached, and the scalpels came erect.

Hutch and Maggie burned them. They hissed, crustacean legs scrabbled wildly, and they turned black and died.

Suddenly they stopped coming and the forest went quiet. They were left with the smell of smoldering meat and burning leaves. Maggie helped Janet up and placed her arm around her shoulder. George lifted Carson. "This way," he said.

Hutch played her lamplight across the path ahead. Nothing moved.

They limped uphill. When they felt it was reasonably safe, they stopped, and Hutch got out the medikit and dispensed painkillers. Then she cut Janet's boot away. The wound was just above the anklebone. It was jagged, bleeding freely, and it had begun to swell. "You'll need stitches," she said. "Be grateful for the boot." She gave her an analgesic, applied a local antiseptic, and dressed it with plastex foam. "How do you feel?"

"Okay. It hurts."

"Yeah. It will. Stay off it." She turned to Carson. "Your turn."

"I hope the thing didn't have rabies," he said. This time, Hutch had a little more trouble: part of his boot had been driven into the ankle. She cut it out, while Carson paled and tried to make light conversation. "It'll be fine," she said.

He nodded. "Thanks," he said.

When she'd finished, Maggie held up her left hand. "Me too," she said.

Hutch was horrified to discover she'd lost the little finger of her right hand. "How'd that happen?"

"Not sure," she said. "I think it got me when I pulled it loose from Janet."

She closed off the wound as best she could. *Son of a bitch.* If they'd been able to recover it, it could have been grafted back by the ship's surgeons. But they weren't going to go back looking.

"Finished?" asked George nervously. "I think they're still around." Hutch could hear them out there, tiny legs scratching against stone, claws clicking. But they seemed to be in the rear now.

Neither Carson nor Janet would be able to walk without help. "We need to make a travois," said Hutch, looking around for suitable dead limbs.

George frowned. "We don't have time for construction work." He found a couple of dead branches and fashioned walking sticks. "Best we can do," he said, distributing them. "Let's go." He directed Maggie to help Janet. And provided a shoulder for Carson. "Hutch, you bring up the rear," he said. "Be careful."

They moved out.

It was slow going. Frank was no lightweight, and George was too tall. He had to bend to support Carson's weight, and Hutch knew they would not make it all the way back to the shuttle. Not like this. Maybe they could find an open spot somewhere. Get Jake to come for them. Use the shuttle to crash through the trees and get them out. If they provided a signal for him to home in on—

George fired his weapon. They heard the familiar crab-shriek. "Damned things are almost invisible," he said. "That one was *ahead* of us."

Where the hell was Jake? Hutch tried again to raise him. But there was still no response. That silence now suggested an ominous possibility.

Hutch looked with frustration at the trees, which could provide no sanctuary since the branches were far beyond their reach.

"This isn't working," said Carson finally, disengaging himself from George and sitting down. "If you didn't have to worry about me, you could carry Janet, and you could move a lot faster. Give me a pulser, and come get me tomorrow."

"Sure," George said. "I'll hold the pass, boys. You go on ahead." He shook his head. "I don't think so."

They were leaving a trail of blood. Hutch traded places with Maggie. Then they started again. Occasionally, Maggie fired her weapon. And it seemed to have gotten personal. "*Little bastard*," she'd say, "*take that*." And: "*Right between the eyes, you son of a bitch*."

She exhausted another pulser. They had three left.

Hutch reluctantly gave Maggie her weapon. "What do you think?" asked Carson.

"We need to get off the ground," said Janet. "We need a tree."

"Find one our size," said Maggie. And then: "How about a *wall*?"

"Yeah," said George. "That should work. The upper level might be safe. If the bastards can't climb." He looked at Hutch. "Can we contact the *Perth*?"

"Not directly. Somebody would need to activate the shuttle relay."

"Wouldn't matter anyhow," said Carson. "They couldn't help. Their shuttle's down here."

His dressing was soaked with blood. Hutch added more foam.

They'd stopped in a small clearing to do repairs, when George held up a hand. "Heads up," he said. "They're here."

Hutch had to fight down an urge to break and run. "Where?" she said.

They came out of the high grass from all directions, and they came in overwhelming numbers. They moved forward with near-military precision. Hutch, Maggie, and George formed a circle around the others and killed with a will. White beams bathed the advancing horde. The brachyids died. They died in rows, but if the lines wavered, they did not stop. Scorched carapaces littered the area, and the grass and bushes caught fire. Carson and Janet, without weapons, squeezed back and tried to keep out of the way. The air filled with the smell of charred meat. A crab trailing smoke caromed off Hutch's foot.

George fought with coolness and calculation. Standing at his side, Hutch almost felt she didn't know him. He was smiling, enjoying himself. The gentle innocence was gone.

Their attackers moved with malice and purpose. Hutch sensed feints and sallies and organization in the attack. Their eyes locked on her and tracked her. No crab on the beaches of her youth had ever seemed so aware of her presence.

Maggie's pulser was fading, going red.

The things came on relentlessly.

The fear that they were not going to get out was beginning to take hold. Oddly, that suspicion induced a series of conflicting emotions in Hutch, like currents in a quiet lake: she was almost simultaneously calm, terrified, resigned. She joined George in taking pleasure in the killing, wielding her beam with deadly satisfaction. And she began to consider how the end might come, what she should do. She decided she would not allow herself, or anyone else, to be taken down alive. She located Carson and Janet with sidewise glances. Carson was riveted by the battle, but Janet caught her eye and nodded. *When the end comes, if it comes, do the right thing.*

The dead, smoking shells continued to pile up. Hutch thought she detected some reluctance in the animals trying to breach the rising barrier, but they were incessantly pushed forward by pressure from behind. She found, increasingly, she could expand her field of fire, and attack the rear ranks. The zone of smoldering meat around them began to act as a shield.

She took a moment to reduce power.

Black smoke was getting into her eyes. She killed two more, and spared one that lurched crazily away from her and ran into a tree.

"We've got to run for it," said George. "Before they regroup."

"I'm in favor," said Hutch. "How do we manage it?"

"The bushes." He pointed to the side. He was shouting, to be heard over the din. Most of the creatures were on the trail, front and rear. "Punch a hole through the bushes," he said.

Hutch nodded.

"Everybody hear that?" called George.

Hutch turned toward Janet and Frank. "Can you guys manage on your own? Until we get clear?"

Carson looked at Janet.

"*I* can hop," she said. "Let's go."

Hutch wasted no time. She swung her pulser toward the shrubbery George had indicated and burned the hole. Several crabs were moving back there, and she killed one while George held the rear. The bushes were thick, and she feared they might bog down in them. Protecting her eyes, she tried to ease the path for Janet. Once, twice, she stopped and drove off attackers.

But by God they were moving again.

Minutes later, they came out on a grassy hillside.

"Where's George?" said Maggie, looking behind them.

Hutch opened a channel. "George, where are you?"

"I'm fine," he said. "I'll be right along."

"What are you doing?"

"Hutch," he said, in a tone she had never heard him use before, "keep going. Get to the wall. I'll meet you there."

"No!" she howled. "No heroes. We need you *here*."

"I'll *be* there, dammit. Frank, will you *talk* to her?" And he signed off.

"He's right," Carson said.

"I'm going back for him—"

"If you do, we're all dead. His only chance is for *us* to get to high ground. Now, *come on*—"

Charred grass and crab-parts crunched underfoot. George followed Maggie, but the crabs came too quickly. He turned and fired. There was no point in his hurrying, because he could go no faster than the people in front of him.

The attack slowed. A few individuals charged, but for the most part, they seemed to understand where the limits of his field of effective fire lay, and they remained outside that range. He backed through the bushes.

They kept pace. And he could hear them on both sides.

He fought down an urge to break and run. He listened for pulsers ahead, and was encouraged to hear only the sounds of people clumping through forest.

In whatever dim perceptions they had, the brachyids understood and avoided the pulser. They did not charge him, at least not in large numbers. They had learned. He needed to use that fact to buy time.

He didn't dare move too quickly. Didn't want to come up on his companions before they'd gained the safety of the wall. So he stopped occasionally, and, when the creatures approached, sometimes singly, sometimes several abreast in their pseudo-military formations, he turned back on them, and drove them off.

Hutch's frantic call unnerved him. He'd been able to hear her both on the link and on the wind. They were still very close. Damn—

The possibilities for ambush were everywhere. But no sudden rush came, no charge from the flank, no surprises. They merely stayed with him. And that was okay. If they were targeting him, they weren't chasing the others. And fast as they were, he was quicker. As long as he didn't have to carry anyone.

He plunged into high grass, too high for him to see them directly, but he could see the stalks moving. He kept going until he came out onto rocky terrain. Where he could see. Where they'd make easy targets.

Let Hutch and the others get as far away as they could.

"Where's the wall?" asked Carson.

They'd reached the top of the slope. Maybe another half klick. "Ten minutes," Hutch said. And, to Janet: "You okay?"

Janet and Carson were limping along as best they could, supported by Hutch and Maggie. "Yeah. I'm fine."

Hutch would have kept George on the circuit, but she had her hands full with her injured comrades, and she didn't want to distract him. But it was hard to keep back the tears.

Carson was quiet. His forehead was cool, and his eyes looked clear. When she tried to talk to him, he only urged her not to stop moving. "I can keep up with you," he said.

They followed their own trail through cut thickets, watching for the foliage to open on their left and give them a view of the wall. *They had to be close now.*

Without warning, Janet collapsed. Hutch caught her, lowered her gently to the ground. "Break," Hutch said. "Take a minute."

Carson did not sit. He hobbled to a tree, and leaned against it.

Janet was pale and feverish. Drenched with sweat. Hutch activated her commlink. "George?"

"Here, Hutch."

"Please come. We need you."

George signed off and committed the misjudgment that cost him his life. He had succeeded in buying adequate time, and might have disengaged and rejoined his friends within a few minutes. But the crustacean army lined up behind him was too tempting a target. He returned to the tactic that had been working so successfully. Thinking to thin out his pursuers, he turned on them, and walked the pulser beam through their ranks. It was red now, failing quickly. But it was enough.

They scattered, making no effort to come after him. And they burned and died as they scuttled away. He pursued with singleminded thoroughness, killing everything that moved. Fires ignited, and the shrieks of the brachyids filled the twilight.

But when he turned back, the ground before him was moving. He played his beam across the new targets. It did not stop them, and he had to concentrate its power on a single animal to kill it.

They advanced deliberately in that sidewise gait, and the scalpels were erect. To his rear, the fire was building. No escape that way.

High on the dark hill, he glimpsed his comrades' lamp.

It looked very far away.

He plunged through an opening in the shrubbery. And they were waiting for him.

24.

Beta Pacifica III. Tuesday, April 12; one hour after sunset.

They saw the flames below, in the dark.

"He'll be okay," said Carson.

Hutch hesitated, looking back. The entire world squeezed down to the flickering light. She wanted to talk to him again, reassure herself. But she remembered Henry's anger: *Where were you when we were trying to get a few answers? All you could contribute was to hang on the other end of that damned commlink and try to panic everybody.*

Miserably, supporting Janet, she set off again. How different everything looked now. The beam from her lamp fell across a tree that had been split by lightning. "I remember this," said Maggie. "We're close—"

Moments later, a scream ripped through the night. It rang across the trees, vibrated in the still air, erupted into a series of short cries. Hutch called out to him and turned back.

But Janet anticipated the move. "No! You can't help him." She grabbed her and held on. "My God, you can't help him, Hutch—"

Janet was considerably stronger, but she could not have restrained her more than a few seconds had Carson not gotten there quickly. They fell in a pile.

"There's nothing you can do," he said.

She screamed.

"You'll make it for nothing." It was Maggie, looking down at her.

"Easy for you," said Hutch, hating the woman. "When other people die, you're always safely away!"

And the tears came.

• • •

The wall looked bright and safe in the glow of the lamp.

Get to the upper level. Hutch's vision had blurred, and she was close to hysteria. "Hold on," Janet told her. "We need you."

The lower strip, the portion they had thought of as resembling a roadway, emerged from the hillside to their right. Halfway across the glade, it rose vertically almost two meters. Not much under ordinary circumstances. But tonight was another matter.

It was a difficult climb with only one foot available. But Carson, supported by Maggie from below, and pulled by Hutch, and perhaps encouraged by the whisper of moving grass, negotiated it, although not without losing more blood. Once he was up, however, Janet became an easy proposition.

Hutch did a quick survey out across the top of the wall to assure herself there would be no surprises. Satisfied, she sat down and got out the medikit. "Let's have another look at everybody," she said in a flat voice.

Janet appeared to be going into shock. Hutch got her legs up, propping them on a mound of earth, removed her own jacket, and drew it over her. Carson was in better shape. When she had done what she could for both, she looked at Maggie's mutilated hand.

"How does it feel?"

"I'll live."

"I'm sorry," Hutch said. "I really didn't mean what I said back there."

"I know."

She changed the dressing. But tears continued to roll down her cheeks and she kept getting everything wet. Maggie had to finish the job herself. Carson hobbled over and sat beside her.

Hutch stared into the dark. The fires had burned out, and the night was growing cool. A crescent moon floated in the trees. "He's gone," she said.

Carson put an arm around her, but said nothing.

"I don't—" She stopped, pulled back, and waited until she had control of her voice. "I don't want to leave him out there."

"We'll get him back," Carson said.

Janet did not look good. *We need to keep her warm.* Maggie contributed her jacket. Hutch gathered some branches and built a fire. The wind began to pick up, and the temperature was dropping. Carson looked pale, and Hutch feared he might go into shock. "It's going to get cold," she said. "We don't want to spend the night out here."

Carson gazed wearily into the fire. "I don't see what choice we have."

"We can get the shuttle."

"How do we do *that*? I can't walk back there. Neither can Janet, for God's sake."

"I don't mean *everybody*. I mean *me*."

"And what would you do after you got there?"

"Bring it here."

The treetops were tied together and shut out the sky. "And do what? You can't get through *that*."

"Sure I can. If we remove a tree or two."

Carson's eyes found hers.

"It's all we've got," she added.

"Wait for daylight."

"We may not have until daylight. Janet's not in good shape." He glanced at Maggie. "What do *you* think?"

Maggie's eyes were wide with fatigue and horror. "I think it's her call," she said.

She hasn't forgotten what I said. Hutch felt desperately tired of it all.

It would have been best, of course, if she could start at once. But there were things that had to be done first.

She needed to find the right tree to take down. She thought they could get away with one, and she found it well out along the wall, past the ruined stairway. It was close enough that they could reach it with a pulser; and she judged that it would leave a hole big enough to get through with the shuttle. That latter point was touch and go, but she was hopeful. If it didn't, they'd deal with it when they had to.

Next, she selected a pickup site, and helped get Janet and Carson to it. Just the use of the term seemed to revive their spirits. Once there, she rebuilt the fire. They were far out over the valley now, and close to the treetops. Branches and leaves reddened in the glow of the flames.

While Hutch got ready to leave, Maggie wandered to the edge, studied the target tree, and looked down. It was about five stories.

"You know what to do now?" Hutch asked.

"Yes. We'll be waiting when you get back."

They had only two functional pulsers left. But Maggie's had gone red. Hutch had the remaining one. She held it out.

Maggie shook her head. "Take it with you. You might need it."

"*You* need it to take the tree down. Anyhow, I'm not going to shoot it out with the little bastards." Janet's breathing didn't sound so good. "Got to go." Their eyes caught and held. "When we get out of here," she said, "I'd like to buy you dinner."

Maggie smiled. It was an uninhibited smile, ringed by tears. "Yeah," she said. "I'd like that."

"Be careful," said Carson.

She strapped the lamp to her wrist and started back along the top of the wall. The night closed over her.

The smell of the sea was strong, and the woods below were full of the sound of insects. George's final cries echoed through her mind, and she was desperately afraid.

Her mind would have conjured up images of his last moments had she allowed it to. But she let the shock effect numb her imagination. She tried to concentrate only on what needed to be done, to push her fears and her loss aside.

She hurried back along the wall, watching the forest floor rise. Ahead, shrubbery blocked her view of the glade.

And she heard them. Directly ahead.

Below, the forest floor was quiet.

Bushes swayed in the wind. She held the lamp up, played its beam across the top of the wall. Everything looked clear. She passed into the screening bushes and emerged in the glade.

They were on the lower level.

She glared down at them.

They were pushing leaves and dirt toward the base of the wall. A chill worked its way up her spine.

Hutch picked up a rock and threw it at them. Incredibly, it missed. But the work stopped momentarily, and eye-stalks swung toward her. Several peeled off and moved into the underbrush on either side of the wall. The others began to back away, and withdrew beyond a distance that George would have recognized.

She opened a channel on her link. "Maggie."

"Here."

"They're out here at the end of the wall. Building a ramp."

She heard a sharp intake of breath. Heard Maggie relay the warning to Carson. "Maybe we should try going down the staircase," Maggie said.

"No," said Hutch. They would never make it. "You've got time yet. Just be ready to go when I get back."

"Okay. Hutch?"

"Yes?"

"I'm looking forward to that dinner."

"Me, too."

She retreated back through the shrubbery, and looked down. It was a healthy jump, about five meters. But she saw only one crab.

She sat down, swung round, and hung by her hands. The thing below began to move. She pushed away from the wall, and let go. The fall took an ungodly long time. While she dropped, she held the lamp away from her body, where it was less likely to get broken or cause injury. She was aware of the wind, and the smell of the woods, and of filtered moonlight.

She hit harder than she'd expected, rolled to her feet, and, without wasting time looking for the brachyid, took off.

The route they had blazed was to her right, uphill, but she thought it wise to stay off it for a while. She chose a parallel course, and resolved to cut over when she was safely away from the area. She had decided she would give the little bastards full credit for military capabilities.

There was no sound of pursuit.

"I'm clear, Maggie," she said into her commlink. "And on my way."

She did not run all out. *Something had happened to Jake.* Keep that in mind. But time pressed. She hurried on, and plunged through blinds and into vegetation that she might otherwise have avoided.

Gradually, she angled uphill, expecting to find the trail.

She didn't. She reached the top of the ridge without knowing where she was. *Son of a bitch.*

She'd missed it. Gone right past it.

Don't panic. She called the wall. Pause. Give her a chance to regroup. "Maggie?"

"Here. How's it going?"

"Still moving. I'm okay."

"Be careful."

"I will. How are you doing with the tree?"

"Slow. The range is a little long."

"Stay with it. I'll keep you posted."

Five minutes later, she stumbled across blackened shrubbery. Okay. This was the way they had come. But the trail barely existed, and her notion that she could sprint back to the shuttle vanished. She realized how little attention she'd paid coming out. And they'd made no effort to mark their passage. No one had considered the possibility of a problem getting back; after all, at worst, it would only be necessary to home in on Jake's signal.

She made several wrong turns. Each time, she retraced her steps and conducted a search. At one point, she came out of the woods and found herself looking across open, moonlit water. The collapsed bridge they'd seen from the air lay in the shallows like a sleeping dinosaur.

The tree did not fall.

Maggie had cut completely through the trunk, but it only leaned to one side, hopelessly tangled in the web of branches. Leaves and broken wood rained down on her, and some went over the side and took the long plunge to the forest floor.

But the canopy was as solid as ever.

"What now?" she asked Carson. She had exhausted her pulser. Only Hutch's weapon remained. She took it out of her belt.

Carson surveyed the trees. "Over there," he said. *Cut that one.* It was the same width, but about four meters farther out. At the extreme limit of the weapon's range. "Get that one, and they might *both* come down."

She looked at him unhappily.

"It's all we've got, Maggie."

She crept to the edge, and reached out. *Get as close as possible.* She pulled the trigger.

Hutch had no idea where she was. There were no stars to guide her. No landmarks. Nothing. She saw no sign of their previous passage, no hill or tree that stirred memory.

She had triangulated on Maggie's link, which sent out a

continuous signal. That told her where she was in relation
to the wall, and allowed her to estimate generally where
the shuttle should be. *It was in this area somewhere.* But
where? She worried that she had already passed it, that it
lay behind her.

"Look out."

The trunk tilted toward them. That shouldn't have happened: Maggie had angled the cut away so it would fall
in the other direction. But instead it came down slowly in
a cacophony of splintering wood. She scrambled back from
the edge. Twigs and leaves and vines came with it. The trunk
slammed into the wall, and the entire structure shuddered. The
general tangle fell across Maggie, a vast leafy net, knocking
her off her feet. Branches cracked and the trunk kept rolling
until it slipped clear and started a long, slow descent into the
abyss. And Maggie realized with horror that she was going
with it.

She was dragged relentlessly toward the edge of the wall.
She tried to free herself. Find something to hold onto. But
everything seemed to be going over the side.

The world was filled with broad flat leaves and a terrible grinding sound. She heard Carson calling her name.
And it occurred to her that she was not going to find out
about Oz. Not *ever*. Nor why the Quraquat had identified the
Monument-Makers with death.

Made no sense.

The tangle paused, balanced high over the forest floor,
allowing her a final glance at the sliver of moon. Mercifully,
it was too dark to see how high she was.

Sorry, Hutch.

"Hutch." The voice was frantic.

"Go ahead, Frank."

"Maggie's dead."

The words hung on the night air. Her eyes slid shut. She
had left the lake front, and was struggling through flowering
plants and oversized ferns. Utterly lost.

"Hutch? Did you hear me?"

"Yes," she said. "How? What happened?" It did not seem
possible. Maggie had been fine. Was too smart—

Carson told her. His voice was thick with sorrow. "I found

her pulser," he added. "She dropped it."

"You're sure she couldn't have survived?"

"Hutch, *she went over the side*." Pause. "Did you get to the shuttle yet?"

"No, Frank. God help me, I have no idea where I am."

"Okay." Carson's voice was gentle. "Do what you can. We've got a hole now. You can get in when you get here."

In the dark, she stared straight ahead. "Out," she said quietly.

Janet had slept through the disaster. Carson looked at her. She seemed unchanged, and her pulse was steady. He sat beside her, grief-stricken. Her eyes fluttered and she touched his wrist. He smiled. "We're doing fine," he said to her unspoken question.

"Can I help?" He had to lean close to hear.

"Not now. Later, maybe." She drifted back to sleep.

Carson buried his head in his hands.

Truscott was listening to several of her passengers outline the future assignments they were expecting when they got home, when Harvey, wearing an irritated frown, asked if he could speak with her in private.

"We've lost contact with the landing party," he said.

That should be no cause for concern. Commlinks failed. "How long?"

"Last check was due forty minutes ago."

She thought about it. "It's a little early to push the button. What do you think? Equipment failure?"

"Unlikely. They would have to be aware of it, though. And the shuttle has several communications methods available. Morris is worried."

"Last status was—?"

"Still on the ground. Carson and the Academy team went off somewhere to look at ruins. They left Jake with the shuttle."

"When were they expected back?"

"Before sunset. It's been dark there for over an hour."

She leaned against the bulkhead. "What options do we have?"

He looked at her. "I hoped you might be able to think of something."

• • •

Hutch was back out on the shoreline, looking at the downed bridge. Here, at least, she had a decent idea which way she wanted to go. But once in the woods, there was no guide. No way to check her course. And she could pass within ten meters of the shuttle and fail to find it.

West. It was toward the west.

She started off, striving to remain within sight of the water.

Earlier, nothing had seemed familiar. Now, she felt as if she'd been everywhere. She moved with frustrated abandon. The brachyids she had feared so much at the beginning of the odyssey had drifted to the back of her mind. *Where was the shuttle?*

Carson's voice broke through the stillness. "Any luck, Hutch?"

"No," she said. "I'm in the neighborhood—"

"Okay. I think we're out of time up here. I can hear them coming."

She did not know what to say.

"I'm going to take Janet down the stairway."

The stairway. It wouldn't work. Probably wouldn't even support their weight. "Don't do it, Frank," she said.

"I'm open to suggestions. We've got maybe ten minutes. At best."

Her lungs heaved. The forest went on forever, trunks and underbrush and roots pushing up through the soil and deep grass and rocks and cane plants.

"Frank."

"Yes?"

"Say something to me. Loud."

"What do you mean?"

"Talk to me."

"Hello."

"Louder."

"Hello."

"Shout it, damn it."

"HELLO!"

"It might work." Jake could not have been attacked unless something got into the shuttle, or he went for a walk. In either case, a hatch, at least, had to be open. Most likely, the cockpit canopy. "Frank, switch to the shuttle's channel, and make as much noise as you can."

She broke contact and listened.

Nothing.

But it was somewhere up ahead. Had to be.

Frank Carson understood that once he left the wall they were dead. Even if he made it down that impossible stairway, they would have no chance. Hutch would not be able to get to them with the shuttle.

Consequently, he bellowed into the commlink. Sometimes he called her name. Sometimes, "SHUTTLE, ONE TWO THREE." Sometimes, "GODDAM, WHERE THE HELL ARE YOU?"

He had stationed himself ten meters in front of Janet. There was still life in the pulser, so they could put up a fight. Ahead, he heard the sound of crustacean claws on rock.

"What's going on?" Janet's voice. She didn't try to move.

Carson explained, in as few words as he could.

"No way off?" she asked.

"No."

"Where's Maggie?"

There was no way to soften it. "Dead," he said. He described how it had happened.

He listened to her breathe. "Little bastards," she said. "Do we have another pulser?"

"No."

She struggled to her feet. Fresh blood welled out of the packing on her ankle. She sorted among broken branches, and picked up one that she could handle.

Carson began talking to the shuttle again. "WE COULD REALLY USE HELP, HUTCH."

Janet stationed herself directly below the opening in the overhang. "If they get here before she does," she said, "I'm going to follow Maggie."

Hutch was fording a stream when she heard it. A whisper, far off, carried away on the wind.

It sounded like: "—Bitch."

She broke into a run.

Carson understood the simple ferocity of a beast look-ing for its dinner. But there was something else at work here. They had expended too much to get him. He wondered at their singlemindedness. Almost as if they perceived the humans as a threat. Was it possible they had dim recollections of the city's former inhabitants, and had made some sort of connection?

Whatever this was about, he was pleased to discover that they hesitated when he showed himself. And there was another piece of good fortune: the brachyids were no quicker on this battered surface than he was. He watched them come, climbing over broken concrete, sliding helplessly into cracks and crevices. One fell off the wall.

He stood adjacent to the stairway. Parts of a handrail had survived. He heard wings, and a large dark-green bird settled on it. The handrail trembled. The bird watched the crabs with interest. Its head bobbed, in the manner of terrestrial avians. It had the wingspread of an eagle, and it leaned forward, made several threatening starts, and suddenly plunged among the creatures. It seized one in outstretched claws, holding it at an angle that prevented the scalpel-claw from doing any damage. The brachyid shrieked, and the bird cackled and rose into the night.

"Where are your relatives?" asked Janet.

Moments later they heard a sharp meaty crack from below.

Last hope of retreat down the stairway was about to go by the boards. Janet looked at him. "You sure we want to let ourselves get cut off?"

He didn't reply.

"We could go sit on it. Climb to the upper level. They couldn't follow us up there."

"The damned thing would collapse. Let's give Hutch more time."

They waited. And eventually the crabs came.

Carson stood with legs braced, the pain in his left ankle pushed into a corner of his mind. They covered the ground before him, a dark horde he could not hope to stop. Nevertheless, they slowed, hesitated, somehow knowing what was coming. When the leading edge had drawn to within a meter, he pointed the weapon at them. They stopped.

He watched.

The moment drew itself out. And finally, as if a signal had been given, scalpels came erect and they swept forward.

The pulser's warning lamp blinked on. He pulled the trigger and played the beam across them, knowing he could not take time to kill them individually. *Hurt large numbers*, he thought, hoping that would be enough to drive them back. They squealed and blackened and crashed together, like tiny vehicles.

They fell back, and the weapon died.

Janet moved close to the edge of the wall. "Okay," she said.

"Hey." Hutch's voice.

"Go ahead."

"I need more noise. I can hear you. The shuttle's right here somewhere."

Carson grunted. "It's a little late, Hutch."

"Talk to me," she raged. "Come on, Carson."

He roared her name to the stars. *"It's too late,"* he cried. *"It's too goddam late."*

"That's good," said Hutch. "Keep at it."

Carson stayed where he was, hoping to intimidate the creatures. He followed Janet's example, and found a branch. He broke off the smaller limbs, and hefted it. When he was satisfied, he joined her. They stood close together.

Carson liked to think of himself as a man of the world. He had taken sex where he could find it, had enjoyed his passions, had been honest with his women. He was not given to sentimentality. Nevertheless some of those women lingered in his affections. Two or three, he might even have settled down with, had circumstances been different. But never in his life had he experienced so strong a rush of emotion, of love for another human being, as he did in those desperate moments, with Janet Allegri, atop the wall in the harbor city.

Hutch's lamplight silhouetted the shuttle, silvered it for all the world to see. Its cold metal hull gleamed, and with desperate joy she thought how it sheltered power she had never appreciated. The cockpit canopy was up, and Carson's profanity spilled out of it in erratic bursts.

"Okay, Frank," she said. "I've got it."

"Good. Move your ass."

It occurred to her that if Jake had been taken inside the ship, it might still be inhabited. But she had no time to monkey with details. She sprinted across the glade, leaped onto the ladder, and was relieved to see that the cockpit, at least, was empty. "On my way," she said into the commlink.

"Keep giving me a signal, turn on the lamps, and don't forget where you're supposed to stand."

She ignited the engines, drew the canopy down, and slammed the door to the cargo section. Checklist. My God, it was hard to ignore old habits. But she had no time for a checklist.

"Negative," said Carson. "All bets are off. The crabs are pushing us to the end of the wall. How far away are you?"

She lifted into the air. "I'll be overhead in two minutes." She locked the DF on Carson's signal, swung around, and hit the burners. The landing gear warning lamp blinked at her: the treads were still down. Leave them that way. The shuttle rolled over a sea of silver-tinged foliage. Look for the *hole*.

Maggie's hole.

She reached behind her into the supply cabinet for a fresh pulser, and laid it on the seat beside her.

Carson and Janet were defending themselves with sticks. Carson clubbed and jabbed the creatures until the wood shattered. Janet swept large numbers of them over the side. But it seemed hopeless, and they had already exchanged a final questioning glance, looking down the side of the wall, when lights blazed overhead.

The shuttle crashed through the vault of the forest. It was wider than its landing surface. But it came down with treads extended and spotlights flashing.

"I see you," said Hutch. "Can you disengage?"

One of the creatures stabbed Carson's good ankle. But he had seen it coming, and he rolled away before the scalpel could penetrate deep.

"Negative," said Janet.

The black hull, ringed by running lights, was coming in directly on top of them. "Heads up," said Hutch.

The top of the wall was alive with the creatures. *How much of us*, wondered Carson, *do they think there is to go around?* In that frightful moment, the notion of all those crabs after two people struck him as absurd. And he laughed.

"Hit the deck," said Hutch. "Look out for the treads."

They went down and one of the brachyids bit Carson's right thigh. Janet hit it with her stick. The agony was blinding.

The treads came in over his head.

• • •

Hutch pushed the stick forward. The top of the wall was ribbon-thin. Alive. The battle disappeared beneath her. The shuttle had visual capabilities below its treads, of course, but Hutch elected not to use them. Just one more distraction. She focused instead on the dimensions of her landing site. Keep level. Keep centered.

Rely on Janet and Frank to get out of the way.

"Stay low," she said. She released the cockpit canopy, and raised it.

Almost down.

Carson screamed. She cut off his channel. No distractions. Not now.

She looked back along the wall. Keep in the middle.

"I'm here, Janet," she whispered.

She jounced down, lifted again. With a little luck, the crabs were running for cover. Do it right. No second chance.

The treads settled.

Contact.

She eased off, got a green board, grabbed the pulser, and leaped out onto the wing.

"Let's go."

Janet already had hold of the boarding ladder. She was covered with blood and dirt and her eyes were wild. Hutch made no effort to be gentle. She seized her shoulder, yanked her up, and pushed her toward the cockpit. Then she went back for Carson.

He wasn't visible. But there *were* crabs down there. Churning, wall-to-wall crabs. Then she heard him, and saw a hand trying to get hold of the port wing, on the other side of the shuttle. "Coming," she said. She took the shortest route, across the cowling rather than back through the cockpit. The hand was gone when she got there. Carson was on the ground, at the edge, trying to beat back the clicking, jabbing horde.

He called her name.

The wing stuck out over the abyss. "Jump for it, Frank," she said. She sprawled down flat on her belly and anchored a foot against the hatch to provide purchase. "Do it—"

He threw a glance toward her. One of the things had fastened onto his leg and was cutting him. Without a word, he leaped, throwing both arms across the wing. She tried to grab his trousers to haul him up but she had to settle for his shirt, his ribs, and she couldn't get a good grip.

He grabbed wildly at the smooth metal. Hutch was dragged half off the wing. *Janet*—

And she was there. She was taller than Hutch, longer, and she scrambled alongside, leaned down, and snatched him back. Snatched them both back.

For years afterward, I was unable to write, or speak, about that terrible night. This was to have been our shining moment, the peak of all our careers. God knows, I felt safe enough when we started. We were well-armed. And we were in a land that had lately served a great civilization. I did not believe that serious predators could have survived such a period.

Nevertheless, I failed to take adequate precautions. It cost the lives of two of the finest people I have ever known.

—Frank Carson
Quoted in "Overnight on Krakatoa,"
by Jane Hildebrand, *The Atlantic*, Oct 11, 2219

Carson sounds as if he forgot he also managed to lose a shuttle pilot on that trip. His name, for the record, was Jake Dickenson.

—Harvey Sill,
Letter published in *The Atlantic*, Oct 25, 2219

25.

On board NCK Catherine Perth. *Wednesday, April 13; 1800 GMT.*

They recovered Maggie's body at about noon, local time. They also found parts of Jake's clothing and equipment. There was no sign of George, other than a few burned-out areas. The brachyids, if they were still in the neighborhood, kept out of the way of the heavily armed landing party.

Harvey Sill led the mission. Hutch went along as guide, but she needed tranks to hold herself together.

On their return to the *Perth*, Maggie's body was placed in refrigeration, a memorial service was scheduled, and formal notifications were sent to Kosmik and the Academy. To Carson's knowledge, it was the first time anyone had been killed in field work by a native life form.

Captain Morris directed preparations for the memorial with a mounting sense of outrage mixed with satisfaction that he had failed to make his point with his superiors but been proved right. However, he could expect to be held responsible by Corporate. He had never before lost a crewman or passenger, and he now had three to account for. Worse, the mission had been unauthorized.

"I hope you're aware," he told Truscott, "what you've got us into."

She was aware. She'd assumed the professionals knew what they were doing, and had trusted them. It was a mistake she'd made before, but she didn't know any other way to operate. You have to trust the people who are close to the action. If once in a while things go wrong, you take the heat. "I'm sorry I've created a problem for you, John," she said.

He missed the quiet irony. "A little late for that. The question is, what do we do now?"

They were in the captain's conference room. Truscott had followed the progress of the recovery party on the command circuit, had watched the body come back, and felt little patience with Morris, enclosed in his own narrow envelope. *How do we get people like you in positions of authority?* "I told you," she said, "that if a problem developed, I would see to it that you were absolved of responsibility. And I will."

"I know you will *try*." Morris's throat trembled. It was unlike him to stand up to anyone who was in a position to damage him. "Nevertheless," he said righteously, "three people are dead."

"I understand that."

"I'm captain here. I expect to be associated with this disaster for the rest of my career. There'll be no escaping it."

It's a terrible thing to listen to a grown man whine. "I rather think," she said, "that the unofficial culpability, if any, will attach to Dr. Carson."

Morris was glad to hear that. But he was too smart to show his satisfaction. Instead, he sat for some moments peering sadly off into a corner, as if he were considering the varieties of disaster which can befall even the most capable men.

Truscott suspected that when she was gone, he would call up a coffee and a cinnamon roll. Emotional encounters, she knew, always left him hungry.

"You'll need some reconstructive surgery when you get home. Meantime, stay off it as much as you can." The ship's physician, a grandmotherly type with an easygoing, upbeat bedside manner, irritated Carson. He had never much liked cheerful people. "Neither of you will be able to walk for about twelve hours," she told him and Janet. "Afterward, I want you both to stay off your feet for several days. I'll let you know when."

Janet was sitting up, examining her anesthetized left leg. "When do we get out?" she asked.

"There's no indication of an infection or complication, but we don't have much experience with this sort of thing. The brachyids injected you with a protein compound that seems to have no purpose. It might make you a little sick, but that will be the extent of it."

"Venom?" asked Carson.

"Probably. But you're not a local life form. So you got off lucky. Anyway, I want to keep an eye on you until morning. If nothing develops by then, you can go back to your quarters." She checked her lightpad. "You have a visitor. May we show him in?"

"Who is it?" asked Carson.

"Me." Harvey Sill appeared in the doorway. "I've got some information for you."

The doctor excused herself, while Sill asked how they were doing. "Pretty good," Carson said. Truth was, he hadn't slept since they'd brought him aboard. "What've you got?"

"A reading on the syzygy."

"On the *what*?"

"The lunar alignment. Remember? You wanted to know how long it had been since the four moons lined up?"

A lot had happened since then, and Carson had forgotten. "Oh, yes," he said. It seemed trivial now.

"It's been a while. We make it 4743 B.C., terrestrial."

He tried to make the numbers fit, and had no luck. "That can't be the one we're looking for."

"Why not?"

"It's too recent. We know they had interstellar travel as early as the twenty-first millenium B.C. The space station is primitive, so it should predate that. Do we have an event that happened more than twenty-three thousand years ago?"

Sill consulted his pad. "One of the moons has an orbit at a steep angle to the others. Which means that they hardly ever line up. Prior to the one in 4743, you have to go back over a hundred thousand years."

"That can't be right."

Sill shrugged. "Let me know if we can do anything else for you." He smiled at Janet, and left the room.

"It was worth a try, I guess," said Carson. "The orbiter may have been up there a long time, but not a hundred thousand years."

"Maybe the photos are simulated."

"Must be." His eyes slid shut. The room was getting sunlight just then. It was warm and sleep-inducing. Something connected with the station had been bothering him when the business with the crabs started. He needed to think about it, to reach back and find it. "Janet," he said, "think about the ruins for a minute."

"Okay."

"We didn't really get to see much of the harbor city. But did it look to you like the kind of city that a high-tech race of star-travelers would have built?"

"You mean the steel and concrete?"

"Yes. And the evidence we had of extensive water travel. I thought the collapsed bridge looked like something *we* might have built."

"*We're* star-travelers."

"We're just starting. These people had been at it for thousands of years. Does it make sense they'd still be using *brick walls*, for God's sake?"

"Maybe," she said. "What are you trying to say?"

"I don't know." The air was thick. It was hard to think. "Is it possible the interstellar civilization came *first*? *Before* the cities and the space station?"

Janet nodded. "The evidence points that way. We tend to assume continual progress. But maybe they slid into a dark age. Or just went downhill." She punched a pillow and finished with a rush of emotion: "That's what it is, Frank. It'll be interesting to see what the excavations show."

"Yes," said Carson. *But somebody else will get to do that. I'm sure as hell not going back down there.*

His legs were anesthetized, and he felt only a pleasant warmth in them.

While Janet slept, Carson withdrew into the back of his mind. The sense of general well-being that should have accompanied the tranks never arrived. He was left only with a sense of disconnectedness. Of watching from a distance.

He went over his decisions again and again. He'd failed to take seriously the possibilities of attack. Failed to consider any danger other than a single, dangerous predator. Failed to provide adequate security.

The room grew dark. He watched the moons appear one by one in his view panel. They were cold and white and *alive*. Maybe everything in this system was alive: the sun, the worlds, the *things* in solar orbit. Even the continents. The moons aligned themselves, formed up like a military unit, like brachyids.

Syzygy.

He was awake. Drenched with sweat.

Beside him, Janet slept peacefully.

Syzygy.

It had last happened in 4743 B.C. And the era of the Monuments had ended, as far as they knew, around 21,000 B.C.

He picked up a lightpad, and began writing it all down. Assume that the people who had lived in the harbor city had put up the space station. Assume also that the station had ended its useful life shortly thereafter, because it was primitive, and would quickly have become obsolete. But there *were* no other stations, more advanced ones, so the harbor city and the planetary civilization had ceased activity. Had they perhaps not outlived their orbiter?

The time span between the last syzygy and the (supposed) end of the Age of Monuments was approximately sixteen thousand years.

	DISCONTINUITIES	
Beta Pac III	Quraqua	Nok
21,000 BC	9000	16,000 BC
4743 BC	1000	400 AD

Again, there were increments of eight thousand years.

He stared at the numbers a long time.

And he thought about the space station. *Why had its occupants tied themselves into their chairs and opened the hatches?*

Carson remembered the old twentieth-century story of the cosmonaut who was stranded in orbit when the Soviet Union dissolved. He was circling the Earth, and one day the country that put him up just wasn't there anymore. Maybe these people got stranded too. Something happened on the ground. Something that cut off all hope of return. And out of grief, or desperation, they had let in the night.

Maybe the discontinuities *weren't* gradual events. Maybe they were sudden, overnight disasters. Okay, that seemed ridiculous. But where did it lead? What other evidence did he have? How could it connect with Oz?

Oz was always the final enigma. *Understand Oz*, he thought, *and we understand the whole puzzle*.

Clockwork.

Whatever it is, it happens every eight thousand years. Had there been an event on Beta Pac III in 13,000 B.C.? And on Nok around 8000 B.C.? *Yes*, he thought, knowing Henry would not have approved this sort of logical leap. But it seemed likely.

What kind of mechanism could produce such an effect?

After a while, he slept again, but not well. He woke to find that daylight had returned. Hutch and Janet were talking, and he got the impression from the way their voices dropped that *he* had been the topic. "How are you doing?" Hutch asked solicitously.

"I'm fine."

Janet pushed her left leg out from under the sheet and flexed it. "It's coming back," she said.

Carson felt better, but was content to lie still.

"Hutch was saying," said Janet, "that there's a memorial service this evening."

He nodded, and felt a fresh twinge of grief. He knew Hutch had gone back to the surface, and he asked about the trip. She described it briefly, in general terms. Maggie had died in the fall. No predator had got at her afterward. Thank God for that. "It must have been pretty quick," she added. "Sill was all business. He wishes we'd go away, and he blames us for Jake's death. He hasn't said it, but it's obvious." She stopped suddenly, and he realized she was sorry she'd said that.

He changed the subject. "Here's something you might be interested in." He fumbled around in the bed, found his lightpad, and passed it over.

Hutch's eyebrows went up. Then she held it so Janet could see. "We've got the eight-thousand-year factor again. I'd say the coincidence is getting pretty long."

Carson agreed. "I can't even begin to formulate an explanation. Could there be something in the wiring of intelligent creatures that breaks out every eight thousand years? Like Toynbee's notions about the cycles of civilizations? Does that make any sense at all?"

"I don't think so," said Janet.

Hutch was still looking at the pad. "All three places," she said, "have strange artifacts. The artifacts are obviously related, and they tie things together. Something *has* to be happening. And we have it by the tail."

"Tail," said Janet. "It's a cosmic horgon that shows up periodically and blows everything away." She was propped up against three pillows, rapping her fingertips against the tray table that stood by the side of her bed.

"Can I get you," she asked Hutch, "to do a diagram?"

"Sure." Hutch picked up the remote and opened the wall to reveal a display. "What do we want?"

"Let's get a look at the relative positions of Beta Pac, Quraqua, and Nok."

Hutch put them up. Beta Pac floated directly on the edge of the Void. Quraqua lay more inshore, fifty-five light-years away, in the general direction of Earth. Nok was lower on the arm, a hundred fifteen light years distant.

"Okay," said Janet. "Let's add the dates of the discontinuities."

Carson understood what Janet was looking for: a connection between dates and distances. But he couldn't see anything. If their guesswork was correct, the earliest known event had happened on Beta Pac III around 21,000 B.C. But there was no discernible order to what happened after that. A second event on Nok five thousand years later. And a third on Quraqua seven thousand years after *that*. It was chaos.

On a whim, Hutch plotted Earth's position. It was *far* out of the picture. They all looked at it, and it seemed to Carson they were missing something.

Janet was already gone from the medical facility when Carson, with some help, dressed and prepared to return to his quarters. They gave him a motorized wheelchair, and he was testing it (and grumbling) when an attendant informed him the captain wanted to see him.

The attendant led Carson to a small examining room. It was furnished with two chairs, a gurney, a basin, and a supply cabinet. "He'll be right with you," he said, withdrawing.

It required little to bring Carson's dislike for Morris to the surface. The symbolic gesture of forcing him to wait, of demonstrating that Carson's time was of less value than the captain's, irritated him. He wondered whether there was any reason he should tolerate this, and was about to leave when

To Sagittarius Arm & Galactic Center

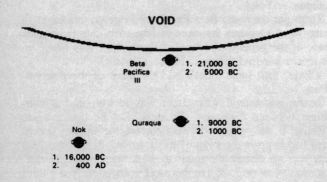

VOID

Beta
Pacifica
III
1. 21,000 BC
2. 5000 BC

Quraqua
1. 9000 BC
2. 1000 BC

Nok

1. 16,000 BC
2. 400 AD

Earth

Light Years
50

Hutch's Star & Event Chart

the captain strode in, told him pontifically to "be at ease," dropped his hat on the gurney, and pulled up a chair with the air of a man who had important business waiting elsewhere. "Well, Carson," he said, "I guess we really stuck our ass in it this time."

"I guess we did, Captain." Carson's blood pressure started to rise.

Morris' gaze had a waxy quality. It slid off Carson's shoulder. "I wanted to say that I'm sorry about the loss of your colleagues."

"Thank you. I appreciate that. And I'm sorry about Jake."

The captain nodded. "He'll be missed." He looked straight ahead, at nothing in particular. Carson's impression was that he was striving for an appearance of stricken contemplation. "You know I was against all this from the beginning. If I'd had my way, none of this would have happened."

I wish you'd been more forceful, Carson thought, but said nothing.

"Tell me, did you learn anything of significance down there?"

Carson was surprised by the question. "Yes," he said. "I think we did."

"Thank God for that, Doctor. With three people dead, we can at least be grateful the mission had a point." He slightly underscored Carson's title, as if it were something that needed to be stepped on.

"It had a point." Carson felt old. "That's not the same as saying it was worth the cost."

"I understand." Morris had a slight wheeze. "I would have you know that the loss of a crewman and two passengers is no small matter. There is paperwork to be done, explanations to be made. And regardless of the fact that the command of this ship is in no way culpable, the incident will nevertheless reflect poorly on me. You have certainly made your presence felt, sir."

"I regret that we have been a problem."

"No doubt. Unfortunately, prudence sometimes comes late. Well, no matter now. There's a memorial service this evening at 1900 on the shuttle deck."

Carson smiled. "Of course." He shifted his weight, uncomfortable at feeling helpless before this man. "Is there anything else?"

"No." Morris' eyes found him again. This time they did not waver. "I'm sorry for you, Doctor."

There was no question that the crew of the *Perth* had liked Jake Dickenson.

Oversized photos of Jake, George, and Maggie dominated the walls. Jake sat in his cockpit; George had been photographed against a rocky shore, hatless and thoughtful; and Maggie, a head shot only, intense eyes, dark hair falling over one shoulder.

Approximately ninety people gathered for the ceremony. The crew wore uniforms with black arm patches; the passengers eschewed the colorful clothing which was the fashion of the time.

It was mercifully short. Jake's friends and shipmates described good times shared, the man's kindness, favors done but never before revealed. Some also recalled brief moments spent with Maggie or George.

Carson was pleased that no one seemed to be blaming *him*. *We are in it together,* they said, in several different ways.

The captain presided, clad in formal dark blue. He noted this was the first time the *Catherine Perth* had lost anyone. He would miss Jake, and although he hadn't really had the opportunity to get to know the deceased members of the Academy team, he was assured they were fine people, and he regretted their loss. Here he paused and his gaze swung slowly around the walls, lingering on each photo, coming finally to rest on the needle-nose prow of the shuttle.

"We can take our consolation," he said somberly, "in knowing they died advancing the cause of human knowledge." His eyes were half-closed. "They understood the risks, but they never hesitated." To Carson, it sounded as if he were already planning his defense before the commission that would surely investigate the accident. "We can offer no higher praise for Jake, Maggie, and George." He glanced toward Carson, and requested the consideration of the Almighty on the assemblage. Carson thought that his friends deserved a better send-off than this hackneyed, dogeared ramble. But Morris rolled on.

When at last he finished, Carson wheeled forward.

He took out his own prepared remarks and glanced at them. They seemed dry and overblown. Too much like the captain's platitudes. Melanie Truscott, watching silently from a position near the statboard, smiled encouragement.

He slid the pad back into his pocket. "I did not know Jake as long, or as well, as you did. But he died with my people, trying to help us." Carson looked at Hutch. "When we lose someone, there can never be an adequate reason. But *they* knew, and it's important that *you* know, that they were not lost on some trivial, arbitrary, sightseeing trip. What lies below *matters*. Jake, George, and Maggie are forever part of it. As are we all." He paused and looked around the assemblage. "I'm sorry. We've paid with our blood. I wish it were otherwise."

The crowd did not disperse. Bound by common loss, they drifted up to the forward lounge, where the lights were brighter than usual and three white candles had been lit. People collected in small groups.

It was the first time Hutch had experienced death on a starship. She had always realized that the interstellars, hauling their fragile cargoes of environment and people, created intense, if temporary, societies. People felt closer, united against a hostile universe. Antagonisms that might have played out to unhappy conclusions on the broad stage of a planetary surface tended to break down in the observation lounges and on the shuttle decks. And the corollary, she realized, was that disaster hit harder. There were no bystanders between the stars.

Most of the tables were occupied. Hutch wandered among them, exchanging stories, sometimes just listening. She was hurting that night. Occasionally, she got up in the middle of a conversation and walked to a spot where she could be alone. No one took offense.

Truscott drifted in, and filled a wineglass. "The *Ashley Tee* is alongside," she told Carson. "They can take your team off when you're ready. But you're welcome to stay with us, if you like. Your survey ship won't have much in the way of medical assistance should you require it."

"Thanks," said Carson. "I'm sorry about all the trouble."

"I'll survive." She managed a smile. "Frank, has John spoken to you?"

"Not in any substantive way. I know he's unhappy."

"He means well. But he's frustrated. He's lost people, and he's worried about his reputation. This isn't a good time for him."

"I know. But considering what others have lost, I have a hard time sympathizing." Truscott, for one, would be in even more trouble. "What will you do now?" he asked.

"Don't know. Write a book, maybe. There's a commission forming to see whether we can adapt terraforming techniques to improving things at home. I'd be interested in joining that."

Carson grimaced. "Can you do much without kicking up tidal waves and earthquakes?"

Her smile illuminated the table. "Yes, we can. We can do quite a lot, as a matter of fact. The problem is that too often the only people who can act don't *want* change. Power doesn't so much corrupt as it breeds conservatism. Keep the status quo." She shrugged. "Caseway thinks the only solution is to move a small, well-educated, well-trained group to a place like Quraqua, and start over. I'm inclined to agree with him that the home world is a lost cause. But I don't think human nature will change just because we send out a contingent with sheepskins."

"You don't believe the Quraqua experiment will work?"

"No." She sipped her drink. "I'm not a pessimist by nature. At least, I don't think I am. But no: I think the nature of the beast is intrinsically selfish. Quraqua is to be the new Earth. And I suspect it *will* be. But education makes a difference in the short run, at best. Train a jerk all you want; in the end, you've still got a jerk."

Carson leaned forward. "You think we're that bad?"

"*Homo jerkus*," she said. "Just read your history." She looked at her watch. "Listen, I have to go. When they write about this, make sure they spell my name right. By the way, I have some messages for you." She fished three envelopes out of a pocket, and handed them to him. Then she turned and walked toward the exit.

The envelopes were standard dispatch holders from the *Perth* communication center. Two were from Ed Horner. The first said: SORRY TO HEAR ABOUT COLLISION. HOPE ALL IS WELL. FIRST PRIORITY IS CREW SAFETY. TAKE ANY ACTION TO PROTECT YOUR PEOPLE.

The second was dated two days later. It authorized Carson to use the *Ashley Tee* as he saw fit. *"Within reason."*

Hutch came up behind him. He showed her the messages. "What do you think?" he asked.

"About what we do now?"

"Yes."

"Restrict ourselves to aerial survey. And then go home."

Carson agreed. He had no heart left for the world of the Monument-Makers. "Tell me what you know about the *Ashley Tee*."

She sat down. "It will have a two-man crew. Their specialty is broad-based survey. They look for terrestrial worlds, and they do some general research on the side. They are not designed for ground work."

"Will they have a shuttle?"

"Yes," she said. "But why would you want a shuttle if we're going to stay off the surface?"

"Hutch, there are whole *cities* down there. We'll want to do some flybys. Find out what we can."

"Okay. The *Ashley Tee* is a Ranger-class EP. It's small, and its shuttle is small. The shuttle is not designed for atmospheric flight, by the way. It's a flying box."

"Not good for atmospheric flight, you say? Can it be done? Can *you* do it?"

"I can do it. It'll be clumsy. And slow. But sure I can do it."

Hutch had never looked better. Candlelight glittered in her dark eyes and off her black onyx earrings. He sensed a depth, a dimension, that had not been there before. He recalled his first meeting with her, among the monoliths at Oz, when she had seemed a trifle frivolous.

Janet joined them. She'd had a little too much to drink, and she looked disheartened. The shimmering rim of the world rolled across the observation port. They were over the night side, but the ocean and the cloud cover glittered.

Hutch was trying to get a look at the third envelope. "What's the other one say?"

"It's from Nok." He tore it open.

FRANK. HAVE COMMANDEERED PACKET. ON MY WAY. HANG ON. DAVID EMORY.

"Well," smiled Janet, "we're getting plenty of help. It would've all been a trifle late. But you have to give them credit for trying."

Carson laughed. "David's figured out that we've got something here. He's interested."

Hutch reassured everyone she was fine, and stayed in the forward lounge long after Carson and Janet had gone. She could not bear the thought of being alone that night.

Alcohol had no effect. Occasionally someone drifted over, sat down, tried to start a conversation. But she could not follow any of it. She almost believed she could will George to come through the door. That he was still at the other end of the commlink.

She forced herself to think about other things. About Carson's idea that the space station was relatively recent. That there had been a dark age.

She cleared the table and took out her lightpad.

Eight-thousand-year cycles.

She drew a line across the top of the field. *Void* here. Beta Pac III *there*. On the edge of the arm. Land's end. And Quraqua? Well back. Fifty-five light-years. Toward Earth. She sketched in Nok, ninety-eight light-years from Quraqua, a hundred fifteen from Beta Pac.

She wrote in the dates of the known events: 21,000 and 5000 B.C. at Beta Pac; 9000 and 1000 B.C. at Quraqua; 16,000 B.C. and A.D. 400 at Nok. Round the 400 date off to zero. Fill out the eight-thousand-year cycle. Assume events on Beta Pac at 13,000 B.C., on Nok at 8000 B.C., and on Quraqua, when? 17,000 B.C.

She looked at the result a long time. Looked out the window at the world of the Monument-Makers. Strings of islands. A jade ocean. The continent around the other side.

They had known something. They had built Oz, and cube moons, and a greater Oz here.

Why?

When she looked back at the lightpad, she saw it. And it was so obvious, she wondered how they could have missed it for so long.

She went back to her quarters, generated a map, and checked the numbers. Everything fit.

TO: COMMISSIONER, WORLD ACADEMY
             OF   SCIENCE   AND   TECHNOLOGY
             SMITHSONIAN SQUARE,
             WASHINGTON, D.C.
FROM: DIRECTOR, BETA PAC TEAM
SUBJECT: MISSION STATUS

WE'VE LOST MAGGIE AND GEORGE DURING ATTACK BY LOCAL LIFE FORMS. PLEASE

MAKE APPROPRIATE NOTIFICATIONS. BOTH
DIED ATTEMPTING TO PROTECT THEIR COL-
LEAGUES. MAJOR DISCOVERIES AWAIT ARRIVAL
OF FULL-SCALE EXPEDITION. REPORT FOLLOWS.
WE WILL REMAIN, AS RESOURCES PERMIT, WITH
THE ASHLEY TEE.

CARSON

PART FOUR

THE ENGINES
OF GOD

26.

The chime brought Carson out of an uneasy sleep.

He let in an ecstatic Hutch. "I think I've got it," she said, waving a lightpad.

"Got what?"

She threw herself into a chair. "If we go to the right place," she said, "and make an Oz, we can find out what this is all about."

"*Make an Oz?* Are you serious? We can't *make an Oz.*" He wondered how much she'd had to drink during the night. "Have you been to bed at all?" he asked accusingly.

"Forget *bed,*" she said. "The numbers work."

Carson put on coffee. "Slow down. What numbers? And where's *the right place*?"

She picked up a remote, and put a star chart on his display. She drew a line along the edge of the Void, and parallel lines through Beta Pac, Quraqua, and Nok. "We always knew we had the eight-thousand-year cycles. But we didn't see any other pattern. Maybe because it was staring us in the face.

"We think we know of two events on Nok, and two on Quraqua. And we may have seen evidence of at least *one* here."

"Okay," said Carson. "Where does that leave us?"

"If there really *is* an eight-thousand-year cycle, and we know there was an event here somewhere around 5000 B.C., then there must have been an earlier event somewhere around 13,000 B.C. Right? And at 21,000 B.C." She posted the numbers in a window:

Event	Beta Pac	Quraqua	Nok
1	21,000 BC		
2	13,000 BC		
3	5000 BC		

"If we stay with the eight-thousand-year cycle," she said, "and we push it backward in time, then there would have been an event on Quraqua at about 17,000 B.C. Yes?"

Event	Beta Pac	Quraqua	Nok
1	21,000 BC	17,000 BC	
2	13,000 BC	9000 BC	
3	5000 BC	1000 BC	

"Okay."

"Good. We're sure of the second and third Quraqua events. In both cases, they start four thousand years later. What does that suggest?"

"Damned if I know."

"Frank, the same kind of thing happens on Nok."

"In what way?"

She filled in the last column, rounding the numbers off.

Event	Beta Pac	Quraqua	Nok
1	21,000 BC	17,000 BC	16,000 BC
2	13,000 BC	9000 BC	8000 BC
3	5000 BC	1000 BC	0

"This time," Carson said, "there's always a thousand-year difference. I see the pattern, but I *don't* see the point."

"It's a *wave*, Frank. Whatever this thing is, it's coming in from the Void. It travels one light-year every seventy-four years. The first one we know about, the A wave, arrived here, at Beta Pac, somewhere around 21,000 B.C."

"I'll be damned," he said.

"Four thousand years later, it hits Quraqua. Then, a thousand or so after that, it shows up at Nok."

Carson thought it over. It sounded like pure imagination. But the numbers worked. "What could it be?"

"The Dawn Treader," she said.

"What?"

Her eyes narrowed. "Remember the Quraquat prayer?" She put it on the screen:

> *In the streets of Hau-kai, we wait.*
> *Night comes, winter descends,*
> *The lights of the world grow cold.*
> *And, in this three-hundredth year*
> *From the ascendancy of Bilat,*
> *He will come who treads the dawn,*
> *Tramples the sun beneath his feet,*
> *And judges the souls of men.*
> *He will stride across the rooftops,*
> *And he will fire the engines of God.*

"Whatever it is," she said, "it's connected somehow with the Oz structures."

The room felt cold. "Could they be talismans?" Carson asked. But the prospect of an advanced race resorting to attempts to invoke the supernatural was disquieting.

"Or targets," said Hutch. "Ritual sacrifices? Symbolic offerings to the gods?" She swung around to face him. "Look, if any of this is right, the wave that went through Nok during A.D. 400 has traveled about thirty-five light years since." She drew another parallel line to mark its location. "There's a star system located along this track. I think we should. go take a look."

Carson called Truscott early. "I need a favor," he said. "I'd like to borrow some equipment."

She was in her quarters. "What do you need, Frank?"

"A heavy-duty particle beam projector. Biggest you have. You *do* have one on board, right?"

"Yes, we have several." She looked perplexed. "You're not going excavating down there?"

"No," Carson said. "Nothing like that. In fact, we're leaving the system."

She registered surprise. "I can arrange it. What else?"

"A pod. Something big enough to use as a command post."

"Okay," she said. "We can do that, too. You'll have to sign for this stuff."

"Thanks. I owe you, Melanie."

"I agree. Now, how about telling me what this is all about?"

He could see no reason for secrecy. "Sure," he said. "How about breakfast?"

The *Ashley Tee* was essentially a group of four cylinders revolving around a central axis. It bristled with sensing and communication devices. Hutch had already talked to them before they made the transfer. "We've got a celebrity," she said, with a smile.

The celebrity was its pilot, the near-legendary Angela Morgan.

Angela was tall and trim with silver hair and gray eyes. Hutch had never met her, but she knew *about* her. Angela had performed many of the pioneer flights during the early days, had pushed the limits of mag technology, and had been the driving force behind many of the safety features now incorporated in FTL deployment.

Her partner was Terry Drafts, a young African physicist not half her age. He was soft-spoken, introspective, intense. He made no secret of his view that riding with Angela was equivalent to getting his ticket punched for greater things.

"If you've really got something, Carson," Angela said, "we'd be happy to help. Wouldn't we, Terry? But don't waste our time, okay?"

Since all starships maintain onboard clocks in correlation with Greenwich, the new passengers suffered no temporal dislocation. It was mid-morning on all the vessels of the various fleets when Angela showed her new passengers to their quarters.

She joined them for lunch, and listened while they talked about their experiences in the system. Eventually, she asked pointedly whether they were certain this was the home world of the Monument-Makers. (They were.) How had the team members been lost? (No one got into graphic details, but they told her enough to elicit both her disapproval and her respect.)

"I see why they wanted me to put the ship at your disposal," she said. "We can stay here. We can take you to Point Zebra. Or we can go all the way back to Earth. Your call." The Point was the staging site for local survey vessels.

"Angela," said Carson, "what we'd like is to take a look

at one of the moons in this system. Then we're going to do some serious traveling."

Angela trained the ship's telescopes on the harbor city. It looked serene: white ruins embedded in soft green hills, thick forest spilling into the sea. The broken bridge that led nowhere.

They spent two days at the Oz-like artifact. They marveled anew at its perpendicularity. It was, announced Drafts, the mecca of right angles. And, unlike the construct on Quraqua's moon, this one had no exception, no round tower.

But it too was damaged. Charred. Cratered.

"I've seen the other one," said Angela. "Why would they make something like this?"

"That's what we hope to find out," said Carson.

That evening, Monday, April 18, 2203, at slightly before 1100 hours, they rolled out of lunar orbit.

Two nights later, Carson ceremonially stored his wheelchair. And Janet added another piece of speculation. She first mentioned it to Hutch. "I was thinking," she said, "about the phrase in that Quraquat prayer—"

" 'The engines of God'? "

"Yes. *The engines of God*—"

"What of it?"

"We might not be far off. *If* there's an A wave, the one that touched Beta Pac in 21,000 B.C.: if it kept going, it would have reached Earth."

Hutch nodded. "Before the rise of civilization, right? Before anybody was there to record it."

"Not exactly. It would have passed through the solar system somewhere around 5000 B.C."

Hutch waited. The date meant nothing to her.

Janet shrugged. "It fits the most recent estimates for Sodom and Gomorrah."

ARCHIVE
(Transmitted via Laserbuoy)

TO: NCA CARY KNAPP
           ATT: DAVID EMORY

FROM: FRANK CARSON, BETA PAC MISSION
           NCA ASHLEY TEE
SUBJECT: OPERATIONAL MOVEMENT
    DAVID. SORRY TO LEAVE BEFORE YOU GET HERE,
BUT BUSINESS PRESSES. WE MAY BE ABLE TO
FIND OUT WHAT HAPPENED AT ORIKON. NEXT
STOP IS LCO4418. JOIN US THERE IF YOU CAN.
CARSON.

27.

On board NCA Ashley Tee, *en route to LCO4418. Wednesday, April 27; 1930 hours.*

"I can't believe," said Drafts, frowning at his pair of deuces, "we're really doing this."

"Doing what?" asked Angela, looking up from a book.

"Chasing a dragon," said Hutch. She wasn't holding anything either.

"It's worth the trip," said Angela. "I don't believe a word of it. But I've been wrong before." She literally radiated vitality. Hutch had no trouble imagining her flying into a volcano.

"By me," said Drafts. He had been winning, and was in an ebullient mood. "The problem I have," he said, "is that I can't imagine what this thing might *look* like. I mean, are we expecting hordes of destructive nanomachines belched into the galaxy from somewhere in the Void every eight thousand years?" He placed his cards face down on the table. "Or fleets filled with psychopaths?"

"Maybe," said Janet, "it's not from the Void, but something out of the center of the galaxy." She was trying not to look pleased with her cards. "I'll open," she said. She pushed a coin into the pot. "It would come from the same direction."

Drafts glanced at Carson. "Forty-four eighteen's already been looked at. If there had been anything going on out there, we'd know about it."

"Maybe not," said Angela. "If this thing exists, it might not be easy to find unless you know what you're looking for."

"Well," said Drafts, still talking to Carson, "I don't want to offend anybody, but I doubt this dragon is likely to stand up to the light of day."

"Ah, Terry, will you never learn?" Angela delivered a sigh they could have heard in the shuttle bay. "You're right. But it's the wrongheaded types who make the big finds."

Carson smiled at her appreciatively.

Drafts shrugged. "Okay," he said.

Hutch folded, and watched Janet scare everyone out of the pot. Carson picked up the cards and began to shuffle. "The Monument-Maker as Death," he said. "Could they have built something that got away from them?"

Hutch tried to wave it away. "Why don't we wait until we get there? Meantime, we can't do anything except guess."

Angela was sitting with her feet doubled under her. She was reading *Matama*, the hundred-year-old Japanese tragedy. "If there *is* a wave," she said without looking up, "it would have to be pretty deep, on an order of a couple of light-years, for us to have a reasonable chance to locate it. What kind of mechanism could be that big?"

"If it exists," said Janet, "it stretches from Quraqua to Nok. That's a hundred light-years. At a minimum." She looked toward Carson. "That would have to be an effect beyond *anybody's* capability to manufacture."

"I just can't see that the evidence amounts to anything," said Drafts. "Look, these people, whoever they were, had a passion for leaving their signature everywhere they've been. They liked *monuments*. The Oz-structures and the cube moons were early efforts. They were getting their sea legs. No hidden meanings; just practice."

"Come on, Terry," said Carson.

"Why not? Why does there have to be some deep-seated significance? Maybe they're just what most other monuments are: somebody's idea of high art. And the eight-thousand-year cycle is hardly established as *fact*. Half of it's pure guesswork, and I bet the rest of it is going to turn out to be wishful thinking."

Carson and Janet looked at Hutch. *Hell, she thought, I made no guarantees.* But she felt forced to defend her speculations. "The dating wasn't mine," she said. "It was done by Henry Jacobi and David Emory and the data technicians on the *Perth*. I just put it together. If the numbers are a coincidence, they're a coincidence. But it's *not* wishful thinking. I have no interest in meeting a dragon out here."

The tension broke, and they all laughed.

• • •

If a cosmic hand were to move the red giant LCO4418 to the center of the solar system, Mercury and Venus would sink beneath its tides, and Earth would swim through its upper atmosphere. The surface simmered serenely at less than 2200 degrees Kelvin. It was an ancient star, far older than Sol. Its blood-colored light spilled across its family of worlds.

Terrestrial planets orbited at either end of the system, separated by four gas giants. The survey team which had visited the system ten years earlier had concluded that there had probably once been other planets, closer to the central luminary, but they had been absorbed as the sun expanded. LCO4418 was now thought to be close to the end of this phase of its cycle. Over the next several million years, it would recede.

Carson watched recordings of its image on the screens. Prominences did not erupt from its interior, nor did sunspots mar its placid surface. It had entered the final stage of its existence, and death would come quickly now. By cosmic standards.

For all that, it would still be here, and still look much the same, when the human race had long since met whatever fate awaited it. Or had evolved into something else.

The flight was somber. The festive mood and the enthusiasm of the days on the *Winckelmann* had gone. The crew and the passengers spent most of their time together. No one drifted off alone. But there were long silences and uncomfortable glances and things left unspoken. It was perhaps not entirely coincidental that on the evening before their arrival at LCO4418, the conversation had centered on how funerals might be improved to aid future archeologists.

Late in the afternoon of May 7, they jumped back into real space, well south of the planetary plain.

On those occasions when Carson was honest with himself, he knew that he did not expect to find anything. He did not really believe in the wave. It was an intriguing concept, but this was not a phenomenon that he could credit. So he stood on *Ashley*'s bridge, and surveyed the vast wastes, and wondered, not for the first time, why he was here.

The three surviving members of the original team found they could no longer hide their feelings from each other, and

Carson was not surprised when Hutch, who had come up behind him, moved right into his mood. "Sometimes," she said, "you just have to take your chance, and let go."

They started by performing a system-wide survey for artificial objects. It showed negative, which did not mean there might not be something present, but only that any such object would be at considerable range, or quite small, or hidden behind a natural body.

In spite of themselves—they agreed, when pressed, that they were chasing ghosts—they were disappointed.

Angela pored over the records of the original mission to 4418. "A fairly typical system," she told Hutch. "What do we do now?"

The red giant dominated the viewscreens. "Verticals and perpendiculars," she said. "We are going to make some right angles."

Carson had been looking for a good construction site. He explained his strategy in detail, and Angela produced topographical maps from the survey. They decided to use an oversized moon orbiting the second planet: 4418-IID. *Delta*.

Drafts put it on the display. In the dim glow of the sun, it was an exotic worldlet, silver and gold by candlelight. Clouds drifted above orange snowfields and nitrogen seas, methane swamps and crooked mountain chains. It lay in the shadow of the big planet's wispy rings.

The atmosphere read out as hydrogen, methane, nitrogen, with substantial amounts of ethane, hydrogen cyanide, ethylene. Distance from the central world was 650,000 kilometers. Period of revolution: 13 days. Diameter: 5300 kilometers. Surface temperature: -165°C, at the equator. Surface gravity: .37. Orbital period: 11.14 days. Age: estimated 4.7 billion years, with an error factor of ten percent. The system was twelve A.U.s from the sun.

They watched an ice volcano erupt in the southern hemisphere. Snow was falling over one of the oceans, and a nearby coastline was whipped by heavy rain. "The rainstorm might be two-hundred proof," said Angela. "There's a lot of ethanol down there, and the temperature's about right." She grinned. "I wouldn't be surprised to find gasoline lakes."

Carson found what he was looking for in the south, about 20 degrees below the equator: a vast plain cluttered with plateaus. "Here." He tapped the screen. "Here's where we want to set up."

With Hutch's help, Drafts disconnected three of the ship's external cameras. The *Ashley Tee* was consequently left with blind spots, but they could get by. They jury-rigged a mount for the laser, and tripods for the cameras.

"Tell me about the communications," Carson asked as they rounded the gas giant early in the afternoon of their third day. They would go into orbit around Delta at breakfast time.

Hutch set up one of the cameras for his inspection, opened the tripod (which they would anchor into the ice), and attached a sensor cluster. "We put the cameras on the ground, around the target. We'll launch two comsats. If the cameras see something, they'll transmit pictures to the comsats, which will send a hyperlight alarm to Point Zebra. The satellites are enclosed in convex casings. No right angles."

"What triggers the cameras?"

"A sudden and substantial increase in electrical activity, or in temperature beyond that normally encountered. Each camera has its own sensor system, and will operate independently. If something *does* happen, we should be able to get pictures."

"How about ordinary electrical storms? Won't they set it off?"

"Angela says lightning will be infrequent here, and quoted pretty good odds against normal phenomena triggering the sensors. If they do," she shrugged, "too bad. Somebody will come out for no reason."

"Somebody will come *out*?" This wasn't exactly the kind of alarm system Carson had in mind. "Won't they be able to tell when they get the pictures at the Point?"

"They won't get any pictures. The pictures are stored in the satellites. All that'll happen is an alarm will go off."

"Why not send the pictures?"

"Can't. Hyperspace communication requires a lot of power. We just can't generate enough for complex transmissions unless we plan to hang around ourselves and use *Ashley's* power plant. So we do the next best thing: we send a beep."

Fine, Carson thought. Every time there was an electrical storm, they would have to dispatch a ship. "I can't say I care much for this arrangement," he grumbled. "How safe will the cameras be if an event occurs?"

"Hard to say, since we really don't know what the event is. They have to be close to the target area, within a few hundred meters, for the short-range sensors to work. If we back it up farther, and go long-range, they'll pick up too much stray activity, and then we *will* get a series of false alarms."

"Okay."

"One other thing. If the kind of action we're looking for develops, there'll be a lot of electricity in the atmosphere, and the transmissions will get scrambled. In that case, the satellites will not get the pictures."

"So package in a delayed broadcast, too."

"I've done that. We will also record everything at ground level. Redundant copies everywhere. So if *anything* survives, we'll have a record." She was proud of her work, and had expected Carson to notice. But he still seemed preoccupied. "I've tried to shield the equipment as best I can," she continued.

"Okay," he said. "Good."

"You'll want to send someone out in a couple of years to replace this stuff. It's not designed for this kind of mission, so it won't last much beyond that."

"I know," he said. They both understood that such a backup flight would be unlikely.

They pinpointed a target area on a broad, snow-covered plain between a mountain range and a swamp filled with nitrogen and hydrocarbon sludge. The plateaus that had drawn Carson's attention were scattered across an otherwise flat landscape. It looked like a piece of the American West, covered with ice, and bathed in the pale red light of the distant sun.

They settled on a group of four mesas which lay within an area approximately sixty kilometers on a side. Each was already roughly rectangular. (The group had been chosen primarily for that reason.) The smallest comprised an area of about six square kilometers, the largest about a hundred. Carson would have given much to find four mesas at the corners of a square, but nature had not provided, not on this world, nor on any other in the system. He was as close as he could get.

They planned to polish off the rough edges, and convert the mesas into perfect rectangles. To that purpose, three would require only minor sculpting. The fourth, the largest, would need a major effort.

"They won't look much like Oz," said Terry.

"Sure they will," said Janet. "When we're finished with them, they'll be all straight lines. No curves. Like the cube moons."

"And you think it's the straight lines that matter?"

"Yes," she said. *Right angles. It always comes back to right angles.* "You know what? Maybe it's just a matter of creating a design that doesn't appear in nature. We were talking about doing some crosscuts. Making it fancy. But that might not matter."

Carson was uncomfortable that no one on board had experience using the big pulser. "We might end by shooting ourselves down," he said.

They installed the mount for the particle beam projector in the cargo area of the shuttle. Janet looked at it uncertainly and grinned at Hutch. "If the thing falls out," she said, "the show's over."

Hutch tried to visualize the way the operation would work. They would have to fly the shuttle at times almost on its side in order to get a good target angle out the cargo door. "I hope none of *us* falls out," she said.

They loaded the pod modules on board, and filled several spare air tanks. There'd be no opportunity to cycle air from *this* environment if things went wrong. For that reason, Carson, who was now thoroughly persuaded to play it safe, brought along enough for a month.

"Why so much?" asked Drafts.

"Shuttle might break down," Carson said. "We could get stuck there."

Hutch didn't like the shuttle. It was boxy, not very aerodynamic, not good for atmospheric flying. It would be a bumpy ride. And slow. And she was not entirely confident, despite what she had told Carson, of her ability to handle it. "I hate to tell you this," she said, "but this is a shoebox with wings. You'd be better off if you could get Angela to pilot the thing. She's used to it, and she's the best there is."

"It can't be that hard."

"You want to bet your life on it?"

Carson looked at her, and smiled his approval. "Thanks," he said.

He took Hutch with him to the bridge, where Angela was examining displays of the target area. "We'd like to have you fly the shuttle," he said without preliminary. "Hutch tells me it's likely to be difficult to handle, and she says you're pretty good."

Angela studied him for a long moment. "Is that what *you* want?" she asked Hutch. She wore a light brown ship's jacket, with *Ashley's* logo, a sail against a circle of stars, displayed prominently on the left breast.

"Yes. I think it would be a good idea."

"Then I'll do it." Hutch thought she looked as if she had something on her mind. "Of course the shuttle's cramped. And four people will crowd the ground station."

Janet leaned in. "I'm not all that excited about carving mountains. If you want, I'll help hold the fort here."

In the morning, the shuttle slipped its moorings, parted from the *Ashley Tee*, and began its descent. Angela had preset a glide path that allowed a methodical entry. They slipped easily into the upper air.

The delicate interaction between the shuttle's flux and local magnetic fields provided all the lift she needed. But as the air pressure rose, they began to bounce around. The wind thumped the panels and blew gobs of thick rain against the windows. Carson, tied into a temporary web in back, complained loudly.

"It's okay," said Angela. "With this kind of vehicle, you've always got a lot of headwind. Don't worry. It's pretty tough."

Mountain ranges and snow dunes and a coffee-colored sea rose to meet them. *No human foot*, Hutch thought. Ever.

An hour later, they approached the target area, coming in over a sludge-filled river. The landscape was mottled with snowdrifts and boulders and gullies. The light was a Halloween mixture from the red sun and the watery-brown ringed giant that floated on the horizon like a Chinese balloon. Gloomy, cold, and forbidding. Not a place to build a country estate.

Angela turned south. "Ten minutes," she said.

The plain smoothed out. The wind came up again, and the surface disappeared beneath blowing snow. The sky was red, not sunset red, but rather like the scorched appearance of clouds in the aftermath of a forest fire.

The first plateaus appeared.

"They're down," said Drafts.

He'd been watching the pictures come in. Janet had shown some concern during the shuttle descent, and was visibly relieved that the mission was on the ground. "Looks like a rainstorm to the west," she said. Orange-gray clouds rode over a mustard-colored mist. "Maybe some of that two-hundred proof."

"Janet." Drafts swung to face her. "Tell me something?"

"Sure."

"What do you do with your spare time when you aren't chasing cosmic waves?"

A bank of displays on her right were dark. These were the long-range scanners, still looking for anything unusual in the system. The sun, the worlds and moons, comets and rocks and assorted debris had been blanked out. Anything else, anything else at all out of the ordinary, out to the edge of the system, would register.

Fool's errand. What else could you call it?

"I'm not sure anymore," she said. "I'm really not sure."

LOG

Ground team reports they have touched down.

We have launched two comsats to ensure round-the-clock communication. We have also orbited a buoy to direct the ship from Nok when it arrives.

I will add that this is the most unusual mission in which I have participated. No one seems to know what we're looking for.

—T. F. Drafts
NCA Ashley Tee
May 14, 2203

28.

The ground blizzard hid the surface, burying everything except the taller mesas, which might have been a gray fleet moving across rust-colored seas. The four they had selected were on the westernmost border of the plain, where the ground began to turn mountainous.

Hutch thought that Carson was being influenced by the towers at the corners of the central square in the Oz-construct on Quraqua's moon. When she mentioned it to him, he seemed surprised, but then agreed that she was probably right. "I'd like to do the same thing here," he said. "Make a square by using squares. We're not quite able to do that, but we can get close."

The largest of the four plateaus merged its rear section with a mountain. This was the one which would present the most difficulty, and they therefore chose its summit as the site for their base. Angela had brought the shuttle down through a stiff wind, and laid it cautiously into the orange snow. Hutch was impressed.

This was a big plateau. They would have needed about ten hours to walk around its rim. Locked in the snow storm, they could not see its sizable dimensions, but they knew they had taken on an ambitious job.

"Let's sit tight for tonight," Carson said. "We'll set up in the morning."

Angela pointed toward a crimson smear in the east. "It *is* morning. But you're right: let's wait 'til the storm blows over. Then this whole project will look reasonable." She smiled drily.

• • •

378

Drafts put the technical manual down when Janet came up onto the bridge. "Anything happening?"

"It's quiet. I think they're all asleep."

"Do we have a reading on the weather?"

"It's bad. I think it's always bad. I'm not sure. My meteorology is weak."

The screens were active. They reflected power drain figures, short- and long-range scans, attitude, orbital configuration. Fuel levels. Life support on both the ship and the shuttle.

Janet was pleased with the way things had turned out. Drafts, despite his hostility to the project, was a congenial companion, armed with a droll sense of humor. The ship was comfortable, and life was easy up here. She couldn't see that the ground assignment was anything but cramped drudgery.

She was about to make some small talk, when he stiffened. Almost immediately, an alert beeped. "Long range," he said.

Two displays brightened. They presented optical and sensor views of a hazy object. Range at twelve A.U.s.

Drafts frowned. "Odd."

Projected diameter: 23,000 km.

"Irregular shape," said Janet.

"We seem to have an extra world." He called up survey records. "Not supposed to be there." He studied the sensor return. "We're not getting much penetration," he said. "It *looks* like a cloud. Hydrogen and dust. Trace iron, carbon, formaldehyde, and silicate particles."

"So it's a cloud." Janet didn't understand why he looked so puzzled.

"Angela would know more about this than I do, but I don't think clouds *come* this small. They tend to be a *lot* bigger."

"What's inside?" asked Janet.

"Don't know. We can't get into it."

He went to mag five and enhanced. It was still a blur.

Delta. Sunday, May 15; 1045 hours.

The winds quit as if a switch had been thrown. The top of the mesa became very still, and they looked out across a crumpled orange wasteland. Angela moved the shuttle out of the snow that had piled up around it, and they got out and began assembling their base.

Within two hours, they erected an RK/107 top-of-the-line

pressurized shelter, which consisted of a triad of interfaced (but fully compartmented) silver and black domes. The snow was wet and heavy and resisted movement, and they were thoroughly tired by the time they collapsed into the unit's compress chairs. Meantime, another storm blew up, and they watched fiery clouds roll overhead. This time, though, it *rained*. It rained thick, syrupy drops that plopped and blatted against the windows and rolled down like amoebas. Lightning flickered.

Angela sat by a window. "So much for the rare electrical storm."

"By the way," said Carson, "if this is really a gasoline atmosphere, why don't the lightning bolts blow the place up?"

"No oxygen," she said. "If there were oxygen in the mix, we'd get a show."

The shelter was state-of-the-art. They had private apartments, a washroom, a kitchen, an operations center, and a conference room. Polarized windows were set in all outside walls. They had comfortable furniture, music, extensive data banks, decent food. "We could have done worse," said Angela, who, like the others, was accustomed to accommodations produced by the lowest bidder.

She seemed thoughtful. And when Hutch asked what was on her mind, she hesitated. "Not sure," she said. "I'm getting near retirement. In fact, they didn't want me to come out on this one. I think this is my swan song." Her gray eyes brightened. "This is the most interesting mission I've been on." Her gaze turned inward. "Yeah. I haven't seen anything like this before. I hope we find something so I can go out in style."

"Even a dragon?"

"Sure," she said. "*Especially* a dragon."

"It won't pass very close."

Janet had been idling through *Ashley's* mission report. The ship had been surveying older stars, mostly middle-aged, stable G-types, prime candidates in the twin searches for habitable worlds and other civilizations. So far, they had nothing to show for their efforts.

The auxiliary screen on her right displayed the cloud. Nothing much had changed. It was somewhat more distinct, a result of enhancement and, to a lesser degree, its decreased range.

"Hey." Drafts stared at his instruments. "I think we've got another one."

"Another what?"

"Another *cloud*."

Janet slid into the seat beside him. "Where?"

"Extreme long range." He jabbed a finger at the readout. She picked it up on a window. "This one is on the other side of the sun, moving away from us. It's out on the edge of the system."

"Can't we get a better picture?"

"It's too far." He was running a search through the data banks. "But it's also not on the charts." He turned toward her. "Neither of these objects was here when the original survey was made."

"Or they got missed."

"I would have thought that was unlikely. Maybe we better let Angela know."

They had just left the dome, just cycled through the airlock and stepped out into the snow, when Drafts's voice broke into their chatter. "We have a couple of anomalies," he said.

They kept walking, plowing through the snow with difficulty. Carson had begun to wonder whether they should try to make snowshoes. "What kind of anomalies?" he asked.

"Clouds, I think. Two of them."

"Here?" asked Angela, looking into a crystal-clear sky, apparently thinking what Carson thought: that they were talking about something in the atmosphere.

"One at twelve A.U.s, approaching; the other on the far side of the sun. Going the other way. Listen, I'm not sure yet, but I don't think they're in orbit."

"Clouds, you say?"

"Yeah. *Clouds*."

"Not possible," she said.

"We'll send you pictures."

"Okay. Yes, do that." She started back inside. "Frank, do you mind?"

"No. Go back and look. We'll see you in the shuttle."

The ATL1600 general-purpose particle beam projector was of the type that had been used to cut shafts in the polar ice packs on Quraqua. It was simple to operate, durable, and effective. The narrow, tightly-focused beam that it generated was capable, even while tied to the shuttle's limited power plant, of slicing the mesas like so much cheese.

On Quraqua, the projectors had been driven by a fusion link with the orbiter. Here, the drain on the shuttle would be considerable, and they could not approach full power. Operations would be limited to seven hours daily. The work would be slow, but they had plenty of time.

The real problem was that the unit was difficult to manage. It had been designed for installation on board a specially fitted CAT. Carson would have to try to aim it from the cargo hold, while the shuttle was in flight. Hutch's mount was really little more than a restraining web to prevent the instrument, or its operator, from falling out. They had one advantage: the half-ton unit weighed only about four hundred pounds in this gravity.

When Angela rejoined them, she was excited. "I don't know whether it has anything to do with what we're looking for, but we've got a couple of very strange beasties out there." She described what the ship had seen. "Terry thinks they're clouds."

"And you don't?"

"No. Clouds would get ripped apart in the gravity fields. They *look* like clouds, but it couldn't be. They have to be solid bodies. The lopsided appearance will turn out to be an illusion."

"They can't be hydrogen clouds?" asked Hutch.

"No."

"I thought there were a lot of hydrogen clouds."

"There are. But they don't come in this size. These are too small. I can't even imagine how such objects would form." She smiled, and looked pleased. "We'll keep an eye on them." Angela helped them lock down the 1600, and then went up front and took the pilot's seat. "Are we ready?"

They were.

"Okay. I'm going to seal off up here. The thing that I'm worried about is that you two and the sixteen hundred are all going to be concentrated on the starboard side. Don't make any sudden changes of position. And if I ask you to shut down, I want you to do it immediately, and move to the other side. Clear on that?

"If the thing *does* break loose and fall out, don't try to stop it. It doesn't weigh nearly as much as it looks, but neither do you. I don't want any dead people."

She wished them luck, and closed off the cockpit. Hutch sat down and made herself comfortable.

They would ride with the outer door open, because the unit's housing stuck out of the vehicle. They fastened tethers to their belts.

Angela engaged her engines, and they lifted off. The shuttle circled the three domes, turned east, and glided out over the plateau. The weather had cleared, and a light wind blew out of the north.

"The plateaus were probably carved by methane glaciers," Angela said. "It would be interesting to know whether this moon has periodic ice ages."

She continued in that vein, while Carson and Hutch endured an uncomfortable ride in back. They looked out at the endless snowscape, watched the edge of the plateau fall away, maybe two hundred meters, and they were cruising over the plain. Carson's idea was to do the easy ones first. Get the hang of the equipment.

Hutch wondered if Angela had ever flown before with an open cargo door. It was unlikely, but the woman knew her shuttle. It developed a drag, and a tendency to turn to starboard, but they seemed to be compensating.

The least challenging of the four mesas was on the south. It was already a passable rectangle, except that one side had partially collapsed and left a big hole in the symmetry. They'd have to square that off. For the rest, they wouldn't have to do much more than straighten the corners.

The projector's phase controls were set in a bright yellow teardrop case; its black mirror housing looked like a rifle barrel. There was provision for both automatic and manual operation. Rewriting the programming to factor in the shuttle was simply too time-consuming, so they had opted to go manual. "When in doubt," said Carson, "fly by the seat of your pants."

There was a pair of handgrips, a sight, and a trigger. But the instrument was unwieldy. So they ignored the trigger, and rigged a remote. The plan was that Carson would aim and, on command, Hutch would push the button.

"Coming up on target," said Angela. "Let's do a couple of flybys and see precisely how we want to do this."

• • •

Janet was surprised to discover that Harley Costa, whom she knew, had flown the original mission to 4418. At the time they'd met he was en route to Canopus. He was a busy little man who talked too fast, and who could not tolerate anyone who didn't share his passion for astronomy. Janet had taken the time to find out about his specialty, asked the right questions, and they'd become fast friends.

Harley didn't have much use for simple sentences. His energy overflowed ordinary syntax. His ideas sallied out to battle. He trampled (rather than refuted) opposing views, lit off objections with glee, and imposed decisions with crushing finality. Harley never expressed an opinion. He delivered truth. She wondered what sort of person his partner had been, cooped up with him for a year or so.

Reading through the report of his visit to 4418, she could hear his voice. Harley had found things to engage his interest here, as he did everywhere. He found volcanic and seismic activity in unlikely places, and an anomalous magnetic pattern around one of the gas giants. He took a series of measurements of the sun, and entertained himself by calculating the date of its eventual collapse.

They had surveyed the individual worlds, and moved on. Since Bode's Law told them where to look for worlds, they might not have bothered doing an intensive sweep, and it was therefore possible to understand how he might have missed other objects in the system, even objects of planetary dimensions.

Had the two objects been here at that time?

"Okay. *Now*."

Hutch punched the button, and a ruby beam flowed from the nozzle. Carson could feel the hair on his arms rise. The beam was pencil-thin. It flashed across the landscape, and bit into the ice.

"That's good," said Hutch. And, to Angela: "Ease it around to port just a mite. *Okay*. Hold it there." Carson knelt behind the unit, aiming it. He tracked vertically down the face of the cliff. A cloud of steam began to form. Ice, snow, and rock fell away. But the cloud grew, and obscured the target.

Carson shut the projector off. "This may take longer than we thought," he said.

The commlink chimed. Channel from *Ashley*. "Go ahead," said Angela's voice. It was Terry.

"Got some more information for you."

"I'm listening."

"Neither of the two objects is in solar orbit. They are passing *through* the system. They are not attached to it."

"Are you *sure*?" Angela sounded skeptical.

"Yes, I'm sure. And here's something else for you: they are maintaining parallel courses. And they're moving at almost the same clip."

Carson grinned at Hutch, *Maybe we've got the son of a bitch*, and the smile widened as they heard Angela inhale the way she might if she were standing in front of an oncoming glidetrain.

Hutch broke in: "The velocity," she said. "What's the velocity?"

"Twenty-eight hundred for the far one and slowing down. Thirty-two and accelerating for the other."

"The speed of the wave," Hutch said hopefully. "They're in the neighborhood of the speed of the wave."

Carson was trying to keep his imagination under control. "Janet, what do you think?"

"Just what you're thinking."

Maybe that was it, that single piece of encouragement from the only other professional archeologist in the area. The old colonel's reserve fell away, and his eyes blazed. "Terry," he said, "how close will they come?"

"To us? One's already past," he said. "The other will get within thirty million klicks. Give or take a few."

"How big did you say it was?"

"It's twenty-three thousand kilometers wide. Sometimes."

"Sometimes?" asked Hutch. "What kind of thing is this?"

"We don't know. It isn't a sphere. We get a lot of different measurements. False readings, maybe. Hard to say."

The steam clung to the cliff wall. "It sounds as if the *dragon* might really be here," said Hutch.

"Premature," he said. But his expression belied detachment.

"I still think it's a *cloud*," said Drafts.

"Let's take another look," said Angela softly.

Thirty minutes later, they had piled back into the shelter, and were studying incoming images. The more distant object was little more than a misty star, a blur seen through heavy rain. But its companion was a thundercloud, lit ominously within, a storm on the horizon just after sunset.

"Well," said Angela, as if that single word summed up the inexplicable. "Whatever it is, just the fact that something is there, that *anything* is there, is significant. The intrusion of an extrasolar object into a planetary system is a rare event. I can't believe it just happened to occur while we're in the area. Since there are *two* of these things, I'd be willing to bet there are more coming. A lot more."

"Sounds like a wave to me," said Hutch.

"I didn't say that."

"Nevertheless it does."

"Unfortunately," said Janet, "if that's our critter, we're not going to get a very good look at it."

"Why not?" demanded Carson.

"Thirty million klicks is not close."

"I wouldn't worry," said Hutch. "If Angela is right, there'll be another along shortly. I think we ought to finish making our Oz, and see what happens."

On the *Ashley*, Janet and Drafts took turns monitoring the commlinks.

Unlike most of the hard-science specialists she knew, he had interests outside his chosen field. He had a sense of humor, he knew how to listen, and he encouraged her to talk about things *she* was interested in. She decided that if her duties required her to be holed up inside a tin can for a year with a single companion, Drafts would be easy to take.

He asked her about the book of Japanese poetry she'd been reading, and challenged her to produce a *haiku*. After a few minutes, and a lot of rewriting, she had one:

> *If they ask for me,*
> *Say, she rides where comets go,*
> *And outpaces light.*

"Lovely," Drafts said.

"Your turn."

"I can't match that."

"Not if you don't try."

He sighed and picked up a pad. She watched him intently

during the process. He smiled tentatively at her, struggled a lot, and finally presented her with one:

> I have walked on stars,
> And sailed the channels of night,
> To sip tea with you.

"I like it," she said.

His dark eyes found her. "I know it's not on a level with yours," he said. "But it's true."

Delta. Tuesday, May 17; 1535 hours.

The corner was *almost* a perfect 90 degrees. The problem was that the ice was brittle, and tended to crumble. But it was good enough. Carson called it a victory, cut power to the 1600, and accepted a handshake from his partner. "That's it, Angela," he said. "We're done for now. Let's go."

She acknowledged, and laid power to the engines.

They wheeled overhead and admired their work. Not bad for amateurs.

Angela spent the evening looking at the data coming in from *Ashley*. She kept moving files around, switching images, talking to herself.

"What's wrong?" asked Hutch.

"These *things*," she said. "There's no way to explain them. And I'm thinking where we're going to be if we let them get away and another one does *not* show up."

"Looking dumb?" suggested Hutch.

"To say the least. We've got a major discovery here. *Whatever it is*. They violate physical law. The one that's approaching us will pass the sun and apparently keep going. I mean, this thing is really *traveling*." She was quiet for a moment. "I don't know what holds them together."

"What are you suggesting, Angela?"

"I think we should arrange to take a close look as it goes by."

"Is there time?"

"We can arrange an intercept. We won't have much time alongside, because the ship can't begin to match the object's velocity in the time available. But we can get a quick glimpse, and maybe the sensors will be more effective up close." She looked at Carson. "What do you think?"

"Can't we catch it later if we have to?" He directed the question to Hutch.

She considered it. "Hazeltines are notoriously poor for pinpoint work. We did pretty well at Beta Pac, but that's the exception. Usually, you pick a star system, and land somewhere in the general neighborhood. With something that's moving the way this thing is, if we let it get away, we might never see it again."

"I don't think running after it right now would be prudent," Carson said.

Angela frowned. "I can't see any problem. Terry's a good pilot. And he will keep a respectful distance."

"No," he said.

"Frank," said Angela, "the real risk is in *not* going."

He rolled his eyes and opened a channel to the ship. "Let's talk about it," he told her.

Janet appeared on the main display. "How's the Neighborhood Improvement Group doing?"

"Not bad," said Carson. "Where's Terry?"

"Right here." The screen split.

"What would you think about intercepting the object? Go out and take a close look?"

He consulted his display and blew unhappily through his fingers. "We'd need to move pretty fast. I make it about two and a half days at max to lay in alongside it."

"Can you wait for us?"

"Frank, this ride is already going to hurt."

"How do you feel about doing it?"

He looked over at Janet. "You game?"

"Sure."

They could see his reluctance. "I don't know," he said.

"Terry," pleaded Angela, "we might not get another chance."

Hutch looked at her. She wanted this badly, and it was clouding her judgment. "It would leave *us* without a ship," she pointed out. "I don't know whether that's a good idea either."

"Don't need one," said Angela.

Janet shrugged. "Don't hesitate because of me."

"I can't see," said Angela, "that there's anything to lose."

Carson wanted to go. That was obvious. But the assorted

shocks on this expedition had taken their toll. Hutch could see his natural instincts struggling with his newfound caution. And she saw them win. "Anybody else with an objection?"

Drafts looked sidewise at his partner. "If Angela wants it, and Janet has no problem, I'd like to do it."

"Okay." Colonel Carson returned. "Let's go."

There were a few last-minute technical conversations. Drafts entered flight requirements into the navigation systems. They would use Flickinger fields to help negate some of the effects of acceleration.

Within thirty minutes of making the decision, the *Ashley Tee* lifted out of orbit into an acceleration that mashed its crew into their seats.

"You okay?" asked Drafts.

"Fine," she said breathlessly.

"It'll be a sixty-two hour run."

In the screens, Delta, the orange ice world, diminished rapidly to a small globe, and then to a point of light. After a while, only the gas giant remained. Soon it too was only a bright star.

LIBRARY ENTRY

Dragon in the dark,
Your eyes move across the stars,
Your breath warms the moon.

—April 24, 2203
(Found in unassigned file on *Ashley Tee*)

29.

Delta. Wednesday, May 18; 0930 hours.

The operation on the small mesa had gone so well that they hoped to finish by the end of the day.

They sliced and buffed until they had three smooth rock walls set at (almost) right angles to each other. Then they turned to the task of straightening the fourth side, with its massive notch. Carson regretted not having the capability to fill the indentation rather than have to pare off the walls on either side. But never mind: he would manage.

They had developed reasonable facility with the 1600, and were now enjoying themselves. Whenever possible, they stationed themselves on the ground. But for the most part it was necessary to take to the air, and work from *above* the mesa. Angela pointed out that they were in violation of a wide variety of safety procedures. But she swallowed her reservations, took them up, and, on signal, rolled the shuttle onto its side. In back, restrained by his tether and Hutch's makeshift harness, Carson rode the 1600, looking straight down. "You're perfectly safe," Hutch assured him.

After about an hour, they changed places. Hutch enjoyed aiming the big cannon, and they learned how to employ the sensors to see through the steam, and so became more proficient. By the time they broke for lunch, a substantial portion of the rear wall lay in rubble. But they had a rectangle!

The limiting factor in getting to the rendezvous point and laying in alongside the cloud was not the capability of the ship, but that of its crew to withstand prolonged acceleration. They would arrive with aching joints and sore backs, and they would have only a few seconds before the target sailed past and left them hopelessly behind. To ameliorate these effects,

Drafts programmed in frequent breaks in the acceleration, during which they could get up and move around. It would not be a comfortable ride, but it would be livable.

Hutch distrusted hastily planned maneuvers as a matter of instinct. She wondered at the necessity for *this* trip. Angela's logic made sense: there was probably another one coming. Why not go after it at their leisure? She was annoyed that Janet had not supported her. Instead, she'd allowed herself to get caught up in the general enthusiasm. They were making snap decisions again, without considering all the consequences. She wondered whether they had learned *anything* at Beta Pac.

She derived some satisfaction from knowing that Janet was now pinned in her webchair by the acceleration. Served her right.

They inspected their work on the south mesa. Seen from the air, it was a child's block, an orange rectangle. "I wish we could change its color," said Carson. "The Oz-structures were highly reflective, and they stood out from their sur- roundings."

"You think that matters?" asked Hutch.

"I don't know. It might."

It occurred to Hutch that the pumpkin-colored block below might be as hard for some future mission to explain as Oz had been.

The eastern mesa was next. It was three times as big as the one they had just worked on, less regular, heavily scored. Moreover, when they started on it, they discovered it was brittle. Its walls shriveled at the touch of the energy beam, and whole sections crumbled away. They experimented with intensity and angle, and discovered that overhead shots with low power worked best. "Like everything else," Carson said as they sliced and polished, "the only thing that succeeds is finesse. The light touch."

Communication with *Ashley* was becoming difficult. After twenty-four hours, the ship had traveled approximately fifteen million kilometers. At that distance, laserburst signals re- quired almost two minutes to make a round trip. Conversa- tions became slow and frustrating, and the two groups began to feel their isolation from each other.

The ground team slept through the night-phase. But all three were up early, anxious to get started. They treated themselves to a substantial breakfast, and went back to the eastern plateau.

They hoped to finish the wall they'd started the previous day, and fashion the corner. Hutch liked doing corners. They were a break from the routine.

Because much of the work was done from the air, Angela was usually alone in the cockpit. There, she watched the visuals coming in from *Ashley*, pictures of the oncoming object. Of the *cloud*, tiny and purple and utterly impossible.

Sometimes she had to draw back, remind herself where she was, remember to keep her mind on the mission, on the people who were hanging out the cargo door. But *My God*, this was a magnificent time.

The only downside was that she was not on board *Ashley*.

On the other end, Drafts was by turns ecstatic and depressed. The sensors still gave them only superficial readings. "What I'd like to do," he told Angela, "is put our money where our mouth is and lay *Ashley* right in front of it. Let it run over us, and see what happens." *That* got her attention, even though she didn't believe he meant it. But she stabbed the Transmit key anyhow and told him to forget anything like that, that she would have his career if he even so much as raised the suggestion again. But he added, long before her threats could have reached him, "Of course I won't. I don't think the probes will do much good, but we'll try to insert one."

Later, when they were back on the ground, Carson came forward for lunch. Hutch remained in back because the cockpit was too crowded for all three. He was munching on a sandwich, and Angela was planning the next day's flight, when, between mouthfuls, he said, "What's that?"

He was looking at the overhead display.

The object had developed *fingers*.

And despite all her training, the intellectual habits of a lifetime, the unshakable conviction that the universe is ultimately rational and knowable, Angela suffered an uneasy twinge. "Don't know," she said, almost angry, as if it were somehow Carson's doing.

Extensions. Not really fingers, but protrusions. Prominences.

"Seven," said Angela. "I count seven."

"One of them's dividing," said Carson.

They grew long and narrow. Hutch thought they looked

like the fingers of the wizard in *The Sorcerer's Apprentice.*

"Have we got measurements?" asked Carson.

Angela checked the status board. "The longest is twenty thousand kilometers, plus or minus six percent. We don't have a reading yet on the expansion rate."

"They're contrails," said Hutch.

Yes. They were. Angela felt relieved, and then foolish, as if she had not known all along it would be something prosaic. "Yes," she said.

The contrails began to lose their definition. They drifted apart, overlapped, bled together. The illusion dissipated. It might have been a wispy comet with a multitude of tails. Or an airship that had exploded.

Got to be enormous disruptions to throw all that off. "I think it's coming apart," Angela said.

The chime sounded, and Drafts's image blinked on. "Take a look at the target," he said.

Carson held up a hand. "We see it." Drafts did not react, of course. His image was delayed by several minutes.

Angela was caught up in a swirl of emotions. "Lovely," she said. Nothing in her life, which had been reasonably full, had prepared her for what she was feeling now. Unable to restrain herself, she let go a cheer, and jabbed a fist skyward. "Good stuff," she said. *"But what is that thing?"*

It looked as if it were unraveling.

Long smoky comets rolled glacially away from the object.

"What the hell's going on?" Drafts's voice again.

The process continued, almost too slowly for the eye to follow. Bursts of conversation passed between the pod and the ship. Drafts thought the object was disintegrating, dissolving as it should have done earlier amid the fierce tides of the gravitational fields.

"But why *now*?" demanded Angela. "Why not yesterday? Why not last week? It's not as if local gravity has changed in any significant way."

"The other one got through," said Hutch. "Why would *this* one explode?"

"I don't think it's really exploding," Angela said without taking her eyes from the screen. "It's hard to see clearly, but I think all that's happening is that some of the outer cloud cover is peeling off."

"What would cause that?"

"I don't know," she said. "This thing doesn't seem to obey physical law."

She took to replaying the entire sequence at fast forward. The object opened slowly and gracefully, a blood-red flower with blooming petals offering itself to the sun.

The ground team continued with their efforts at block carving. They wielded the 1600 and shaped and molded the ice, and took pleasure in their growing skills. And they watched the numbers coming in on the dragon.

Toward the end of the day's operations, Angela called Carson's attention to the screens. But Carson was riding the saddle. "Neither of us is in a position to look right now," he said. "What is it?"

The object might have been a comet whose head had exploded. "It's *turning*," she said. "I'll be damned. It's changing course. That's what all the earlier activity was about. It's been pitching material off into space."

"Isn't that impossible?" Hutch asked. "I mean, natural objects *don't* throw *turns*, do they?"

"Not without help." *Outside, the land looked empty and cold and inhuman. Soaked in ruby light, where anything could happen.*

"Where is it going?" Carson asked.

"Don't know. We won't be able to tell until it completes the maneuver. But it *has* turned inside *Ashley*'s projected course. *Toward us*, actually." She tried to keep the sense of melodrama out of her voice, but it was difficult not to scream the words.

"You sure?" That was Hutch.

"I'm sure that it's turning in our general direction."

Nobody said anything for a long time.

Hutch's face appeared on one of the screens. That was good. They needed to be able to see each other now.

"Son of a bitch," said Hutch. "Is it possible the thing knows we're here?"

"What the hell," said Carson, "*is* that thing?"

"That's the question," said Angela, "we keep asking, isn't it?"

"You'd better let *Ashley* know," said Hutch.

"I've got a call in."

They stared at one another for a long moment. "Maybe we

ought to think about getting out of here," said Hutch.

Carson put a hand on her shoulder but said nothing.

Angela had the same thought. But they needed to avoid jumping to conclusions. Celestial bodies do not chase *people*. "I don't know whether you two are aware of it," she said, "but we've got the daddy of all anomalies here. We are all going down in the history books."

"Just so we don't all go down," said Hutch.

"Angela." It was Drafts, looking confused. "I don't know where it's going, but it sure as hell isn't going to the same place we are. It's swinging inside us, and we can't brake quickly enough to adjust to its new course. Whatever *that* turns out to be. We'll have to loop around and try again. This is going to become a marathon. We'll need several extra days now to make a rendezvous. Can't really be specific until the thing settles down." He shook his head. "This can't be happening. I'll get back to you as soon as we know what's going on."

Angela was a study in frustration. "That can't be right," she said. "They had just enough time to get out to it before. Now he thinks he can take a couple of days to turn around, and catch up to it?"

"He just hasn't thought it out yet," said Carson.

"Maybe. But he might know something we don't."

"If he did, wouldn't he mention it?"

"Sure. Unless he assumed we all had the same information."

"Ask him."

"Maybe there's no need." Angela looked at the numbers again and started her subroutines. Meantime, she noted that her power cells had dropped inside safety margins. "That's it, kids," she said. "Saddle up. We're going home."

Nobody talked much on the way back, but once they got inside the shelter she told them what Drafts had known: "It's decelerating. It's thrown on the brakes."

"That's why it's coming apart," said Hutch.

"Yes, I would say so. Despite appearances, it's apparently pretty tightly wrapped, considering what it's able to do. But this maneuver is a bit much even for the mechanism that holds it together."

Carson asked the question that might have been on everyone's mind: "Is it a *natural* object?"

"Of course it is," said Angela. But she was speaking from common sense, not from knowledge.

"How can it change directions?" asked Hutch. "And what sort of braking mechanism could it have?"

"Maybe there's something out there exerting force on it," Angela said. "A superdense object, possibly."

"You think that's what's happening?" asked Carson. He had thrown off his jacket, and was making for the coffee pot.

"No." There would have been other effects, advance indications, orbital irregularities. There was none of that. "No," she said. "I have no explanation. But that doesn't mean we need to bring in malevolent agencies."

"Who said *malevolent*?" asked Hutch.

They exchanged looks, and Angela let the question hang. "It's reacting to something. Has to be. Magnetic fields, maybe. Maybe there's been a solar burp of some kind. Hard to tell, sitting down here." She shrugged. "We'll just have to wait and see."

"Angela," said Hutch, "Is this thing *like* a cloud? Chemically?"

"Yes," she said. "It's constructed of the same kind of stuff as the big clouds that stars condense from: particles of iron, carbon, silicates. Hydrogen. Formaldehyde. And there's probably a large chunk of iron or rock inside."

Hutch tasted her coffee. It was spiced with cinnamon. "There were concentrations of formaldehyde," she said, "in the soil around Oz."

"I didn't know that," said Angela. "Is that true?"

"Yes, it is."

She looked out at the sun, which was still high in the southwest. It was only marginally closer to the horizon than it had been when they arrived.

"So how does it brake?" asked Hutch again.

Angela thought about it. "One way would be what we've seen: to hurl material outward. Like a rocket. Another way would be to manipulate gravity fields."

"Is that possible?" asked Carson.

"Not for us. But if anti-gravity is possible, and the evidence suggests it *is*, then *yes*, it could be done." Angela fell silent for a few moments. "Listen: let's cut to reality here. Just the *existence* of this thing implies wholesale manipulation of gravity, of tidal forces, and of damned near every other kind of force I can think of. It's almost as if the thing exists in a dimensional vacuum, where nothing from the outside touches it."

"Almost?"

"Yes. Almost. Look: there are *two* clouds. Let's assume both were traveling at the same velocity when they entered the planetary system. They should have broken up, but they didn't. The one on the far side of the sun is moving more slowly than this one. That's as it should be, because it's contending with solar drag, while our baby here is getting pulled along as it moves toward the sun. So there *is* some effect. But don't ask me to explain it."

Angela drifted out of the conversation while she watched the object, and the readouts. The cometary tail, which (in obedience to physical law) was leading the object, had become harder to see as the head turned toward them. Now its last vestiges virtually disappeared into the red cloudscape. After a while she turned back to them. "It's coming here," she said.

They watched the image. Watched for the tail to appear on the other side. It did not.

Their eyes touched. "Target angle stable," she added.

Hutch paled. "When?"

Carson said, "This can't be happening. We're being chased by a *cloud?*"

"If it continues to decelerate at its present rate, I would say Monday. About 0100."

"We'd better let Terry know," said Carson. "Get them back here and pick us up."

Hutch shook her head. "I don't think so. They're moving away from us at a pretty good clip. My guess is that it will be noon Sunday before they can even get turned around."

Bedtime. Angela noticed Hutch in front of a display, her expression wistful, perhaps melancholy. She sat down with her. "We'll do fine," she said. "It can't really be after *us.*"

"I know," said Hutch. "It's an illusion."

The screen was filled with poetry.

"What is it?" Angela asked.

"Maggie's notebooks." Her eyes met Angela's, but looked quickly away. "I think there was a lot about the woman that I missed."

Angela's gaze intensified, but she didn't speak.

Hutch brought up a file. "This is from *Urik at Sunset*."

It was a group of prayers and songs celebrating the deeds of the Quraquat hero. Epic in tone, they retained a highly personal flavor. "Urik was to be experienced up close," Maggie commented in the accompanying notes, "and not from a distance in the manner of terrestrial heroes."

She went on: "Show me what a people admire, and I will tell you everything about them that matters."

And, finally, a prayer that seemed particularly pertinent:

> *My spirit glides above the waters of the world,*
> *Because you are with me.*

They looked east across the sky. *It will come from that direction. Over there.* It would come in over the coffee-colored sea. If the sun would set, which of course it won't for several more days, they'd be able to see it now. "It'll probably become visible during the next twelve hours," Angela said.

What was the old line from the *Rubaiyat*?

But who was now the potter?

And who the pot?

The snowfields were broad and serene.

Delta. Friday, May 20; 0900 hours.

Hutch was not happy. "What are our options?" she asked.

"How about clearing out now?" suggested Carson. "Get in the shuttle and *go*. Get away from Delta altogether."

Angela considered it. "I don't think the odds would be good. The shuttle was designed for ship-to-ship operations. It was never intended for use in gravity wells. It doesn't have much power. We can't really get clear, and I don't think we want to play tag with that monster. No. Listen, it's moving pretty slowly now. I suggest we stay where we are. Go around the other side of the world and *hide*."

"I agree," said Hutch. She depolarized the viewing panels, letting the red daylight in. "We know there were survivors on Quraqua and Nok: these things don't kill everybody. Let's just dig in."

"Listen," said Carson, "is it really going to score a direct hit on *us*?"

"Yes," Angela said. "I don't think there's any doubt about

it. It'll come in about thirty degrees off the horizon, and it'll land right in our coffee. Incidentally, its timing is perfect. If it were a little earlier, or a little later, it wouldn't have a clear shot at us. At the mesas, I mean."

Carson's stomach tightened. *Its timing is perfect.* "Okay," he said. "Let's make for the other side. Let the moon absorb the impact. After that happens, we clear out. If we can." His face was grim. "So now we know about Oz. It was intended to draw the goddam thing. I can't believe it. The sons of bitches deliberately arranged to bomb the civilizations on Nok and Quraqua. They must have been psychos."

"Let's talk about it later," said Angela. "We've got things to do."

"Right," said Carson. "Let's start by rearranging the cameras to get the best record we can."

"There *is* something else we could try," said Hutch. "Maybe our blocks worked better than we expected. We could blow them up. Pull the bait out of the water."

Angela shook her head. "I don't think it would matter now. It's late. That thing is coming for dinner no matter what we do."

The outermost moon in the system orbited the gas giant at a range of eighteen million kilometers. It was little more than a barrel-shaped rock, with barely the surface area of Washington, D.C. It was a fairly typical boulder, battered and ill-used. An observer in that moon's northern hemisphere would, during these hours, have been looking at a fearsome sky, a blood-red sky, filled by a vast fiery river. The river knew no banks and no limits: it drove the stars before it, and even the sun was lost in the brilliance of its passage.

30.

Delta. Saturday, May 21; 1010 hours.

They watched the dragon rise, a massive cloudbank, swollen and infected. Streamers and tendrils rolled toward them, over the eastern horizon.

The cameras had optical, infrared, X-ray, and short-range sensor capabilities. They were state-of-the-art stuff, but Hutch didn't think they were going to last long when things began to happen.

They picked three sites, each a half-kilometer outside the general target area. Two were on high ground. They slipped the cameras into makeshift housings, and bolted the units into the ice. One was set to track the approach of the dragon, and the others to scan the target area.

When they'd finished they ran tests, adjusted the power cells, and executed a successful drill from the cockpit. Afterward, they retired to the dome for a turkey luncheon. Hearty meal, thought Hutch. Good for morale.

They cracked a couple of bottles of Chablis, and made jokes about the weather.

No one had much appetite. In a world that had lost its anchor to reality, it was hard to get seriously involved with a turkey sandwich. Anything now seemed possible.

Long ago, when she was nine years old, Hutch had gone with her father to see Michael Parrish, the magician. It had been an evening filled with floating cabinets, people getting sawed in half, and a black box that yielded an unending supply of doves, rabbits, and red and white kerchiefs. Priscilla Hutchins had tried to fathom the methods used by the magician, but she had been astonished time and again. And although she knew that trickery was involved, that magic wasn't real, she had nevertheless lost touch with the physical world, and reached a point at which the impossible failed to surprise her.

She was at that point now.

After dinner, she went outside and sat down in the snow. She let the alienness of the scene suck at her, as if it might extract some hidden part, and infuse a portion of itself, a particle of enchantment that would re-establish a cable to comprehension. It was almost as if this world had been placed here exclusively for her and her companions, that it had waited through billions of unchanging years for precisely this moment.

The others joined her after a while, en route to other tasks, but they too paused in the growing radiance of the thing in the east.

Ashley continued to relay updates on the dragon, which was still running hot and true. Drafts was sliding from professional acceptance to near-panic, and had begun urging them to use the shuttle to get off-world. Janet, who had perhaps been through too much with Hutch and Carson, merely told them she knew they'd be okay.

After a while, they got up and straggled over to the shuttle. They disconnected the 1600 and carried it inside the dome. Not that it would matter when the fire fell out of the sky.

They began packing.

"I don't think we should wait until tomorrow," said Angela. "I'd feel better if we cleared out tonight."

"We live better here," said Carson. "There's no point in scrunching up in the shuttle for an extra day." He went inside and came back with more Chablis. To prove the point.

So they waited under the hammer and debated whether they would be safer on the ground or in the air at the moment of impact. Whether it wasn't paranoid to think they were actually being chased by this thing. ("It's not *us*," each of them said, in one form or another. "It's seen the *mesas*. It's the *mesas* it's coming after.") Whether, if they made a run for it, the object would adjust course again and come after them. *Them*, and damn the mesas. After a while, despite the tension, Hutch couldn't keep her eyes open. No one went to bed that night; they all slept in the common room, stretched out in chairs.

Hutch woke, it seemed, every few minutes. And she decided, if she ever went through anything like this again (which she would, but that's another story), she'd by God, clear out at the first hint of funny business.

Somewhere around five, she smelled coffee. Angela held out a cup.

"Hi," said Hutch.

The dragon was an angry smear in the sky.

"I'll be glad," said Angela, "when we're out of here."

There was a ring around the sun, and a thick haze over the plain. A half-moon had broken through in the southwest.

Fresh snow lay on the ground when Angela and Hutch came out of the dome, carrying their bags. There were a few flakes in the air. "It's frustrating when you think about it," said Angela. "Cosmic event like this, and we have to go hide on the other side of the world."

Hutch climbed into the shuttle. "I suppose we could stay, if you insist," she said.

"No. I didn't mean that." Angela handed her bags through, took her place at the controls, and studied her checklist. "But I wish we had a ship, so we could lay off somewhere and watch the fireworks." Hutch activated the commlink, and picked up the feed from *Ashley*. The dragon blinked on. The view wasn't good now because the ship was very distant. And still retreating.

Angela thought the main body might be more than a million kilometers behind the forward spouts. Yet the mind still saw it as a thundercloud. An ominous thundercloud. Belching and roiling and flickering. But still only a thundercloud. She tried to imagine a similar visitation over the Temple of the Winds. What would a nontechnological race have made of this harpy? And she wondered about the Monument-Makers. Why had they sicked it on that unfortunate race? And left their final ironic taunt? *Farewell and good fortune. Seek us by the light of the horgon's eye.*

And, in that moment, she understood.

The comm panel blinked. "Incoming," said Angela.

David Emory's face blinked on. "Hello, ground station," he said. "What's happening? Do you need help?"

Relief and pleasure swept through Hutch. "David, hello. Where are you?" But he did not react. She watched and counted off the seconds while her signal traveled outward to him, and her newborn hope died. He was too far away.

Carson climbed through the hatch. "I see the cavalry has arrived," he said. "Where are they?"

David broke into a wide smile. "Hutch. It's good to see you. I'm on the *Cary Knapp*. What is that *thing*? What's going on?"

Hutch gave him a capsulized version.

"We'll get there as quickly as we can."

"Stay clear," she said. "Stay clear until the dust settles."

By mid-morning they were in the air.

They all watched the dragon: Emory on the *Knapp*, Janet and Drafts on *Ashley*, and Carson's group in the shuttle.

The pictures now were coming from the *Knapp*. They were clearer than anything they'd had before. Delta resembled a child's ball floating before a cosmic wall of black cloud.

They were about to be swallowed.

Enormous fountains of gas and vapor billowed away; vast explosions erupted in slow time, as if occurring in a different temporal mode. Fiery blossoms disconnected and drifted away. "It's disintegrating," Angela said. "It's moving quite slowly now, and I'd guess it's thrown off seventy percent of its mass. It's coming here, but afterward it won't be going anywhere else."

They'd left the plain and its mesas behind, and were gliding above a nitrogen swamp, bathed in the shifting light. Carson was in the right-hand seat. He kept making remarks like "My God, I don't believe this," and "No wonder they all got religion."

Gales battered the craft. Hutch, in back, wondered whether they'd be able to stay in the air. She watched the pictures coming in from *Knapp*. "The gas giant's tearing it up," she said, straining to make herself heard over the wind. "If we're lucky, maybe there won't be any of it left when it gets here."

"Forget that idea," said Angela. She took a deep breath. "It's a Chinese puzzle. Have you noticed anything odd?"

Carson studied the display. "Have I noticed anything *odd*?" He stifled laughter.

She ignored the reaction. "No quakes," she said.

"I don't follow."

But Hutch did. "It's fifteen hours away. Does this place *have* plates?"

"Yes."

She looked at Carson. "A celestial body that close should be raising hell with local tectonics. Right?"

"That's right." Angela poked her keyboard, asked for new data. "If nothing else, we should be getting major tidal surges." The swamp had given way to a mud-colored sea. Thick, slow waves rolled ashore. A few meters higher up, the rock was discolored. "That would be high tide," she said. "This doesn't look like anything unusual."

"What's the point?" asked Carson.

"The point is that these oceans, even these kinds of oceans, ought to be jumping out of their beds. Hold on." She opened the *Knapp* channel, and asked David to get readings on the positions of the satellites. While she waited, she brought up the entire file on the gas giant and its family of moons. She established orbits, computed velocities, and calculated lunar positions.

When the ship began relaying its information, she checked her predictions.

Tau, the misshapen rock at the edge of the system, had strayed out of its orbit. But by only about four hundred kilometers. Negligible. Rho was two hundred kilometers in advance of her predicted position. Everything else, within tolerances, was correct.

The sun was rising again as the shuttle gained on it. They were moving out over a gasoline swamp. Behind them, the sky burned.

"It's not solid," said Hutch.

"That's right," Angela announced with finality. "It's a dust cloud, after all. Has to be. There might be a solid core in there somewhere, but it must be *small*."

"But a rock," said Hutch, "even a *big* rock, isn't going to hold that thing together."

"That's right, Hutch. Find the glue and win yourself a Nobel."

Sunday; 1146 hours.

The *thing* on the monitors seemed like a visitant out of the old tales. A messenger from the Almighty. Carson wondered what the skies had looked like over Egypt on the first Passover? What the weather report had been for Sodom? What they'd seen from the walls at Jericho?

Something deep in his instincts signaled the approach of the supernatural. Out here, pursued by an apparently angry cosmic anomaly, watching it close in, Carson was getting religion.

He made no effort to shrug the idea off; rather he aggressively entertained it, wondering where it might lead. Might beings with cosmic power actually exist? If they were confronting one here, it was manifesting a disquieting interest in the more primitive races. A stupid god, driven to destroy right angles. A thing dispensing serious trouble to those who defied the divine edict to build only in the round.

He scanned through the religious and romantic art of Nok and Quraqua, as recorded in Maggie's records, looking for correlations. He found some. *Here* was a cloud demon of terrifying similarity to the thing in the sky. And *there*, a dark god with red eyes and lunging talons emerging from a storm.

1411 hours.

Lightning flickered through the gasoline-drenched skies. Ethyl rain swept in torrents across the windscreen, and clung to the shuttle's wings. Angela would have gone higher, above the atmosphere, but the turbulence was strong, and intensifying. She was not certain she could make it safely back down when the time came.

It was, by turns, terrifying and ecstatic. The shuttle rolled and plunged. When she wasn't fighting for control of the vehicle, she was dreaming of glory. She would always be associated with this phenomenon. It might even one day carry her name: the *Morgan*. She liked the sound of it, rolled it around her tongue. Visualized future scholars addressing seminars: *Several categories of* Morgans *are known to exist.*

Well, maybe not.

Carson was imagining a wave of dragon clouds, perhaps thousands of light-years long, swirling out of the Void, an irresistible, diabolical tide. Drowning entire worlds, with clocklike precision. Pumped into the system by the rhythm of a cosmic heart. And not *one* wave. *Three* waves. Maybe a *thousand* waves, their crests separated by 108 light-years.

To what purpose?

Was it happening everywhere? All along the Arm? On the other side of the Galaxy? "The big telescope," he said.

Hutch looked at him. "Pardon?"

"I was thinking about the telescope at Beta Pac. It was pointed toward the Magellanic Clouds."

"You figure out why?"

"Maybe. The Monument-Makers knew about the dragons. Do you think they might have been trying to find out whether other places were safe? Beyond this galaxy?"

Hutch listened to her pulse. "That's a good question," she said.

1600 hours.

The *Knapp* was approaching from sunward. Carson talked at length with David Emory. Despite the time delay, the conversations distracted him from the moment-to-moment terrors of the ride through that fierce sky. Emory asked about everything, the conditions in the city by the harbor, what they had seen at the space station, how they had found the dragon. He expressed his sorrow at the loss of their colleagues. He had known Maggie, had worked with her, admired her. "I never met George," he said.

Carson had by then changed places with Hutch. In the cockpit, Angela asked if she understood why Emory was so inquisitive.

"He doesn't expect us to survive," she guessed. "He doesn't want mysteries afterward. So he's getting all his questions in now."

1754 hours.

They had left the dragon behind, and the sun as well, and passed onto the night side. But an eerie red glow lay on the horizon. Below, the land flowed past, rendered soft and glossy by the snow. "We'll go another hour or so," Angela said, "and then we'll look for a plain somewhere, as flat as we can find, where nothing can fall on us."

The pictures coming in from *Knapp* revealed that the anomaly had become so tenuous, so inflated, so unraveled, that one could not say precisely *where* it was. It seemed to have spilled across the system of moons and rings.

At the target area, monitored by the cameras, boiling light filled the sky.

1952 hours.

The shuttle cleared a range of glaciers and glided low over country that was flat and featureless, save for a few hills on the horizon. They had come approximately halfway around the globe. "Ideal," said Carson. "Let's park it right here."

On board NCA Ashley Tee. 2006 hours.
Ashley reached the end of its forward flight. For a microsecond, a flicker of a moment, it came to an absolute halt, relative to Delta. Then the instant was gone, and it reversed course and began its return. Inside the ship, the moment would have gone unnoticed (the thrust, after all, continued unabated from the same quarter of the vessel), had not a green console lamp blinked on.

"Closing," said Drafts. He knew that Janet had seen the signal, had in fact been watching for it. But it was something to say. A benchmark to be noted. They were, at last, on their way.

2116 hours.
Angela gave up trying to raise the ships. "It's getting worse," she said. Her gauges were all over the park. "That thing is putting out a hurricane of low-frequency radiation, mostly in the infrared, microwave, and radio bands. But we're lucky: it could just as easily be generating X-rays, and fry us all."

Their own sky was almost serene, save for the angry glow on the horizon.

2304 hours.
Two hours to impact. More or less. With so ephemeral an object, who could know?

Transmissions from the mesa site were garbled beyond recovery. Angela switched away from them. She also shut down all nonessential systems, and did a strange thing: she turned out the cockpit lights, as if to conceal the location of the shuttle.

The conversation was desultory. They talked about incidentals, how strange the sky looked, how nobody was going to leave home again. And they reassured one another.

Had long-dead Pinnacle experienced these things? "They *have* to be part of the natural order," Carson said. "Every eight thousand years they come in and take you out. Why?"

"It's almost as if," said Angela, "the universe is wired to attack cities. Is that possible?"

Jack McDevitt

Hutch sat in the darkness, feeling like prey. What was the line Richard had quoted? *Something there is that doesn't love a wall*. "It might be," she said, "that it's part of a program to protect life."

Carson's brows drew together. "By blowing it up?"

"By discouraging the rise of dominant species. Maybe it's a balancing effect. Maybe the universe doesn't approve of places like New York."

In the west, they saw lightning. *Coming this way*.

"Air pressure's going down fast," said Angela. The ground shook. It was only a tremor, a wobble. "Maybe we should get back upstairs."

"No." Carson sank into his chair and tried to relax. "We're safer here."

Monday; 0004 hours.

Ashley was accelerating. But whatever was going to happen would be over long before they arrived on the scene. Janet had spent much of her time trying to talk with Emory, but the signals had faded in the electromagnetic flux created by the dragon. On her screens, Delta and the thing had joined. Drafts was frantic, and had grown worse as the hour approached. He was not helped by the loss of communications. And being pinned in his web chair did nothing to ease his frustration.

Janet tried to sound optimistic. Hutch and Angela Morgan together! If there was a way to survive, she knew one or the other would find it.

0027 hours.

The skies flowed past, churned, *exploded*. Heavy bolts ripped the night, and the wind howled around them. Snow and ice rattled against the shuttle.

The plain trembled. One by one, the shuttle's monitors died.

Carson hovered in the rear doorway, between the two women. "We're doing okay," he said.

"Never better," said Hutch.

"You betcha," said Angela, with mock cheer. "Here we sit with God coming after us."

"We'll be fine," said Carson.

There was no point at which it could be said that *contact* actually occurred. The dragon no longer possessed definitive limits. It had opened out. Filaments tens of thousands of kilometers long had broached Delta's atmosphere hours earlier. But Carson and the women knew that the moon was now firmly in the embrace of its fierce visitor.

The air was thick with ash and snow. It drifted down onto the plain, and a black crust began to form.

"Maybe," said Angela, "there really *is* no core."

"Let's hope not," said Carson. And he was about to add, optimistically, that maybe it wouldn't be much worse than a large storm after all, when white light exploded overhead, and a fireball roared out of the sky and ripped into the snowscape.

It wasn't close, but they all flinched.

"What was that?"

"Meteor?"

"Don't know—"

"Damn," said Hutch.

Carson took a deep breath. "Angela, how long do you think this will last?"

"Hard to tell. The worst of it should end within a day or two. It's still moving pretty quickly. And it's not tracking Delta's orbit, so we should come out of it fairly soon." They could hear her breathing in the dark. "I think this place is going to have even lousier weather than usual for a while though."

"I'm scared," said Hutch.

So was Carson. But he knew it would be improper to concede the point. Someone needed to show strength. "We'll be okay," he told her. He wished they could get pictures from the ground cameras. What was happening at the site?

The dragon's head dissolved. Billows and fountains expanded, collapsed, and blew apart. They rubbed together like great cats. Chunks of rock and ice, apparently buried within the thick atmosphere, were expelled.

On Delta, methane seas exploded into nearby low-lying areas. Tornado-force winds, generated by sudden changes in pressure, roared around the globe. Everywhere, it was midnight.

Rock and ice fell out of the sky. Their fiery trails illuminated the general chaos. Most were small, too small to penetrate even the relatively thin atmosphere. Others plowed into ice fields, and blasted swamps and seas.

Volcanoes erupted.

Out on their plain, Hutch, Angela, and Frank crouched in the shuttle and waited. Waited for the world-cracking collision that would come when the core of the dragon struck ground. As it must. As Angela, despite her assurances to the contrary, sincerely believed it must.

But it never happened.

The winds hammered at them, and the plain trembled, and black rain and ice and thick ashes poured down.

The night rumbled and flared.

Gradually, they became persuaded that the worst was over, that the hurricane-force winds were diminishing. They *would* survive; they needed only ride out the storm. And they grew talkative. An atmosphere that might best be described as nervous festive set in. Things banged and exploded and crunched in the night. But they were still there. And they silently congratulated themselves on their good luck. At one point, their rising spirits were helped along when they thought they heard Janet's voice in the ocean of static pouring out of the receivers.

Navigation lights were mounted low on both sides of the cowling, behind the cockpit on the fuselage, and beneath the wings. Periodically, Angela blew the snow and soot off the windscreen and turned them on. Mounds were building high around them.

"I'll make you a bet, Frank," said Hutch.

"Which is—?"

"When we start reading the history of the Monument-Makers, we're going to discover that a lot of them cleared out."

"How do you mean?"

"Left the Galaxy. Probably went to one of the Magellanic Clouds. Somewhere where they don't have these things."

"Maybe. I think they entertained themselves bringing them down on the heads of whatever primitives they could find. I don't think the Monument-Makers were very decent critters."

"I think you've got it wrong," she said.

"In what way?"

She took Carson's wrist. "Oz was a decoy," she said.

He leaned closer to her. "Say again."

"Frank, they were *all* decoys. The cube moons. The Oz-creation at Beta Pac. They were supposed to draw these things off."

"Well, if they were," he said, "they apparently didn't work."

"No. I guess they did the best they could. But you're right. They didn't work. In the end, the Monument-Makers couldn't even save themselves."

He sat down on the deck behind her seat. "You think *they* got hit by one of these things?"

"I think they got hit *twice*. The interstellar civilization probably got nailed. They collapsed. Maybe they ran. I don't know. Maybe they got out and made for the Lesser Magellanic. Ran from these *things* because they couldn't divert them, and couldn't stop them."

"What about the space station?" he asked. "What do you think happened there?"

"—Survivors. Somebody rebuilt. But they didn't get as far the second time. They didn't go interstellar. Maybe it was a different type of civilization. Maybe they lost too much. They were just at the beginning of their space age when the wave came again." She was glad now for the dark. "Frank, think what their technology must have been at its height. And how much advance warning they had. Maybe thousands of years. They knew these things were out there, and they tried to help where they could. But you're right: they didn't succeed."

"The goop is getting a little high," said Angela. "I think it would be a good idea to shift locations. We don't want to get buried."

"Do it," said Carson.

She took them up. Their navigation lights, freed, spilled out over the black snow. The wind rocked the vessel, swept it clean.

Lightning lanced through the night. They timed the distant rumble, guessed at the effect of local air pressure. It was about twelve kilometers away. Cautiously, she set back down.

They passed coffee around. "It figures," said Carson. "We knew all along that the natives lived through these. Except, I guess, the urban populations." He looked hard at Hutch. "I think you're right. About Oz. When did you figure it out?"

"A few hours ago. I kept thinking how much Oz looked like a city. Who were they trying to fool?" She kissed Carson lightly on the cheek. "I wonder if they understood what these things really are? Where they come from?"

"I wonder," Angela said, "if this is the way organized religion got started." They all laughed.

More lightning. Closer.

"Maybe we should start paying attention to the storm," said Hutch.

Angela nodded. "It *does* seem to be walking this way, doesn't it?"

Another bolt glided to ground, illuminating the cockpit.

"I think it's seen us," Hutch said.

"Hey." Angela caught her shoulder. "Don't let your imagination get overloaded."

"It's only lightning out there," whispered Carson.

Angela, as a precaution, powered up.

"What kind of sensor range do we have?" asked Hutch.

"Zip. If we have to go, we'll be flying blind."

A long, liquid bolt flowed between land and sky. Hills and plain stood out in quick relief, and vanished. Thunder rolled across them. "It *is* coming this way," whispered Angela.

"I don't think we want to go up in this wind if we can avoid it," said Carson. He was about to add something, when another fireball appeared. It sliced across the sky. They watched it move through the dark, right to left, watched it stop and begin to brighten.

"Son of a bitch," squealed Angela. "It's turning toward *us*." Simultaneously, she pulled back the yoke, and the shuttle bucked into the air. The wind howled. The thing in the night burned, a blue-white star churning to nova.

"Button up," called Hutch, sliding into her harness and igniting the energy field. Carson scrambled for a handhold.

Hutch locked Angela down in her web seat, and sealed off cargo, where Carson was seated. Then she clipped on her own restraints.

"Frank?"

"I'm okay," he said. "Get us out of here."

Angela put the juice to the magnets, and the shuttle leaped forward, and up, and the light passed beneath them. They heard the subsequent roar and felt the shock wave, and came around in time to see a white geyser climbing skyward.

Hutch looked toward Angela. "Strange meteor."

She nodded. "I'd say so."

The wind dragged at them, blew them across the sky.

Angela was trying to ease back onto the surface when a thunderbolt exploded alongside and the night filled with light. Their electronics went down, and the vehicle lurched wildly. Smoke leaked into the cockpit.

Angela activated her fire-retardants, fought the shuttle into near-level flight, and started back up. "Safer upstairs," she said.

"No," said Carson. "Down. Take us down."

"Frank, we need to be able to maneuver. We're a sitting duck down there."

"Do it, Angela. Get us on the ground."

"You're crazy," said Hutch.

Angela looked distraught. "Why?"

Another bolt hammered them.

"Just do it," Carson said. "As quick as you can."

Hutch watched him on the monitor. He was pulling together the air tanks they'd stored.

Angela pushed the stick forward. "We should be trying to get above this," she protested.

"How do you get above *meteors*?" demanded Carson.

Status lamps blinked off, came back on. Something exploded in back and a roar filled the vehicle. They began to fall.

"We're holed," cried Hutch.

Angela banked left and whacked the navigation console. "Portside rear stabilizers are gone," she said. Through the bedlam of escaping air, howling wind, raining rock and ice, she managed to comment coolly, "Looks like you'll get your way. We are sure as hell going down."

The sky was filled with lightning.

"Fifty meters," said Angela.

They jounced back onto the plain, throwing up gouts of snow and soot. Another meteor was tracking across the sky to their rear. They watched it pause and begin to brighten.

"Out," Carson cried.

Angela started to argue, but Hutch reached over and punched the air cyclers. "It's okay," she said.

They grabbed the tanks and dragged them out as soon as the hatch had opened. Hutch tumbled into the snow, got up, and kept going.

Carson was right behind her.

"Run," he cried. He had three tanks, lost one, but did not go back for it.

The fireball was coming in over a range of hills to the north.

They ran. The snow was crusted and kept breaking underfoot. Hutch went down again. Damn.

Hang onto the tanks!

"You sure he knows what he's doing?" Angela asked.

"Yes," said Hutch. "I think so. *Go.*"

The women struggled to put distance between themselves and the shuttle. Carson stayed with them.

The meteor trailed fire. Pieces broke off and fell.

"Everybody down!" cried Carson. They threw themselves into the snow.

The fireball roared in and blasted the shuttle. Direct hit.

The ground buckled, the icescape brightened, and a hurricane of snow and earth rolled over them. Rocks and debris struck Hutch's energy field.

When it subsided, Carson switched on his lamp. They saw only a crater where the shuttle had been.

Angela shivered. She looked at the sky, and back at the lamp. "For God's sake," she said, "turn it off."

Carson complied. "If you like," he said. "But I think we'll be all right now."

She tried to bury herself in the snow, to hide from the clouds.

"It was never after *us*," said Carson.

"How can you *say* that?" Angela asked.

More lightning. "Right angles," he said. "It wanted the shuttle. Your flying box."

Over the next few hours, the electricity drained out of the heavens. They sat quietly, watching the storms clear off. "I think I understand why the Quraquat used the image of a Monument-Maker to portray Death," Frank said.

"Why?" asked Angela.

"Shoot the messenger. The Monument-Makers probably had no compunctions about landing, introducing themselves, and telling the Quraquat what the problem was." He smiled. "You know, Richard was right. There are no aliens. They all turn out to be pretty human."

"Like George," said Hutch.

Carson drew up his knees and wrapped his arms around them. "Yes," he said. He looked at Angela and explained: "They couldn't stop the goddam things, so they created a diversion. Made something else for them to attack."

"Well, something occurs to *me*," said Angela. "This *thing*"—she waved in the general direction of the sky—"was part of the wave that struck Beta Pac about 5000 B.C., Quraqua around 1000 B.C., and Nok in AD 400. More or less. Right?"

"Yes," said Carson.

"It's headed toward Earth." She looked unsettled.

Carson shrugged. "We've got nine thousand years to deal with it."

"You know," Hutch said, "Janet mentioned that we may already have had some direct experience with these things. She thinks the A wave correlates to Sodom."

Angela's eyes narrowed. "Sodom? Maybe." She fixed Carson with a tight smile. "But I'm not sure we've got as much time as you think. The B wave is still out there."

Hutch moved closer to her companions. The B wave, the wave that had struck Beta Pac in 13,000 B.C., and Quraqua four thousand years later, would be relatively close to Earth. "About a thousand years," she said.

"Well," said Carson, "whatever. Nine or one, I still think we've got plenty of time."

A shadow crossed Angela's face. "I suspect that's close to what the Monument-Makers said."

LIBRARY ENTRY

No successful probe of an Omega cloud in flight has been made. Efforts to transmit signals through the objects have yielded no results as of this writing. (See Adrian Clement's excellent monograph, The Omega Puzzle, *quoted in full in Appendix iii, for a lucid discussion of the theoretical problems involved.)*

The only attempts to take a manned vehicle beneath the outer layers were made 3 and 4 July, 2211, by Meg Campbell, on the Pasquarella. *Campbell made consecutive descents to 80 meters and 650 meters. She failed to return from a third try.*

*A detailed analysis of the Omega clouds must apparently
await the development of new technology.*

—Janet Allegri, *The Engines of God*
Hartley & Co., London (2213)

AFTERWORD

Institute for Advanced Studies, Princeton, NJ. April 2231.

To date, there are few substantive answers about the Monument-Makers. A vast ruin exists deep beneath the harbor city on Beta Pacifica III. It is known to be from the *Cholois*, or Monument-Maker, era. (The term means *the Universal People*, and it seems to have been used to include other intelligent species.) Excavation is proceeding with due caution. What *is* currently known is that Priscilla Hutchins' suggestion that a substantial number of the Cholois fled their home is correct. They planned, initiated, and may have completed, an intergalactic leap.

Surviving members of the species still exist on the home world. They are few, and have been reduced to a state of near-savagery. None have been found with any memory of their former greatness, save in their myths.

Recent investigations support the view that the inhabitants of the space station at Beta Pac III witnessed the destruction of their world by an Omega cloud, and chose to die in space rather than return to a devastated homeland. Investigation continues.

Attempts to inspect the Omega clouds (which were *not* named for Angela Morgan) have been uniformly unproductive. Strong electromagnetic fields are believed to contribute to the clouds' ability to retain their structure, but no one has explained satisfactorily how this could be.

They have turned out to be much less numerous than formerly supposed. It was something of an aberration that the *Ashley Tee* found two of them simultaneously in the same system. They are nevertheless uncomfortably plentiful, and there is no realistic hope that the solar system will not receive one or two unwelcome visitors in its own distant future.

Conferences have already been convened to plan a strategy, and to ensure that future generations are warned of the danger.

The central processing unit recovered by Maggie Tufu from the space station has been a trove of information about the so-called City-Builder era. The natives of that period were aware of their early exploits. But rather than serving as a source of pride, they provoked a sense of lost greatness and decay which slowed development, promoted decay, and induced dark ages.

The existence of the Omega clouds has raised deep-seated philosophical questions about the position of the human race in a universe now seen by many to be actively hostile. Return-to-nature movements have sprung up around the world, and there has also been a resurgence of fundamentalist religious groups, which had been in decline for decades.

Project Hope has proceeded successfully, and it now appears that the first human settlers will arrive on Quraqua well ahead of schedule.

Six additional monuments have been found. The Braker Society (named for its founder, Aran Braker, who died of a stroke during a demonstration outside the Smithsonian) has led a strong effort in recent years to recover the Great Monuments, and place them in Earth orbit. This effort has been encouraged by technological advances which would render the project feasible. Although the idea has found considerable popularity among the general public, opposition has come principally from the Academy and its allies, one of the more vocal of whom has been Melanie Truscott. These have been characterized as "Arconuts" by the Braker Society.

Starship design has improved significantly as a result of the experience of the *Winckelmann*. Secondary life support systems, capable of full manual operation, are now standard features.

Melanie Truscott's career went into eclipse for several years, owing to the Richard Wald incident. She came to the public's attention again in 2207 when she opposed an effort to resume massive logging in the Northwest. She lost that struggle, but was elected to the Senate in 2208.

Ian Helm, who was Kosmik's director of southern icecap operations on Quraqua, escaped all blame for pushing the button. He has served several agencies and corporations in high-level posts, and is currently Commissioner of the NAU Park Service.

The Great Telescope in Beta Pacifica shares many of the characteristics of a living organism, although it is not quite precise to say it is *alive*. It was once fully capable of collecting data across the spectrum. Its signals have never been translated satisfactorily into optical images. It is now believed that the software, whose methodology is only dimly understood, has malfunctioned.

Henry Jacobi died in Chicago after a long illness. His last years were embittered by a series of simmy versions of the rescue at the Temple, all of which portrayed him as reckless and blundering.

Frank Carson never did take the job with the Academy's personnel division. And despite his resolution after the deaths of Maggie Tufu and George Hackett, he returned to Beta Pacifica III, where he headed the Working Group for six years. He received full credit for leading the original expedition, and ranks in his own lifetime with Champollion, Larimatsu, and Wald. He married Linda Thomas, from the Temple mission, and is now the father of two redheaded girls. He is also Chairman of the Margaret Tufu Foundation, which provides research grants and educational aid to budding mathematicians.

Tourists at the Academy in Washington, D.C., often visit the George Hackett wing of the main library. A striking photograph of Hackett, superimposed over a copy of the Casumel script which he helped rescue at Quraqua, dominates the west wall.

Maggie Tufu's brilliant account of the search for the meaning of the inscription at Oz, *Philological Aspects of Casumel Linear*, was published several years ago to unanimous acclaim. Edited by Janet Allegri, it is already recognized as a mathematical classic.

Allegri is now teaching at Oxford.

Priscilla Hutchins continues to pilot the Academy's ships. She has established a reputation of her own, and people meeting her for the first time are always surprised to discover that she is not quite as tall, or as beautiful, as they had expected. That comes later.

—David Emory

Red Mars
Kim Stanley Robinson

WINNER OF THE NEBULA AWARD

MARS. THE RED PLANET.
Closest to Earth in our solar system,
surely life must exist on it?

We dreamt about the builders of the canals we could see by telescope, about ruined cities, lost Martian civilisations, the possibilities of alien contact. Then the Viking and Mariner probes went
up, and sent back - nothing. Mars was a barren planet: lifeless,
sterile, uninhabited.

In 2019 the first man set foot on the surface of Mars: John
Boone, American hero. In 2027 one hundred of the Earth's finest
engineers and scientists made the first mass-landing. Their
mission? To create a New World.

To terraform a planet with no atmosphere, an intensely cold
climate and no magnetosphere into an Eden full of people, plants
and animals. It is the greatest challange mankind has ever faced:
the ultimate use of intelligence and ability: our finest dream.

'A staggering book . . . The best novel on the colonization of
Mars that has ever been written'   *Arthur C. Clarke*

'First of a mighty trilogy, *Red Mars* is the ultimate in future
history'   *Daily Mail*

'*Red Mars* may simply be the best novel ever written about Mars'
                                                       Interzone

ISBN 0 586 21389 9